The New York/Mid-Atlantic Gardener's Book of Lists

The New York/Mid-Atlantic Gardener's

BOOK OF LISTS

Bonnie Lee Appleton
and Lois Trigg Chaplin

Series Editor
Lois Trigg Chaplin

Taylor Trade Publishing
Dallas, Texas

To Joe and Albie who so patiently and lovingly accepted "when the book is finished" as an answer.

Designed by David Timmons

Published by Taylor Publishing Company
1550 West Mockingbird Lane
Dallas, Texas 75235

Library of Congress Cataloging-in-Publication Data

Appleton, Bonnie Lee, 1948–
    The New York/Mid-Atlantic gardener's book of lists / Bonnie Appleton and Lois Trigg Chaplin.
        p.   cm.
    Includes bibliographical references (p.   ).
    ISBN 0-87833-261-8 (pbk.)
    1. Landscape plants—New York (State) 2. Landscape plants—Mid-Atlantic States. 3. Landscape gardening—New York (State) 4. Landscape gardening—Middle Atlantic States. I. Chaplin, Lois Trigg. II. Title—.

SB408.A66 2001
635.9'09747—dc21   00-066670

10   9   8   7   6   5   4   3   2   1

Printed in the United States of America

CONTENTS

DEDICATION

A special thanks goes to Bonnie Appleton for all the hard work she has put into this title. Her experience, contacts, and enthusiasm make her the perfect author for this book. Although I am listed as coauthor here because I am the creator of the original title, *The Southern Gardener's Book of Lists*, Bonnie has done all the work and deserves all the credit. I know this book will be helpful to both experienced and new gardeners for years to come. Use it as a workbook to add plants as you discover them. Happy gardening.

Lois Trigg Chaplin

ACKNOWLEDGMENTS

Many people—professional horticulturists, nursery men and women, arborists, extension agents, fellow university professors, gardeners, and garden writers—shared their time, expertise, and support in helping to compile the lists for this book. Some have been friends and colleagues for many years, while others responded quickly and positively to the phone call or e-mail of a complete stranger. They helped not only with the plant lists but also with the lists of references, and with suggestions of just what lists seemed appropriate to include.

Only one will be singled out by name—Dr. H. Marc Cathey—president emeritus of the American Horticultural Society, and a former director of the U.S. National Arboretum in Washington, D.C. When asked if he would share his heat zone database so that the plants in this book's lists could be coded with the cold hardiness ratings and the newer and more difficult to find heat zone ratings, he offered to go one better. Dr. Cathey personally coded all of the plants in the main chapters himself. His selfless desire to share information with everyone has greatly increased the value of this book, and I am very grateful for his contribution.

Bonnie Lee Appleton

TO THE READER

One of the questions I've been asked most often during my career in university extension was whether I had lists of plants to fit particular landscape sites and niches. I quickly learned to stuff my files full of these lists, collected from trade and consumer magazines, as handouts at presentations, and as appendices in various reference books. The only problem with that was I ended up with bulging files and too much to copy and send to people, but no nicely organized way of sharing all of this collected knowledge and experience.

I decided this situation needed to be remedied, and that starting to organize this information would be a good writing assignment for our graduate students. So the students in a special topics course on trees that I taught a few years ago were all assigned a landscape situation. They were told to research the situation (wet soil, alkaline pH, etc.) and to write an extension publication that described it and included a list of trees that should survive in that landscape situation.

One of the references I suggested they consult was a book I had recently purchased—*The Southern Gardener's Book of Lists* by Lois Trigg Chaplin. Many of them used the book, and as a result of the lists they found in it and elsewhere, Virginia Tech has a new, and still evolving, series of extension publications called "Trees for Problem Landscape Sites" (available at www.ext.vt.edu).

So appreciate my surprise and amusement when Lois's agent called and asked me first if I was familiar with the book, and second if I would be interested in writing the New York and Mid-Atlantic version. I shared with her my firsthand knowledge of Lois's book, and decided I really couldn't pass up the chance to not only finally get even more of my list files organized, but to get paid to do so. Little did I know how little I knew about many of this region's plants until I began to do more in-depth research, and until my various "guest listers" started supplying me lists containing the names of plants with which I was totally unfamiliar.

This has been a wonderful opportunity, and I appreciate Lois entrusting the task to me. I hope you will be able to use this book in combination with more detailed plant references you may have, or that have been suggested at the back of this book in order to populate your various landscape situations, problems, challenges, and niches with a host of wonderful, and I hope to many of you, new plants. I hope the lists will also help remind you of plants you know but may have overlooked, especially our Mid-Atlantic region natives.

These lists are not all inclusive; they're intended to get you started in your garden or landscape. If any plants were not included in a list, but from experience you believe they should be there, please add them for your reference and perhaps for someone else's future guidance. Also, if a certain plant just won't work for you, scratch it from the list and try something else.

Bonnie Lee Appleton
Norfolk, Virginia

INTRODUCTION

Whether you're gardening in a small townhouse backyard, or on a mini-estate of many acres, you're bound to find sites and situations which challenge your plant selecting ability: too much sun or too little water; hungry deer you don't want to attract but hummingbirds that you do. These lists are focused to help you wade through the wonderful diversity that greets you when you walk into a garden center or thumb through a mail-order catalog. But first you need to know a bit about the information contained within the lists, and how to best use that information.

The "Backwards Landscaping Process"
To get started, try using a backwards landscaping process. By making a series of ever narrowing decisions, you can find one or more plants to fill your garden and landscape needs:

* Do you want or does the site require a tree, shrub, vine, ground cover, etc.?
* Do you want the plant to be evergreen or deciduous?
* What plant characteristics do you want: for example, flowers, fruit, fall color?
* Do you want a plant with multiseasonal interest?
* How large can that plant realistically get (height and spread) and how fast (growth rate)?
* For what degree of maintenance do you have time or money? Must it be the near perfect plant that gets no pests, needs no pruning, and doesn't require supplemental fertilizer or water, or are you willing to lend a helping hand so that your plant will establish and grow in your garden or landscape?
* Under what site and environmental conditions must the plant grow? Soil characteristics, light intensity and duration, available moisture, temperature, and wind conditions are all critical selection factors.

Once you think through these questions and analyze your landscape site, you should have narrowed down the type of plant for which you're looking. You may be able to consult just one or two lists, or you may need to cross-reference several, in order to make your selection and purchase.

Plant Names
Most plants listed in this book have two names—first their common name, then their taxonomic or botanical name (the italicized name in parentheses). We generally ask for a plant by its common name, but unfortunately that sometimes causes confusion, and sometimes the purchase of an unwanted plant.

Common names vary from region to region. Within the New York and Mid-Atlantic region, we get a wonderful mixing of people from other areas, but a confusing mixture of plant common names. You may call the stately native tree with the large green tulip-shaped leaves and yellow tulip-shaped flowers a tulip tree, but someone else may call it a tulip poplar or a yellow poplar, or even a tulip magnolia. This tree is not a true poplar (the genus *Populus*), and it's not a magnolia (the genus *Magnolia*), although it is a relative of the southern and deciduous magnolias in the larger classification of the magnolia family.

What the tree is, regardless of the common name you pick, is *Liriodendron tulipifera*. That Latin name is the same in any region of the United States, or any region of the world. It is a name that only changes if the plant is reclassified or taxonomically renamed, something that doesn't happen very frequently. Most of the taxonomic names

SUNFLOWER

used in this book are the latest ones, unless the newer classification has not yet become widely adopted and would cause confusion. If you ask for or order a plant by its taxonomic name, you should (unless tags are mixed or plants just completely misidentified) get exactly what you want.

Variety, Cultivar, and Trade Names

Most of our more common landscape plants now come in more sizes, shapes, and colors than the basic form. Take Japanese maples. A Japanese maple is not a Japanese maple is not a Japanese maple. There are tall ones and short ones, green-leaved ones and red-leaved ones. These variations of the original plant may be botanical *varieties* (if they reproduce naturally on their own), or *cultivars*—cultivated varieties (if they need us to reproduce and keep them in the landscape).

Varieties are designated by "var." after the genus (first Latin name, first letter capitalized) and species (second Latin name, lowercased). Japanese boxwood, for example, is *Buxus microphylla* var. *japonica*. Cultivar names, which are usually but not always in English, are capitalized and listed in single quotes after the species name. For example, *Acer palmatum* is Japanese maple, while *Acer palmatum* 'Burgundy Lace' is the Burgundy Lace Japanese maple (a cultivar), and *Acer palmatum* var. *dissectum* is the thread-leaf Japanese maple (a botanical variety).

Commercial horticulture, however, has added a new twist in recent years: trademarked or registered names. So a plant may have one cultivar name attached to it but be known by a different trademarked common name. One example would be *Acer rubrum* 'Franksred,' Red Sunset® maple. Another would be *Tilia americana* 'DTR 123,' Legend® linden. This trademarking is done to give special ownership to the plant and economic return to its originator. When in doubt, use the Latin name in combination with common names to be sure you're getting what you want.

Most of the lists in this book do not include cultivar names because the lists would be just too long. In a few cases, however, when especially good cultivars exist for a particular characteristic or use, they are listed. Generally, use the lists to get you to the right plant for the right location, then investigate the fascinating variety available at the cultivar level.

An x Here and an x There

In some binomial or Latin plant names you'll see an x. Most of the times the x is between the genus and the species for the plant, standing for an intrageneric hybrid (a cross between two species in the same genus). For example, the Anglojapanese yew, *Taxus* x *media*, is a cross or hybrid between the English yew, *Taxus baccata*, and the Japanese yew, *Taxus cuspidata*.

On rare occasions, a cross may occur between two different genera, resulting in an intergeneric hybrid. One of the most common examples of an intergeneric hybrid is the Leyland cypress, x *Cupressocyparis leylandii*, a cross between the Monterey cypress (*Cupressus macrocarpa*) and the Alaskan cedar (*Chamaecyparis nootkatensis*).

Cold Hardiness and Heat Tolerance

Most of the plants listed in the main chapters of this book are accompanied by two sets of numbers. One set indicates a plant's cold hardiness; the other indicates its heat tolerance. These numbers are important because they help to better define where plants *should* be successful within the New York and Mid-Atlantic region. A typical entry would be:

Fragrant snowbell (*Styrax obassia*)	6-8, 8-6
Pond cypress (*Taxodium ascendens*)	5-11, 12-5

These numbers are based on temperatures, which are only part of what contributes to plant hardiness. Other factors—rainfall, snow cover, soil types, winds, elevation, pollution—also contribute to hardiness but are far more difficult to quantify and standardize. Furthermore, they all have confounding effects—one affecting the other. Then factor in plant genetics and vigor or condition and it really gets confusing.

To an extent, we can do things culturally to modify some of the other factors. We can add irrigation if it fails to rain, or try to improve drainage if it's soggy. We can amend soils to change their pH or texture. Yet we can't do much to change the overall temperatures in an area. Sure, there are microclimates around all buildings and in each landscape, and we should learn where they are and use them to our advantage. A marginally cold-hardy plant might make it if we place it in a warm southwestern exposure, or a heat-intolerant plant that we just must have might make it if we put it in a northern exposure. But our overall temperature ranges can't be changed that much, and therefore they're the basis of the two ratings.

In the lists in this book, the first set of numbers represents the cold hardiness zones within which a plant will be most successful. Each zone represents a change of 10 degrees F. Within each zone, there are two sub-zones—*a* and *b*—with 5 degree differences. These numbers are based on the average annual minimum temperature recorded for a particular location. You may drive miles before you change zones, or go literally just around the corner to arrive in a different zone. When you begin to use the lists in this book, locate your hardiness zone on the map, and use that as your first guide to plant suitability.

The first hardiness zone map was issued by the USDA in the 1930s. It was developed by Henry Skinner, who was the director of the National Arboretum at the time. The map was revised in 1965 and again in 1990 with the help of Marc Cathey. That 1990 revision is the current version and includes eleven zones that range from the warmest areas (zone 11 in Florida, California, and Hawaii) to the coldest areas (zone 1 in Alaska). This book predominantly covers zones 5 through 7. This range excludes portions of northern and western New York, for which *The New England Gardener's Book of Lists* by Karan Davis Cutler should be used.

It is important to note that Marc Cathey used the 1990 version of the USDA Hardiness Zone Map to code plant lists in this book. This version has eleven zones where previous versions had ten. You will find, therefore, that as you consult other references for additional plant specifics, the zones may in some cases vary for the same plant. It all depends on the version of the USDA Hardiness Zone Map that was used. For a few references—in particular Donald Wyman's excellent tree and shrub books—the USDA map wasn't used for zoning. Wyman's books use the zone map compiled in 1971 by the Arnold Arboretum in Jamaica Plains, Massachusetts, and you will find that the dividing lines for the zones, and therefore the zone coding for plants, are different from the USDA system.

Through the American Horticultural Society, Marc Cathey helped to develop the system for indicating heat zones, the second set of numbers you will find in the plant lists in this book. The Heat Zone Map was published in 1998 as part of the AHS's 75th anniversary celebration. The map divides the United States into twelve zones based on the number of days each year that the daily high temperatures reach or exceed 86 degrees F, the temperature at which plants begin to sustain physiological damage.

Find your heat zone on the map in this book, combine that with your cold hardiness zone, and use this wonderful new combination of numbers to your advantage to select the right plant for the right location. Some plants will have very narrow zone ratings, some very wide, but as long as your two numbers appear within the ranges, you should be able to grow your desired plant (we'll assume you'll provide proper care).

For more information on these maps, consult the United States National Arboretum website—www.ars-grin.gov—or the American Horticultural Society website—www.ahs.org. By the way, the maps have been refined down to the county and zip code level, so little confusion need exist as to where you are located.

Don't assume that if you live in the warmest part of your state in the winter you are therefore in the warmest part in the summer. Masses of asphalt and bodies of water can have interesting effects on temperature. These numbers are a guide, not an absolute. Get to know the microclimates of your garden or landscape to help you refine your plant selections. Visit local botanical and display gardens, and arboreta, to see what succeeds there, or see what plants grow well for your neighbors. Consult the publications and websites of your state Cooperative Extension Service for additional information. (See the list of websites at the back of this book.)

A few last things to keep in mind. If you can buy plants grown either locally or as close to your cold and heat zones as possible, that will help. These plants will already be acclimated to your temperatures. Sometimes if you baby a plant a little bit extra the first year while its roots are getting established, that will help offset negative stresses that might affect the plant later in its life. No matter what, remember there will always be a plant that doesn't know the rules, didn't read the books or study the zones, or doesn't realize which list it's been put on, and yet will survive and flourish despite the odds. Such is the exciting and frustrating nature of plants. Happy plant selecting!

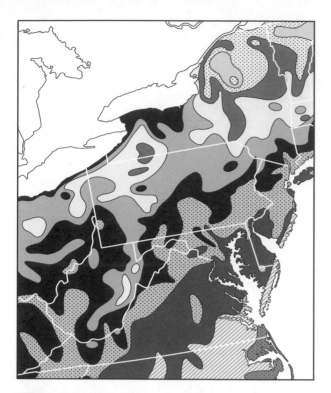

USDA Hardiness Zone Map for the New York/Mid-Atlantic Region

AVERAGE ANNUAL MINIMUM TEMPERATURES

Temperature (°C)			Temperature (°F)
-34.5 to -37.2		3b	-30 to -35
-31.7 to -34.4		4a	-25 to -30
-28.9 to -31.6		4b	-20 to -25
-26.2 to -28.8		5a	-15 to -20
-23.4 to -26.1		5b	-10 to -15
-20.6 to -23.3		6a	-5 to -10
-17.8 to -20.5		6b	0 to -5
-15.0 to -17.7		7a	5 to 0
12.3 to -15.0		7b	10 to 5
-9.5 to -12.2		8a	15 to 10

"The effects of cold on a plant are very apparent and immediate. When a plant's lower limit of temperature is reached, ice forms in its cells and tears them apart beyond hope of repair, so that the plant dies quickly. Heat damage to plants may first appear in many different parts of the plant: flower buds may wither, leaves may droop or become more appealing to insects, chlorophyll may disappear, or roots may stop growing. These signs may continue reappearing for several summers, until desiccation reaches a high enough level that the enzymes that control growth are deactivated. Death from heat stress is slow and lingering."

Marc Cathey is president of the American Horticultural Society in Alexandria, Virginia, and helped develop the heat-zone categories for plants.

USDA Heat-Zone Map for the New York/Mid-Atlantic Region

AVERAGE NUMBER OF DAYS PER YEAR ABOVE 86°F (30°C)

< 1		1
1 to 7		2
> 7 to 14		3
> 14 to 30		4
> 30 to 45		5
> 45 to 60		6
> 50 to 90		7
> 90 to 120		8

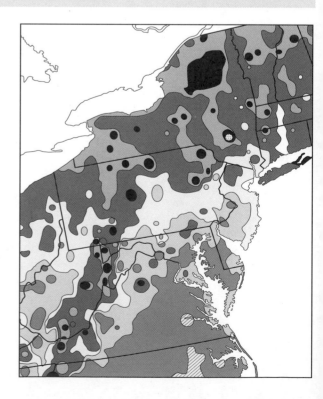

TREES

Not only are trees the largest plants in most gardens and landscapes, but they also represent, on a plant-by-plant basis, the largest capital investments as well. Surveys of improvements to residential properties have shown that landscaping is the item that generally nets the largest return on investment when a property is sold. Adding appropriate shade, street, and flowering trees to your landscape, or taking proper care of existing trees, will generally contribute the most to landscape improvement.

While many people have sticker shock when they learn the cost to buy, and sometimes also to install a tree, keep in mind that trees generally cost the least to maintain of any of your landscape plants. If they're planted in good soil, and properly mulched and watered, they rarely need fertilization. They don't need deadheading, as many perennials do. They don't need yearly or more frequent pruning or shearing, as shrubs do. They don't need yearly replacement, as annuals do. Though trees get insect and disease problems, they rarely die from an attack of aphids that might kill an annual very quickly.

ELM

Add to these pluses some of the more intangible or harder to quantify economic, recreation, social, and therapeutic benefits of trees. Trees provide shade, they help to combat air pollution in a variety of ways, their roots help to reduce soil and water erosion, they redirect and slow down winds, and more. They can be used to screen views, soften or enhance buildings, reduce traffic noise and glare, and attract wildlife. Trees are also believed to reduce crime and to speed recovery time for hospital patients. Trees are very good investments in a bottom-line world.

By definition a tree is generally a single-stemmed woody plant whose height at maturity is at least 15 feet. As with most of nature, there are exceptions. Clump birches and redbuds and serviceberries have multiple trunks, for example, and some Japanese maple cultivars and dwarf Alberta spruces will never grow to 15 feet. Trees provide ample variety and variation for you to meet any aesthetic, climatic, engineering, architectural, economic, social, recreational, therapeutic, or other need you might have.

Tips for Selecting and Succeeding with Trees

- Diversify. A wonderful rule of selection suggested by the late Dr. Frank Santamour, tree geneticist with the National Arboretum in Washington, D.C. , is that of 30%–20%–10%: never use more than 30% of plants from any one plant family, more than 20% of plants from any one genera, or more than 10% of plants from any one species. We have a habit when we select trees, more than with selecting any other group of plants, to use monocultures. Throughout the New York and Mid-Atlantic region you see street after street, or parking lot after parking lot, lined, ringed, and rowed with only one or two species of trees, such as red maples, green ashes, or pin oaks. In the city of Norfolk, Virginia, city arborist David Sivyer reports that 50% of the street trees are crape myrtles. Sure they're beautiful in the summer with their incredible canopies of flowers, and out-of-towners wish they lived on such red-and-pink-lined streets, but when it's cool and humid in the summer, the old cultivars that are so prevalent end up with leaves covered with powdery mildew. Monocultures are pest smorgasbords. Garden pests start at one end of a group of red maples, for example, and infect or infest until they reach the other end.
- Use references that will help you determine tree sizes and growth rates. Once the tree is too tall or too broad, it's usually very difficult or too expensive to move.

- Shop for a quality tree. Look not only for an unscarred trunk and well-spaced branches, but also be sure you're buying an adequate root system, whether the tree was container or field grown.
- Dig a proper planting hole—much wider but no deeper than the root ball. Spend the extra time to assure that roots quickly establish into the soil. Be sure to remove containers and unpack field root balls (cut ropes and the tops of wire baskets, peel back the burlap).
- Do not amend the backfill soil for individual planting holes—instead, save organic matter for mulch. Water well at planting and for the next year, and generally forget trunk wrapping or staking. Prune only to remove problems the first year, but then prune some each year to train a good branch structure and to remove codominant (double) leaders.
- Monitor for pest problems and get them properly identified before applying control measures. Few trees die quickly from pests the way smaller plants may. Stored reserves in trees may sustain them for years even as they're beginning to decline.
- Recycle nutrients by using leaves as mulch, preferably composted first. Apply mulch over as much of the tree's root system (which generally extends beyond the crown or dripline by two or more times) as possible, and minimize soil disturbance, compaction, chemicals, and anything that might cut or damage the roots within that zone.
- Water drought-sensitive trees if summer rainfall is scarce. Fertilize only if signs (e.g., pale leaves) or soil tests reveal a deficiency. Routine fertilization is unneeded, wasteful, and polluting.
- Lawn mowers, weed eaters, and root damage kill more trees than any insects or diseases do. Respect the tree above and below ground.

TREES FOR THE 21ST CENTURY

This list of trees for the 21st century includes new releases along with readily available and proven urban trees. Many of these are native trees that have long been overlooked for their landscape potential.

One of the favorite flowering trees for the New York and Mid-Atlantic region is the native flowering dogwood (*Cornus florida*). Due to concern over the destructive fungal disease *Discula* anthracnose, which has killed many native dogwoods in the woods and in landscapes, a series of hybrid dogwoods is of major interest. The Rutgers University Stellar series is a result of twenty-five years of hybridizing by Elwin Orton. One of the parents is the native dogwood, which was crossed with the kousa dogwood (*Cornus kousa*). The results are several very floriferous trees that are more vigorous than either parent, and that bloom after the flowering dogwood but before the kousa. They are very showy, with large bracts (the modified leaves that look like petals). In addition, the Stellar dogwoods are resistant to both anthracnose and borers. Dr. Orton also produced many new Japanese and deciduous hollies.

For those who like flowering trees, there are several genera where many new hybrids and cultivars seem to be introduced yearly. These include the crabapples, various deciduous and the southern magnolia, and redbuds. Magnolia relatives that should be watched as exciting future trees are the mangletias, a group with evergreen leaves and white to pinkish flowers.

If you're looking for shade trees, you won't be disappointed either. New introductions seem to appear yearly in the red and sugar maples, and there is a red by silver maple hybrid—the Freeman maple (*Acer × freemanii*). There are also new green ashes, little-leaf lindens, lacebark elms, zelkovas, and other popular deciduous trees grown for shade and used frequently as street trees.

This list of trees for the 21st century was compiled with the help of Jim Sellmer, an assistant professor of ornamental horticulture with Penn State University in State College, Pennsylvania.

Street Wise trident maple (*Acer buergerianum* 'BNMTF')	5-9, 9-3
Amur maple (*Acer ginnala*)	2-7, 7-1
Paperbark maple (*Acer griseum*)	4-8, 8-1
Full-moon maple (*Acer japonicum*)	5-7, 7-4
Miyabe maple (*Acer miyabei*)	5-8, 8-5
Legacy and Green Mountain sugar maples	4-8, 8-1
(*Acer saccharum* 'Legacy' and 'Green Mountain')	
Three-flowered maple (*Acer triflorum*)	5-7, 7-5
Shantung maple (*Acer truncatum*)	4-8, 8-1

Briotii red horse chestnut (*Aesculus* x *carnea* 'Briottii')	7-8, 8-6
Red buckeye (*Aesculus pavia*)	5-8, 8-4
Autumn Brilliance serviceberry (*Amelanchier* x *grandiflora* 'Autumn Brilliance')	5-8, 8-4
Dura-Heat river birch (*Betula nigra* 'BNMTF')	5-7, 7-2
Whitespire gray birch (*Betula populifolia* 'Whitespire')	3-7, 7-2
European hornbeam (*Carpinus betulus*)	4-8, 8-1
American hornbeam (*Carpinus caroliniana*)	3-9, 9-1
Oklahoma redbud (*Cercis reniformis* 'Oklahoma')	6-9, 9-3
Chinese fringe tree (*Chionanthus retusus*)	6-8, 8-5
White fringe tree (*Chionanthus virginicus*)	5-9, 9-3
Yellowwood (*Cladrastis kentukea*)	4-9, 9-1
Turkish filbert (*Corylus colurna*)	3-9, 9-1
Pagoda dogwood (*Cornus alternifolia*)	4-8, 8-1
Wonderberry dogwood (*Cornus florida* 'Wonderberry')	5-8, 8-1
Stellar series dogwoods (*Cornus* x 'Aurora,' 'Celestial,' 'Constellation,' 'Ruth Ellen,' 'Stardust,' and 'Stellar Pink')	5-8, 8-1
Japanese cornelia dogwood (*Cornus officinalis*)	2-8, 8-1
Smoke trees (*Cotinus coggygria, C. obovatus*)	5-8, 8-1
Carolina silverbell (*Halesia carolina*)	5-8, 8-4
Possumhaw (*Ilex decidua*)	5-9, 9-5
Winterberry (*Ilex verticillata* cvs. and hybs.)	5-8, 8-5
Fruitless sweetgum (*Liquidambar styraciflua* 'Rotundiloba')	6-9, 9-1
Amur maackia (*Maackia amurensis*)	5-7, 7-5
Little Girl magnolias (*Magnolia* x 'Ann,' 'Betty,' 'Jane')	5/6-9, 9-6
Galaxy and Spectrum magnolias (*Magnolia* x 'Galaxy' and 'Spectrum')	6-9, 9-6
Ashe magnolia (*Magnolia ashei*)	7-9, 9-7
Alta southern magnolia (*Magnolia grandiflora* 'TMGH')	7-9, 9-3
Big-leaf magnolia (*Magnolia macrophylla*)	6-9, 9-6
Sweet bay magnolia (*Magnolia virginiana*)	6-9, 9-6
Black gum, sour gum, black tupelo (*Nyssa sylvatica*)	5-9, 9-5
Persian parrotia (*Parrotia persica*)	4-7, 7-1
Lacebark pine (*Pinus bungeana*)	4-7, 7-1
Chinese pistache (*Pistacia chinensis*)	6-9, 9-6
Mountain stewartia (*Stewartia ovata*)	5-8, 8-5
Japanese snowbell (*Styrax japonicus*)	6-8, 8-6
Fragrant snowbell (*Styrax obassia*)	6-8, 8-6
Japanese tree lilac (*Syringa reticulata*)	4-7, 7-1
Pond cypress (*Taxodium ascendens*)	5-11, 12-5
Valley Forge elm (*Ulmus americana* 'Valley Forge')	3-9, 9-1
Accolade elm (*Ulmus japonica* x *U. wilsoniana* 'Morton')	5-9, 9-4
Lacebark elm (*Ulmus parvifolia* 'Allee,' 'Athena,' Dynasty')	5-11, 12-5

"Invariably we must wear many hats including that of the landscape designer, urban forester, nursery operator, tree breeder, and horticulturist when selecting trees for the future to assure that your choices will survive and thrive in the environment in which they are placed. We often can't wear all of those hats, so that is where groups like METRIA (Metropolitan Tree Improvement Alliance) are so important and vital. Like-minded people (tree breeders, nursery operators, urban foresters, landscape designers, and horticulturists) come together biennially to discuss and share their research addressing the many issues impacting the success and future of our urban trees. If you would like to learn more about METRIA, visit our website at http://fletcher.ces.state.nc.us/programs/nursery/metria."

Jim Sellmer is past executive director of METRIA and an assistant professor of ornamental horticulture with Penn State University in State College, Pennsylvania.

JAPANESE MAPLES

A gardener searching for a winsome dwarf to enliven an intimate corner, or for a stately ornamental to adorn an expanse of lawn, will find his or her reward within the Japanese maples. Delightful with each turn of season, these highly adaptable and long-lived maples display an incredible variety of form, texture, color, and habit. Japanese maples are not prone to specific pest or disease problems in the landscape and prefer a low nitrogen environment. For what more could one ask than an element of grace and astounding beauty that thrives on inattention?

All Japanese maples have certain preferences, but most will acclimate to less than optimum conditions. They prefer filtered light during the heat of the day. If you have used up all of the shady spots in the garden or have need of a larger-growing specimen for an open area, don't despair. Merely select a cultivar more tolerant of full sun and maintain proper watering to insure success. Red cultivars need significant sunlight to color well, while yellows require more shade. Overhead watering during the heat of the day should be avoided, as it may cause leaf scorch. Unless you have a known soil deficiency, do not add amendments or fertilizer when planting. If your tree should develop a pest or disease problem, have it properly diagnosed before treatment. Many common garden chemicals can cause cosmetic or systemic damage in Japanese maples.

There are hundreds of cultivars within the two species *Acer palmatum* and *Acer japonicum* (also known as full-moon maple). Even those not included have valuable characteristics worthy of consideration. A good starting point is this list from Elizabeth Gardner, who selected cultivars with proven performance that should be commercially available in the New York and Mid-Atlantic region.

Hardiness and heat zones are 5-8 and 8-2. Cultivars denoted with an asterisk (*) will show variable red and green tones depending on season and cultural conditions.

Red Upright Form
Acer palmatum 'Bloodgood,' 'Burgundy Lace,' 'Emperor 1,' 'Fireglow,' 'Moonfire,' 'Nuresagi,' 'Red Baron,' 'Tsukushigata,' 'Trompenburg,' 'Suminagashi'

Green Upright Form
Acer japonicum 'Aconitifolium'
Acer palmatum 'Aoygi,' 'Arakawa,' 'Christy Ann,' 'Hogyoku,' 'Killarney,' 'Omuryama,' 'Osakasuki,' 'Sango kaku,' 'Seiryu,' 'Shishigashira'

Red Weeping
Acer palmatum 'Crimson Queen,' 'Garnet,' 'Orangeola'*, 'Raraflora'*, 'Red Dragon,' 'Red Feather,' 'Red Filigree Lace,' 'Red Select,' 'Shojo shidare,' 'Tamukeyama'

Green Weeping
Acer japonicum 'Green Cascade'
Acer palmatum 'Baldsmith'*, *dissectum* 'Flavecens,' *dissectum* 'Palmatifidium,' 'Germaine's Gyration,' 'Green Mist,' 'Green Hornet,' 'Viridis,' 'Waterfall'

Red Linearilobum (long, narrow lobes)
Acer palmatum 'Atrolineare,' 'Beni otake,' 'Hubb's Red Willow,' 'Red Pygmy,' 'Villa Taranto'*

Green Linearilobum
Acer palmatum 'Linearilobum,' 'Koto no ito,' 'Scolopendrifolum,' 'Scolopendrifolum rubrum'*, 'Shino buga oku'

Large Shrub to Small Tree (spring color; summer green)
Acer palmatum 'Beni maiko,' 'Bonfire,' 'Corallinum,' 'Kashima,' 'Katsura,' 'Tsuma gaki,' 'Shishio Improved'

Red Dwarf Shrub or Witch's Broom
Acer palmatum 'Beni hime,' 'Beni komachi,' 'Beni fushigi,' 'Shaina,' 'Skeeter's Broom'

Green Dwarf Shrub or Witch's Broom
Acer palmatum 'Coonara Pygmy,' 'Garyu,' 'Hanami nishiki,' 'Kamagata,' 'Koto hime,' 'Mikawa yatsubusa,' 'Sharp's Pygmy'

Variegated Upright Tree
Acer palmatum 'Asahi zuru,' 'Beni schischihenge,' 'Butterfly,' 'Kagiri nishiki,' 'Orido nishiki,' 'Sagara nishiki,' 'Ukigumo'

Variegated Weeping
Acer palmatum 'Beni shidare tricolor,' 'Goshiki shidare,' 'Toyama nishiki,' *dissectum* 'Variegatum'

Variegated Large Shrub
Acer palmatum 'Aka shigitatsu sawa,' 'Higaseyama,' 'Peaches & Cream,' 'Shigitatsu sawa'
Variegated Dwarf
Acer palmatum 'Goshiki kotohime,' 'Wilson's Pink Dwarf'

"Most of the gardeners with whom I am acquainted have become intoxicated with the charm of Japanese maples. Where they had first planned to include only one in the landscape, they have subsequently added several, enjoying the attributes of all the diverse forms. As your imagination wanders down the garden path of your mind, consider these botanical wonders and their promise to provide beauty for generations to come."

Elizabeth Gardner, a certified nurseryman, is general manager of Acer Acres (a.k.a. Twin Ponds), a Beaverdam, Virginia, wholesale container nursery and landscaping company that propagates and grows more than 250 different cultivars of Japanese maples.

LOW-PEST TREES

When people call and ask for lists of trees, they generally request trees with few or no pest problems, and trees that quickly provide shade. The use of pest-resistant and pest-tolerant trees is one of the principles of IPM—Integrated Pest Management. IPM is an approach to managing plant pests which combines biological, chemical, cultural, and physical controls in order to maximize plant health while minimizing human and environmental risks.

This list was compiled by arborist Paul Wolfe of Integrated Plant Care in Rockville, Maryland, with additions by Virginia Tech clinicians Mary Ann Hansen and Eric Day. According to Paul, "Many low-pest trees and shrubs have multiseasonal interest, which adds to their value. With the crape myrtles, select newer varieties that have proven to be powdery mildew resistant, including cultivars with American Indian names that were developed at the National Arboretum in Washington, D.C."

Trees marked with an asterisk (*) are recommended as beneficial native landscape trees by the Virginia Native Plant Society.

Small Deciduous, 25 to 35 feet

Paperbark maple (*Acer griseum*)	4-8, 8-3
Japanese maple (*Acer palmatum*)	5-8, 8-2
Serviceberry (*Amelanchier arborea, A. canadensis*)	4-9, 9-4
White fringe tree (*Chionanthus virginicus*)*	5-9, 9-3
Kousa dogwood (*Cornus kousa*)	5-8, 8-3
Golden-rain tree (*Koelreuteria paniculata*)	5-9, 8-5
Crape myrtle (*Lagerstroemia indica*)	7-9, 9-7/6
Star magnolia (*Magnolia stellata*)	5-9, 9-5
Crabapple (*Malus* spp.)	4-8, 8-1
Autumnalis cherry (*Prunus subhirtella* var. *autumnalis*)	6-8, 8-6
Japanese tree lilac (*Syringa reticulata*)	4-7, 7-1

Medium Deciduous, 35 to 60 feet

European hornbeam (*Carpinus betulus*)	4-8, 8-1
Yellowwood (*Cladrastis kentukea*)	4-9, 9-1
European beech (*Fagus sylvatica*)	5-7, 7-5
Carolina silverbell (*Halesia carolina*)	5-8, 8-4
Sweet bay magnolia (*Magnolia virginiana*)*	6-9, 9-6
Sourwood (*Oxydendrum arboreum*)	5-9, 9-4
Persian parrotia (*Parrotia persica*)	4-7, 7-1
Amur cork tree (*Phellodendron amurense*)	3-7, 7-1

Yoshino cherry (*Prunus* × *yedoensis*)	6-8, 8-6
Japanese stewartia (*Stewartia pseudocamellia*)	5-8, 8-5
Japanese snowbell (*Styrax japonicus*)	6-8, 8-6
Littleleaf linden (*Tilia cordata*)	4-8, 8-1
Lacebark elm (*Ulmus parvifolia*)	5-9, 9-5
Japanese zelkova (*Zelkova serrata*)	5-8, 8-5

Large Deciduous, more than 60 feet

Red maple (*Acer rubrum*)	3-9, 9-1
River birch (*Betula nigra*)	5-7, 7-2
Katsura (*Cercidiphyllum japonicum*)	4-8, 8-1
American beech (*Fagus grandifolia*)*	3-9, 9-1
Ginkgo (*Ginkgo biloba*)	5-9, 9-2
Sweetgum (*Liquidambar styraciflua*)*	6-9, 9-1
Tulip tree, tulip poplar, yellow poplar (*Liriodendron tulipifera*)*	5-9, 9-2
Dawn redwood (*Metasequoia glyptostroboides*)	5-11, 12-5
Black gum (*Nyssa sylvatica*)*	5-9, 9-5
White oak (*Quercus alba*)	5-9, 9-5
Red oak (*Quercus rubra*)	5-9, 9-4
Bald cypress (*Taxodium distichum*)*	5-11, 12-5
American linden (*Tilia americana*)*	3-9, 9-1
American elm, new cvs. (*Ulmus americana*)	3-9, 9-1

GINKGO

Evergreen, varying heights

White fir (*Abies concolor*)	2-7, 7-1
Fraser fir (*Abies fraseri*)	4-7, 7-2
Blue Atlas cedar (*Cedrus atlantica* 'Glauca')	6-9, 9-6
Hinoki false cypress (*Chamaecyparis obtusa*)	4-8, 8-1
Japanese cryptomeria (*Cryptomeria japonica*)	6-9, 9-6
American holly (*Ilex opaca*)	5-9, 9-5
Southern magnolia (*Magnolia grandiflora*)*	7-9, 9-3
Norway spruce (*Picea abies*)	3-8, 8-1
Limber pine (*Pinus flexilis*)	3-7, 7-1

TREES THAT HAVE NO BUSINESS BEING IN A LANDSCAPE

The title of this list comes from Paul Wolfe, who contributed the Low-Pest Trees list. He says you'd have to be a glutton for punishment to plant some of these problem trees. Ed Milhous from Haymarket, Virginia, who is a consulting arborist and a former Cooperative Extension agent, put together this list of trees and their major flaws, with some additions from Paul Wolfe and from Mary Ann Hansen and Eric Day at Virginia Tech. Everyone may not agree with the choices of these tree and pest specialists, because many of these trees also have good landscape features. However, if you decide to plant any of them, or let existing ones remain in place in your landscape, this list lets you know the problems you may encounter. For example, Paul calls willows "a plumber's best friend" because the roots get in sewers and pipes—but only if there are openings or defects. Tree roots can't bore into these items!

If you want to use the wonderful native sweetgum that's on this list but don't want to contend with the messy fruit, plant the generally fruitless cultivar 'Rotundiloba.'

Box elder (*Acer negundo*)	Grows quickly, rots even faster; magnet for box elder bugs
Norway maple (*Acer platanoides*)	Dense shade under which nothing will grow; invasive in some areas
Silver maple (*Acer saccharinum*)	Becomes massive quickly; short-lived; surface roots

Tree of heaven (*Ailanthus altissima*)	Short-lived; invasive
Mimosa (*Albizia julibrissin*)	Short-lived, especially due to wilt disease; seeds volunteers
White-barked birches (*Betula papyrifera*, *B. pendula*)	Quickly killed by bronze birch borers
Paper mulberry (*Broussonetia papyrifera*)	A weedy tree with obnoxious roots
Catalpa (*Catalpa speciosa*)	Brittle wood; seeds everywhere; occasional caterpillar problems
Deodar cedar (*Cedrus deodara*)	Sudden cold temperatures can kill out the top of large trees
White dogwood (*Cornus florida*)	Not for hot, sunny spots; being killed by *Discula* anthracnose fungus and borers
English hawthorn (*Crataegus laevigata*)	Thorny; defoliated in summer by rust disease
Leyland cypress (× *Cupressocyparis leylandii*)	Dying from wet feet and *Seridium* canker
Green ash (*Fraxinus pennsylvanica*)	Numerous pest problems, especially borers
Honeylocust (*Gleditsia triacanthos*)	Multiple insect problems; thorns and seeds are problems, except with the seedless cultivars
Black walnut (*Juglans nigra*)	Drops large fruit and leaves early; allelopathic to other plants
Sweetgum (*Liquidambar styraciflua*)	Fruit gumballs are a hazard; litter and maintenance problem
Osage orange (*Maclura pomifera*)	Thorns; falling fruit
Crabapples (*Malus* spp.)	Attacked by bacterial and fungal diseases, unless newer resistant cultivars
White and red mulberries (*Morus alba* and *M. rubra*)	Smelly fruit that birds use to paint cars and houses purple
Princess or empress tree (*Paulownia tomentosa*)	Invasive due to massive seed production
White pine (*Pinus strobus*)	Not tolerant of poorly drained, compacted urban soils
Virginia pine (*Pinus virginiana*)	Uproots easily
American sycamore (*Platanus occidentalis*)	Annual defoliation due to anthracnose disease; lacebug; fruit litter
Cottonwood (*Populus deltoides*)	Surface roots; cotton on seeds coats everything
Lombardy poplar (*Populus nigra* 'Italica')	Short-lived; grows too fast; aggressive roots
Flowering cherries (*Prunus* spp.)	Trunk cankers can cause gradual death
Flowering plums (*Prunus* spp.)	Black knot fungal disease can cause severe dieback
Bradford pear (*Pyrus calleryana* 'Bradford')	Crotch angles split easily
Pin oak (*Quercus palustris*)	Frequent chlorosis problems due to overliming lawns; numerous insect pests
Black locust (*Robinia pseudoacacia*)	Thorns, shallow roots, and suckers; insects; topples easily in storms
Willows (*Salix* spp.)	Grow fast and split easily; trunk cankers; roots invade pipe openings
Mountain ashes (*Sorbus* spp.)	Numerous pest problems
Canadian hemlock (*Tsuga canadensis*)	Plagued with mites, scales, and woolly adelgids
American elm (*Ulmus americana*)	Killed by Dutch elm disease; look for new resistant hybrids and cultivars
Siberian elm (*Ulmus pumila*)	Breaks easily in storms; defoliated by elm leaf beetles

"When planting a tree in your yard, it is nice to know exactly what you're getting into. Often someone will buy a tree at the garden center, enjoy if for a few years, and then discover some unfortunate disadvantages to the particular kind of tree just about the time the tree is beginning to have an effect in the landscape. While no plant is perfect, remember: when you make a mistake planting a tree, as time passes it only gets to be a bigger mistake."
Ed Milhous is a consulting arborist from Haymarket, Virginia.

LOW-PEST CRABAPPLES AND DOGWOODS

Deborah Smith-Fiola of Rutgers Cooperative Extension has compiled an extremely useful manual of landscape plants that have been documented to be resistant to specific insects and diseases. It's not surprising that the following lists are among the most often requested. They give species and cultivars of two of our most popular spring-flowering trees—crabapples and dogwoods—that are resistant to some of our region's most damaging pests. (More lists can be found in Debby's manual, *Pest Resistant Ornamental Plants*.)

**Crabapple Cultivars Resistant to Cedar-Hawthorn Rust, Scab,
and Frog Eye Leaf Spot**   4-8, 8-1
Malus 'Beverly,' 'Bob White,' 'Centennial,' 'Christmas Holly,' 'Coralburst,' 'David Makamik,' 'Doglo,' 'Donald Wyman,' 'Golden Gem,' 'Golden Hornet,' 'Jewelberry,' 'Klehm's Improved,' 'Liset,' 'Narragansett,' 'Ormiston Roy,' 'Prairie Fire,' 'Prince George,' 'Professor Sprenger,' 'Profusion,' 'Red Jade,' 'Red Jewel,' 'Selkirk,' 'Sentinel,' 'Silver Moon,' 'Snowdrift,' 'Strawberry Parfait,' 'Sugar Tyme,' 'Velvet Pillar,' 'White Angel,' '*Malus* x *zumi* 'Calocarpa'

Dogwoods Resistant to Spot Anthracnose (*Elsinoe*)   5-8, 8-5
Cornus florida 'Junior Miss'

Dogwoods Resistant to Anthracnose (*Discula*)   5-8, 8-5
Cornus canadensis, C. florida 'Spring Grove' and 'Sunset,' *C. kousa* 'Milky Way' and 'Steeple,' *C. kousa* x *C. florida* hybrids, *C. kousa* var. *chinensis, C. racemosa*

Dogwoods Resistant to Dogwood Borer   5-8, 8-5
Cornus kousa, C. kousa x *C. florida* hybrids

ALTERNATIVES TO BRADFORD PEAR

One of the best spring-flowering trees for the New York and Mid-Atlantic region is the callery pear (*Pyrus calleryana*). Its prolific showing of white flowers makes it extremely popular. But the most popular callery pear cultivar—'Bradford'—has gained a bad reputation. 'Bradford' pear is easy for the nursery industry to grow, so when the landscape industry saw its beautiful flowers, glossy green leaves, red fall color, and wonderful form, they demanded and planted tens of thousands of them. Soon after its introduction, it gave the crabapple a run for its money for honors as favorite flowering tree. Unfortunately, a structural problem—narrow crotch angles, where the branch attaches to the stem—plagues the tree after it's been in the landscape for 15 to 20 years. Then large branches begin to break away, especially in storms, and its beauty gets destroyed. This wonderful landscape beauty is now in disfavor.

If you still want a callery pear of some form, try one of the cultivars with fewer structural problems than you'll find with the 'Bradford.' Those are listed below. Some of the narrower forms better fit the limited space allotted to street trees. These cultivars must each be evaluated on other characteristics, however, including susceptibility to fire blight, a bacterial disease that can be heavy on some cultivars. In addition, many other trees have one or more of the callery pear's landscape attributes, so consider using some of the alternatives that follow. These lists are from Waynesboro, Virginia, horticulturist C. Dwayne Jones.

Callery Pears with Good Structure

'Aristocrat'	broader crown than 'Bradford'
'Redspire'	columnar, more reliable fall color
'Cleveland Select'	narrow
'Whitehouse'	narrow
'Capital'	very narrow

Trees to Substitute for Callery Pears

Trident maple (*Acer buergerianum*)	5-9, 9-3
Flame amur maple (*Acer ginnala* 'Flame')	2-7, 7-1
Three-flowered maple (*Acer triflorum*)	5-7, 7-5
Norwegian Sunset maple (*Acer truncatum* x *platanoides* 'Keithsform')	3-7, 7-1
Autumn Brilliance serviceberry (*Amelanchier* x *grandiflora* 'Autumn Brilliance')	4-9, 9-4
Fox Valley river birch (*Betula nigra* 'Little King')	5-7, 7-2
Tea-oil camellia (*Camellia oleifera*)	6-9, 9-5
Korean hackberry (*Celtis koraiensis*)	6-8, 8-6
Chinese fringe tree (*Chionanthus retusus*)	6-8, 8-5
White fringe tree (*Chionanthus virginicus*)	5-9, 9-3
Pagoda dogwood (*Cornus alternifolia*)	4-8, 8-1
Spring Glow dogwood (*Cornus mas* 'Spring Glow')	5-8, 8-3
Two-winged silverbell (*Halesia diptera*)	5-8, 8-4
Golden-rain tree (*Koelreuteria paniculata*)	5-9, 8-5
Wada's Memory magnolia (*Magnolia kobus* 'Wada's Memory')	5-9, 9-5
Dr. Merrill magnolia (*Magnolia* x *loebneri* 'Merrill')	5-9, 9-5
Galaxy magnolia (*Magnolia* x 'Galaxy')	6-9, 9-5
Snowdrift crabapple (*Malus* x 'Snowdrift')	4-8, 8-1
Village Shade photinia (*Photinia villosa* 'Village Shade')	4-9, 9-1
Chinese pistache (*Pistacia chinensis*)	6-9, 9-6
Rosemary Clarke apricot (*Prunus mume* 'Rosemary Clarke')	6-8, 8-6
Okame cherry (*Prunus* x 'Okame')	5-8, 8-4
Jacktree (*Sinojackia rehderiana*)	6-10, 10-6
Pagoda tree (*Sophora japonica*)	7-11, 12-7
Korean mountain ash (*Sorbus alnifolia*)	5-8, 8-5
Emerald Pagoda snowbell (*Styrax japonicus* 'Emerald Pagoda')	6-8, 8-6
Snowfall Japanese snowbell (*Styrax japonicus* 'Snowfall')	6-8, 8-6
Fragrant snowbell (*Styrax obassia*)	6-8, 8-6
Ivory Silk tree lilac (*Syringa reticulata* 'Ivory Silk')	4-7, 7-1

"When approached by citizens about suitable trees to replace Bradford pears, I always ask: What part of the tree do you want to keep—its form, flower, toughness, size, or fall color? If size and shape are important and bloom color is not critical, then the pink flowering Okame cherry closely matches the Bradford's characteristics. Then they can tell their neighbors they have the only pink-flowered Bradford pear."

C. Dwayne Jones is a horticulturist for the City of Waynesboro, Virginia, and is very active in educational programs about tree care.

TOUGH CITY TREES

When we think of city trees, we most often look at them as a means to offset the visual negative. We use them as a means to bring beauty and visual relief to a hardscape, or we may look at them as an asset to a city park, a public building site, or even to provide shade along a coastal road or resort area. The trees in this list from Roger Huff, city arborist for Virginia Beach, Virginia, have proven themselves in some of these situations.

Amur maple (*Acer ginnala*)	2-7, 7-1
Red maple (*Acer rubrum* cvs.)	3-9, 9-1
Green Mountain sugar maple (*Acer saccharum* 'Green Mountain')	4-8, 8-3
Serviceberry (*Amelanchier canadensis*)	3-7, 7-1
Southern catalpa (*Catalpa bignonioides*)	5-9, 9-3
Northern catalpa (*Catalpa speciosa*)	4-8, 8-1
Sugar hackberry (*Celtis laevigata*)	5-9, 9-3
Common hackberry (*Celtis occidentalis*)	2-9, 9-1
Eastern redbud (*Cercis canadensis*)	6-9, 9-6
Katsura (*Cercidiphyllum japonicum*)	4-8, 8-1
Leyland cypress (× *Cupressocyparis leylandii*)	6-9, 9-4
Marshall's Seedless green ash (*Fraxinus pennsylvanica* 'Marshall's Seedless')	6-9, 9-3
Ginkgo, males only (*Ginkgo biloba*)	5-9, 9-2
Thornless honeylocust (*Gleditsia triacanthos* var. *inermis* cvs.)	3-7, 7-1
Eastern red cedar (*Juniperus virginiana*)	3-9, 9-1
Golden-rain tree (*Koelreuteria paniculata*)	5-9, 8-5
Golden chain tree (*Laburnum anagyroides*)	6-8, 8-5
Japanese crape myrtle (*Lagerstroemia fauriei*)	6-9, 9-6
Fruitless sweetgum (*Liquidambar styraciflua* 'Rotundiloba')	6-9, 9-1
Little Gem magnolia (*Magnolia grandiflora* 'Little Gem')	6/7-9, 9-3
Sweet bay magnolia (*Magnolia virginiana*)	6-9, 9-6
Amur cork tree (*Phellodendron amurense*)	3-7, 7-1
Japanese black pine (*Pinus thunbergiana*)	5-8, 8-4
Bloodgood London plane tree (*Platanus* × *acerifolia* 'Bloodgood')	6-8, 8-3
Japanese flowering cherry (*Prunus serrulata* cvs.)	5-8, 8-3
Yoshino cherry (*Prunus* × *yedoensis*)	6-8, 8-6
Sawtooth oak (*Quercus acutissima*)	6-9, 9-5
Swamp white oak (*Quercus bicolor*)	4-8, 8-3
Water oak (*Quercus nigra*)	7-9, 9-7
Willow oak (*Quercus phellos*)	6-9, 9-5
Red oak (*Quercus rubra*)	5-9, 9-5
Pagoda tree (*Sophora japonica* cvs.)	5-9, 9-5
Bald cypress (*Taxodium distichum*)	5-11, 12-5
Lacebark elm (*Ulmus parvifolia*)	5-9, 9-5
Japanese zelkova (*Zelkova serrata*)	5-9, 9-5

"City trees have many benefits, but the selection process needs to include an evaluation of the harsh environment in which they are to be planted. In some instances, a 'weed tree' may be the only solution. Frank Lloyd Wright's comment 'form follows function' says it all when selecting city trees. Business-district trees must possess aesthetics and be able to tolerate poor soils, limited exposure to sunlight, poor drainage, people pressure, reflected heat, and vehicle emissions. Heavy industry and junkyards need to be screened or buffered. City neighborhoods need trees that are infrastructure friendly, safe, and attractive. Coastal trees need to be tolerant of high-velocity, salt-laden winds."
Roger Huff is the city arborist for Virginia Beach, Virginia.

STREET TREES

Street trees have to be among the toughest of all trees. They're challenged daily by adverse urban conditions, such as climate extremes, poor soil, pollutants, lack of maintenance, and a variety of abuses perpetrated by people in the New York and Mid-Atlantic region. Nina Bassuk, who provided us with this list, suggests that by seeking to plant the "perfect urban tree" over and over again, we set ourselves up for a disaster in the future. "I believe a reasonable goal for most urban plantings is to place a 5% limit on any one species within the total municipal tree population," Nina states. "Therefore, if a disease or an insect infestation should occur, 95% of a tree population would remain intact. Unfortunately, in most urban areas, perhaps only five or fewer species make up the great majority of trees planted."

Small Trees (suitable for planting under utility wires or in restricted spaces)

Trident maple (*Acer buergerianum*)	5-9, 9-3
Amur maple (*Acer ginnala*)	2-7, 7-1
Shantung maple (*Acer truncatum*)	4-8, 8-1
Serviceberry (*Amelanchier arborea*)	4-9, 9-4
American hornbeam (*Carpinus caroliniana*)	3-9, 9-1
Thornless cockspur hawthorn (*Crataegus crus-galli inermis*)	4-7, 7-1
Washington hawthorn (*Crataegus phaenopyrum*)	4-8, 8-1
'Ohio Pioneer' hawthorn (*Crataegus punctata* 'Ohio Pioneer')	5-7, 7-1
'Winter King' hawthorn (*Crataegus viridis* 'Winter King')	5-7, 7-1
Accolade flowering cherry (*Prunus sargentii* 'Accolade')	5-9, 9-5
Canada Red choke cherry (*Prunus virginiana* 'Canada Red')	3-8, 8-1
Swedish mountain ash (*Sorbus intermedia*)	5-8, 8-3
Columnar Oakleaf mountain ash (*Sorbus thuringiaca fastigiata*)	5-7, 7-5
Japanese tree lilac (*Syringa reticulata*)	4-7, 7-1

Medium to Large Trees

Freeman maple (*Acer* x *freemanii*)	4-7, 7-1
Norway maple (*Acer platanoides*)	3-7, 7-1
Sycamore maple (*Acer pseudoplatanus*)	4-7, 7-1
Red maple (*Acer rubrum*)	3-9, 9-1
Red horse chestnut (*Aesculus* x *carnea*)	7-8, 8-6
Black alder (*Alnus glutinosa*)	3-7, 7-1
Heritage river birch (*Betula nigra* 'Heritage')	5-7, 7-5
European hornbeam (*Carpinus betulus*)	4-8, 8-1
Hackberry (*Celtis occidentalis*)	2-9, 9-1
Katsura (*Cercidiphyllum japonicum*)	4-8, 8-1
Yellowwood (*Cladrastis kentukea*)	4-9, 9-1
Turkish filbert (*Corylus colurna*)	3-9, 9-1
Hardy rubber tree (*Eucommia ulmoides*)	4-7, 7-1
White ash (*Fraxinus americana*)	6-9, 9-6
European ash (*Fraxinus excelsior*)	6-9, 9-6
Green ash (*Fraxinus pennsylvanica*)	4-9, 9-1
Ginkgo (*Ginkgo biloba*)	5-9, 9-2
Thornless honeylocust (*Gleditsia triacanthos* var. *inermis*)	3-7, 7-1
Kentucky coffee tree (*Gymnocladus dioica*)	5-9, 9-2
Golden-rain tree (*Koelreuteria paniculata*)	5-9, 8-5
Sweetgum (*Liquidambar styraciflua*)	6-9, 9-1
Tulip tree (*Liriodendron tulipifera*)	5-9, 9-2
Dawn redwood (*Metasequoia glyptostroboides*)	5-11, 12-5
Black gum (*Nyssa sylvatica*)	5-9, 9-5
American hop hornbeam (*Ostrya virginiana*)	5-9, 9-2
Amur cork tree (*Phellodendron amurense*)	3-7, 7-1
London plane tree (*Platanus* x *acerifolia*)	5-8, 8-3

Sargent cherry (*Prunus sargentii*)	5-9, 9-5
Callery pear (*Pyrus calleryana*)	5-8, 8-2
Sawtooth oak (*Quercus acutissima*)	6-9, 9-5
Swamp white oak (*Quercus bicolor*)	4-8, 8-3
Shingle oak (*Quercus imbricaria*)	5-8, 8-4
Bur oak (*Quercus macrocarpa*)	3-9, 9-1
Chinkapin oak (*Quercus muehlenbergii*)	4-8, 8-2
Pin oak (*Quercus palustris*)	5-8, 8-4
Willow oak (*Quercus phellos*)	6-9, 9-5
English oak (*Quercus robur*)	5-8, 8-4
Northern red oak (*Quercus rubra*)	5-9, 9-4
Shumard oak (*Quercus shumardii*)	5-8, 8-5
Black locust (*Robinia pseudoacacia*)	4-9, 9-4
Pagoda tree (*Sophora japonica*)	5-9, 9-5
Korean mountain ash (*Sorbus alnifolia*)	5-8, 8-5
Bald cypress (*Taxodium distichum*)	5-11, 12-5
American linden or basswood (*Tilia americana*)	3-8, 8-1
Littleleaf linden (*Tilia cordata*)	4-8, 8-1
Crimean linden (*Tilia euchlora*)	4-8, 8-1
Silver linden (*Tilia tomentosa*)	4-8, 8-1
Elm hybrids (*Ulmus* spp.)	3-9, 9-1
Lacebark elm (*Ulmus parvifolia*)	5-9, 9-5
Japanese zelkova (*Zelkova serrata*)	5-9, 9-5

"If there is no one perfect urban tree, it is also important to understand that there is no one urban environment. The urban environment is a varied conglomeration of microclimates. Above ground or below ground, site conditions can change dramatically within the space of a few feet. This list of recommended urban trees will only accomplish half the task of choosing an appropriate tree. A reasonable site assessment should be completed prior to selection. For more details consult http://www.cals.cornell.edu/dept/flori/uhi/urbantrees1.html."

Nina Bassuk, a professor of horticulture and program leader of the Urban Horticulture Institute at Cornell University in Ithaca, New York, focuses on the physiological problems of plants grown in urban environments.

TREES FOR UTILITY EASEMENTS

Choosing an appropriate tree based on use and available space will determine the long-term health and environmental impact of the plant. Locating large trees under or too near overhead facilities creates future maintenance expenses for the entire community, increases the potential for service interruptions during inclement weather, and never allows the plant to achieve its full potential. A carefully chosen species located where it can develop and not conflict with utility wires, signage, or access to essential service equipment such as transformer pads will add beauty and value to the landscape. A "utility line arboretum," a demonstration and trial site for large shrubs and small trees for use in utility easements, was started by Bonnie Appleton and graduate student Barbara Touchette at Virginia Tech's Hampton Roads Agricultural Research and Extension Center in Virginia Beach in 1992. This ongoing project is a cooperative effort between Virginia Tech and Dominion Virginia Power, with additional assistance from the Virginia Department of Forestry and the Virginia Nursery and Landscape Association. In addition, the J. Frank Schmidt Co. of Boring, Oregon, has a series of trees called Utilitrees™ selected for use in easement areas. Included in this series are ashes, maples, and many members of the *Prunus* genus, such as ornamental cherries and plums.

Trident maple (*Acer buergeranum*)	5-9, 9-3
Hedge maple (*Acer campestre*)	6-8, 8-4

Amur maple (*Acer ginnala*)	2-7, 7-1
Paperbark maple (*Acer griseum*)	4-8, 8-3
Japanese maple (*Acer palmatum*)	5-8, 8-2
Serviceberries (*Amelanchier arborea, A. canadensis*)	4-9, 9-4
American hornbeam (*Carpinus caroliniana*)	3-9, 9-1
Japanese hornbeam (*Carpinus japonica*)	3-9, 9-1
Redbuds (*Cercis canadensis, C. mexicana,* other spp.)	6-9, 9-6
Chinese fringe tree (*Chionanthus retusus*)	6-8, 8-5
White fringe tree (*Chionanthus virginicus*)	5-9, 9-5
Kousa dogwood (*Cornus kousa*)	5-8, 8-3
Stellar series dogwoods (*Cornus* x *rutgersensis*)	5-8, 8-3
Thornless cockspur hawthorn (*Crataegus crus-galli* var. *inermis*)	4-7, 7-1
Washington hawthorn (*Crataegus phaenopyrum*)	4-8, 8-1
Franklinia (*Franklinia alatamaha*)	6-9, 9-6
Golden-rain tree (*Koelreuteria paniculata*)	5-9, 8-5
Crape myrtle (*Lagerstroemia indica*)	7-9, 9-7/6
Galaxy magnolia (*Magnolia* 'Galaxy')	6-9, 9-6
Little Gem magnolia (*Magnolia grandiflora* 'Little Gem')	7-9, 9-3
Saucer magnolia (*Magnolia* x *soulangeana*)	6-9, 9-6
Star magnolia (*Magnolia stellata*)	5-9, 9-5
Sweet bay magnolia (*Magnolia virginiana*)	6-9, 9-6
Flowering crabapple (*Malus* spp.)	4-8, 8-1
Sourwood (*Oxydendrum arboreum*)	5-9, 9-4
Persian parrotia (*Parrotia persica*)	4-7, 7-1
Thundercloud cherry plum (*Prunus cerasifera* 'Thundercloud')	5-9, 9-4
Flowering apricot (*Prunus mume* 'Bonita' and 'Peggy Clark')	6-8, 8-6
Yoshino cherry (*Prunus* x *yedoensis*)	6-8, 8-6
Evergreen oak (*Quercus myrsinifolia*)	7-9, 9-7
Japanese stewartia (*Stewartia pseudocamellia*)	5-8, 8-5
Japanese snowbell (*Styrax japonicus*)	6-8, 8-6
Fragrant snowbell (*Styrax obassia*)	6-8, 8-6
Doublefile viburnum (*Viburnum plicatum* var. *tomentosum*)	6-8, 8-6
Japanese tree lilac (*Syringa reticulata*)	4-7, 7-1

"All trees and shrubs reaching a mature height over 15 feet should be planted a minimum of 20 feet from any overhead utility wires, including electric, communication, or TV cable. Trees over 40 feet high should be placed a minimum of 45 feet from any overhead conductors."
   Jeff Smith, based in Norfolk, Virginia, is a regional forester in the coastal area of Dominion Virginia Power.

SALT-TOLERANT TREES

During the winter in many parts of the New York and Mid-Atlantic region, de-icing salts are applied to roads, sidewalks, parking lots, and other hard surfaces to help melt snow and ice. As a result, trees and other plants may have problems with salt in the soil, which damages roots, and salt spray splashed up by cars onto leaves, buds, and twigs. One easy solution is to use de-icing materials that are less toxic to plants (gypsum, calcium chloride, ammonium nitrate, ash, sand, and newer commercial de-icers). Other solutions are to establish windbreaks from tolerant shrubs and ornamental grasses, or to use solid barriers such as concrete. Or you can select salt-tolerant trees like the ones in this list.

Amur maple (*Acer ginnala*)	2-7, 7-1
Norway maple (*Acer platanoides*)	3-7, 7-1

European hornbeam (*Carpinus betulus*)	3-9, 9-1
White ash (*Fraxinus americana*)	6-9, 9-3
Ginkgo (*Ginkgo biloba*)	5-9, 9-2
Honeylocust (*Gleditsia triacanthos* var. *inermis*)	3-7, 7-1
American holly (*Ilex opaca*)	5-9, 9-5
Golden-rain tree (*Koelreuteria paniculata*)	5-9, 8-5
Sweetgum (*Liquidambar styraciflua*)	6-9, 9-1
Sweet bay magnolia (*Magnolia virginiana*)	6-9, 9-6
Black gum (*Nyssa sylvatica*)	5-9, 9-5
Austrian pine (*Pinus nigra*)	5-8, 8-4
Japanese black pine (*Pinus thunbergiana*)	5-8, 8-4
London plane tree (*Platanus* × *acerifolia*)	5-8, 8-3
Callery pear (*Pyrus calleryana*)	5-8, 8-2
White oak (*Quercus alba*)	5-9, 9-5
Water oak (*Quercus nigra*)	7-9, 9-7
Willow oak (*Quercus phellos*)	6-9, 9-5
Red oak (*Quercus rubra*)	5-9, 9-4
Pagoda tree (*Sophora japonica*)	6-9, 9-6
Japanese tree lilac (*Syringa reticulata*)	6-8, 8-6
Bald cypress (*Taxodium distichum*)	5-11, 12-5
Lacebark elm (*Ulmus parvifolia*)	5-9, 9-5

Some trees to avoid planting along streets that may be de-iced include red maple (*Acer rubrum*), sugar maple (*Acer saccharum*), hackberry (*Celtis occidentalis*), Eastern white pine (*Pinus strobus*), and little-leaf linden (*Tilia cordata*).

BLACK WALNUT—THE TREE THAT POISONS OTHER PLANTS

Though grown primarily for their wood and nuts, black walnuts often serve as shade trees. When certain other landscape plants are planted near or under a black walnut, however, those plants tend to yellow, wilt, and die. This decline occurs because black walnut produces a colorless chemical called hydrojuglone in its leaves, stems, fruit hulls, inner bark, and roots. When exposed to air or soil compounds, hydrojuglone is oxidized into juglone, which is highly toxic (phytotoxic) to many other plants. Juglone is one of many plant-produced chemicals that can harm other plants in a process known as *allelopathy*. Additional common landscape trees causing allelopathic effects are sugar maple, tree of heaven, hackberries, southern wax myrtle, American sycamore, cottonwood, black cherry, red oak, black locust, sassafras, and American elm.

Allelopathic effects can be reduced by:

- Regularly cleaning up all fallen leaves and fruit, and keeping debris away from desired landscape plants.
- Maintaining high organic matter levels in the soil. Organic matter encourages healthy soil microbial populations that can metabolize toxins.
- Planting tolerant trees, shrubs, vines, ground covers, flowers, and grasses under the trees, or in areas that might contain the roots.

The following plants are generally tolerant of black walnut toxins, unless under drought conditions.

Trees and Shrubs That Tolerate Juglone

American arborvitae, white ash, barberry, American beech, black and 'Heritage' river birch, box elder, Ohio buckeye, catalpa, black cherry, crabapple, daphne, flowering dogwood, elderberry, American elm, forsythia, fringe tree, golden-rain tree, globeflower, black gum, hawthorn, Canadian hemlock, hibiscus, hickory, American holly, honeylocust, honeysuckle, hydrangea, lilac, black locust, red, sugar, Japanese and black maple, ninebark, white, red and scarlet oak, pawpaw, callery pear, Virginia pine, privet, eastern red cedar, eastern redbud, sassafras, serviceberry, Carolina silverbell, Norway spruce, St. John's wort, sumac, sweetgum, sycamore, tulip tree, viburnums (some species), witch hazel

Other Plants That Tolerate Juglone

anemone, aster, astilbe, bee balm, begonia, bittersweet, calendula, clematis (virgin's bower), coral bells, Virginia creeper, daffodil, shasta daisy, daylily, evening primrose, ferns, hardy geraniums, goldenrod, wild grapes, hollyhock, hosta, grape hyacinth, siberian iris, ironweed, Jack-in-the-pulpit, lambs' ears, liriope, lobelia, may apple, morning glory, mullein, phlox, primrose, black raspberry, wild rose, rudbeckia, scilla, sedum, speedwell, spiderwort, sunflower, trillium, tulip, violet, wisteria, yarrow

Plants Damaged by Juglone

apple, azalea, white birch, blackberry, blueberry, chrysanthemum, autumn crocus, forget-me-not, domestic grape, lily-of-the-valley, linden, mountain laurel, peony, pine, potato, rhododendron, thyme, tomato

FLOWERING TREES

DOGWOOD

A flowering tree in full bloom is one of the most magnificent sights in nature. Landscapes large and small come alive with color and texture from a few strategically placed flowering trees. While most flowering trees will be more "floriferous" in full sun, many, like the native dogwood, actually are better suited to partial shade that duplicates the light intensity under which they naturally grow. In this list from Norman Grose, who is the tree and shrub manager for McDonald's Garden Center in Chesapeake, Virginia, trees that tolerate partial shade are marked with an asterisk (*); they are good choices as understory trees—small trees that grow under or in the shade of larger, taller trees.

White	Bloom Season	
White redbud (*Cercis canadensis alba*)*	Early spring	6-9, 9-3
White fringe tree (*Chionanthus virginicus*)*	Mid spring	5-9, 9-3
Chinese fringe tree (*Chionanthus retusus*)*	Mid spring	6-8, 8-5
American yellowwood (*Cladrastis kentukea*)	Late spring	4-9, 9-1
Dogwood (*Cornus florida*)*	Early spring	5-8, 8-3
Kousa dogwood (*Cornus kousa*)*	Mid spring	5-8, 8-3
Washington hawthorn (*Crataegus phaenopyrum*)	Late spring	4-8, 8-1
Green hawthorn (*Crataegus viridis*)	Late spring	5-7, 7-1
Crape myrtles (*Lagerstroemia indica, L. fauriei,* and hybs.)	All summer	7-9, 9-7/6
Southern magnolia (*Magnolia grandiflora*)	All summer	7-9, 9-3
Star magnolia (*Magnolia stellata*)*	Early spring	5-9, 9-5
Sweet bay magnolia (*Magnolia virginiana*)*	Late spring, summer	6-9, 9-5
Sourwood (*Oxydendrum arboreum*)*	Mid summer	5-9, 9-4
Yoshino cherry (*Prunus* x *yedoensis*)	Early spring	6-8, 8-6
Weeping cherry (*Prunus* x 'Snow Fountain')	Early spring	6-8, 8-6
Flowering pear (*Pyrus calleryana*)	Early spring	5-8, 8-2
Pagoda tree (*Sophora japonica*)	Mid summer	6-9, 9-6
Japanese snowbell (*Styrax japonicus*)	Mid spring	6-8, 8-6
Violet or Lavender		
Crape myrtle (*Lagerstroemia indica* and hybrids)	All summer	7-9, 9-7/6
Magnolia hybrids (*Magnolia* x)	Early spring	5-9, 9-5
Chaste tree (*Vitex agnus-castus*)	Early summer	6-9, 9-6
Yellow		
Cornelian cherry (*Cornus mas*)	Early spring	5-8, 8-3
Golden-rain tree (*Koelreuteria paniculata*)	Late spring	5-9, 8-5
Golden chain tree (*Laburnum* x *watereri*)	Mid spring	6-8, 8-5
Elizabeth magnolia (*Magnolia* x 'Elizabeth')	Mid spring	6-9, 9-6
Red		
Red horse chestnut (*Aesculus* x *carnea*)	Late spring	7-8, 8-6

Crape myrtle (*Lagerstroemia indica* and hybs.)	All summer	7-9, 9-7/6

Pink

Eastern redbud (*Cercis canadensis*)*	Early spring	6-9, 9-3
Chinese redbud (*Cercis chinensis*)*	Early spring	6-9, 9-3
Dogwood (*Cornus florida* cvs.)*	Early spring	5-9, 9-3
Crape myrtle (*Lagerstroemia indica* and hybs.)	All summer	7-9, 9-7/6
Saucer magnolia (*Magnolia* x *soulangeana*)*	Early spring	6-9, 9-6
Magnolia hybrids (*Magnolia* x)*	Early spring	6-9, 9-6
Thundercloud plum (*Prunus cerasifera* 'Thundercloud')	Early spring	5-9, 9-4
Flowering apricot (*Prunus mume*)	Late winter/early spring	6-8, 8-6
Kwanzan cherry (*Prunus serrulata* 'Kwanzan')	Early spring	5-8, 8-5
Weeping cherry (*Prunus subhirtella* 'Pendula')	Early spring	6-8, 8-6

"The crape myrtle's long lasting and brilliant summer blooms are a great addition to any landscape. The hybrids developed by the National Arboretum are all quality selections. These can be easily identified because they are named after Native American tribes. 'Natchez,' 'Tuscarora,' and 'Catawba' are three of my favorite cultivars. Also, the native fringe tree is a treasure, if you can find it. Its lacy, lightly fragrant white blooms are delightful. Unfortunately, it can be hard to find because it is not easy to produce. I like the golden-rain tree because it is one of the most interesting and beautiful trees. Its bright yellow blooms do appear like a golden rain shower. After it is finished blooming, colorful seed pods form all over the tree."

Norman Grose is the tree and shrub manager for McDonald's Garden Center in Chesapeake, Virginia.

TREES WITH FRAGRANT FLOWERS

Fragrance is not often considered a priority when planning a landscape, but it can add immeasurably to the overall enjoyment, interest, and lasting impression of the garden. Trees with fragrant flowers provide all the usual benefits of trees in the landscape with a surprise at some special time. If you're planning a landscape, try to include some trees to scent the air in the spring or summer while you'll be outside. If you're lucky enough to already have any of these trees in your yard or on your fence line, be sure to enjoy them during bloom time.

Don't forget that there are trees with fragrant leaves. Most of them are evergreens such as firs (*Abies*), cedars (*Cedrus*), pines (*Pinus*), and arborvitae (*Thuja*). Leaves of these plants are wonderful to crush and sniff when you're working in the yard.

Amur maple (*Acer ginnala*)	2-7, 7-1
Mimosa (*Albizia julibrissin*)	6-9, 9-6
White fringe tree (*Chionanthus virginicus*)	5-9, 9-3
Yellowwood (*Cladrastis kentukea*)	4-9, 9-1
Common persimmon (*Diospyros virginiana*)	7-9, 9-7
Russian olive (*Elaeagnus angustifolia*)	3-8, 8-1
Franklinia (*Franklinia alatamaha*)	6-9, 9-4
Kentucky coffee tree (*Gymnocladus dioica*)	5-9, 9-2
Carolina silverbell (*Halesia carolina*)	5-8, 8-4
American holly (*Ilex opaca*)	5-9, 9-5
Crape myrtle (*Lagerstroemia indica*)	7-9, 9-7/6
Yulan magnolia (*Magnolia denudata*)	6-9, 9-6
Southern magnolia (*Magnolia grandiflora*)	7-9, 9-3
Star magnolia (*Magnolia stellata*)	5-9, 9-5
Sweet bay magnolia (*Magnolia virginiana*)	6-9, 9-6
Sargent crabapple (*Malus sargentii*)	4-8, 8-1

Sourwood (*Oxydendrum arboreum*)	5-9, 9-4
Hardy orange (*Poncirus trifoliata*)	5-9, 9-5
Amur choke cherry (*Prunus maackii*)	3-7, 7-1
Japanese flowering cherry (*Prunus serrulata*)	5-8, 8-3
Yoshino cherry (*Prunus* x *yedoensis*)	6-8, 8-6
Fragrant epaulette tree (*Pterostyrax hispida*)	5-8, 8-5
Black locust (*Robinia pseudoacacia*)	4-9, 9-4
Pagoda tree (*Sophora japonica*)	5-9, 9-5
Fragrant snowbell (*Styrax obassia*)	6-8, 8-6
Japanese snowbell (*Styrax japonicus*)	6-8, 8-6
Japanese tree lilac (*Syringa reticulata*)	6-8, 8-6
Common lilac (*Syringa vulgaris*)	4-8, 8-1
American linden or basswood (*Tilia americana*)	3-8, 8-1
Littleleaf linden (*Tilia cordata*)	4-8, 8-1
Silver linden (*Tilia tomentosa*)	4-8, 8-1

"A whiff of a mimosa still evokes pleasant childhood memories for me, even though many people consider it a weed tree. Other fragrant trees for the New York and Mid-Atlantic region are the crape myrtle and lilac, which can be trained into tree form."

Mary Bean, from Clifton, Virginia, is a former Cooperative Extension agent who now consults and coordinates professional development seminars for the horticulture industry.

TREES WITH NON-GREEN LEAVES

Some people want trees with leaves that are anything but green during the growing season, not just during the fall. Generally, it is not the straight species of the trees that has non-green leaves, but various cultivars, which in some cases are so numerous (Japanese maples for example—see the list on pp. 8 and 9) that cultivars are not listed here. For details on available cultivars of the species in this list, consult a plant reference book, or talk with the staff at your local nursery. Many cultivars of these species have variegated leaves, with whites, yellows, creams, and pinks.

Deciduous
Box elder (*Acer negundo*)	5-8, 8-3
Japanese maple (*Acer palmatum*)	5-8, 8-2
Norway maple (*Acer platanoides*)	3-7, 7-1
Redbud (*Cercis canadensis*)	6-9, 9-4
Flowering dogwood (*Cornus florida*)	5-8, 8-3
Cornelian cherry (*Cornus mas*)	5-8, 8-3
Smoke tree (*Cotinus coggygria*)	5-8, 8-1
European beech (*Fagus sylvatica*)	5-7, 7-5
Honeylocust (*Gleditsia triacanthos* var. *inermis*)	3-7, 7-1
Crabapple (*Malus* spp.)	4-8, 8-1
Cherries and plums (*Prunus* spp.)	5-8, 8-5

Evergreen
Concolor fir (*Abies concolor*)	3-7, 7-2
Blue Atlas cedar (*Cedrus atlantica glauca*)	6-9, 9-3
False cypress (*Chamaecyparis* spp.)	4-8, 8-1
China fir (*Cunninghamia lanceolata*)	7-9, 9-7
Leyland cypress (x *Cupressocyparis leylandii*)	6-9, 9-4
English holly (*Ilex aquifolium*)	7-9, 9-1

American holly (*Ilex opaca*)	5-9, 9-5
Junipers (*Juniperus* spp.)	3-9, 9-1
Colorado spruce (*Picea pungens*)	3-8, 8-1
Eastern white pine (*Pinus strobus*)	4-9, 9-3
Arborvitaes (*Thuja occidentalis* and *T. orientalis*)	2-7, 7-1

FALL COLOR TREES

Frank Gifford, an arborist with Gifford Brothers Tree Service in Telford, Pennsylvania, compiled this color list. As days shorten and temperatures drop during the fall, these trees consistently provide good fall color in the New York and Mid-Atlantic region. As production of the green chlorophyll pigment ceases, existing yellow pigments are revealed. Red pigments develop in the fall only if the shortening days are sunny and the nights are cool, below 45 degrees F. Genetic variation and the introduction of new cultivars are additional factors that affect fall color.

Some trees are listed here with multiple colors, for varying reasons. Many of the maples (*Acer*) will have all of the listed colors on one tree at the same time, and often within the same leaf. Bradford pear (*Pyrus calleryana* 'Bradford') will be yellow to red in some locations, and red to purple in others. Black tupelo or sour gum (*Nyssa sylvatica*) will change from its summer dark green to a fluorescent yellow, then to orange to scarlet to purple.

B = bronze
P = purple/maroon/burgundy
Y = yellow/gold
O = orange
R = red /crimson/scarlet

Trident maple (*Acer buergerianum*)	Y, O, R	5-9, 9-3
David maple (*Acer davidii*)	Y, O	5-7, 7-5
Amur maple (*Acer ginnala*)	Y, R	2-7, 7-1
Paperbark maple (*Acer griseum*)	R	4-8, 8-3
Full-moon maple (*Acer japonicum* 'Vitifolium')	P, O, R	5-7, 7-4
Japanese maple (*Acer palmatum* 'Bloodgood')	R	5-8, 8-2
Striped maple (*Acer pensylvanicum*)	Y	3-7, 7-1
Red maple (*Acer rubrum* 'October Glory,' 'Red Sunset')	Y, O, R	3-9, 9-1
Sugar maple (*Acer saccharum*)	Y, O, R	4-8, 8-3
Three-flowered maple (*Acer triflorum*)	Y, O, R	5-7, 7-5
Ohio buckeye (*Aesculus glabra*)	B, Y, O, R	3-7, 7-1
Serviceberry (*Amelanchier arborea*)	O, R	4-9, 9-4
Sweet birch (*Betula lenta*)	Y	3-7, 7-2
Paper birch (*Betula papyrifera*)	Y	2-7, 7-1
European hornbeam (*Carpinus betulus*)	Y	3-9, 9-1
American hornbeam (*Carpinus caroliniana*)	Y, O, R	3-9, 9-1
Pignut hickory (*Carya glabra*)	Y	5-8, 8-4
Chinese chestnut (*Castanea mollissima*)	B	4-8, 8-1
Katsura (*Cercidiphyllum japonicum*)	Y, O	4-8, 8-1
American yellowwood (*Cladrastis kentukea*)	Y	4-9, 9-1
Flowering dogwood (*Cornus florida*)	P, R	5-8, 8-3
Kousa dogwood (*Cornus kousa*)	P, R	5-8, 8-3
American smoke tree (*Cotinus obovatus*)	P, Y, O, R	5-8, 8-5
Green hawthorn (*Crataegus viridis* 'Winter King')	P, R	5-7, 7-1
American beech (*Fagus grandifolia*)	B, Y	3-9, 9-1
European beech (*Fagus sylvatica* 'Asplenifolia')	B	5-7, 7-5
Franklinia (*Franklinia alatamaha*)	O, R	6-9, 9-4
White ash (*Fraxinus americana*)	P, Y, R	6-9, 9-3
Raywood ash (*Fraxinus oxycarpa* 'Raywood')	P	6-9, 9-3

Ginkgo (*Ginkgo biloba*)	Y	5-9, 9-2
Japanese larch (*Larix kaempferi*)	Y	3-6, 6-1
Sweetgum (*Liquidambar styraciflua*)	P, Y, R	6-9, 9-1
Tulip tree (*Liriodendron tulipifera*)	Y	5-9, 9-2
Tea crabapple (*Malus hupehensis*)	Y, R	4-8, 8-1
Dawn redwood (*Metasequoia glyptostroboides*)	B	5-11, 12-5
Black gum (*Nyssa sylvatica*)	P, Y, O, R	5-9, 9-5
Sourwood (*Oxydendrum arboreum*)	P, Y, R	5-9, 9-4
Persian parrotia (*Parrotia persica*)	Y, O, R	4-7, 7-1
Amur cork tree (*Phellodendron amurense*)	B, Y	3-7, 7-1
Chinese pistache (*Pistacia chinensis*)	R, O	6-9, 9-6
Sargent cherry (*Prunus sargentii*)	B, Y, R	5-9, 9-5
Golden larch (*Pseudolarix kaempferi*)	Y, O	5-9, 9-5
Fragrant epaulette tree (*Pterostyrax hispida*)	Y	5-8, 8-5
Bradford callery pear (*Pyrus calleryana* 'Bradford')	P, Y, R	5-8, 8-2
Scarlet oak (*Quercus coccinea*)	R	5-9, 9-4
Pin oak (*Quercus palustris*)	B, R	5-8, 8-4
Willow oak (*Quercus phellos*)	B, R	6-9, 9-5
Red oak (*Quercus rubra*)	R	5-9, 9-4
Shumard oak (*Quercus shumardii*)	R	5-8, 8-5
White willow (*Salix alba* 'Tristis')	Y	4-9, 9-4
Sassafras (*Sassafras albidum*)	P, Y, O, R	5-8, 8-4
Korean mountain ash (*Sorbus alnifolia*)	B, Y, O, R	5-8, 8-3
Korean stewartia (*Stewartia koreana*)	P, R	5-8, 8-4
Tall stewartia (*Stewartia monadelpha*)	P, R	6-9, 9-6
Japanese stewartia (*Stewartia pseudocamellia*)	P, Y, R	5-8, 8-5
Bald cypress (*Taxodium distichum*)	B	5-11, 12-5
Littleleaf linden (*Tilia cordata*)	Y	4-8, 8-1
Japanese zelkova (*Zelkova serrata*)	R, P, Y, O	5-8, 8-5

"Enjoy the more subtle fall colors as much as the most vibrant ones in the neighborhood. Fall color should accent your landscape, not overwhelm it. Be patient—some trees need to reach a certain stage of maturity or have optimal weather conditions before achieving their full fall color potential. Don't shy away from bronze and yellow. A larch (*Larix*) or dawn redwood (*Metasequoia glyptostroboides*) provides an excellent backdrop for a more dramatic full-moon maple (*Acer japonicum* 'Vitifolium'). A halo of bright yellow paper birch (*Betula papyrifera*) leaves on a rich green front lawn can be as beautiful as the most brilliant sassafras (*Sassafras albidum*). Finally, don't forget the old-fashioned way to have a colorful fall landscape: inherit it. A property with mature oaks (*Quercus*), ash (*Fraxinus*), maples (*Acer*), and hickories (*Carya*) would take nearly a lifetime to grow."

Frank Gifford is a certified arborist with Gifford Brothers Tree Service in Telford, Pennsylvania.

TREES WITH ATTRACTIVE FRUIT

Showy fruits, be they berries or pods, lend wonderful fall and winter interest to the landscape and often provide food for birds and other wildlife. Colors range from yellows and greens to purples and blacks. The berries of the Chinese pistache (*Pistacia chinensis*) come in pink and robin's-egg blue. Don't forget the cones on the deciduous and evergreen conifers—bald cypress, cedars, cryptomeria, dawn redwood, firs, hemlocks, larches, pines, spruces. What we call juniper berries are actually cones. Cones range from very small (arborvitae and hemlocks) to often very large and flashy, especially some that sit upright atop the branches, like the true cedars (*Cedrus*).

Some trees in this list are dioecious—that is, the male and female flowers are on separate trees. You need both kinds in the same general area in order for pollination and fruit set to occur. Dioecious trees in this list are marked with an asterisk (*).

Yellow or Green Berries or Pods

American holly (*Ilex opaca* 'Canary,' 'Goldie')	5-9, 9-5
Pagoda tree (*Sophora japonica*)	5-9, 9-5

Orange or Red Berries

Serviceberries (*Amelanchier* spp.)	4-9, 9-4
Flowering dogwood (*Cornus florida*)	5-8, 8-4
Chinese dogwood (*Cornus kousa*)	5-8, 8-4
Cornelian cherry (*Cornus mas*)	5-8, 8-3
Hawthorns (*Crataegus* spp.)	4-8, 8-1
Common persimmon (*Diospyros virginiana*)*	4-9, 9-1
English holly (*Ilex aquifolium*)*	7-9, 9-5
Foster's holly (*Ilex* x *attenuata* 'Fosteri')*	6-9, 9-4
Deciduous hollies (*Ilex decidua, I. verticillata*)*	5-9, 9-5
American holly (*Ilex opaca*)*	5-9, 9-5
Yaupon holly (*Ilex vomitoria*)*	7-10, 12-7
Crabapples (*Malus* spp., hybs., and cvs.)	4-8, 8-1
Mountain ash (*Sorbus* spp.)	5-8, 8-5
Yews (*Taxus* spp.)*	5-7, 7-5

Blue, Purple, or Black Berries

Serviceberries (*Amelanchier* spp.)	4-9, 9-1
White fringe tree (*Chionanthus virginicus*)*	7-9, 9-7
Junipers (*Juniperus* spp.)*	3-9, 9-1
Black gum (*Nyssa sylvatica*)	5-9, 9-5
Amur cork tree (*Phellodendron amurense*)*	3-7, 7-1
Chinese pistache (*Pistacia chinensis*)*	6-9, 9-6
Nannyberry (*Viburnum lentago*)	2-8, 8-1
Siebold viburnum (*Viburnum sieboldii*)	5-8, 8-5

Dry Fruit and Seedpods

Amur maple (*Acer ginnala*)	2-7, 7-1
Japanese maple (*Acer palmatum*)	5-8, 8-2
Red maple (*Acer rubrum*)	3-9, 9-1
Korean evodia (*Evodia danielli*)	5-8, 8-5
Kentucky coffee tree (*Gymnocladus dioica*)	5-9, 9-2
Carolina silverbell (*Halesia carolina*)	5-8, 8-4
Golden-rain tree (*Koelreuteria paniculata*)	5-9, 8-5
Southern magnolia (*Magnolia grandiflora*)	7-9, 9-3
Sourwood (*Oxydendrum arboreum*)	5-9, 9-4
Fragrant epaulette tree (*Pterostyrax hispida*)	5-8, 8-5
American bladdernut (*Staphylea trifolia*)	4-9, 9-4
Japanese snowbell (*Styrax japonicus*)	6-8, 8-6

TREES WITH WONDERFUL BARK

My love of great bark can be attributed to Steve Dubik, professor of landscape technology at Montgomery College, who is a fanatical bark nut," says Amanda Laudwein, who compiled this list. Amanda is a landscape consultant specializing in integrated pest management in Silver Spring, Maryland.

Many trees have intricately colored bark that is striking from afar (London plane tree), fascinating on closer inspection (snakebark maple), hidden under foliage (yews), or require patience as the beauty only

appears with age (Japanese zelkova). Some bark is attractive because of its color, such as the white bark of many of the birches, or the tans and rusts of the crape myrtles. Other bark is attractive because of its smoothness (beeches and cherries), or because it's shaggy (shagbark hickory), or peels or exfoliates (river birch or lacebark elm). The snakebark and moosewood maples have colored twigs, as do many willows: *Salix alba* has cultivars with red and yellow twigs, and weeping willow twigs are yellowish green. Two trees with really green twigs are hardy orange (*Poncirus trifoliata*) and pagoda tree (*Sophora japonica*).

Trident maple (*Acer buergerianum*)	orange brown, exfoliating
Snakebark or striped maple (*Acer capillipes*)	green and white striped, smooth
Paperbark maple (*Acer griseum*)	cinnamon, exfoliating
Coralbark maple (*Acer palmatum* 'Sango Kaku,' 'Senkaki')	coral red, smooth
Moosewood (*Acer pensylvanicum*)	green and white striped, smooth
Redvein maple (*Acer rufinerve*)	bluish white young stems, later green and white stripe
Heritage river birch (*Betula nigra* 'Heritage')	cream and cinnamon, exfoliating
Paper or white birch (*Betula papyrifera*)	chalky white, peeling
Asian white birch (*Betula platyphylla* var. *japonica*)	white, smooth
American hornbeam (*Carpinus caroliniana*)	gray, smooth, "muscled"
Shagbark hickory (*Carya ovata*)	dark gray, exfoliating
Katsura tree (*Cercidiphyllum japonicum*)	brown, slightly shaggy
Chinese fringe tree (*Chionanthus retusus*)	gray, peeling
American yellowwood (*Cladrastis kentukea*)	gray, smooth
Flowering dogwood (*Cornus florida*)	gray brown, blocky like alligator hide
Kousa dogwood (*Cornus kousa*)	gray/tan/brown patches
Japanese cedar (*Cryptomeria japonica*)	reddish brown, long peeling strips
Dove tree or handkerchief tree (*Davidia involucrata*)	reddish brown, scaly
Common persimmon (*Diospyros virginiana*)	dark gray, checkerboard pattern
American beech (*Fagus grandifolia*)	light gray, smooth
European beech (*Fagus sylvatica*)	medium gray, smooth
Rocky mountain juniper (*Juniperus scopulorum*)	gray or reddish brown, shredding
Eastern red cedar (*Juniperus virginiana*)	light grayish brown shredding with rust beneath
Crape myrtles (*Lagerstroemia indica* hybs. and cvs.)	gray, smooth, exfoliates with tans and browns beneath
Fantasy crape myrtle (*Lagerstroemia fauriei* 'Fantasy')	tan and rust, smooth
Crabapple (*Malus* spp.)	gray-brown, scaly
Dawn redwood (*Metasequoia glyptostroboides*)	reddish brown, long exfoliating strips
American hop hornbeam (*Ostrya virginiana*)	grayish brown, long strips
Sourwood (*Oxydendrum arboreum*)	graying brown to black with slight checkerboard
Persian parrotia (*Parrotia persica*)	gray, exfoliates with green/white/brown beneath
Lacebark pine (*Pinus bungeana*)	greenish with white or brown patches
London plane tree (*Platanus* x *acerifolia*)	cream/olive/light brown, exfoliating
Amur choke cherry (*Prunus maackii*)	red to cinnamon brown, some exfoliating
Birchbark cherry (*Prunus serrula*)	shiny reddish brown, peels, major lenticels
Chinese quince (*Pseudocydonia sinensis*)	gray/green/brown, exfoliating
Korean stewartia (*Stewartia koreana*)	gray/brown/cinnamon, exfoliating
Tall stewartia (*Stewartia monadelpha*)	cinnamon, exfoliating
Japanese stewartia (*Stewartia pseudocamellia*)	gray and reddish brown, exfoliating
Fragrant snowbell (*Styrax obassia*)	gray, exfoliating with red and green marks
Japanese tree lilac (*Syringa reticulata*)	reddish brown, smooth, cherry-like

Bald cypress (*Taxodium distichum*)	reddish brown, fibrous
English yew (*Taxus baccata*)	reddish brown, scaly or flaky
Japanese yew (*Taxus cuspidata*)	reddish brown, exfoliates
Lacebark elm (*Ulmus parvifolia*)	gray/green/brown/rust, exfoliating
Japanese zelkova (*Zelkova serrata*)	gray, smooth to later mildly exfoliating

SHADE-TOLERANT TREES

Behind the successful establishment of every tree lies careful consideration of three key factors: the desires of the home owner, the characteristics of the site, and the needs of the tree. While some factors, such as soil, can be modified, others such as light or exposure cannot be effectively changed. Although shade is a challenge, it is also an opportunity for a gardener to shine! The trees in this list, from Virginia Lerch in New Carrollton, Maryland, will put up with varying degrees of shade. Shade can be infinitely variable, but for simplicity this list is divided into two groups: light to medium shade, and dense shade. If adequate moisture and nutrients are provided, these trees will do well. Many of the smaller entries listed here are often referred to as understory trees because they will grow under the canopies of taller trees.

Light to Medium Shade

Concolor fir (*Abies concolor*)	3-7, 7-2
Hedge maple (*Acer campestre*)	6-8, 8-4
Variegated box elder (*Acer negundo* 'Flamingo,' 'Variegatum')	5-8, 8-3
Red maple (*Acer rubrum*)	3-9, 9-1
Freeman maple (*Acer* x *freemanii*)	4-7, 7-1
Red buckeye (*Aesculus pavia*)	5-8, 8-4
Black alder (*Alnus glutinosa*)	3-7, 7-1
Serviceberries (*Amelanchier arborea, A. canadensis*)	4-9, 9-1
Redbud (*Cercis chinensis*)	6-9, 9-6
Atlantic white cedar (*Chamaecyparis thyoides*)	3-8, 8-1
Yellowwood (*Cladrastis kentukea*)	4-9, 9-1
Flowering dogwood (*Cornus florida*)	5-8, 8-4
Stellar dogwoods (*Cornus* x *rutgersensis*)	5-8, 8-4
European beech (*Fagus sylvatica*)	5-7, 7-5
Carolina silverbell (*Halesia carolina*)	5-8, 8-4
Foster's holly (*Ilex* x *attenuata* 'Fosteri')	6-9, 9-4
Yaupon holly (*Ilex vomitoria*)	7-10, 12-7
Southern magnolia (*Magnolia grandiflora*)	7-9, 9-3
Black gum (*Nyssa sylvatica*)	5-9, 9-5
Sourwood (*Oxydendrum arboreum*)	5-9, 9-4
White spruce (*Picea glauca*)	3-6, 6-1
Staghorn sumac (*Rhus typhina*)	3-8, 8-1
Japanese stewartia (*Stewartia pseudocamellia*)	5-8, 8-5
Japanese snowbell (*Styrax japonicus*)	6-8, 8-6
Giant or western arborvitae (*Thuja plicata*)	2-7, 7-1
Canadian hemlock (*Tsuga canadensis*)	4-8, 8-1
American elm (*Ulmus americana* 'Valley Forge')	3-9, 9-1
Lacebark elm (*Ulmus parvifolia*)	5-9, 9-5

Dense Shade

Japanese maple (*Acer palmatum*)	5-8, 8-2
Sugar maple (*Acer saccharum*)	4-8, 8-3
Allegheny serviceberry (*Amelanchier laevis*)	5-9, 9-3
Pawpaw (*Asimina triloba*)	6-8, 8-6
European hornbeam (*Carpinus betulus*)	4-8, 8-1
Possumhaw (*Ilex decidua*)	5-9, 9-5

American holly (*Ilex opaca*)   5-9, 9-5
Sweet-bay magnolia (*Magnolia virginiana*)   6-9, 9-6
American linden (*Tilia americana*)   3-8, 8-1

"Lack of attention to light intensity is usually costly! The consequences not only include the death of the tree, but futile attempts to manage inappropriate tree size, and constant dissatisfaction with an unshowy tree in that special site! Unhealthy trees also are prone to insect and disease problems."

Virginia Lerch, a board member of the Mid-Atlantic chapter of the International Society of Arboriculture and the Maryland Community Forest Council, is a consultant in New Carrollton, Maryland, who specializes in training tree-care professionals.

TREES FOR WET SITES

A number of trees, many of them native throughout bottomlands (flood plains) and along bodies of fresh water in the New York and Mid-Atlantic region, are tolerant of wet soil, and even occasional flooding. This list of trees for wet sites is from A. William Graham Jr., a consultant with the Morris Arboretum in Philadelphia, Pennsylvania. But don't plant these moisture-loving trees near a septic field or old pipes that are cracked or paper thin. Tree roots can't bore through pipes, but they are opportunistic, and if a crack or hole exists through which they can penetrate, through they will go.

If you note that many of these water-tolerant trees also seem to show up frequently as street or parking lot trees where the soil may get very dry, you're right. Many of them are very tolerant of soil moisture extremes and therefore make good urban trees.

Red maple (*Acer rubrum*)   3-9, 9-1
Silver maple (*Acer saccharinum*)   4-8, 8-1
Alder (*Alnus glutinosa*)   3-7, 7-1
Downy serviceberry (*Amelanchier arborea*)   4-9, 9-4
River birch (*Betula nigra*)   5-7, 7-2
American hornbeam (*Carpinus caroliniana*)   3-9, 9-1
Northern catalpa (*Catalpa speciosa*)   4-8, 8-1
Hackberry (*Celtis occidentalis*)   2-9, 9-1
Atlantic white cedar (*Chamaecyparis thyoides*)   3-8, 8-1
White fringe tree (*Chionanthus virginicus*)   5-9, 9-3
Japanese cryptomeria (*Cryptomeria japonica*)   6-9, 9-4
Common persimmon (*Diospyros virginicus*)   4-9, 9-1
Green ash (*Fraxinus pennsylvanica*)   4-9, 9-1
Thornless honeylocust (*Gleditsia triacanthos* var. *inermis*)   3-7, 7-1
Possumhaw (*Ilex decidua*)   5-9, 9-5
Winterberry (*Ilex verticillata*)   5-8, 8-5
American holly (*Ilex opaca*)   5-9, 9-5
Sweetgum (*Liquidambar styraciflua*)   6-9, 9-1
Southern magnolia (*Magnolia grandiflora*)   7-9, 9-3
Sweet bay magnolia (*Magnolia virginiana*)   6-9, 9-6
Dawn redwood (*Metasequoia glyptostroboides*)   5-11, 12-5
Water tupelo (*Nyssa aquatica*)   5-9, 9-5
Black gum (*Nyssa sylvatica*)   5-9, 9-5
London plane tree (*Platanus* x *acerifolia*)   6-8, 8-3
American sycamore (*Platanus occidentalis*)   5-8, 8-3
Austrian pine (*Pinus nigra*)   5-8, 8-4
White poplar (*Populus alba*)   4-9, 9-1
Swamp white oak (*Quercus bicolor*)   4-8, 8-3
Water oak (*Quercus nigra*)   7-9, 9-7

Pin oak (*Quercus palustris*)	5-8, 8-4
Willow oak (*Quercus phellos*)	6-9, 9-5
Red oak (*Quercus rubra*)	5-9, 9-4
Weeping willow (*Salix babylonica*)	6-9, 9-5
Bald cypress (*Taxodium distichum*)	5-11, 12-5
American arborvitae (*Thuja occidentalis*)	2-7, 7-1
Oriental arborvitae (*Thuja orientalis*)	2-7, 7-1
Lacebark elm (*Ulmus parvifolia*)	5-9, 9-5
Japanese zelkova (*Zelkova serrata*)	5-9, 9-5

"I have witnessed half the growth of an extraordinary grove of dawn redwoods (*Metasequoia glyptostroboides*) during my twenty-seven years at the Morris Arboretum. The dawn redwood seems to prefer the small streamside location where several of the thirty or so planted in a grove have topped 100 feet. These trees are still babies, some having been planted in 1948. Our grove is just starting to give the awesome feeling one gets when in a grove of their close relatives, the California Redwoods (*Sequoia sempervirens*)."

A. William Graham Jr. is an arboricultural consultant with the Morris Arboretum of the University of Pennsylvania in Philadelphia, Pennsylvania.

TREES FOR DRY SITES

A dry site is one at which tree water deficits are likely to be more frequent, severe, or longer than is normal for the region. Sites become dry due to insufficient rainfall (drought) or irrigation, or insufficient soil volume in planting areas. Dry areas also develop where soil is compacted and water quickly runs off, or where the soil is high in sand. High temperatures and wind can increase the effects of drought, and therefore steps should be taken to provide shade or windbreaks if possible in areas with dry soil. Applying mulch over as much of a tree's root system as possible, not just token small circles, will help not only with water conservation, but will also keep the soil cooler.

The trees in this list are appropriate for dry locations, and can be considered for other benefits as well. "I tend to prefer plants with several seasons of interest, such as good flowering characteristics, interesting bark, and fall color," notes Scott Clark, nursery specialist of the Cornell Cooperative Extension for Suffolk County, Long Island, and an adviser to commercial businesses involved in ornamental horticulture. "Several of my favorites that tolerate dry conditions are yellowwood (*Cladrastis kentukea*), pagoda tree (*Sophora japonica*), and Japanese tree lilac (*Syringa reticulata*)."

Hedge maple (*Acer campestre*)	6-8, 8-4
Amur maple (*Acer ginnala*)	2-7, 7-1
Tatarian maple (*Acer tataricum*)	3-7, 7-1
Ohio buckeye (*Aesculus glabra*)	3-7, 7-1
Pawpaw (*Asimina triloba*)	6-8, 8-6
European hornbeam (*Carpinus betulus*)	4-8, 8-1
Chinese chestnut (*Castanea mollissima*)	4-8, 8-1
Hackberry (*Celtis occidentalis*)	2-9, 9-1
Eastern redbud (*Cercis canadensis*)	6-9, 9-6
White fringe tree (*Chionanthus virginicus*)	5-9, 9-3
American yellowwood (*Cladrastis kentukea*)	4-9, 9-1
Turkish filbert (*Corylus colurna*)	3-9, 9-1
Smoke trees (*Cotinus coggygria, C. obovatus*)	5-8, 8-1
Hawthorn (*Crataegus* spp.)	4-7, 7-1
European beech (*Fagus sylvatica*)	5-7, 7-5
Green ash (*Fraxinus pennsylvanica*)	4-9, 9-1
Ginkgo (*Ginkgo biloba*)	5-9, 9-2

HACKBERRY

Thornless honeylocust (*Gleditsia triacanthos* var. *inermis*)	3-7, 7-1
Black walnut (*Juglans nigra*)	5-9, 9-5
Eastern red cedar (*Juniperus virginiana*)	3-9, 9-1
Golden-rain tree (*Koelreuteria paniculata*)	5-9, 8-5
Crabapples (*Malus* spp.)	4-8, 8-1
American hop hornbeam (*Ostrya virginiana*)	5-9, 9-2
Chinese pistache (*Pistacia chinensis*)	6-9, 9-6
London plane tree (*Platanus* × *acerifolia*)	6-8, 8-3
Hardy orange (*Poncirus trifoliata*)	5-9, 9-5
Purple leaf plum (*Prunus cerasifera*)	5-9, 9-4
Callery pear (*Pyrus calleryana*)	5-8, 8-2
Bur oak (*Quercus macrocarpa*)	3-9, 9-1
Red oak (*Quercus rubra*)	5-9, 9-4
Black locust (*Robinia pseudoacacia*)	4-9, 9-4
Sassafras (*Sassafras albidum*)	5-8, 8-4
Pagoda tree (*Sophora japonica*)	5-9, 9-5
Japanese tree lilac (*Syringa reticulata*)	4-7, 7-1
Lacebark elm (*Ulmus parvifolia*)	5-9, 9-5
Japanese zelkova (*Zelkova serrata*)	5-9, 9-5

TREES THAT TOLERATE CLAY SOIL

Go into any new subdivision and with rare exception you'll find that the topsoil has been stripped away and a heavy clay subsoil is what's left for planting. Though desirable to amend the entire area with compost or some other organic matter before planting, that's not always possible if landscaping is required before an occupancy permit will be issued. Generally, do not amend with sand, because adding small amounts of sand will actually help turn the soil into concrete. As with wet and dry soil extremes, many native bottomland trees will tolerate—tolerate, not flourish!—in these shouldn't-be-left-but-are soils.

Hedge maple (*Acer campestre*)	6-8, 8-4
Red maple (*Acer rubrum*)	3-9, 9-1
Silver maple (*Acer saccharinum*)	4-8, 8-1
River birch (*Betula nigra*)	5-7, 7-3
American hornbeam (*Carpinus caroliniana*)	3-9, 9-1
Hackberry (*Celtis occidentalis*)	2-9, 9-1
Redbud (*Cercis canadensis*)	6-9, 9-3
Washington hawthorn (*Crataegus phaenopyrum*)	4-8, 8-1
Hardy rubber tree (*Eucommia ulmoides*)	4-7, 7-1
Green ash (*Fraxinus pennsylvanica*)	4-9, 9-1
Thornless honeylocust (*Gleditsia triacanthos* var. *inermis*)	3-7, 7-1
Possumhaw (*Ilex decidua*)	5-9, 9-5
Winterberry (*Ilex verticillata*)	5-8, 8-5
Golden-rain tree (*Koelreuteria paniculata*)	5-9, 8-5
Sweetgum (*Liquidambar styraciflua*)	6-9, 9-1
Sweet bay magnolia (*Magnolia virginiana*)	6-9, 9-6
Crabapples (*Malus* spp. and cvs.)	4-8, 8-1
Amur cork tree (*Phellodendron amurense*)	3-7, 7-1
Norway spruce (*Picea abies*)	3-8, 8-1
Colorado blue spruce (*Picea pungens glauca*)	3-8, 8-1
London plane tree (*Platanus* × *acerifolia*)	6-8, 8-3
American sycamore (*Platanus occidentalis*)	4-8, 8-1
Callery pear (*Pyrus calleryana* cvs.)	5-8, 8-2
Sawtooth oak (*Quercus accutissima*)	6-9, 9-5
White oak (*Quercus alba*)	5-9, 9-5

Swamp white oak (*Quercus bicolor*)	4-8, 8-3
Cherrybark oak (*Quercus falcata*)	6-9, 9-5
Bur oak (*Quercus macrocarpa*)	3-9, 9-1
Pin oak (*Quercus palustris*)	5-8, 8-4
Red oak (*Quercus rubra*)	5-9, 9-4
Weeping willow (*Salix babylonica*)	6-9, 9-5
Bald cypress (*Taxodium distichum*)	5-11, 12-5
Lacebark elm (*Ulmus parvifolia*)	5-9, 9-5
Japanese zelkova (*Zelkova serrata*)	5-8, 8-5

"When planting in clay soils it is especially important to excavate the root collar of the tree or shrub to make sure that it is planted at or just slightly above the existing grade level. If the trees are to be planted very high, do not leave them on a small mound. Taper additional topsoil into the existing grade and till the two together, outside the root ball. This will lessen the soil interface and improve water movement and root growth. Also remember that when clay soils dry out, they shrink and become as hard as brick. It takes a long slow watering to filter into this soil. Mulching the whole area under the drip line of the tree can greatly reduce this severe drying out."

Barbara White is the Community Tree Planting Program Director for the National Tree Trust in Washington, D.C.

TREES FOR ALKALINE SOIL

Most of the time when a soil has a high pH (over 7), it is due to naturally occurring limestone deposits in the soil, or to someone overliming their lawn as they strive for perfect turf. In either case, trees like pin oaks and shrubs like azaleas signal that the pH is too high via their chlorotic leaves. The leaf tissue between the veins becomes yellow, most often because the high pH ties up iron and causes a deficiency. If you live in an area with an alkaline soil—often referred to as "limy" or "chalky"—don't despair. Throughout this book are lists of plants that can tolerate, and in some cases even prefer, alkaline soils.

Hedge maple (*Acer campestre*)	6-8, 8-4
Amur maple (*Acer ginnala*)	2-7, 7-1
Norway maple (*Acer platanoides*)	3-7, 7-1
Sugar maple (*Acer saccharum*)	4-8, 8-3
Horse chestnut (*Aesculus hippocastanum*)	3-8, 8-1
Common alder (*Alnus glutinosa*)	3-7, 7-1
European hornbeam (*Carpinus betulus*)	4-8, 8-1
Pecan (*Carya illinoensis*)	5-9, 9-1
Hackberry (*Celtis occidentalis*)	2-9, 9-1
Eastern redbud (*Cercis canadensis*)	6-9, 9-6
Yellowwood (*Cladrastis kentukea*)	4-9, 9-1
Cornelian cherry (*Cornus mas*)	5-8, 8-3
American filbert (*Corylus americana*)	3-9, 9-1
Smoke tree (*Cotinus coggygria*)	5-8, 8-1
Hawthorn (*Crataegus* spp.)	4-7, 7-1
Leyland cypress (x *Cupressocyparis leylandii*)	6-9, 9-4
Persimmon (*Diospyros virginiana*)	4-9, 9-1
White ash (*Fraxinus americana*)	6-9, 9-3
Green ash (*Fraxinus pennsylvanica*)	4-9, 9-1
Ginkgo (*Ginkgo biloba*)	5-9, 9-2
Honeylocust (*Gleditsia triacanthos* var. *inermis*)	3-7, 7-1
Kentucky coffee tree (*Gymnocladus dioica*)	5-9, 9-2
Possumhaw (*Ilex decidua*)	5-9, 9-5

Yaupon holly (*Ilex vomitoria*)	7-10, 12-7
Rocky mountain juniper (*Juniperus scopulorum*)	4-7, 7-1
Eastern red cedar (*Juniperus virginiana*)	3-9, 9-1
Golden-rain tree (*Koelreuteria paniculata*)	5-9, 8-5
Waterer laburnum (*Laburnum* x *watereri*)	6-8, 8-5
Japanese crape myrtle (*Lagerstroemia fauriei*)	6-9, 9-6
Sweetgum (*Liquidambar styraciflua*)	6-9, 9-1
Tulip tree (*Liriodendron tulipifera*)	5-9, 9-2
Amur maackia (*Maackia amurensis*)	5-7, 7-5
Cucumber magnolia (*Magnolia acuminata*)	4-8, 8-2
Crabapple (*Malus* spp.)	4-8, 8-1
American hop hornbeam (*Ostrya virginiana*)	5-9, 9-2
Amur cork tree (*Phellodendron amurense*)	3-7, 7-1
Japanese black pine (*Pinus thunbergiana*)	5-8, 8-4
Chinese pistache (*Pistacia chinensis*)	6-9, 9-6
London plane tree (*Platanus* x *acerifolia*)	6-8, 8-5
Purple-leaf plum (*Prunus cerasifera*)	5-9, 9-4
Douglas fir (*Pseudotsuga menziesii*)	5-7, 7-4
Bur oak (*Quercus macrocarpa*)	3-9, 9-1
Chinkapin oak (*Quercus muehlenbergii*)	4-8, 8-2
English oak (*Quercus robur*)	5-8, 8-4
Shumard oak (*Quercus shumardii*)	5-8, 8-5
Black locust (*Robinia pseudoacacia*)	4-9, 9-4
Weeping willow (*Salix babylonica*)	6-9, 9-5
Pagoda tree (*Sophora japonica*)	5-9, 9-5
Japanese tree lilac (*Syringa reticulata*)	4-7, 7-1
American arborvitae (*Thuja occidentalis*)	2-7, 7-1
American linden (*Tilia americana*)	3-8, 8-1
Littleleaf linden (*Tilia cordata*)	4-8, 8-1
Lacebark elm (*Ulmus parvifolia*)	5-9, 9-5
Japanese zelkova (*Zelkova serrata*)	5-9, 9-5

"Low pH is one of the most common soil fertility problems we have, yet it is a problem we often create ourselves. Most nitrogen fertilizers we use on our lawns make the soil more acid, and if we don't counterbalance this acidity with periodic limestone applications, trees and shrubs growing in our landscape can be adversely affected. It takes approximately 1.8 pounds of lime to offset the acidity produced by each pound of ammonium nitrate or urea fertilizer, and 5.3 pounds of lime to offset acidity produced by each pound of ammonium sulfate fertilizer. Having the soil tested every three to five years, and liming when needed, is a good hedge against soil acidity problems."

Steve Donohue is a professor of soil science and manager of the soils testing lab for Virginia Tech University in Blacksburg, Virginia.

TREES THAT NEED ACID SOIL

Most soils throughout the New York and Mid-Atlantic region are mildly acid—6.0 to 6.5. That pH range is actually the preferred, or a well tolerated range, for a majority of our landscape plants. However, just as most people know that rhododendrons and azaleas like an even more acid soil (4.5 to 5.5), so too are there trees that tolerate or prefer to have the soil considerably more acid. One of these trees, sourwood or lily-of-the-valley tree, from which bees make great honey, is a rare tree member of the rhodie family.

A major shade and street tree that often serves as an indicator tree when the pH gets too high or alkaline, tying up iron that it needs, is the pin oak (*Quercus palustris*). This happens especially where the tree roots grow into turf areas that are heavily limed.

Balsam fir (*Abies balsamea*)	3-6, 6-1
Fraser fir (*Abies fraseri*)	4-7, 7-2
Red maple (*Acer rubrum*)	3-9, 9-1
Serviceberries (*Amelanchier* spp.)	4-9, 9-1
River birch (*Betula nigra*)	5-7, 7-2
Chinese chestnut (*Castanea mollissima*)	4-8, 8-1
Hinoki false cypress (*Chamaecyparis obtusa*)	4-8, 8-1
White fringe tree (*Chionanthus virginicus*)	5-9, 9-3
Flowering dogwood (*Cornus florida*)	5-8, 8-3
Kousa dogwood (*Cornus kousa*)	5-8, 8-3
Japanese cedar (*Cryptomeria japonica*)	6-9, 9-1
China fir (*Cunninghamia lanceolata*)	7-9, 9-7
American beech (*Fagus grandifolia*)	3-9, 9-1
Franklinia (*Franklinia alatamaha*)	6-9, 9-4
Carolina silverbell (*Halesia carolina*)	5-8, 8-4
Hollies (*Ilex* spp.)	5-9, 9-5
Larch (*Larix decidua*)	3-6, 6-1
Southern magnolia (*Magnolia grandiflora*)	7-9, 9-3
Saucer magnolia (*Magnolia* x *soulangeana*)	6-9, 9-5
Star magnolia (*Magnolia stellata*)	5-9, 9-5
Sweet bay magnolia (*Magnolia virginiana*)	6-9, 9-6
Black gum (*Nyssa sylvatica*)	5-9, 9-5
Sourwood (*Oxydendrum arboreum*)	5-9, 9-5
Norway spruce (*Picea abies*)	3-8, 8-1
Colorado spruce (*Picea pungens*)	3-8, 8-1
Eastern white pine (*Pinus strobus*)	4-9, 9-3
Scotch pine (*Pinus sylvestris*)	3-7, 7-1
Douglas fir (*Pseudotsuga menziesii*)	5-7, 7-4
White oak (*Quercus alba*)	5-9, 9-5
Scarlet oak (*Quercus coccinea*)	5-9, 9-4
Pin oak (*Quercus palustris*)	5-8, 8-4
Willow oak (*Quercus phellos*)	6-9, 9-5
English oak (*Quercus robur*)	5-8, 8-4
Red oak (*Quercus rubra*)	5-9, 9-4
Weeping willow (*Salix babylonica*)	6-9, 9-6
Sassafras (*Sassafras albidum*)	5-8, 8-4
Mountain ash (*Sorbus aucuparia*)	4-7, 7-1
Japanese stewartia (*Stewartia pseudocamellia*)	5-8, 8-5
Japanese snowbell (*Styrax japonicus*)	6-8, 8-6
Canadian hemlock (*Tsuga canadensis*)	4-8, 8-1

CONTAINER TREES

Planting trees in above-ground containers and planters is a common practice on sites that aren't suited for in-ground planting. Containers differ from raised planters in that they are usually smaller in volume and moveable, whereas planters are generally larger and often built as part of the permanent hardscape. The greatest challenge in selecting trees for containers and planters is choosing trees that can survive temperature extremes and that can establish roots in a limited volume of substrate (potting soil). Several factors that need to be considered when selecting containers and trees include environmental influences, container and planter design, substrate type, and tree characteristics. Many of the trees in this list have dwarf cultivars that will work best under the demanding and often stressful conditions of container life.

Deciduous

Trident maple (*Acer buergeranum*)	5-9, 9-3
Hedge maple (*Acer campestre*)	6-8, 8-4
Amur maple (*Acer ginnala* 'Flame')	2-7, 7-1
Paperbark maple (*Acer griseum*)	4-8, 8-3
Full-moon maple (*Acer japonicum*)	5-7, 7-4
Japanese maple (*Acer palmatum*)	5-8, 8-2
Serviceberry (*Amelanchier* spp.)	5-9, 9-3
Eastern redbud (*Cercis canadensis* 'Forest Pansy,' 'Silver Cloud,' 'Texas White')	6-9, 9-5
Chinese fringe tree (*Chionanthus retusus*)	6-8, 8-5
White fringe tree (*Chionanthus virginicus*)	5-9, 9-3
Kousa dogwood (*Cornus kousa*)	5-8, 8-3
Cornelian cherry (*Cornus mas*)	5-8, 8-3
Smoke tree (*Cotinus coggygria*)	5-8, 8-1
Thornless cockspur hawthorn (*Crataegus crus-galli* var. *inermis*)	4-7, 7-1
Downy hawthorn (*Crataegus mollis*)	3-6, 6-1
Crape myrtle (*Lagerstroemia indica*)	7-9, 9-7/6
Ann magnolia (*Magnolia* x 'Ann')	5/6-9, 9-5
Star magnolia (*Magnolia stellata*)	5-9, 9-5
Purple-leaf plum (*Prunus cerasifera*)	5-9, 9-4
Korean stewartia (*Stewartia koreana*)	5-8, 8-4
Japanese stewartia (*Stewartia pseudocamellia*)	5-8, 8-4
Japanese snowbell (*Styrax japonicus*)	6-8, 8-6
Fragrant snowbell (*Styrax obassia*)	6-8, 8-6

Evergreen

False cypress (*Chamaecyparis* spp.)	3-8, 8-1
Nellie R. Stevens holly (*Ilex* x 'Nellie R. Stevens')	7-7, 9-7
Juniper (*Juniperus* spp.)	3-9, 9-1
Little Gem southern magnolia (*Magnolia grandiflora* 'Little Gem')	7-9, 9-3
Lacebark pine (*Pinus bungeana*)	4-7, 7-1
Swiss stone pine (*Pinus cembra*)	3-7, 7-1
Mugo pine (*Pinus mugo*)	3-7, 7-1
American arborvitae (*Thuja occidentalis*)	2-7, 7-1
Canadian hemlock (*Tsuga canadensis*)	4-8, 8-1

FAST-GROWING SHADE TREES

One of the most common questions posed to employees of garden centers and Cooperative Extension Services is "What's a fast-growing shade tree?" Often, people move into a new subdivision, where builders removed the existing trees, and then quickly find that not only is their house hot because there are no shade trees, but it's hot trying to work or play in the yard. The trees in this list are among the fastest growing for the region, both for shade and in some cases for other landscape features. Keep in mind, however, that many fast-growing trees (especially silver maple, poplars, and willows) have weak or brittle wood, which may make them short-lived. Others shed many parts that become litter problems. If you plant the brittle trees, think of them as only temporary, and at the same time plant one or two trees that are slower growing but that will be able to take the place of the fast-growing tree when it dies or falls apart. A few of the trees listed here, such as red maple and lacebark elm, aren't weak and don't litter objectionably, and they make fine shade as well as specimen trees.

Red maple (*Acer rubrum*)	3-9, 9-1
Silver maple (*Acer saccharinum*)	4-8, 8-1
Black alder (*Alnus glutinosa*)	3-7, 7-1
River birch (*Betula nigra*)	5-7, 7-2

Northern catalpa (*Catalpa speciosa*)	4-8, 8-1
Southern catalpa (*Catalpa bignonioides*)	5-9, 9-3
Green ash (*Fraxinus pennsylvanica*)	4-9, 9-1
Sweetgum (*Liquidambar styraciflua*)	6-9, 9-6
London plane tree (*Platanus* x *acerifolia*)	6-8, 8-3
Poplars (*Populus* spp.)	3-9, 9-1
Water oak (*Quercus nigra*)	7-9, 9-7
Pin oak (*Quercus palustris*)	5-8, 8-4
Willow oak (*Quercus phellos*)	6-9, 9-5
Bradford pear (*Pyrus calleryana* 'Bradford')	5-8, 8-2
Black locust (*Robinia pseudoacacia*)	4-9, 9-4
Weeping willow (*Salix babylonica*)	6-9, 9-3
Bald cypress (*Taxodium distichum*)	5-11, 12-3
Lacebark elm (*Ulmus parvifolia*)	5-9, 9-5

TREES THAT LITTER

An important aspect of tree selection is evaluating the size, volume, and maintenance requirements of parts—leaves, bark, branches, fruit—that are dropped by trees. Such annual shedding is part of the natural life cycle of all trees, deciduous or evergreen. The cycle can be viewed as either a beneficial recycling challenge or a maintenance nightmare, but as long as you're prepared for it, you can plan for it, or unplan (not plant a species or remove it).

This list was contributed by Jim Sellmer, a Penn State assistant professor of horticulture.

Hard to Rake Leaves
Norway maple (*Acer platanoides*)
Red maple (*Acer rubrum*)
Silver maple (*Acer saccharinum*)
Horse chestnut (*Aesculus hippocastanum*)
Hickories (*Carya* spp.)
Northern catalpa (*Catalpa speciosa*)
Southern catalpas (*Catalpa bignonioides*)
Black walnut (*Juglans nigra*)
Tulip tree (*Liriodendron tulipifera*)
Cucumber tree magnolia (*Magnolia acuminata*)
Southern magnolia (*Magnolia grandiflora*)
Princess tree (*Paulownia tomentosa*)
London plane tree (*Platanus* x *acerifolia*)
American sycamore (*Platanus occidentalis*)
Bur oak (*Quercus macrocarpa*)

Drop Twigs
Silver maple (*Acer saccharinum*)
River birch (*Betula nigra*)
Paperbark birch (*Betula papyrifera*)
Southern catalpa (*Catalpa bignonioides*)
Northern catalpa (*Catalpa speciosa*)
Pecan (*Carya illinoensis*)
Common hackberry (*Celtis occidentalis*)
Black walnut (*Juglans nigra*)
London plane tree (*Platanus* x *acerifolia*)
American sycamore (*Platanus occidentalis*)
Poplars (*Populus* spp.)
Oaks (*Quercus* spp.)
Black locust (*Robinia pseudoacacia*)
Weeping willow (*Salix babylonica*)
Siberian elm (*Ulmus pumila*)

Quick to Clog Gutters
Maple (*Acer* spp.)
River birch (*Betula nigra*)
Paperbark birch (*Betula papyrifera*)
European white birch (*Betula pendula*)
Gray birch (*Betula populifolia*)
Tulip tree (*Liriodendron tulipifera*)
Pines (*Pinus* spp.)
Black cherry (*Prunus serotina*)
Oaks (*Quercus* spp.)
Willow oak (*Quercus phellos*)
Weeping willow (*Salix babylonica*)

Messy, Hazardous Seeds and Fruit
Norway maple (*Acer platanoides*)
Ohio buckeye (*Aesculus glabra*)
Horse chestnut (*Aesculus hippocastanum*)
Tree of heaven (*Ailanthus altissima*)
Pecans and hickories (*Carya* spp.)
Southern catalpa (*Catalpa bignonioides*)
Northern catalpa (*Catalpa speciosa*)
Persimmon (*Diospyros virginiana*)
Ginkgo (*Ginkgo biloba*)
Honeylocust (*Gleditsia triacanthos*)
Kentucky coffee tree (*Gymnocladus dioica*)

Black walnut (*Juglans nigra*)
Sweetgum (*Liquidambar styraciflua*)
Tulip tree (*Liriodendron tulipifera*)
Osage orange (*Maclura pomifera*)
Crabapples (*Malus* spp.)
Mulberries (*Morus* spp.)
Princess tree (*Paulownia tomentosa*)
Pines (*Pinus* spp.)
London plane tree (*Platanus* x *acerifolia*)

American sycamore (*Platanus occidentalis*)
Cottonwood (*Populus deltoides*)
Black cherry (*Prunus serotina*)
Douglas fir (*Pseudotsuga menziesii*)
Oaks (*Quercus* spp.)
Common buckthorn (*Rhamnus cathartica*)
Glossy buckthorn (*Rhamnus frangula*)
Black locust (*Robinia pseudoacacia*)
Siberian elm (*Ulmus pumila*)

"I find a lawn mower to be invaluable in reducing my need to rake leaves. By mowing a couple of times during the peak of leaf drop, I can work the leaves back into the lawn as mulch before they become a problem. This goes for the large leaves like sycamore and Norway maple or for the sticky, thin leaves of silver maple that tend to mat together after becoming wet. Messy fruits and seeds come in many forms, from too many seeds like tree of heaven, Norway maple, and buckthorn (which assists their invasive habit), to the downright dangerous like the large green grapefruit-like fruit of osage orange."

Jim Sellmer, assistant professor of horticulture for Penn State University, fights messy trees in State College, Pennsylvania.

TREES PRONE AND RESISTANT TO STORM DAMAGE

There are certain genera of trees that are more inherently susceptible to storm damage than others, but any tree has the potential to become a storm-damaged victim," says Joel Koci, the owner of Arbor Care Professional Tree Service in Rockville, Virginia. Joel, who teaches arboriculture at J. Sargeant Reynolds Community College in Richmond, helped compile this list. Any tree that exhibits the following may incur storm damage:

- Sharp v-crotching
- Extreme lean or growth in one direction
- Over-pruning, which allows scaffold limbs to be sun scalded, leading to rot
- Heavy fruit set; hickory, walnut, pecan, apple, and white oak are more prone to damage when they are laden with fruit

It's not only tree genetics that determine a tree's potential for failure, but also its growing position and aerial microclimate that may predispose it to failure. Unfortunately, tree roots are also subject to failure, creating another potential for storm damage. Tree roots that have been cut due to grade changes, ditch lines, or for utility installation cause the trees to be less sturdy and more prone to storm damage. The cut roots also allow soil-borne root rots to enter the trees and begin consuming their roots, thus reducing the trees' anchorage system. In addition to cut roots, a raised water table can cause root rot and a decline in tree anchorage, again making it susceptible to wind throw or failure.

Trees Prone to Storm Damage
Red maple (*Acer rubrum*)
Box elder (*Acer negundo*)
Silver maple (*Acer saccharinum*)
Birches (*Betula* spp.)
Hickories (*Carya* spp.)
Hackberry (*Celtis occidentalis*)
Katsura (*Cercidiphyllum japonicum*)
Leyland cypress (x *Cupressocyparis leylandii*)
Green ash (*Fraxinus pennsylvanica*)
Honeylocust (*Gleditsia triacanthos*)

Golden-rain tree (*Koelreuteria paniculata*)
Tulip tree (*Liriodendron tulipifera*)
Pines (*Pinus* spp.)
Cherries, plums (*Prunus* spp.)
Douglas fir (*Pseudotsuga menziesii*)
Bradford pear (*Pyrus calleryana* 'Bradford')
Oaks (*Quercus* spp.)
Hemlock (*Tsuga canadensis*)
American elm (*Ulmus americana*)
Siberian elm (*Ulmus pumila*)

Storm-Resistant Trees

Sugar maple (*Acer saccharum*)
American hornbeam (*Carpinus caroliniana*)
Beech (*Fagus* spp.)
Ginkgo (*Ginkgo biloba*)

Kentucky coffee tree (*Gymnocladus dioica*)
Sweetgum (*Liquidambar styraciflua*)
Bald cypress (*Taxodium distichum*)
Littleleaf linden (*Tilia cordata*)

EVERGREEN SCREENS AND WINDBREAKS

Using trees as screens can easily enhance living and working spaces. Before selecting trees for screening, first determine the screen's purpose, whether functional or environmental. Screening can be used to define an area, modify or hide a view, create privacy, block wind, dust, salt and snow, control noise, filter light, and direct traffic flow. Avoid using only one species of tree as your screen because an unexpected pest, weather event, or cultural mistake could kill your monoculture. Make your screen of two or more plants—mix evergreen trees with deciduous ones, or with evergreen or deciduous shrubs.

If a screen or windbreak is needed in an area with little ground into which to plant, consider using trees with narrow crowns, or planting trees in containers, either as a temporary or a long-term screen. Use a large container so that annuals, perennials, or ground covers can be planted at the base of the tree to give a more landscaped effect. If a tree that can be sheared is needed, consider using Leyland cypress, eastern white pine, or hemlock.

False cypress (*Chamaecyparis* spp).	3-8, 8-1
Japanese cedar (*Cryptomeria japonica*)	6-9, 9-6
Leyland cypress (x *Cupressocyparis leylandii*)	6-9, 9-4
Foster's holly (*Ilex* x *attenuata* 'Fosteri')	6-9, 9-4
Nellie Stevens holly (*Ilex* x 'Nellie R. Stevens')	7-9, 9-7
American holly (*Ilex opaca*)	5-9, 9-5
Chinese juniper (*Juniperus chinensis* 'Torulosa')	3-9, 9-1
Rocky Mountain juniper (*Juniperus scopulorum* 'Mountbatten,' 'Skyrocket')	4-7, 7-1
Eastern red cedar (*Juniperus virginiana* 'Glauca')	3-9, 9-1
Southern magnolias (*Magnolia grandiflora* 'Hasse,' 'Little Gem')	7-9, 9-3
Sweet bay magnolia (*Magnolia virginiana*)	6-9, 9-6
Spruces (*Picea* spp.)	3-8, 8-1
Pines (*Pinus* spp.)	4-9, 9-1
Arborvitae (*Thuja* spp.)	2-7, 7-1
Canadian hemlock (*Tsuga canadensis*)	4-8, 8-1

ROCKY MOUNTAIN JUNIPER

TREES FOR NARROW SPACES

About 300 years ago in Italy, a tree was found that created much interest—the Lombardy poplar (*Populus nigra* 'Italica'), a mutation of the black poplar. Prized for its rapid growth into a uniquely narrow, columnar form, it was quickly planted throughout Europe and the United States, especially for allees, street plantings, and narrow screens. Unfortunately, as with the Bradford pear, along with the Lombardy's unique form came two flaws: brittle wood and susceptibility to a devastating fungal canker disease. Though screening rows of Lombardy poplars still stand—often with a tree or two missing or of shorter height as they die back—it is no longer a recommended landscape tree.

There are, however, many other trees whose cultivars offer a narrow crown for areas where spreads more than 15 to 20 feet are undesirable or hazardous. This becomes more important each year as the amount of space we have for plants seems to constantly shrink. Generally, when you see a tree cultivar described as fastigiate or columnar, you can assume it's a tree whose crown can take a tight fit. Upright cultivars of many of these trees were introduced by Princeton Nursery of Princeton, New Jersey, with some bearing the nursery's name. Evergreen trees are marked with an asterisk (*).

White or concolor fir (*Abies concolor*)*	3-7, 7-2
Freeman maple (*Acer* x *freemanii* 'Armstrong,' 'Celebration,' 'Scarlet Sentinel')	4-7, 7-1

Paperbark maple (*Acer griseum*)	4-8, 8-3
Greencolumn black maple (*Acer nigrum* 'Greencolumn')	4-8, 8-2
Striped maple (*Acer pensylvanicum*)	4-9, 9-1
Norway maples (*Acer platanoides* 'Columnare,' 'Crimson Sentry,' 'Easy Street,' 'Olmsted')	3-7, 7-1
Red maples (*Acer rubrum* 'Armstrong,' 'Bowhall,' 'Karpick,' 'Scarlet Sentinel')	3-9, 9-1
Sugar maples (*Acer saccharum* 'Apollo,' 'Endowment,' 'Goldspire,' 'Newton Sentry,' 'Seneca Chief,' 'Skybound,' 'Temple's Upright')	4-8, 8-3
Serviceberries (*Amelanchier* × *grandiflora* 'Autumn Brilliance,' 'Princess Diana')	5-8, 8-4
Brilliant Red chokeberry (*Aronia arbutifolia* 'Brilliantissima')	5-9, 9-4
Fastigiate European white birch (*Betula pendula* 'Fastigiata')	2-7, 7-1
Whitespire Asian white birch (*Betula platyphylla* 'Whitespire')	3-7, 7-1
European hornbeams (*Carpinus betulus* 'Columnaris,' 'Fastigiata')	4-8, 8-1
Hinoki false cypress (*Chamaecyparis obtusa*)*	4-8, 8-1
Atlantic white cedar (*Chamaecyparis thyoides*)*	3-8, 8-1
American smoke tree (*Cotinus obovatus*)	5-8, 8-1
Crimson Cloud hawthorn (*Crataegus laevigata* 'Crimson Cloud')	5-8, 8-3
Lavalle hawthorn (*Crataegus* × *lavallei*)	5-8, 8-3
Fastigiate Washington hawthorn (*Crataegum phaenopyrum* 'Fastigiata')	4-8, 8-1
Japanese cryptomeria or cedar (*Cryptomeria japonica*)*	6-9, 9-4
China fir (*Cunninghamia lanceolata*)*	7-9, 9-7
Leyland cypress (× *Cupressocyparis leylandii*)*	6-9, 9-4
European beech (*Fagus sylvatica* 'Dawyck Purple,' 'Fastigiata')	5-7, 7-5
White ashes (*Fraxinus americana* 'Empire,' 'Greenspire')	6-9, 9-3
Green ashes (*Fraxinus pennsylvanica* 'Leprechaun,' 'Skyward,' 'Summit')	4-9, 9-1
Ginkgo (*Ginkgo biloba* 'Fairmount,' 'Fastigiata,' 'Magyar,' 'Princeton Sentry')	5-9, 9-2
Foster's hybrid hollies (*Ilex* × *attenuata* 'East Palatka,' 'Fosteri')*	6-9, 9-4
Hollywood juniper (*Juniperus chinensis* 'Torulosa')*	3-9, 9-1
Rocky Mountain juniper (*Juniperus scopulorum* 'Gray Gleam,' 'Skyrocket,' 'Wichita Blue')*	4-7, 7-1
Canaert eastern red cedar (*Juniperus virginiana* 'Canaertii,' 'Glauca')	3-9, 9-1
Fastigiate golden-rain tree (*Koelreuteria paniculata* 'Fastigiata')	5-9, 8-5
Columnar golden chain (*Laburnum anagyroides* 'Columnaris')	6-8, 8-5
Vossii golden chain (*Laburnum* × *watereri* 'Vossii')	6-8, 8-5
Sweetgums (*Liquidambar styraciflua* 'Festival,' 'Moraine,' 'Rotundiloba')	6-9, 9-1
Columnar tulip tree (*Liriodendron tulipifera* 'Fastigiatum')	5-9, 9-2
Amur maackia (*Maackia amurensis*)	5-7, 7-5
Galaxy magnolia (*Magnolia* 'Galaxy')	6-9, 9-6
Southern magnolias (*Magnolia grandiflora* 'Alta,' 'Bracken's Brown Beauty,' 'Edith Bogue,' 'Glen St. Mary,' 'Hasse,' 'Little Gem,' 'Majestic Beauty')*	7-9, 9-3
Sweet bay magnolia (*Magnolia virginiana*)	6-9, 9-6
Crabapples (*Malus* 'Adirondack,' 'Centurion,' 'Pink Spires,' 'Red Baron,' 'Royalty,' 'Sentinel,' 'Velvet Pillar')	4-8, 8-1
Sourwood (*Oxydendrum arboreum*)	5-9, 9-4
Persian parrotia (*Parrotia persica*)	4-7, 7-1
Bakeri blue spruce (*Picea pungens* 'Bakeri')*	3-8, 8-1
Hoopsii blue spruce (*Picea pungens* 'Hoopsii')*	3-8, 8-1
Swiss stone pine (*Pinus cembra*)*	3-7, 7-1
Fastigiate white pine (*Pinus strobus* 'Fastigiata')*	4-9, 9-3
Thundercloud plum (*Prunus cerasifera* 'Thundercloud')	5-9, 9-4
Big Cis plum (*Prunus* × *cistena* 'Schmidtcis')	4-8, 8-1
Newport plum (*Prunus* 'Newport')	5-9, 9-4
Okame cherry (*Prunus* 'Okame')	5-8, 8-3

Columnar sargent cherry (*Prunus sargentii* 'Columnaris')	5-9, 9-5
Japanese flowering cherries (*Prunus serrulata* 'Amanogawa,' 'Kwansan,' 'Royal Burgundy')	6-8, 8-6
Canada Red choke cherry (*Prunus virginiana* 'Canada Red')	3-8, 8-1
Fastigiate Douglas fir (*Pseudotsuga menziesii* 'Fastigiata')	5-7, 7-4
Callery pears (*Pyrus calleryana* 'Capital,' 'Cleveland Select,' 'Whitehouse')	5-8, 8-2
Crimson Spire oak (*Quercus alba* × *Q. robur* 'Crimschmidt')	5-9, 9-3
English oak (*Quercus robur* 'Fastigiata,' 'Skyrocket')	5-8, 8-4
Japanese umbrella pine (*Sciadopitys verticillata*)*	5-9, 9-4
Pagoda tree (*Sophora japonica* 'Fastigiata,' 'Princeton Upright')	5-9, 9-5
European mountain ash (*Sorbus aucuparia* 'Fastigiata')	4-7, 7-1
Japanese stewartia (*Stewartia pseudocamellia*)	5-8, 8-5
Ivory Silk Japanese tree lilac (*Syringa reticulata* 'Ivory Silk')	4-7, 7-1
Pond cypress (*Taxodium ascendens*)	5-11, 12-5
Eastern arborvitae or white cedar (*Thuja occidentalis* 'Elegantissima,' 'Pyramidalis,' 'Wintergreen')*	2-7, 7-1
Columnar western or giant arborvitae (*Thuja plicata* 'Fastigiata')*	2-7, 7-1
American linden (*Tilia americana* 'Boulevard,' 'Fastigiata,' 'Redmond')	3-8, 8-1
Littleleaf linden (*Tilia cordata* 'Chancellor,' 'June Bride')	4-8, 8-1
Musashino zelkova (*Zelkova serrata* 'Musashino')	5-9, 9-5

"Seasonal effects on transplant establishment will vary with climate since new roots need warm soil for growth, and cold winds can desiccate stems. In addition, trees that are marginally hardy in your region should generally be transplanted in spring."
Roger Harris is an associate professor of horticulture for Virginia Tech in Blacksburg, Virginia.

TREES WITH SPECIAL TRANSPLANT TIMING

According to Gary Watson and Gene Himelich in their book *Principles and Practices of Planting Trees and Shrubs*, "Many trees are transplanted most easily when dormant. The most pronounced state of dormancy corresponds closely with the coldest winter months. Dormancy variations occur between evergreen and deciduous plants. Dormancy is initiated in many plant species at the time of the formation and maturation of terminal buds. Many plants are moved more readily after terminal buds have matured. In general, evergreens can be moved earlier in the fall and later in the spring than deciduous plants. Root growth potential of seedlings increases the longer harvest is delayed in the fall." They include this list of trees that they suggest are best transplanted in the spring. (Their book is available from the International Society of Arboriculture, Champaign, Illinois, or www.isa-arbor.org).

Fir (*Abies* spp.)	3-7, 7-1	kentukea)	
Freeman maple (*Acer* × *freemanii*)	4-7, 7-1	Flowering dogwood (*Cornus florida*)	5-8, 8-3
Paperbark maple (*Acer griseum*)	4-8, 8-3	Hawthorn (*Crataegus* spp.)	4-7, 7-1
Red maple (*Acer rubrum*)	3-9, 9-1	Persimmon (*Diospyros virginiana*)	4-9, 9-1
Pawpaw (*Asimina triloba*)	6-8, 8-6	American beech (*Fagus grandifolia*)	3-9, 9-1
Birch (*Betula papyrifera, B. pendula*, etc.)	2-7, 7-1	European beech (*Fagus sylvatica*)	5-7, 7-5
except river birch (*B. nigra*)	5-7, 7-2	Ginkgo (*Ginkgo biloba*)	5-9, 9-4
American hornbeam (*Carpinus caroliniana*)	3-9, 9-1	Carolina silverbell (*Halesia carolina*)	5-8, 8-4
		American holly (*Ilex opaca*)	5-9, 9-5
Hickory (*Carya* spp.)	5-9, 9-1	Walnut (*Juglans nigra*)	5-9, 9-5
Pecan (*Carya illinoensis*)	5-9, 9-1	Golden-rain tree (*Koelreuteria paniculata*)	6-9, 9-6
Katsura (*Cercidiphyllum japonicum*)	4-8, 8-1	Golden chain tree (*Laburnum* × *watereri*)	6-8, 8-5
American yellowwood (*Cladrastis*	4-9, 9-1	Larch (*Larix* spp.)	3-6, 6-1

Sweetgum (*Liquidambar styraciflua*)	6-9, 9-1	Golden larch (*Pseudolarix kaempferi*)	5-9, 9-5
Tulip tree (*Liriodendron tulipifera*)	5-9, 9-2	Callery pear cultivars (*Pyrus calleryana* 'Aristocrat,' 'Bradford,' 'Capital,' etc.)	5-8, 8-2
Southern magnolia (*Magnolia grandiflora*)	7-9, 9-3		
Saucer magnolia (*Magnolia* x *soulangeana*)	6-9, 9-6	Oak (*Quercus* spp.) except English (*Q. robur*) and pin (*Q. palustris*)	4-8, 8-1
Star magnolia (*Magnolia stellata*)	5-9, 9-5		
Sweet bay magnolia (*Magnolia virginiana*)	6-9, 9-6	Willow (*Salix alba, S. babylonica, S. matsudana*, etc.)	6-9, 9-5
Black gum (*Nyssa sylvatica*)	5-9, 9-5		
American hop hornbeam (*Ostrya virginiana*)	5-9, 9-2	Sassafras (*Sassafras albidum*)	5-8, 8-4
		Bald cypress (*Taxodium distichum*)	5-11, 12-5
Sourwood (*Oxydendrum arboreum*)	5-9, 9-4		
Cork tree (*Phellodendron amurense*)	3-7, 7-1	Silver linden (*Tilia tomentosa*)	3-8, 8-1
London plane tree (*Platanus* x *acerifolia*)	6-8, 8-3	Canadian hemlock (*Tsuga canadensis*)	4-8, 8-1
Poplar (*Populus alba, P. deltoides*, etc.)	4-9, 9-1	Japanese zelkova (*Zelkova serrata*)	5-9, 9-5
Flowering apricot, cherry, peach, plum (*Prunus* spp.)	3-9, 9-1		

LIVING CHRISTMAS TREES

Many people hate to use cut trees at Christmas, preferring instead to use living trees that can be transplanted to the landscape. All of the conifers in this list from Larry Kuhns, a Penn State professor of ornamental horticulture and owner of a tree farm, are grown as Christmas trees and as landscape plants. However, their range of adaptability varies greatly. "Of the trees that are commonly grown as Christmas trees, only a few make very good plants for the landscape," Larry advises. "My favorites are southwestern white pine for large open areas, Serbian spruce for smaller, confined areas, and Douglas fir or Colorado spruce for hedges or screens." In general, the pines are the most adaptable and will grow well throughout the New York and Mid-Atlantic region. Southwestern white pine is a relatively new introduction to the region and is superior in the landscape to the traditional eastern white pine. Because of their growth habits and tendency to open up with age, they do not serve well as landscape screens in the long run.

Spruces and Douglas fir are widely adapted in all but the hottest parts of the region, and they hold together well to provide dense screens for many years. Norway spruce tends to get more rangy and open than the other spruces listed here. Serbian spruce stays relatively narrow and is a good choice for small properties. Of the true firs, white fir is the most widely adapted to the region. Balsam, Canaan, and fraser fir only survive in cooler parts of the region, which tend to be in the higher elevations. As the average temperature of the area goes up, the true firs are stressed and become more susceptible to insect problems such as spider mites. Leyland cypress is not the best Christmas tree, but does make a wonderful hedge or screen.

When using a living Christmas tree, limit the amount of time that the tree is inside to no more than two weeks. Locate the tree in a cool area of the house and keep the root ball moist. You may need to pre-dig a planting hole in case the ground is frozen when you're ready to plant your tree after Christmas.

Balsam fir (*Abies balsamea*)	3-6, 6-1	Serbian spruce (*Picea omorika*)	5-8, 8-3
Canaan fir (*Abies balsamea lephrolepsis*)	3-6, 6-1	Colorado spruce (*Picea pungens*)	3-8, 8-1
White fir (*Abies concolor*)	3-7, 7-2	Austrian pine (*Pinus nigra*)	5-8, 8-4
Fraser fir (*Abies fraseri*)	4-7, 7-2	Red pine (*Pinus resinosa*)	3-7, 7-1
Leyland cypress (x *Cupressocyparis leylandii*)	6-9, 9-4	Eastern white pine (*Pinus strobus*)	4-9, 9-3
		Southwestern white pine (*Pinus strobiformis*)	4-9, 9-1
Norway spruce (*Picea abies*)	3-8, 8-1		
Engelmann spruce (*Picea engelmannii*)	3-8, 8-1	Scotch pine (*Pinus sylvestris*)	3-7, 7-1
White spruce (*Picea glauca*)	3-6, 6-1	Douglas fir (*Pseudotsuga menziesii*)	5-7, 7-4

SHRUBS

Shrubs—woody, multi-stemmed plants that usually don't grow over 15 feet tall—are the backbones of any landscape design. You can select shrubs to fill any need, ranging from a low ground cover on a steep slope to a hedge or screen to keep views or things in or out. Small shrubs can fit into containers on a deck or patio, and large shrubs can function as small pseudo-trees for utility easement plantings. But aside from filling utilitarian needs in a landscape, shrubs make aesthetic contributions. With equally large numbers of both deciduous and evergreen species, and thousands of cultivars, there are shapes, textures, and colors to fit any landscape theme or specimen requirement. Many shrubs have two or more seasons of interest, whether from leaf or flower colors, interesting fruit, delightful fragrances, or bark that is colored or textured.

Shrubs are more forgiving than trees if we make a selection error and need to modify their size or form. Many of the deciduous shrubs can be cut back to ground level and retrained when new stems develop. Many of the broad-leaved evergreens will also tolerate heavy pruning, although generally not as severe as the deciduous species.

Shrubs can be the lowest maintenance plants in your landscape if you give them plenty of room and allow them to grow, unpruned or unsheared, to their own mature size. Or they can be the highest maintenance plants if you want a formal hedge that must be sheared every few weeks to keep a particular shape and size.

Tips for Selecting and Succeeding with Shrubs

- Be sure you select the right shrub for the right location. If you need an upright shrub, select a species or cultivar that has the growth habit you want. Don't spend unnecessary time shearing a naturally horizontal habit into a spike, or a spike into a pathetic little ball.
- Be aware that many popular deciduous and evergreen shrubs (arborvitae, barberry, boxwood, euonymus, false cypress, holly, juniper, spirea, viburnum) have dwarf forms for use in small, low, or tight places. Also keep in mind that many evergreen shrubs (arborvitae, boxwood, false cypress, Japanese holly, juniper) have very upright or pyramidal forms that can be used in narrow spaces, without constant shearing.
- Learn proper shrub pruning, and start pruning early. Don't wait until a shrub has overgrown your windows or sidewalk or created a hazard. Shearing, however, too often results in mathematicians' delights—round, square, or other geometric forms that rarely do justice to the natural shape of the plant. In addition, tight shearing will result in a dense layer of leaves on the shrub's exterior that will reduce air circulation through the shrub and often increase insect and disease problems. Learn to prune naturalistically, and start that pruning the first year you plant the shrub.
- Keep 2 to 4 inches of mulch around the base of your shrubs to conserve moisture and to protect their shallow roots from temperature extremes and cultivation damage. Supply supplemental irrigation during the growing season if water deficits develop.
- If shrubs are growing in mulched beds, little supplemental fertilization should be necessary. Monitor for signs of nutrient deficiencies, especially micronutrients such as iron and magnesium, which are evidenced by chlorosis (yellowing) patterns on the leaves.
- Monitor for diseases and insects. If populations get large enough to cause significant damage, apply appropriate control measures. Contact your local Cooperative Extension Service for lists of chemical and nonchemical products.

PROBLEM-FREE SHRUBS

N o shrub is totally problem free. Problems—either abiotic or physiological (soil, climate), or biotic or pathological (diseases, insects)—can occur when shrubs are used in environments (soil type and pH, moisture and light levels) that are not conducive to their growth. But here are some of the most problem-free shrubs for the New York and Mid-Atlantic region. This list comes from two Virginia Tech specialists in Blacksburg, Virginia: MaryAnn Hansen, manager of the Plant Disease Clinic, and Eric Day, manager of the Insect Clinic, who note, "Though both Chinese and yaupon hollies are susceptible to scales and sooty mold, they were included because there are few evergreen shrubs on the list, and these species do perform well in many landscapes. Many Chinese juniper cultivars are susceptible to two diseases—Phomopsis blight and Kabatina tip blight—but some cultivars, including 'Keteleeri,' 'Pfitzeriana,' 'Pfitzeriana Aurea,' var. *sargentii*, and var. *sargentii* 'Glauca,' have resistance to both diseases."

Those marked with an asterisk (*) are recommended as beneficial native landscape plants by the Virginia Native Plant Society.

Buttonbush (*Cephalanthus occidentalis*)*	5-11, 12-3
Summersweet or sweet pepperbush (*Clethra alnifolia*)*	3-9, 9-1
Winged euonymus (*Euonymus alatus*)	4-9, 9-1
Border forsythia (*Forsythia* x *intermedia*)	6-9, 9-3
Dwarf fothergilla (*Fothergilla gardenii*)	5-9, 9-3
Large fothergilla (*Fothergilla major*)	5-8, 8-2
Smooth hydrangea (*Hydrangea arborescens*)*	4-9, 9-1
House or bigleaf hydrangea (*Hydrangea macrophylla*)	6-9, 9-3
Oakleaf hydrangea (*Hydrangea quercifolia*)	5-9, 9-3
Chinese holly (*Ilex cornuta*)	7-9, 9-7
Winterberry (*Ilex verticillata*)*	5-8, 8-5
Yaupon holly (*Ilex vomitoria*)	7-10, 12-7
Chinese juniper (*Juniperus chinensis*)	3-9, 9-1
Shore juniper (*Juniperus conferta*)	5-9, 9-1
Oregon holly grape (*Mahonia aquifolium*)	5/6-9, 9-1
Leatherleaf mahonia (*Mahonia bealei*)	6/7-8, 8-3
Northern bayberry (*Myrica pensylvanica*)*	3-6, 6-1
Staghorn sumac (*Rhus typhina*)	3-8, 8-1
Meyer lilac (*Syringa meyeri*)	4-7, 7-1
Burkwood viburnum (*Viburnum* x *burkwoodii*)	4-8, 8-1
Arrowwood (*Viburnum dentatum*)*	3-8, 8-1
Linden viburnum (*Viburnum dilatatum*)	5-8, 8-5
Blackhaw viburnum (*Viburnum prunifolium*)*	3-9, 9-1

SHRUBS THAT TOLERATE OR PREFER SHADE

T he majority of shrubs, especially the deciduous ones with showy flowers, need to be grown in full sun. Full sun, however, doesn't exist in all landscapes, or in all parts of all landscapes, and therefore it's helpful to know that there are many shrubs that will tolerate a range of shade from light or filtered to relatively dense. Shade may reduce flowering and fruiting on some species, but often that is acceptable in order to find a shrub that will tolerate shade.

In addition to the shrubs listed here, check with your local nursery about the various species, hybrids, and cultivars available for azaleas, rhododendrons, yews, and viburnums that would do well in your particular hardiness and heat zones. Also, blueberries and their relatives in the *Vaccinium* genus are other good choices for shady locations.

Shrubs marked with an asterisk (*) in this list should be grown in the shade, because their leaves burn badly if exposed to direct sunlight from mid-morning until late afternoon.

Glossy abelia (*Abelia* x *grandiflora*)	5-9, 9-1
Five-leaved aralia (*Acanthopanax sieboldianus*)	5-8, 8-3
Japanese aucuba (*Aucuba japonica*)*	6-11, 12-
Wintergreen barberry (*Berberis julianae*)	6-9, 9-4
Japanese barberry (*Berberis thunbergii*)	4-8, 8-3
Littleleaf boxwood (*Buxus microphylla*)	6-9, 9-5
Common boxwood (*Buxus sempervirens*)	6-8, 8-1
Japanese camellia (*Camellia japonica*)	7-9, 9-5
Sasanqua camellia (*Camellia sasanqua*)	7-9, 9-5
Hinoki false cypress (*Chamaecyparis obtusa*)	4-8, 8-1
Wintersweet (*Chimonanthus praecox*)	7-9, 9-6
Summersweet (*Clethra alnifolia*)	3-9, 9-1
Red osier dogwood (*Cornus sericea*)	5-8, 8-3
Buttercup winter hazel (*Corylopsis pauciflora*)	6-9, 9-3
Hazels (*Corylus* spp.)	3-9, 9-1
Burkwood daphne (*Daphne* x *burkwoodii*)*	5-8, 8-5
Winter daphne (*Daphne odora*)*	7-9, 9-7
Poet's laurel (*Danae racemosa*)*	6-9, 9-6
Redvein enkianthus (*Enkianthus campanulatus*)	5-8, 8-3
Wintercreeper (*Euonymus fortunei*)	5-9, 9-3
Spreading euonymus (*Euonymus kiautschovicus*)	6-8, 8-6
Dwarf fothergilla (*Fothergilla gardenii*)	5-9, 9-3
Vernal witch hazel (*Hamamelis vernalis*)	4-8, 8-1
Common witch hazel (*Hamamelis virginiana*)	3-8, 8-1
Oakleaf hydrangea (*Hydrangea quercifolia*)	5-9, 9-3
St. John's wort (*Hypericum calycinum*)	5-9, 9-4
Hollies (*Ilex* spp.)	7-9, 9-7
Anise (*Illicium floridanum*)	7-9, 9-7
Virginia sweetspire (*Itea virginica*)	6-9, 9-6
Mountain laurel (*Kalmia latifolia*)	5-9, 9-5
Globeflower or Japanese kerria (*Kerria japonica*)	4-9, 9-1
Drooping leucothoe (*Leucothoe fontanesiana*)	5-8, 8-3
Privet (*Ligustrum amurense*)	3-7, 7-2
Spice bush (*Lindera benzoin*)	5-9, 9-4
Winter honeysuckles (*Lonicera fragrantissima*)	5-8, 8-2
Oregon grape holly (*Mahonia aquifolium*)	5/6-9, 9-1
Leatherleaf mahonia (*Mahonia bealei*)	6/7-8, 8-1
Wax myrtle (*Myrica cerifera*)	6-9, 9-6
Bayberry (*Myrica pensylvanica*)	3-6, 6-1
Nandina or heavenly bamboo (*Nandina domestica*)	6-11, 12-1
Holly osmanthus (*Osmanthus heterophyllus*)	7-9 9-7
Mock orange (*Philadelphus coronarius*)	5-8, 8-3
Japanese pieris (*Pieris japonica*)	6-8, 8-5
Pyracantha (*Pyracantha coccinea*)	6-9, 9-6
Jetbead (*Rhodotypos scandens*)	5-8, 8-4
Staghorn sumac (*Rhus typhina*)	3-8, 8-1
Sweet box (*Sarcococca hookeriana* var. *humilis*)*	6-9, 9-5
Japanese skimmia (*Skimmia japonica*)*	7-9, 9-7

"I define shade as an area that gets less than five hours of direct sunlight per day, or only ever gets dappled or indirect light that might be reflected from a building or body of water. All plants need some sun to photosynthesize, but shade-tolerant plants are those that prefer cool, filtered sunlight. With lots of moist compost on a well-drained site and some protection from the hot, drying sun, these plants literally have it made in the shade."

Joel Lerner, founder and CEO of Environmental Design, Capitol View Park, Maryland, is a *Washington Post* columnist and has authored several books, including *The Complete Home Landscape Designer* (St. Martin's Press).

EVERGREEN AZALEAS

Evergreen azaleas are one of the most popular shrubs in the New York and Mid-Atlantic region. Their popularity comes from their profuse flowering that to many people assures that spring has arrived. However, there are now azaleas like the Encore series that bloom in the fall. There are also beautiful deciduous azaleas, many species of which are native in our region, and many of which have flower colors (yellows, oranges) and fragrance that are unavailable in the evergreen azaleas. Few retail nurseries carry a very good selection of deciduous azaleas, but several mail-order nurseries are a good source.

This list of azalea cultivars that perform well for the New York and Mid-Atlantic region was compiled by two eastern shore of Virginia azalea growers: Robin Rinaca, owner of Eastern Shore of Virginia Nursery in Keller, and Bill Daley, owner of Broadleaf Gardens in Onancock. "The way to succeed with azaleas is location, location, location," advises Robin. Azaleas prefer a soil with even moisture and an acid pH, and grow best in a site protected from the hot afternoon sun.

All azaleas belong to the genus *Rhododendron*, with the different cultivars coming from a variety of hybrid groups.

Red
Girard's Crimson, Girard's Rose, Hershey Red, Hino Crimson, Marilee, Mother's Day, Sherwood Red
Pink
Blaauw's Pink, Higasa, Kaempo, Mary Elizabeth, Nancy of Robin Hill, Rose Bud, Sir Robert, Tradition
White
Delaware Valley White, Helen Curtis, Pleasant White, White Moon
Orchid
Corsage, Elsie, Poukhanense
Purple
Girard's Fuchsia, Purple Splendor, Red-Eyed Orchid Queen
Bicolor
Ben Morrison, Peggy Ann

REALLY GOOD RHODIES—RHODODENDRONS

Whereas azaleas may be the undisputed queens of the spring-flowering shrubs in the southern part of our region, as you progress north you note a distinct increase in the use of their generally larger-leaved relatives, the rhododendrons. To distinguish the two from each other, it helps to remember that azaleas bear their flowers individually, whereas the flowers of the rhododendrons are clustered into terminal heads. Most people are familiar with rhododendrons as fairly large 5 to 8 foot shrubs, but great diversity exists within this genus. There are actually dwarf rhodies that fit nicely into small spaces in rock gardens. With rhododendrons, the diversity is great, but here's a really short list that grower Tom Saunders has selected as a starting point. Tom is a former president of the Virginia Nursery and Landscape Association and supervises production for his family's nursery, Saunders Bros., in Piney River, Virginia.

"Red rhododendrons are breathtaking to behold," Tom says. "Nothing tells one more that summer is coming than the bloom of a red rhodo." Tom notes that the most common flower color on rhododendrons is lilac or purple. In this color range, he recommends 'Purple Gem' and 'PJM,' which offer the homeowner smaller leaves and lower growth habits, making them perfect for use as foundation plants.

RHODODENDRON

White
Catawbiense Album, Chionoides, Yaku Princess
Pink
English Roseum, Rocket, Roseum Pink, Scintillation
Peach
Percy Wiseman
Red
Henry's Red, Jean Marie de Montague, Nova Zembla
Lavender, Lilac, or Purple
Catawbiense Boursault, Catawbiense Grandiflorum, Northern Starburst, PJM, Purple Gem

BOXWOODS

Visit many of the historical sites throughout our region and one of the more frequent and revered shrubs in those landscapes will be boxwood (often called just "box"). Boxwoods are utilitarian or functional shrubs that make wonderful hedges and screens. They serve as good foundation plants if you select appropriately sized cultivars. Also, they make excellent backgrounds for colorful deciduous shrubs, annuals, and perennials because of their glossy, generally dark-green leaves, which help to highlight brightly colored flowers. Some boxwoods, though, have gold and silver variegations.

Though considered an "old" landscape shrub, boxwoods are even more popular today due to their animal resistance. Deer and other wildlife will not eat boxwood because it is toxic to them. There are more than one hundred distinct and different types that go far beyond the traditional English boxwood. More can be learned about them from the *Boxwood Handbook: A Practical Guide to Knowing and Growing Boxwood*, written by Lynn R. Batdorf, curator of boxwood at the U.S. National Arboretum in Washington, D.C., and International Boxwood Registrar. (Lynn's handbook, with more than fifty color pictures, is available from the American Boxwood Society, P.O. Box 85, Boyce, VA 22620-0085.)

Joan Butler, a boxwood consultant for the State Arboretum of Virginia in Boyce, compiled this list.

Littleleaf boxwood (*Buxus microphylla*)
Kingsville dwarf boxwood (*Buxus microphylla* 'Compacta')
Curlylocks littleleaf boxwood (*Buxus microphylla* 'Curly Locks')
Grace Hendrick Phillips boxwood (*Buxus microphylla* 'Grace Hendrick Phillips')
Green Pillow boxwood (*Buxus microphylla* 'Green Pillow')
John Baldwin boxwood (*Buxus microphylla* 'John Baldwin')
Japanese boxwood (*Buxus microphylla* var. *japonica*)
Green Beauty boxwood (*Buxus microphylla* var. *japonica* 'Green Beauty')
Morris Midget boxwood (*Buxus microphylla* var. *japonica* 'Morris Midget')
Common boxwood (*Buxus sempervirens*)
Narrow-leaved or willow boxwood (*Buxus sempervirens* 'Angustifolia')
Columnar boxwood (*Buxus sempervirens* 'Dee Runk')
Variegated silver or olive boxwood (*Buxus sempervirens* 'Elegantissima')
Graham Blandy boxwood (*Buxus sempervirens* 'Graham Blandy')
Weeping boxwood (*Buxus sempervirens* 'Pendula')
Prostrate boxwood (*Buxus sempervirens* 'Prostrata')
Pyramid boxwood (*Buxus sempervirens* 'Pyramidalis')
English boxwood (*Buxus sempervirens* 'Suffruticosa')
Yugoslavian boxwood (*Buxus sempervirens* 'Vardar Valley')
Korean boxwood (*Buxus sinica* var. *insularis*)
Justin Brouwers boxwood (*Buxus sinica* var. *insularis* 'Justin Brouwers')

"Boxwoods need excellent drainage, and most cultivars benefit from high, dappled shade to exhibit their best color. Shallow planting and adequate moisture are necessities because their absorbing roots grow in the top 8 inches of soil or mulch. A neutral soil pH is preferred, and if fertilizer is needed for faster growth, apply it in November or December. Some protection is valuable on windswept sites, particularly on a western exposure where afternoon sun is hot and drying."

Joan Butler has grown boxwood for over thirty years and is a boxwood consultant for the State Arboretum of Virginia in Boyce, Virginia.

SHRUBS THAT WON'T EAT THE HOUSE

One of the biggest landscape mistakes most people make is in the selection of shrubs to go in front of a house. These shrubs are traditionally referred to as foundation plants, and all too often they quickly overgrow and appear to eat the house. While to some this may seem like just a maintenance hassle due to the extra pruning that may become necessary, in reality these overgrown shrubs detract from the aesthetic appeal and real estate value of the house. In addition, they may become a hazard by obscuring house numbers or giving potential vandals a hiding place.

Today's houses use an increasing array of colors and textures in building materials, often with no visible house foundation. This has expanded the use of color and texture in the plants chosen for foundation plantings. Splashes of bright color from deciduous shrubs like spirea, clethra, nandina, and crape myrtle have given the somber greens of holly, yew, juniper, and arborvitae a shot in the arm. Plus, many extraordinary cultivars of old favorites like azalea, rhododendron, boxwood, and barberry are introduced each year. There are also many low-growing cultivars of hydrangea and juniper.

This list of low-growing shrubs is from Andrew Gerachis, formerly an environmental horticulture extension agent with Virginia Cooperative Extension in Leesburg. "Cramming all of your plants up against the foundation makes your house look taller from the street and reduces your opportunities for creating nice views from indoors," Andrew cautions. "By expanding your landscape out from the foundation, you are able to expose the attractive features of your foundation and windows while giving people both inside and out something attractive to look at. This has the added effect of making your house look more in scale with the overall landscape."

Edward Goucher abelia (*Abelia* x 'Edward Goucher')	6-9, 9-6
Glossy abelia (*Abelia* x *grandiflora* 'Sunrise,' 'Confetti,' 'Sherwood')	5-9, 12-6
Dwarf crimson Japanese barberry (*Berberis thunbergii atropurpurea* 'Nana' or 'Crimson Pygmy')	4-8, 8-3
Japanese barberry (*Berberis thunbergii* 'Aurea,' 'Aurea Nana,' 'Bagatelle,' 'Kobold,' 'Royal Cloak')	4-8, 8-3
Hybrid boxwoods (*Buxus* x 'Green Velvet,' 'Green Mountain')	6-8, 8-1
Littleleaf boxwood (*Buxus microphylla* 'Winter Gem,' 'Wintergreen')	6-9, 9-5
Common boxwood (*Buxus sempervirens* 'Vardar Valley')	6-8, 8-1
Japanese false cypress (*Chamaecyparis pisifera* 'Filifera Aurea Nana,' 'Squarossa Minima')	4-8, 8-1
Sweet pepperbush, summersweet (*Clethra alnifolia* 'Hummingbird')	3-9, 9-1
Japanese cedar (*Cryptomeria japonica* 'Globosa Nana')	6-9, 9-4
Burning bush (*Euonymus alatus* 'Rudy Haag')	4-9, 9-4
Forsythia (*Forsythia* x *intermedia* 'Courtacour,' 'Goldilocks,' 'Courtasol,' 'Gold Tide')	6-9, 9-3
Green-stem forsythia (*Forsythia viridissima* 'Bronxensis')	6-8, 8-5
Hills-of-snow hydrangea (*Hydrangea arborescens* 'Annabelle')	4-9, 9-1
Bigleaf hydrangea (*Hydrangea macrophylla*)	6-9, 9-3
Oakleaf hydrangea (*Hydrangea quercifolia* 'Sike's Dwarf,' 'Pee Wee')	5-9, 9-3
St. John's wort (*Hypericum* 'Albury Purple')	5-9, 9-4
Japanese holly (*Ilex crenata* 'Helleri,' 'Soft Touch,' 'Hogendoorn')	5-7, 7-3
Inkberry holly (*Ilex glabra* 'Shamrock')	5-9, 9-6
Deciduous holly (*Ilex verticillata* 'Red Sprite')	5-8, 8-5

Virginia sweetspire (*Itea virginica* 'Sprich,' 'Saturnalia')	6-9, 9-5
Chinese juniper (*Juniperus chinensis*)	3-9, 9-1
Common juniper (*Juniperus communis*)	3-9, 9-1
Shore juniper (*Juniperus conferta*)	5-9, 9-3
Creeping juniper (*Juniperus horizontalis*)	3-9, 9-1
Japanese-garden juniper (*Juniperus procumbens*)	4-9, 9-2
Singleseed juniper (*Juniperus squamata*)	4-7, 7-3
Crape myrtle (*Lagerstroemia* 'Chickasaw,' 'Pocomoke,' 'Centennial,' 'Hope,' 'Victor')	7-9, 9-7/6
Nandina (*Nandina domestica* 'Gulfstream,' 'Moon Bay,' 'Harbour Dwarf')	6-11, 12-4
Holly osmanthus (*Osmanthus heterophyllus* 'Goshiki,' 'Rotundifolius')	7-9, 9-7
White spruce (*Picea glauca* 'Globe')	3-6, 6-1
Mugo pine (*Pinus mugo* 'Mops,' 'Aurea,' 'Sherwood Compact')	3-7, 7-1
Japanese stone pine (*Pinus pumila*)	6-9, 9-6
Cherry laurel (*Prunus laurocerasus* 'Otto Luyken')	6-9, 9-5
Pyracantha (*Pyracantha coccinea* 'Santa Cruz')	6-9, 9-6
Mountain rosebay rhododendron (*Rhododendron catawbiense* 'Chionoides')	5-8, 8-1
Rhododendrons (*Rhododendron* 'Purple Gem,' 'Ramapo')	5-8, 8-1
Yakushima rhododendron (*Rhododendron yakushimanum* 'Black Satin')	5-8, 8-1
Fragrant sumac (*Rhus aromatica* 'Gro-Low')	2-8, 8-1
Sweet box (*Sarcococca hookeriana* var. *humilis*)	6-9, 9-5
Japanese skimmia (*Skimmia japonica*)	7-9, 9-7
Bumalda Japanese spirea (*Spiraea* × *bumalda* 'Dart's Red,' 'Goldflame')	3-8, 8-1
Japanese spirea (*Spiraea japonica* 'Gold Mound,' 'Neon Flash')	3-8, 8-1
English yew (*Taxus baccata* 'Repandens')	5/6-7, 7-5
Japanese yew (*Taxus cuspidata* 'Dark Green Spreader')	4-7, 7-5
American arborvitae (*Thuja occidentalis* 'Hetz Midget,' 'Danica,' 'Little Gem')	2-7, 7-1
Lowbush blueberries (*Vaccinium angustifolium*)	2-5/6, 6-1
Koreanspice viburnum (*Viburnum carlesii* 'Compactum')	5-8, 8-4
European cranberry-bush viburnum (*Viburnum opulus* 'Compactum,' 'Nanum')	4-8, 8-1
American cranberry-bush viburnum (*Viburnum trilobum* 'Compactum')	2-7, 7-1

EVERGREEN SHRUBS FOR SCREENS AND BACKGROUNDS

Shrubs used as screens and backgrounds need to be tough so that they can be planted in a variety of soils and exposures. They also need to be as low maintenance as possible, in particular because they are often used in large masses or long rows to get the desired effect. Horticultural consultant Vincent Simeone of Long Island, New York, compiled this list of good evergreen choices for our region.

Chinese abelia (*Abelia chinensis*)	5-9, 12-6
Glossy abelia (*Abelia* × *grandiflora*)	5-9, 12-6
Wintergreen barberry (*Berberis julianae*)	6-9, 9-4
Common boxwood (*Buxus sempervirens*)	6-8, 8-1
Japanese camellia (*Camellia japonica*)	7-9, 9-5
Sasanqua camellia (*Camellia sasanqua*)	7-9, 9-5
Plum yew (*Cephalotaxus harringtonia* cvs.)	6-9, 9-3
Spreading euonymus (*Euonymus kiautschovicus*)	6-8, 8-6
Burford holly (*Ilex cornuta* 'Burfordii')	7-9, 9-7
Japanese holly (*Ilex crenata* cvs.)	5-7, 7-5
Inkberry (*Ilex glabra*)	5-9, 9-5
Meserve holly (*Ilex* × *meserveae* cvs.)	5-9, 9-5
Japanese anise tree (*Illicium anisatum*)	7-9, 9-7
Florida anise (*Illicium floridanum*)	7-9, 9-7
Small anise tree (*Illicium parviflorum*)	7-9, 9-7
Chinese juniper (*Juniperus chinensis* cvs.)	3-7, 7-1

Mountain laurel (*Kalmia latifolia*)	3-9, 9-1
Japanese privet (*Ligustrum japonicum*)	7-11, 12-7
Holly osmanthus (*Osmanthus heterophyllus*)	7-9, 9-7
Cherry laurel (*Prunus laurocerasus* cvs.)	6-9, 9-5
Portuguese laurel (*Prunus lusitanica*)	7-9, 9-7
Catawba rhododendron (*Rhododendron catawbiense*)	5-8, 8-1
Rosebay rhododendron (*Rhododendron maximum*)	5-8, 8-1
Yakushima rhododendron (*Rhododendron yakushimanum* and hybs.)	6-9, 9-1
English yew (*Taxus baccata* cvs.)	5/6-7, 7-5
Japanese yew (*Taxus cuspidata* cvs.)	5-7, 7-5
Hybrid yew (*Taxus* × *media* cvs.)	5-7, 7-5
Burkwood viburnum (*Viburnum* × *burkwoodii*)	4-8, 8-1
Prague viburnum (*Viburnum* × *pragense*)	6-8, 8-6
Leatherleaf viburnum (*Viburnum rhytidophyllum*)	6-8, 8-6

> "Evergreen plants can be extremely functional in the landscape. They can create an aesthetically pleasing environment while offering privacy and acting as a buffer against unwanted sounds such as vehicular traffic. It is important to select shrubs that can offer a dense evergreen screen as well as vigorous growth and resistance to pest problems. Of all of the good evergreens available, viburnums are among the best."
>
> **Vincent Simeone is a Long Island, New York, consultant who has been involved in many facets of horticulture, such as public gardens, teaching, lecturing, and garden traveling.**

EVERGREEN SHRUBS FOR FORMAL SHAPES

Sometimes you want a row of shrubs with a formal appearance—as a hedge (a clipped screen), topiary (a trained form), or low border for an herb or knot garden. Or you might need some shrubs to fit a tight or narrow spot and opt not to use an upright or narrow cultivar. Most deciduous and some evergreen shrubs such as boxwoods, hollies, and yews can be sheared back fairly hard and still regrow adequate density. Others, especially the narrow-leaved evergreens like junipers, can't take that degree of shearing. If you cut into wood on junipers where no needles exist, you'll leave a hole that won't fill back in. Notice that the next time you go by overgrown junipers that have been sheared back too hard and are left with nothing but dry, brown, dead needles. Explore the various cultivars of these species to find the ones with the best characteristics for your particular location or need.

EUONYMUS

Glossy abelia (*Abelia* × *grandiflora*)	5-9, 12-6
Japanese barberry (*Berberis thunbergii*)	4-8, 8-2
Boxwoods (*Buxus* spp.)	6-8, 8-1
False cypress (*Chamaecyparis* spp.)	4-8, 8-1
Thorny elaeagnus (*Elaeagnus pungens*)	7-9, 9-7
Winged euonymus (*Euonymus alatus*)	4-9, 9-4
Wintercreeper (*Euonymus fortunei*)	5-9, 9-5
Evergreen euonymus (*Euonymus japonicus*)	6-9, 9-5
Spreading euonymus (*Euonymus kiautschovicus*)	6-8, 8-6
Chinese holly (*Ilex cornuta*)	7-9, 9-7
Japanese holly (*Ilex crenata*)	5-7, 7-5
Inkberry (*Ilex glabra*)	5-9, 9-5
Yaupon holly (*Ilex vomitoria*)	7-10, 12-7
Junipers (*Juniperus chinensis, J. communis, J. virginiana*)	3-9, 9-1
Privets (*Ligustrum amurense, L. japonicum, L. lucidum, L. sinense, L. vulgare*)	7-11, 12-7
Box honeysuckle (*Lonicera nitida*)	6-9, 9-5

Holly osmanthus (*Osmanthus heterophyllus*)	7-9, 9-7
Cherry laurel (*Prunus laurocerasus*)	6-9, 9-6
Pyracantha (*Pyracantha coccinea*)	6-9, 9-6
Rosebay rhododendron (*Rhododendron maximum*)	5-8, 8-1
Yews (*Taxus baccata, T. cuspidata, T. × media*)	5-7, 7-5

SHRUBS TO USE ON SLOPES AND AS GROUND COVERS

Nothing says that the plants used as ground covers or on slopes have to be either turf grasses or herbaceous plants of some form. Often a woody plant—either a vine or a low shrub—is just as appropriate. Usually a low shrub will require limited maintenance, especially on steep slopes or areas prone to erosion. Some will have stems that may root in place, like forsythia, while others, like red-twig dogwood, may spread by stolons (horizontal stems). Many bring with them leaf colors or flowers or fruits that add a different dimension to the covering over the ground.

Prostrate glossy abelia (*Abelia × grandiflora* 'Prostrata')	5-9, 12-6
Sherwood glossy abelia (*Abelia × grandiflora* 'Sherwoodii')	5-9, 12-6
Crimson Pygmy Japanese barberry (*Berberis thunbergii* 'Crimson Pygmy')	4-8, 8-1
Japanese quince (*Chaenomeles japonica*)	6-9, 9-1
Red-twig dogwood (*Cornus alba*)	2-8, 8-1
Bearberry cotoneaster (*Cotoneaster dammeri*)	6-8, 8-6
Rockspray cotoneaster (*Cotoneaster horizontalis*)	5-7, 7-4
Slender deutzia (*Deutzia gracilis*)	5-8, 8-3
Heath (*Erica carnea*)	5-7, 7-5
Wintercreeper (*Euonymus fortunei* 'Colorata')	5-9, 9-5
Arnold Dwarf forsythia (*Forsythia × 'Arnold Dwarf'*)	6-9, 9-3
Siebold forsythia (*Forsythia suspensa sieboldii*)	6-9, 9-3
Bronx forsythia (*Forsythia viridissima* 'Bronxensis')	6-9, 9-3
St. John's wort (*Hypericum calycinum*)	5-9, 9-4
Dwarf Japanese hollies (*Ilex crenata* 'Kingsville Green Cushion,' 'Mariesii')	5-7, 7-5
Compact inkberry (*Ilex glabra* 'Compacta')	5-9, 9-5
Dwarf yaupon holly (*Ilex vomitoria* 'Nana')	5-8, 8-5
Winter jasmine (*Jasminum nudiflorum*)	6-9, 9-7
Chinese juniper (*Juniperus chinensis* 'San Jose,' var. *sargentii*)	3-9, 9-1
Shore juniper (*Juniperus conferta* 'Blue Pacific,' 'Emerald Sea')	5-9, 9-5
Creeping juniper (*Juniperus horizontalis* 'Bar Harbor,' 'Douglasii,' 'Plumosa,' 'Wiltonii')	3-9, 9-1
Japanese-garden juniper (*Juniperus procumbens* 'Nana')	3-9, 9-1
Tamarisk savin juniper (*Juniperus sabina tamariscifolia*)	4-7, 7-1
Dwarf crape myrtles (*Lagerstroemia × indica* dwarf cvs.)	7-9, 9-7/6
Dwarf drooping leucothoe (*Leucothoe fontanesiana* 'Nana')	5-8, 8-3
Dwarf nandina (*Nandina domestica* 'Fire Power,' 'Harbour Dwarf,' 'Nana')	6-11, 12-4
Dwarf mugo pine (*Pinus mugo* 'Compacta')	3-7, 7-1
Potentilla or bush cinquefoil (*Potentilla fruticosa*)	3-7, 7-1
Otto Luyken cherry laurel (*Prunus laurocerasus* 'Otto Luyken')	6-9, 9-6
Fragrant sumac (*Rhus aromatica*)	2-8, 8-1
Roses (*Rosa* spp. and cvs.)	3-11, 12-1
Little Princess spirea (*Spiraea japonica* 'Little Princess')	4-9, 9-1
Snowmound spirea (*Spiraea nipponica* 'Snowmound')	4-8, 8-1
Spreading English yew (*Taxus baccata* 'Repandens')	5/6-7, 7-5
Japanese yew (*Taxus cuspidata* 'Densa')	5-7, 7-5
Yucca (*Yucca filamentosa*)	5-11, 12-5

THORNY SHRUBS FOR BARRIERS

Occasionally you want to keep people out of an area, or direct foot traffic in a particular direction. Most people—although there are always exceptions—won't cut through a hedge or shrubs with thorns. Close spacing is essential so that individual plants quickly overlap. Heights given are approximate if left unpruned. The height of hardy orange (*Poncirus trifoliata*) will be less in colder areas.

6 to 7 Feet

Wintergreen barberry (*Berberis julianae*)	6-9, 9-6
Korean barberry (*Berberis koreana*)	5-8, 8-5
Mentor barberry (*Berberis* x *mentorensis*)	5-8, 8-5
Japanese barberry (*Berberis thunbergii*)	4-8, 8-1
Flowering quince (*Chaenomeles speciosa*)	6-9, 9-1
Rugosa rose (*Rosa rugosa*)	3-9, 9-1

8 to 15 Feet

Thorny elaeagnus (*Elaeagnus pungens*)	7-9, 9-7
Chinese holly (*Ilex cornuta*)	7-9, 9-7
Holly osmanthus (*Osmanthus heterophyllus*)	7-9, 9-7
Pyracantha (*Pyracantha coccinea*)	6-9, 9-6

15 to 25 Feet

Hardy orange (*Poncirus trifoliata*)	5-9, 9-6

SHRUBS THAT BLOOM IN FALL AND WINTER

What a rare treat to find shrubs, both deciduous and evergreen, that flower during the fall or winter. Though many fall-blooming perennials exist, it's a very special treat when a utilitarian shrub screen or hedge suddenly bursts into flower at an unexpected time of year. An even rarer treat is the fragrance that emanates from some of the off-peak bloomers. Some of these shrubs are less well known and underused, but most are available in local nurseries. If not, several mail-order nurseries offer them. The fragrant bloomers in this list are marked with an asterisk (*).

Japanese camellia (*Camellia japonica*)	7-9, 9-5
Sasanqua camellia (*Camellia sasanqua*)	7-9, 9-5
Fragrant wintersweet (*Chimonanthus praecox*)*	7-9, 9-6
Winter daphne (*Daphne odora*)*	7-9, 9-7
Thorny elaeagnus (*Elaeagnus pungens*)*	7-9, 9-7
Witch hazel (*Hamamelis virginiana*)*	3-8, 8-1
Winter jasmine (*Jasminum nudiflorum*)	6-9, 9-7
Dwarf sarcococca (*Sarcococca hookeriana* var. *humilis*)*	6-9, 9-5

COLD-HARDY CAMELLIAS

Reigning queen of the broadleaf evergreens in southern gardens, the camellia is now enjoying popularity in more northern areas. Through proper variety selection and a few winter protection techniques, New York and Mid-Atlantic gardeners are now having success with camellias. Gardeners may select from several of the hardier-than-average *Camellia japonica* varieties or relatively new cold-hardy hybrids. Hardy hybrids are now available in both spring and fall bloomers.

Bob Black from Bennett's Creek Nursery in Suffolk, Virginia, compiled this list of cold-hardy camellias, which includes the flower color, size, and type as well as the plant's overall growth habit and bloom season. The list also indicates hardiness zones.

Camellia Flower Sizes:

miniature	2.5 inches or less
small	2.5 to 3 inches
medium	3 to 4 inches
large	4 to 5 inches
very large	over 5 inches

Camellia Flower Forms:

single	one row of up to eight petals plus stamens
semi-double	two rows of petals plus stamens
anemone	one row of outer petals plus a center cluster of petaloids
peony	loose petals mixed with petaloids and stamens
rose form	several rows of overlapping petals with a concave center showing stamens
formal double	many rows of overlapping petals and never showing stamens

Camellia japonica Hardy to Zone 7a

'Adolfe Audusson': Dark red. Large, semi-double. Average, compact growth. Mid-season bloom.

'Bernice Boddy': Light pink. Medium, semi-double. Loose, upright growth. Mid-season bloom.

'Blood of China': Deep salmon red. Medium, loose peony. Vigorous, compact growth. Late-season bloom.

'Clower White': White. Medium, loose peony. Vigorous open growth. Mid-season bloom.

'Governor Mouton': Red with white splotches. Medium, semi-double. Average, upright growth. Mid-season bloom.

'Grace Albritton': Light pink. Miniature to small, formal double. Vigorous, bushy, upright growth. Mid to late-season bloom.

'Jerry Hill': Pink. Medium, formal double. Vigorous, busy, upright growth. Late-season bloom.

'Kumasaka': Rose pink. Medium, rose form double. Average, compact growth. Mid to late-season bloom.

'Lady Vansittart': White striped rose pink. Medium, semi-double. Average, bushy growth. Handsome holly-like foliage. Mid-season bloom.

'Les Marbury': White to pale pink with rose pink streaking. Small, formal double. Slow, compact, upright growth. Mid-season bloom.

'Leucantha': White. Medium, semi-double. Vigorous, compact, upright growth. Mid-season bloom.

'Paulette Goddard': Red. Medium, semi-double. Average, upright growth. Mid to late-season bloom.

'Professor Charles Sargent': Dark red. Medium, full peony. Average, compact growth. Mid-season bloom.

'R.L.Wheeler': Rose pink. Very large, semi-double with showy circle of stamens. Vigorous, upright growth. Mid-season bloom.

'Sea Foam': White. Medium, formal double. Vigorous, upright growth. Mid-season bloom.

April Series *Camellia japonica* Hybrids, Hardy to Zone 6 with Winter Protection

'April Blush': Shell pink. Medium, semi-double. Slow, compact growth. Mid-season bloom.

'April Dawn': Pink and white. Medium, formal double. Vigorous, upright growth. Mid- to late-season bloom.

'April Remembered': Cream to pink. Large, semi-double. Vigorous, upright growth. Early to late-season bloom.

'April Snow': White. Medium, rose form double. Slow, compact growth. Late season blooms.

'April Tyrist': Red. Anemone form. Average, upright growth. Mid-season bloom.

Fall-Blooming Winter Series *Camellia oleifera* x *Camellia sasanqua* Hybrids, Hardy to Zone 6b

'Winter's Beauty': Shell pink. Small, loose peony. Average upright growth.

'Winter's Fire': Red. Medium, semi-double. Average upright growth.

'Winter's Interlude': Pink. Miniature to small, anemone form. Average upright growth.

'Winter's Rose': Shell pink. Miniature, formal double. Slow compact growth.

'Winter's Snowman': White. Small semi-double to anemone form. Average upright growth.

'Winter's Star': Lavender pink. Medium, single form. Vigorous upright growth.

"To help ensure your success with camellias along the northern edge of the camellia hardiness range, a few basic winter protection techniques are advisable. A generous layer of mulch will provide insulation for root systems. When choosing a material remember that camellias are acid loving. Pine needles are an excellent choice. Windbreaks in the form of fences, walls, or shrubbery will help reduce potential damage from the coldest winter winds. Finally, a canopy providing filtered shade will help prevent frost injury and sun scald. Pines, oaks, and other similar trees with somewhat open canopies are good choices."

Bob Black is the propagation manager and camellia grower at Bennett's Creek Nursery in Suffolk, Virginia, and vice president of the Virginia Camellia Society.

DECIDUOUS SHRUBS WITH INTERESTING BARK OR STEMS

The shrubs in this list from horticultural consultant Signe Hanson may already have given form, colorful flowers, fragrance, and fall color to the landscape, but once their leaves drop, their stems and bark provide one more season of interest. Some of these plants have brightly colored stems, so in planning your landscape, think about a dark-green background to show them off. Even an expanse of snow will highlight those with red stems, or a brick wall those with yellow stems.

The characteristic of colorful stems is usually associated with young wood. Pruning regularly will emphasize the color. Cutting out the oldest one-third of the stems every few years will accomplish this without losing the overall size of the plant. For a more dramatic effect, prune back all the stems to let a new burst of color grow.

Those shrubs listed as exfoliating have bark that naturally peels off in layers or sheets. While this is a wonderful landscape feature, you will do harm if you help the shrub peel. Let the bark naturally fall away from the stems.

Japanese clethra (*Clethra barbinervis*)	exfoliating tan and gray bark	5-9, 8-3
Red-twig, red osier dogwood (*Cornus alba, C. sericea*)	bright-red stems	2-8, 8-1
Golden-twig dogwood (*Cornus sericea* 'Flaviramea')	yellow stems	2-8, 8-1
Harry Lauder's walking stick (*Corylus avellana* 'Contorta')	contorted gray stems	3-9, 9-1
Scotch broom (*Cytisus scoparius*)	dark-green stems	6-8, 8-6
Winged euonymus (*Euonymus alatus*)	green to brown corky ridges	4-9, 9-1
Seven-son flower (*Heptacodium miconioides*)	exfoliating, sandy-color bark	5-9, 9-1
Oakleaf hydrangea (*Hydrangea quercifolia*)	exfoliating cinnamon-color bark	5-9, 9-3
Virginia sweetspire (*Itea virginica* 'Henry's Garnet')	dark-burgundy stems	6-9, 9-6
Winter jasmine (*Jasminum nudiflorum*)	dark-green stems	6-9, 9-7
Globeflower or Japanese kerria (*Kerria japonica*)	bright-green stems	4-9, 9-1
Aureo-vittata globeflower (*Kerria japonica* 'Aureo-vittata')	green and white striped bark	4-9, 9-1
Beautybush (*Kolkwitzia amabilis*)	exfoliating light-tan bark	5-9, 9-5
Crape myrtle (*Lagerstroemia × indica*)	exfoliating tan and rust bark	7-9, 9-7/6
Ninebark (*Physocarpus opulifolius*)	exfoliating tan bark	3-7, 7-1
Hardy orange (*Poncirus trifoliata*)	bright-green stems	5-9, 9-5
Highbush blueberry (*Vaccinium corymbosum*)	red stems	5-9, 9-2

"Bark is my favorite woody-plant characteristic. The color and texture are striking, especially in winter when the trunk is exposed. It is worth planning a garden around one of these plants."

Signe Hanson of Denton, Maryland, is an independent horticultural consultant serving nurseries and greenhouses in Maryland and Delaware. She writes a regular monthly column for the *Mid-Atlantic Grower*.

SPRING-BLOOMING SHRUBS

For most of us, to see the first crocus and daffodils blooming is reassurance that winter can't last much longer. But numerous shrubs also bloom in the spring. The following sampling lists plants in approximate order of bloom, beginning with the vernal witch hazel, which generally starts to bloom in late January or early February in the warmer sections of our region. For the colder reaches of New York and the Mid-Atlantic, add to that date at least a month or more for plants to start blooming. The basic flower color is given, but many of these shrubs have additional cultivars of diverse colors.

LEUCOTHOE

Vernal witch hazel (*Hamamelis vernalis*)	yellow to red	4-8, 8-1
Filberts or hazels (*Corylus avellana*)	·yellowish catkins	3-9, 9-1
Witch hazels (*Hamamelis* x *intermedia* cvs.)	yellow, orange, copper, red	5-9, 9-2
Chinese witch hazel (*Hamamelis mollis*)	yellow	5-9, 9-2
Winter daphne (*Daphne odora*)	white to pinkish purple	7-9, 9-7
Spring heath (*Erica carnea*)	white, pink, red	2-8, 8-1
Winter jasmine (*Jasminum nudiflorum*)	yellow	6-9, 9-7
White false forsythia (*Abeliophyllum distichum*)	white	5-9, 9-5
Fragrant winter hazel (*Corylopsis glabrescens*)	pale yellow	6-9, 9-3
Forsythia (*Forsythia* x *intermedia* cvs.)	yellows	6-9, 9-3
Spice bush (*Lindera benzoin*)	greenish yellow	5-9, 9-5
Flowering quince (*Chaenomeles speciosa*)	white, pink, red	6-9, 9-6
Winter honeysuckle (*Lonicera fragrantissima*)	white	5-8, 8-2
Japanese pieris (*Pieris japonica*)	white, pink	6-8, 8-6
Korean rhododendron (*Rhododendron mucronulatum*)	pink, purple	5-8, 8-5
Mountain pieris (*Pieris floribunda*)	white	5-8, 8-4
Hardy orange (*Poncirus trifoliata*)	white	5-9, 9-5
Flowering almond (*Prunus triloba*)	pink	6-8, 8-6
PJM rhododendrons (*Rhododendron* cvs.)	white, red, purple	4-8, 8-1
Bridalwreath spirea (*Spiraea prunifolia*)	white	5-8, 8-5
Oregon holly grape (*Mahonia aquifolium*)	yellow	5/6-9, 9-1
Leatherleaf mahonia (*Mahonia bealei*)	yellow	6/7-8, 8-3
Dwarf flowering almond (*Prunus glandulosa*)	white, pink	5-8, 8-3
Beach plum (*Prunus maritima*)	white	3-6, 6-1
Snow azalea (*Rhododendron mucronatum*)	white, purple	5-8, 8-1
Fragrant sumac (*Rhus aromatica*)	pale yellow	2-8, 8-1
Thunberg spirea (*Spiraea thunbergii*)	white	5-8, 8-2
Barberries (*Berberis* spp.)	yellow	4-8, 8-1
Sweetshrub or Carolina allspice (*Calycanthus floridus*)	reddish brown	5-9, 9-1
Redvein enkianthus (*Enkianthus campanulatus*)	white, yellow, pale orange, red	5-8, 8-3
Burning bush (*Euonymus alatus*)	greenish yellow	4-9, 9-1
Pearlbush (*Exochorda racemosa*)	white	5-9, 9-5
Dwarf fothergilla (*Fothergilla gardenii*)	white	5-9, 9-3
Globeflower (*Kerria japonica*)	orange	4-9, 9-1
Evergreen azaleas (*Rhododendron* spp., hybs., and cvs.)	white, pink, red, lavender, bicolors	5-9, 9-5
Carolina rhododendron (*Rhododendron carolinianum*)	rosy purple	5-8, 8-5
Pinkshell azalea (*Rhododendron vaseyi*)	light rose	5-8, 8-4
Jetbead (*Rhodotypos scandens*)	white	5-8, 8-4
Common lilac (*Syringa vulgaris*)	white, pink, red, purple	4-8, 8-1
Hardy gardenia (*Gardenia jasminoides* 'Chuck Hayes,' 'Kleim Hardy')	white	7-11, 12-1
Burkwood viburnum (*Viburnum* x *burkwoodii*)	white, pink	4-8, 8-1
Koreanspice (*Viburnum carlesii*)	white, pink	5-8, 8-4

Weigela (*Weigela florida*)	white, pink, red	5-8, 8-1
Chokeberry (*Aronia arbutifolia*)	white	5-9, 9-4
Red-twig, red osier dogwood (*Cornus alba, C. sericea*)	white	2-8, 8-1
Creeping cotoneaster (*Cotoneaster adpressus*)	pink	5-8, 8-1
Cranberry cotoneaster (*Cotoneaster apiculatus*)	pink	5-7, 7-1
Spreading cotoneaster (*Cotoneaster divaricatus*)	pink	6-8, 8-6
Slender deutzia (*Deutzia gracilis*)	white	5-8, 8-3
Fetterbush (*Leucothoe racemosa*)	white	6-9, 9-3
Tatarian honeysuckle (*Lonicera tatarica*)	white, pink	3-9, 9-1
Red-tip photinia (*Photinia × fraseri*)	white	7-9, 9-7
Potentilla (*Potentilla fruticosa*)	white, yellow, orange, red	3-7, 7-1
Cherry laurel (*Prunus laurocerasus*)	white	6-9, 9-6
Scotch broom (*Cytisus scoparius*)	yellow, pink	6-8, 8-6

SUMMER-BLOOMING SHRUBS

It's hard to draw a real dividing line between spring and summer relative to bloom times because so many factors—temperature, rainfall, exposure—affect when a shrub may bloom. However, these shrubs, listed in approximate bloom order, will start flowering in mid to late May or early June in the southern sections of our region.

One of the most interesting of the summer shrubs is the bigleaf hydrangea (*Hydrangea macrophylla*). If the soil is acid, the flowers are blue, but if alkaline, they're pink. As a soil undergoes a natural pH shift, becoming more acid as organic matter decomposes, a hydrangea that once flowered pink will change to purple and then to blue. Some people change a hydrangea's flower color by adding lime to turn it pink, or adding iron (alum or sulfate) or copper, often as pennies! Modern breeding now gives us cultivars which will relatively reliably remain one color or the other despite soil pH.

Persian lilac (*Syringa × persica*)	white, purple	3-7, 7-1
Flame azalea (*Rhododendron calendulaceum*)	yellow, orange, scarlet	5-8, 8-4
Catawba rhododendron (*Rhododendron catawbiense* hybs.)	white, pink, red, purple	4-8, 8-1
Pinxterbloom azalea (*Rhododendron nudiflorum*)	white, pink	6-9, 9-3
Nippon spirea (*Spiraea nipponica*)	white	4-8, 8-1
Vanhoutte spirea (*Spiraea × vanhouttei*)	white	4-8, 8-1
Highbush blueberry (*Vaccinium corymbosum*)	white	5-9, 9-2
European cranberry bush (*Viburnum opulus*)	white	4-8, 8-1
Leatherleaf viburnum (*Viburnum rhytidophyllum*)	white	6-8, 8-6
Japanese snowball (*Viburnum plicatum*)	white	4-8, 8-1
Doublefile viburnum (*Viburnum plicatum tomentosum*)	white	4-8, 8-1
American cranberry bush (*Viburnum trilobum*)	white	2-7, 7-1
New Jersey tea (*Ceanothus americanus*)	white	4-8, 8-1
Smoke bush (*Cotinus coggygria*)	pale green, pink, burgundy	5-8, 8-1
Beautybush (*Kolkwitzia amabilis*)	pink	5-9, 9-5
Drooping leucothoe (*Leucothoe fontanesiana*)	white	5-8, 8-3
Mock orange (*Philadelphus coronarius*)	white	5-8, 8-5
Ninebark (*Physocarpus opulifolius*)	white, pink	3-7, 7-1
Rugosa rose (*Rosa rugosa*)	white, yellow, pink, red	2-9, 9-1
Late lilac (*Syringa villosa*)	white, purple	4-7, 7-1
Arrowwood (*Viburnum dentatum*)	white	3-8, 8-1
Bearberry cotoneaster (*Cotoneaster dammeri*)	white	6-8, 8-6
Rockspray cotoneaster (*Cotoneaster horizontalis*)	white, pink	5-7, 7-5
Hollies (*Ilex* spp.)	white	7-9, 9-7
Mountain laurel (*Kalmia latifolia*)	white, pink, red	5-9, 9-5
Privets (*Ligustrum* spp.)	white	7-11, 12-7
Pyracantha or firethorn (*Pyracantha coccinea*)	white	6-9, 9-6

Shrub roses (*Rosa* spp. and hybs.)	many colors	2-9, 9-1
Willowleaf cotoneaster (*Cotoneaster salicifolius*)	white	6-8, 8-6
Elderberry (*Sambucus canadensis*)	white	4-9, 9-1
Crape myrtle (*Lagerstroemia* x *indica*)	white, pink, red, purple	7-9, 9-7/6
Bumalda spirea (*Spiraea* x *bumalda*)	pink, red	3-8, 8-1
Japanese spirea (*Spiraea japonica*)	white, pink, red	4-9, 9-1
Japanese beautybush (*Callicarpa japonica*)	white, pink	6-8, 8-6
Swamp azalea (*Rhododendron viscosum*)	white, pink	5-9, 9-4
Bottlebrush buckeye (*Aesculus parviflora*)	white	5-9, 9-4
St. John's wort (*Hypericum calycinum*)	yellow	5-9, 9-4
Butterfly bush (*Buddleia davidii*)	white, yellow, pink, purple	6-9, 9-3
Chaste tree (*Vitex agnus-castus*)	white, blue-purple	6-9, 9-6
Oakleaf hydrangea (*Hydrangea quercifolia*)	white	5-9, 9-3
Tamarisk (*Tamarix pentandra*)	pink	4-8, 8-2
Yucca (*Yucca filamentosa*)	white	5-11, 12-5
Sweet pepperbush, summersweet (*Clethra alnifolia*)	white, pink	3-9, 9-1
Nandina, heavenly bamboo (*Nandina domestica*)	white	6-11, 12-4
Buttonbush (*Cephalanthus occidentalis*)	white	5-11, 12-3
Glossy abelia (*Abelia* x *grandiflora*)	white, pink	5-9, 9-1
Rose of Sharon (*Hibiscus syriacus*)	white, pink, red, purple	5-9, 9-1
Bluebeard (*Caryopteris* x *clandonensis*)	blue	6-9, 9-2
Bigleaf hydrangea (*Hydrangea macrophylla*)	pink, blue	6-9, 9-3
Panicled hydrangea (*Hydrangea paniculata*)	white	4-8, 8-1
Saltbush (*Baccharis halimifolia*)	white	3-7, 7-1

CRAPE MYRTLES

Crape myrtle, the "tree of one hundred days" or the "lilac of the south," can be grown successfully in much of our region, including New York. However, although anecdotal evidence abounds, no cultivar has been proven reliably top-hardy in any location colder than zone 7. This cutoff may be pushed by planting in a protected site or in a container, as with the new miniature cultivars. The roots of most crape myrtle cultivars are hardy to zone 6, allowing the plant to be grown as a perennial, since it flowers on new growth. Usually, the hardiness and heat zone ratings for crape myrtles are 7-10, 10-6.

This list of crape myrtles is from Margaret Pooler, a plant breeder at the National Arboretum in Washington, D.C. It indicates flower color and the plant's growth habit as well as its mature height.

3 to 5 feet

Caddo	bright pink	low spreading
Centennial	purple	compact globose
Chickasaw	pink-lavender	compact miniature
Pocomoke	rose-pink	compact miniature
Victor	red	upright dwarf

10 to 20 feet

Acoma	white	low spreading
Apalachee	light lavender	dense upright
Catawba	violet purple	globose multi-stem
Lipan	lavender	broad upright
Osage	clear pink	pendulous globose
Regal Red	red	broad upright
Sioux	dark clear pink	dense upright
Tonto	red	globose multi-stem
Tuskegee	dark pink	broad spreading
Zuni	lavender	upright vase

20 to 30 feet

Choctaw	medium clear pink	globose tree
Dynamite	red	upright
Natchez	white	broad tall tree
Wichita	lavender	upright vase

"Hundreds of cultivars of crape myrtles have been named, but the most popular are the *Lagerstroemia indica* x *L. fauriei* hybrids developed by the late Don Egolf at the U.S. National Arboretum. Named after Native American tribes, these mildew-tolerant cultivars offer the grower almost every combination of flower color, growth habit, and bark characteristic imaginable. All of Dr. Egolf's hybrids can be observed in a landscaped setting in the Gotelli Collection at the National Arboretum, Washington, D.C."

Margaret Pooler is a breeder of woody ornamental landscape plants at the U.S. National Arboretum in Washington, D.C.

SHRUBS WITH INTERESTING LEAF COLOR

Many shrubs, both deciduous and evergreen, have leaves that are colors other than green, or that are green variegated with splotches of white, yellow, or pink to red. Use these shrubs sparingly so that instead of fighting with each other, their wonderful colors and patterns serve as specimens or points of interest where additional color is needed in the landscape. With new cultivars being introduced yearly, this is only a sampling of what is available. Of the many that are too numerous to include here are dozens of different junipers (*Juniperus chinensis, J. communis, J. conferta, J. horizontalis, J. procumbens, J. sabina, J. scopulorum*) offering an array of colors, such as yellow, green, blue and gray, plus white and yellow variegations, and several that have purplish winter tints.

Deciduous

Japanese barberries (*Berberis thunbergii*)	4-8, 8-3
'Aurea'—yellow; 'Crimson Pygmy'—crimson; 'Rose Glow'—green, white, pink, rose	
Red-twig dogwood (*Cornus alba*)	2-8, 8-1
'Argentea-marginata'—green and white; 'Spaethii'—green and yellow	
Smoke bush (*Cotinus coggygria* f. *purpureus*)	5-8, 8-1
'Royal Purple'—purple; 'Velvet Cloak'—purple	
Bigleaf hydrangea (*Hydrangea macrophylla*)	6-9, 9-3
'Variegata'—light and dark green with cream	
Globeflower (*Kerria japonica*)	4-9, 9-1
'Aureo-variegata'—green and yellow; 'Picta'—green and white	6-8, 8-6
Golden vicary privet (*Ligustrum* x *vicaryi*)	
golden yellow	
Purpleleaf sand cherry (*Prunus* x *cistena*)	4-8, 8-1
maroon	
Bumalda spirea (*Spiraea* x *bumalda*)	7-9, 9-6
'Candle Light'—yellow; 'Fire Light'—red-orange; 'Goldflame'—orange; 'Goldmound'—yellow-green	
Japanese spirea (*Spiraea japonica*)	4-9, 9-1
'Gold Mound'—golden yellow; 'Limemound'—lime; 'Magic Carpet'—chartreuse	
Thunberg spirea (*Spiraea thunbergii*)	5-8, 8-2
'Mellow Yellow'—yellow	
Chaste tree (*Vitex agnus-castus*)	6-9, 9-6
gray-green	
Weigela (*Weigela florida*)	5-8, 8-1
'Java Red'—red; 'Rubidor'—yellow-green and variegated; 'Variegata'—green and yellow; 'Wine and Roses'—burgundy	

Evergreen

Japanese aucuba (*Aucuba japonica*)	6-11, 12-6
'Crotonifolia'—green spotted with white; 'Picturata'—yellow blotch in center;	
'Variegata'—green spotted with yellow	
Common boxwood (*Buxus sempervirens*)	6-8, 8-1
'Argenteo-variegata'—green with white; 'Aureo-variegata'—green with yellow	
Lawson false cypress (*Chamaecyparis lawsoniana*)	4-8, 8-1
'Aurea Densa'—golden yellow; 'Forsteckensis'—gray-green	
Hinoki false cypress (*Chamaecyparis obtusa*)	4-8, 8-1
'Crippsii'—golden yellow; 'Mariesii'—green tipped with white	
Japanese false cypress (*Chamaecyparis pisifera*)	4-8, 8-1
'Aurea Nana'—yellow; 'Boulevard'—gray-blue; 'Golden Mop'—yellow;	
'Nana Variegata'—green with white; 'Plumosa Rogersii'—yellow	
Winter daphne (*Daphne odora*)	7-9, 9-7
'Marginata'—green and cream	
Thorny elaeagnus (*Elaeagnus pungens*)	7-9, 9-7
'Aureus'—green with yellow; 'Maculata'—green with yellow blotch;	
'Tricolor'—green with yellow and pinkish white; 'Variegata'—green with yellowish white	
Wintercreeper (*Euonymus fortunei*)	5-9, 9-5
'Emerald and Gold,' 'Golden Prince'—green and yellow; 'Emerald Gaiety,' 'Gracilis'	
—green and white	
Evergreen euonymus (*Euonymus japonicus*)	6-9, 9-5
'Albomarginata,' 'Silver King,' 'Silver Queen'—green and white; 'Aureovariegatus,'	
'Gold Center,' 'Golden'—green and yellow	
Drooping leucothoe (*Leucothoe fontanesiana*)	5-8, 8-1
'Girard's Rainbow'—cream, pink and green	
Nandina (*Nandina domestica*)	6-11, 12-4
'Fire Power'—red; 'Gulfstream,' 'Harbour Dwarf'—red part of year	
Red-tip photinia (*Photinia* x *fraseri*)	7-9, 9-7
red on green	
Variegated Japanese pieris (*Pieris japonica* 'Variegata')	6-8, 8-5
green and white	
English yew (*Taxus baccata*)	5/6-7, 7-5
'Aurea,' 'Washingtonii'—yellow; 'Elegantissima'—green and yellow	
American arborvitae (*Thuja occidentalis*)	2-7, 7-1
'Aurea,' 'Lutea'—yellow; 'Umbracilifera'—gray-blue	

FRAGRANT SHRUBS

Robert Stiffler, veteran garden writer for the *Virginian-Pilot* newspaper in Virginia Beach, contributed these lists of shrubs with fragrant flowers and with fragrant leaves. "Fragrance is a garden element for which we should plan and plant," he advises. "Use these shrubs near a door or walkway where you can enjoy their fragrance the most. It's just as easy to plant a fragrant shrub as a non-fragrant one. Keep that in mind when visiting your favorite nursery."

According to Carlsons Gardens, in Salem, New York, you will have a nearly continuous succession of fragrances from spring to summer if you plant these native azaleas, which bloom in the following order: pinxterbloom azalea (*Rhododendron periclymenoides*; formerly *R. nudiflorum*), rose-shell azalea (*R. prinophyllum*; formerly *R. roseum*), coast azalea (*R. atlanticum*), sweet azalea (*R. arborescens*), swamp azalea (*R. viscosum*).

Fragrant Flowers

Glossy abelia (*Abelia* x *grandiflora*)	5-9, 12-6
Globe butterfly bush (*Buddleia globosa*)	7-9, 9-7
Sweetshrub (*Calycanthus floridus*)	5-9, 9-1

Sasanqua camellia (*Camellia sasanqua*)	7-9, 9-5
New Jersey tea (*Ceanothus americanus*)	4-8, 8-1
Buttonbush (*Cephalanthus occidentalis*)	5-11, 12-3
Wintersweet (*Chimonanthus praecox*)	7-9, 9-7
Sweet pepperbush, summersweet (*Clethra alnifolia*)	3-9, 9-1
Carol Mackie daphne (*Daphne × burkwoodii* 'Carol Mackie')	5-8, 8-4
Winter daphne (*Daphne odora*)	7-9, 9-7
Slender deutzia (*Deutzia gracilis*)	5-8, 8-5
Thorny elaeagnus (*Elaeagnus pungens*)	7-9, 9-7
Dwarf fothergilla (*Fothergilla gardenii*)	5-9, 9-3
Hardy gardenia (*Gardenia jasminoides* 'Chuck Hayes,' 'Kleim Hardy')	7-11, 12-1
Witch hazels (*Hamamelis* spp.)	5-9, 9-2
Sweetspire (*Itea virginica*)	6-9, 9-5
Spice bush (*Lindera benzoin*)	5-9, 9-4
Winter honeysuckle (*Lonicera fragrantissima*)	5-8, 8-2
Bush honeysuckles (*Lonicera* spp.)	5-9, 9-2
Devilwood (*Osmanthus americana*)	7-10, 10-7
Holly osmanthus (*Osmanthus heterophyllus*)	7-9, 9-7
Mock orange (*Philadelphus coronarius*)	5-8, 8-3
Japanese pieris (*Pieris japonica*)	6-8, 8-5
Native azaleas (*Rhododendron* spp.)	4-8, 8-1
Roses (*Rosa* spp.)	3-11, 12-1
Sweet box (*Sarcococca hookeriana* var. *humilis*)	6-9, 9-5
Japanese skimmia (*Skimmia japonica*)	7-9, 9-7
Lilac (*Syringa vulgaris*)	4-8, 8-1
Burkwood viburnum (*Viburnum × burkwoodii*)	4-8, 8-1
Fragrant snowball (*Viburnum × carlcephalum*)	6-8, 8-5
Koreanspice viburnum (*Viburnum × carlesii*)	6-8, 8-5
Chaste tree (*Vitex agnus-castus*)	6-9, 9-6

WINTER HONEYSUCKLE

Fragrant Leaves

English boxwood (*Buxus sempervirens* 'Suffruticosa')	6-8, 8-1
Sweetshrub (*Calycanthus floridus*)	5-9, 9-1
St. John's wort (*Hypericum calycinum*)	5-9, 9-4
Junipers (*Juniperus* spp.)	3-9, 9-1
Spice bush (*Lindera benzoin*)	5-9, 9-4
Wax myrtle (*Myrica cerifera*)	6-9, 9-6
Bayberry (*Myrica pensylvanica*)	3-6, 6-1
Fragrant sumac (*Rhus aromatica*)	4-9, 9-3
Siebold viburnum (*Viburnum sieboldii*)	4-8, 8-1
Chaste tree (*Vitex agnus-castus*)	6-9, 9-6

SHRUBS FOR FALL COLOR

The cool, crisp air of fall provides a welcome relief from the heat and humidity of summer, while the gorgeous reds, oranges, and yellows of deciduous shrubs add to the celebration. New York and Mid-Atlantic gardeners are fortunate in having many plant choices available for good fall color. This list from Karen Carter, a Cooperative Extension agent in Richmond, Virginia, offers abundant possibilities for adding fall color at eye-level. In some cases specific cultivars have been suggested, but they are not exhaustive. Also, keep in mind that some evergreens exhibit fall color (*Nandina* for example), and trees like black gum (*Nyssa sylvatica*) and the maples (*Acer* spp.) provide the ceiling for the room your landscape creates.

Red to Purple or Maroon

Red chokeberry (*Aronia arbutifolia*)	5-9, 9-4

Japanese barberry (*Berberis thunbergii* var. *atropurpurea* 'Bagatelle,' 'Crimson Pygmy,'   4-8, 8-1
   'Rose Glow')

Red-twig, red osier dogwood (*Cornus alba, C. sericea*)   2-8, 8-1

Smoke bush (*Cotinus coggygria* 'Flame,' 'Royal Purple,' 'Velvet Cloak')   5-8, 8-1

Cranberry cotoneaster (*Cotoneaster apiculatus*)   5-7, 7-4

Spreading cotoneaster (*Cotoneaster divaricatus*)   5-7, 7-4

Rockspray cotoneaster (*Cotoneaster horizontalis*)   5-7, 7-5

Disanthus (*Disanthus cercidifolius*)   5-8, 8-5

Winged euonymus (*Euonymus alatus*)   4-9, 9-4

Dwarf winged euonymus (*Euonymus alatus* 'Compactus')   4-9, 9-4

Oakleaf hydrangea (*Hydrangea quercifolia*)   5-9, 9-3

Virginia sweetspire (*Itea virginica* 'Henry's Garnet')   6-9, 9-5

Pinkshell azalea (*Rhododendron vaseyi*)   5-8, 8-5

Fragrant sumac (*Rhus aromatica*)   4-9, 9-1

Shining sumac (*Rhus copallina*)   5-9, 9-4

Smooth sumac (*Rhus glabra*)   2-8, 8-1

Staghorn sumac (*Rhus typhina*)   3-8, 8-1

Rugosa rose (*Rosa rugosa*)   2-9, 9-1

Bridalwreath spirea (*Spiraea prunifolia*)   5-8, 8-2

Early lilac (*Syringa oblata* var. *dilatata*)   4-6, 6-4

Highbush blueberry (*Vaccinium corymbosum*)   5-9, 9-2

Mapleleaf viburnum (*Viburnum acerifolium*)   4-8, 8-1

Arrowwood viburnum (*Viburnum dentatum* 'Cardinal')   3-8, 8-1

Doublefile viburnum (*Viburnum plicatum* var. *tomentosum*)   4-8, 8-1

Blackhaw viburnum (*Viburnum prunifolium*)   3-9, 9-1

Orange to Red

Redvein enkianthus (*Enkianthus campanulatus*)   5-8, 8-3

Large fothergilla (*Fothergilla major* 'Mount Airy')   5-9, 9-3

Flame azalea (*Rhododendron calendulaceum*)   5-9, 9-4

Royal azalea (*Rhododendron schlippenbachii*)   5-9, 9-4

Chinese sumac (*Rhus chinensis*)   4-9, 9-1

Bumalda spirea (*Spiraea* × *bumalda* 'Goldflame')   3-8, 8-1

Thunberg spirea (*Spiraea thunbergii*)   5-8, 8-2

Yellow

Bottlebrush buckeye (*Aesculus parviflora*)   5-9, 9-4

Sweetshrub (*Calycanthus floridus*)   5-9, 9-1

Cinnamon clethra (*Clethra acuminata*)   5-8, 8-3

Sweet pepperbush, summersweet (*Clethra alnifolia*)   3-9, 9-1

Leatherwood (*Dirca palustris*)   4-9, 9-1

Forsythia (*Forsythia* × *intermedia*)   6-9, 9-6

Japanese kerria (*Kerria japonica*)   4-9, 9-1

Witch hazel (*Hamamelis* × *intermedia* 'Arnold Promise,' 'Diane,' 'Jelena,' 'Pallida,'   5-9, 9-2
   'Ruby Glow')

Japanese witch hazel (*Hamamelis japonica*)   5-9, 9-2

Chinese witch hazel (*Hamamelis mollis*)   5-9, 9-2

Vernal witch hazel (*Hamamelis vernalis*)   4-8, 8-1

Common witch hazel (*Hamamelis virginiana*)   3-9, 9-1

Spice bush (*Lindera benzoin*)   5-9, 9-4

Yellowroot (*Xanthorhiza simplicissima*)   3-9, 9-1

Multicolor

Smoke bush (*Cotinus coggygria*)   5-8, 8-1

Witch hazels (*Hamamelis* spp.)	3-9, 9-1
Crape myrtle (*Lagerstroemia indica*)	7-9, 9-7/6

"The first species that come to mind when I think of fall color are natives like the black gum tree (*Nyssa sylvatica*), and shrubs like sumacs, blueberry, and sweetpepper bush (*Clethra alnifolia*). Many of these plants have shown up all by themselves in my landscape and I try to encourage them wherever possible. I also supplement their show by planting Japanese barberry, nandina, winged euonymus, and sweetshrub (*Calycanthus floridus*), all good plants that are tough enough to survive minimal maintenance."

Karen Carter is an environmental horticulture extension agent for the Virginia Cooperative Extension in Richmond, Virginia.

SHRUBS WITH COLORFUL FRUITS

From late summer through winter, among the showiest landscape features are shrubs with fruits in orange, red, blue, and purple. Occasionally you'll also find yellow- and white-fruited cultivars, but these colors are generally less dramatic. Often the fruit attract birds, which is another reason to use these plants.

This list comes from horticulturist David Yost of Fairfax, Virginia. Perhaps one of the most outstanding and easiest to grow is the native beautyberry. Its clusters of purple berries are spaced every inch or two along the stem and are magnificent enough for flower arrangers to spend the day scouring the roadsides in search of them. There will be some variation in how long berries last in your garden, based on the weather and the hunger of birds. It often just depends on when the birds spot your landscape and say, "There's lunch."

Some of the prettiest fruits occur on plants that can be very invasive—such as elaeagnus and several shrub honeysuckles. The use of these plants should be very restricted.

Red chokeberry (*Aronia arbutifolia*)	5-9, 9-4
Aucuba (*Aucuba japonica*)	6-11, 12-6
Japanese barberry (*Berberis thunbergii*)	4-8, 8-1
American beautyberry (*Callicarpa americana*)	5-10, 12-3
Purple beautyberry (*Callicarpa dichotoma*)	6-8, 8-5
Cranberry cotoneaster (*Cotoneaster apiculatus*)	5-7, 7-1
Spreading cotoneaster (*Cotoneaster divaricatus*)	5-7, 7-4
Rockspray cotoneaster (*Cotoneaster horizontalis*)	5-7, 7-4
Willowleaf cotoneaster (*Cotoneaster salicifolius*)	6-8, 8-6
Strawberry bush (*Euonymus americana*)	4-9, 9-1
Seven-son flower (*Heptacodium miconioides*)	5-9, 9-1
Burford holly (*Ilex cornuta* 'Burfordii,' 'Dwarf Burford')	7-9, 9-7
Possumhaw (*Ilex decidua*)	5-9, 9-5
Meserve hollies (*Ilex* x *meserveae*)	5-9, 9-5
Winterberry (*Ilex verticillata*)	5-8, 8-5
Deciduous hollies (*Ilex verticillata* x *I. serrata* hybs. and cvs.)	5-8, 8-5
Spice bush (*Lindera benzoin*)	5-9, 9-4
Oregon grape holly (*Mahonia aquifolium*)	5/6-9, 9-1
Leatherleaf mahonia (*Mahonia bealei*)	6/7-8, 8-3
Northern bayberry (*Myrica pensylvanica*)	3-6, 6-1
Nandina or heavenly bamboo (*Nandina domestica*)	6-11, 12-7
Trifoliate orange (*Poncirus trifoliata*)	5-9, 9-6
Pyracantha or firethorn (*Pyracantha coccinea*)	6-9, 9-6
Rugosa rose (*Rosa rugosa*)	2-9, 9-1
Japanese skimmia (*Skimmia japonica*)	7-9, 9-7
Snowberry (*Symphoricarpos albus laevigatus*)	2-6, 6-1
Coralberry (*Symphoricarpos orbiculatus*)	2-6, 6-1
Highbush blueberry (*Vaccinium corymbosum*)	5-9, 9-2
European cranberry bush (*Viburnum opulus*)	4-8, 8-1

Doublefile viburnum (*Viburnum plicatum*)	4-8, 8-1
Blackhaw viburnum (*Viburnum prunifolium*)	3-9, 9-1
Tea viburnum (*Viburnum setigerum*)	5-7, 7-5
American cranberry bush (*Viburnum trilobum*)	2-7, 7-1

"I have a preference towards native plants and encourage gardeners to include them whenever possible. Chokeberry, winterberry, spice bush, and blackhaw viburnum will thrive under difficult growing conditions as well as providing landscape beauty. There are so many new introductions and varieties available to gardeners, it's hard to decide what plants to choose. Just for fun, try something different. 'Sparkleberry,' a hybrid deciduous holly, is spectacular in the fall and winter. 'Blue Princess,' a Meserve holly, has year-round interest, with bright-red berries showing against the blue-green foliage. The list of nandinas is endless, and seven-son flower is definitely something different, if you have lots of room in which it can grow."

David Yost of Fairfax, Virginia, is a former Cooperative Extension agent who works for Merrifield Garden Center, where he helps to diagnose plant problems, teaches, and appears on Merrifield's *Gardening Advisor* weekly TV program.

SHRUBS THAT NEED PARTNERS

A few genera of shrubs whose flowers or fruits we value for landscape color are dioecious. Unlike plants whose flowers are perfect (male and female reproductive organs within each flower) or that are monoecious (separate male and female flowers on the same plant), dioecious plants have male and female flowers on separate plants. If we want to assure that the fruits we value will develop, we need both plants. Male plants will never bear fruit, but the pollen from the male plant is needed to pollinate the flowers on the female plant in order for the ovaries in the female flowers to mature into fruit.

The male and female plants must be within a reasonable distance of each other. If both are in your yard, pollination—whether by wind or insects—should occur. If the female plant is in your yard and the male plant is in an immediate neighbor's yard or even down the street, your plant will probably bear fruit. But how much farther apart the sexes can be is relatively unknown. Some experts recommend grafting a male branch onto a female plant, but should that branch die or be mistakenly pruned away, there would go pollination. Others have suggested planting one of each plant in the same hole and just keeping the male plant pruned small, but again, that's not very reliable pollination insurance. The best method is to plant one or more of each sex, unless these shrubs are commonly planted where you live.

Aucuba (*Aucuba japonica*)	6-11, 12-6
Smoke bush (*Cotinus coggygria*)	5-8, 8-1
Hollies (*Ilex* spp.)	5-9, 9-5
Junipers (*Juniperus* spp.)	3-9, 9-1
Spice bush (*Lindera benzoin*)	5-9, 9-4
Wax myrtle (*Myrica cerifera*)	6-9, 9-6
Bayberry (*Myrica pensylvanica*)	3-6, 6-1
Sumacs (*Rhus* spp.)	4-9, 9-1
Pussy willow (*Salix discolor*)	4-8, 8-1
Skimmia (*Skimmia japonica*)	7-9, 9-7
Yews (*Taxus* spp.)	5-7, 7-5

SHRUBS THAT LIKE ACID SOIL

Most shrubs, and for that matter, most landscape plants, grow best in soils that are slightly acid—pH 6.0 to 6.5. Several, however, need to be grown at pH's considerably lower or more acid, such as 5.5. Some, such as azaleas, will even tolerate 4.5. A majority of these shrubs are in the *Ericaceae* family, which includes the heaths (*Erica* spp.) and heathers (*Calluna vulgaris*) used as ground covers, and trees such as sourwood (*Oxydendrum arboreum*). Though these plants are often planted in less acid soils, their growth will be inferior, and considerable chlorosis (pale leaf color) may develop due to nutrient imbalances. These same shrubs (and other species in these same genera) definitely should not be grown in alkaline soil unless major steps are taken to drop the soil's pH.

Summersweet (*Clethra alnifolia*)	3-9, 9-1
Scotch broom (*Cytisus scoparius*)	6-8, 8-6
Redvein enkianthus (*Enkianthus campanulatus*)	5-8, 8-3
Dwarf fothergilla (*Fothergilla gardenii*)	5-9, 9-3
Hollies (*Ilex* spp.)	5-8, 8-5
Anise (*Illicium floridanum*)	7-9, 9-7
Virginia sweetspire (*Itea virginica*)	6-9, 9-5
Common juniper (*Juniperus communis*)	3-9, 9-1
Mountain laurel (*Kalmia latifolia*)	5-9, 9-5
Drooping leucothoe (*Leucothoe fontanesiana*)	5-8, 8-3
Japanese pieris (*Pieris japonica*)	6-8, 8-5
Azaleas and rhododendrons (*Rhododendron* spp., hybs., and cvs.)	5-9, 9-5
Blueberries and relatives (*Vaccinium* spp.)	5-9, 9-2

ALKALINE-TOLERANT SHRUBS

Some shrubs need neutral (7.0) to slightly alkaline (above 7.0) soils if they're to thrive. Nutrient imbalances will be to blame if leaves are off color or chlorotic, but different minerals or elements are involved with the shrubs that need a "sweeter" soil. These are shrubs that will usually do well around rock out-croppings or where lots of cement or paving or foundation rubble has been buried.

Flowering quince (*Chaenomeles speciosa*)	6-9, 9-1
Yaupon holly (*Ilex vomitoria*)	7-10, 12-7
Creeping juniper (*Juniperus horizontalis*)	3-9, 9-1
Crape myrtle (*Lagerstroemia indica*)	7-9, 9-7/6
Nandina or heavenly bamboo (*Nandina domestica*)	6-11, 12-4
Mock orange (*Philadelphus coronarius*)	5-8, 8-5
Pyracantha or firethorn (*Pyracantha coccinea*)	6-9, 9-6
Spireas (*Spiraea* spp.)	4-9, 9-1
Chaste tree (*Vitex agnus-castus*)	6-9, 9-6

FLOWERING
QUINCE

SHRUBS THAT TOLERATE CLAY SOIL

It hardly seems fair to stick a shrub into a soil that could be baked into bricks or pottery, but sometimes in new subdivisions, or on commercial properties—especially around parking areas—that's all you're left with. If so, these are shrubs that, while they'll always grow better in a less heavy soil, can at least be used to land-scape in a less-than-desirable soil environment.

Chokeberry (*Aronia arbutifolia*)	5-9, 9-4
Barberries (*Berberis* spp.)	4-8, 8-1
Flowering quince (*Chaenomeles speciosa*)	6-9, 9-1
Red osier dogwood (*Cornus sericea*)	2-8, 8-1
Deutzia (*Deutzia gracilis*)	5-8, 8-5
Burning bush (*Euonymus alatus*)	4-9, 9-4
Forsythia (*Forsythia* × *intermedia*)	6-9, 9-6
Witch hazel (*Hamamelis* spp.)	4-8, 8-1
Junipers (*Juniperus* spp.)	4-8, 8-1
Beautybush (*Kolkwitzia amabilis*)	5-9, 9-5
Privets (*Ligustrum* spp.)	7-11, 12-7
Honeysuckles (*Lonicera* spp.)	4-9, 9-1
Bayberry (*Myrica pensylvanica*)	3-6, 6-1
Pyracantha or firethorn (*Pyracantha coccinea*)	6-9, 9-6

Sumacs (*Rhus* spp.)	4-9, 9-1
Currant (*Ribes alpinum*)	3-7, 7-1
Rugosa rose (*Rosa rugosa*)	3-9, 9-1
Goat willow (*Salix caprea*)	6-8, 8-6
Pussy willow (*Salix discolor*)	4-8, 8-1
Spireas (*Spiraea* spp.)	4-9, 9-1
Snowberry (*Symphoricarpos albus laevigatus*)	3-7, 7-1
Yews (*Taxus* spp.)	5-7, 7-5
American arborvitae (*Thuja occidentalis*)	2-7, 7-1
Arrowwood (*Viburnum dentatum*)	3-8, 8-1
Cranberry viburnum (*Viburnum opulus*)	4-8, 8-1
Blackhaw viburnum (*Viburnum prunifolium*)	3-9, 9-1
Sargent viburnum (*Viburnum sargentii*)	4-7, 7-1

SHRUBS FOR WET SITES

Many plants—like azaleas, rhododendrons, and yews—won't survive where the soil drains poorly; they tend to rot when their roots are exposed to moisture and deprived of oxygen. Some shrubs, however, are quite at home with sogginess. Many grow naturally in water or other wet areas and can be used for beautification, screening, wildlife habitat, and erosion control. So don't let that wet spot discourage you! Try some of the shrubs in this list, which comes from Roxanne Stonecypher, a landscape designer and owner of the Dismal Swamp Nursery in Chesapeake, Virginia. "When you are purchasing shrubs for wet areas," she advises, "you'll find that small half-gallon container-grown plants survive the best. Check their roots, and look for white, healthy-looking roots with no circling."

Smooth alder (*Alnus serrulata*)	5-8, 8-5
False indigo bush (*Amorpha fruticosa*)	2-8, 8-1
Red chokeberry (*Aronia arbutifolia*)	5-9, 9-4
Black chokeberry (*Aronia melanocarpa*)	4-9, 9-4
Saltbush (*Baccharis halimifolia*)	3-7, 7-1
Sweetshrub (*Calycanthus floridus*)	3-9, 9-1
Buttonbush (*Cephalanthus occidentalis*)	5-11, 12-3
Summersweet (*Clethra alnifolia*)	3-9, 9-1
Silky dogwood (*Cornus amomum*)	5-8, 8-5
Graystem dogwood (*Cornus racemosa*)	4-8, 8-1
Red osier dogwood (*Cornus sericea*)	2-8, 8-1
Strawberry bush (*Euonymus americana*)	4-9, 9-1
Possumhaw (*Ilex decidua*)	5-9, 9-1
Inkberry holly (*Ilex glabra*)	5-9, 9-5
Winterberry (*Ilex verticillata*)	5-8, 8-5
Yaupon holly (*Ilex vomitoria*)	7-10, 12-7
Anise (*Illicium parviflorum*)	7-9, 9-7
Virginia sweetspire (*Itea virginica*)	6-9, 9-5
Mountain laurel (*Kalmia latifolia*)	5-9, 9-5
Coastal leucothoe (*Leucothoe axillaris*)	6-9, 9-6
Drooping leucothoe (*Leucothoe fontanesiana*)	5-8, 8-3
Fetterbush (*Leucothoe racemosa*)	6-9, 9-3
Spice bush (*Lindera benzoin*)	5-9, 9-4
Wax myrtle (*Myrica cerifera*)	6-9, 9-6
Bayberry (*Myrica pensylvanica*)	3-6, 6-1
Devilwood (*Osmanthus americana*)	7-10, 10-7
Flame azalea (*Rhododendron calendulaceum*)	5-9, 9-4
Pinxterbloom azalea (*Rhododendron nudiflorum*)	5-9, 9-4
Swamp azalea (*Rhododendron viscosum*)	5-9, 9-4

Swamp rose (*Rosa palustris*)	5-9, 9-4
Goat willow (*Salix caprea*)	6-8, 8-6
Pussy willow (*Salix discolor*)	4-8, 8-1
Basket willow (*Salix purpurea*)	4-7, 7-1
Elderberry (*Sambucus canadensis*)	4-9, 9-1
American arborvitae (*Thuja occidentalis*)	2-7, 7-1
Highbush blueberry (*Vaccinium corymbosum*)	5-9, 9-2
Arrowwood (*Viburnum dentatum*)	3-8, 8-1
Highbush cranberry (*Viburnum trilobum*)	2-7, 7-1

SHRUBS FOR DRY SITES

Rare is the shrub that really requires dry conditions, but luckily there are some tough shrubs that can tolerate dry sites. These sites range from heavy clay soils that crack open in the middle of summer droughts to sites along the seashore where the soils are pure sand. Incorporating compost into the entire planting bed, irrigating if at all possible, and mulching to conserve moisture and moderate soil temperatures will sure help survival in these less-than-desirable locations.

Five-leaved aralia (*Acanthopanax sieboldianus*)	5-8, 8-3
Lead plant (*Amorpha canescens*)	2-6, 6-1
Saltbush (*Baccharis halimifolia*)	3-7, 7-1
Mentor barberry (*Berberis mentorensis*)	5-8, 8-3
Japanese barberry (*Berberis thunbergii*)	4-8, 8-3
New Jersey tea (*Ceanothus americanus*)	4-8, 8-1
Flowering quince (*Chaenomeles speciosa*)	6-9, 9-1
Gray dogwood (*Cornus racemosa*)	4-8, 8-1
Smoke bush (*Cotinus coggygria*)	5-8, 8-5
Broom (*Cytisus* spp.)	6-9, 9-4
Evergreen euonymus (*Euonymus japonicus*)	6-9, 9-6
Witch hazel (*Hamamelis virginiana*)	3-8, 8-1
St. John's wort (*Hypericum calycinum*)	5-9, 9-4
Indigos (*Indigofera* spp.)	6-9, 9-5
Common juniper (*Juniperus communis*)	2-6, 6-1
Shore juniper (*Juniperus conferta*)	5-9, 9-1
Creeping juniper (*Juniperus horizontalis*)	3-9, 9-1
Eastern red cedar (*Juniperus virginiana*)	3-9, 9-1
Beautybush (*Kolkwitzia amabilis*)	5-9, 9-5
Fetterbush (*Leucothoe racemosa*)	6-9, 9-3
Privets (*Ligustrum* spp.)	7-11, 12-7
Wax myrtle (*Myrica cerifera*)	6-9, 9-6
Bayberry (*Myrica pensylvanica*)	3-6, 6-1
Eastern ninebark (*Physocarpus opulifolius*)	3-7, 7-1
Potentilla or bush cinquefoil (*Potentilla fruticosa*)	3-7, 7-1
Beach plum (*Prunus maritima*)	3-6, 6-1
Buckthorns (*Rhamnus* spp.)	5-9, 9-4
Sumacs (*Rhus* spp.)	4-9, 9-3
Rose acacia (*Robinia hispida*)	6-11, 12-4
Rugosa rose (*Rosa rugosa*)	3-9, 9-1
Scotch rose (*Rosa spinosissima*)	3-9, 9-1
Virginia rose (*Rosa virginiana*)	3-9, 9-1
Tamarisk (*Tamarix* spp.)	5-8, 8-5
Nannyberry (*Viburnum lentago*)	2-8, 8-1
Chaste tree (*Vitex agnus-castus*)	6-9, 9-6
Yuccas (*Yucca* spp.)	5-11, 12-5

"Although some plants are naturally more drought tolerant than others, horticulture by definition means growing plants in a protected, artificial environment where stresses are different than in nature. No plant can survive becoming completely desiccated. Heat damage is always linked to an insufficient amount of water being available to the plant. Herbaceous plants are 80 to 90 percent water, and woody plants are about 50 percent water. Plant tissues must contain enough water to keep their cells turgid and to sustain the plant's processes of chemical and energy transport. Watering directly at the roots of a plant—through drip irrigation for instance—conserves water that would be lost to evaporation or runoff during overhead watering. In addition, plants take in water more efficiently when it is applied to their roots rather than their leaves. Mulching will also help conserve water."

Marc Cathey is president of the American Horticultural Society in Alexandria, Virginia, and helped develop the heat-zone categories for plants.

OLD-FASHIONED SHRUBS

Why make a list of old-fashioned shrubs? Because they are among the toughest plants, surviving before we had sophisticated irrigation systems and equipment or a myriad of inorganic chemicals to baby our plants through less-than-ideal conditions. They're tough, many are fragrant, and they remind you of the good old days when your grandmother grew these plants. Over the past ten to fifteen years, many of these old-fashioned shrubs have come back into the limelight as plant breeding and selection have developed new and outstanding cultivars. "We find more of our visitors wanting to see old-fashioned shrubs," says Mike Andruczyk, curator for the Norfolk, Virginia, Botanical Garden. "There is renewed interest in the plants people grew up with. One reason is they're often easier to grow than some of the more modern imports. They also bring back childhood memories."

Butterfly bush (*Buddleia davidii*)	6-9, 9-3
Boxwood (*Buxus sempervirens*)	6-8, 8-1
Buttonbush (*Cephalanthus occidentalis*)	5-11, 12-3
Early deutzia (*Deutzia gracilis*)	5-8, 8-3
Forsythia (*Forsythia* × *intermedia*)	6-9, 9-3
Rose of Sharon (*Hibiscus syriacus*)	5-9, 9-1
Bigleaf hydrangea (*Hydrangea macrophylla*)	6-9, 9-3
Chinese juniper (*Juniperus chinensis*)	3-9, 9-1
Globeflower or Japanese kerria (*Kerria japonica*)	4-9, 9-1
Mock orange (*Philadelphus coronarius*)	5-8, 8-5
Sweet azalea (*Rhododendron arborescens*)	7-9, 9-7
Roses (*Rosa* spp.)	3-9, 9-1
Elderberry (*Sambucus canadensis*)	4-9, 9-1
Bridalwreath spirea (*Spiraea prunifolia*)	5-8, 8-2
Thunberg spiraea (*Spiraea thunbergii*)	5-8, 8-2
Common lilac (*Syringa vulgaris*)	4-8, 8-1
Chaste tree (*Vitex angus-castus*)	4-9, 9-1
Weigela (*Weigela florida*)	5-8, 8-1

DEUTZIA

SHRUBS TO TRAIN AS SMALL TREES

Some shrubs, although multi-stemmed, have a crown that is tree form, or "limbed up"—the bottom branches are removed. Such a shrub can be used in a utility easement, under an overhang, or as a specimen, even in a large container. Several shrubs can be trained into tree form very effectively, but be forewarned that limbing them up often results in an increase in suckers from the base or roots. If these suckers are removed periodically, these large shrubs can be used in place of small trees.

Chinese witch hazel (*Hamamelis mollis*)	5-9, 9-2
Common witch hazel (*Hamamelis virginiana*)	3-8, 8-1
Rose of Sharon (*Hibiscus syriacus*)	5-9, 9-1
Deciduous hollies (*Ilex decidua, I. verticillata*)	5-8, 8-5
Crape myrtle (*Lagerstroemia indica*)	7-9, 9-7/6
Staghorn sumac (*Rhus typhina*)	3-8, 8-1
English yew (*Taxus baccata*)	5-7, 7-5
Arrowwood viburnum (*Viburnum dentatum*)	3-8, 8-1
European cranberry viburnum (*Viburnum opulus*)	4-8, 8-1
Blackhaw viburnum (*Viburnum prunifolium*)	3-9, 9-1
Siebold viburnum (*Viburnum sieboldii*)	5-8, 8-5
American cranberry viburnum (*Viburnum trilobum*)	2-7, 7-1
Chaste tree (*Vitex agnus-castus*)	6-9, 9-1

"Any shrub that may appear to have grown out of scale with the landscape can be trained up to become a small canopy for a micro niche in the landscape. To avoid basal sprouts when limbing up a large shrub to be a small tree, be patient. Remove no more than one-quarter to one-third of the total crown in any one year until the desired form is attained."

Howard Eyre is an assistant professor of ornamental horticulture and environmental design at Delaware Valley College in Doylestown, Pennsylvania.

ADULT IVY SHRUBS

Interesting shrubs for landscapes are the adult forms of ivy (*Hedera*). When propagated, they exhibit an upright growth habit with an extended floral display (greenish white) and beautiful berries (bluish black). The adult forms of ivy exhibit all the attributes of the juvenile, vine-like forms: soil-variation tolerance, drought tolerance, and minimal pests. The various cultivars vary by leaf color and texture. These adult ivies lend themselves to many landscape uses—foundation plants, hedges, screens, specimens, and even container plants. They are easy to maintain, rarely requiring supplemental irrigation, and need only minimal fertility and pruning.

The growth rate of ivy adults initially can be quite rapid; they often grow more than 18 inches in one season. But as the plants mature, internode growth (stem space between leaf attachments) decreases until growth becomes minimal in the mature plant. If initial juvenile shoots or runners develop, they should be removed the following spring, and the plant will eventually stop sending these out. Adults forms of ivy prefer some shade, although most of the green cultivars will tolerate even full sun.

Richard Davis, who does all of the adult ivy propagation and evaluation at the Ivy Farm in Locustville, Virginia, compiled this list. "New cultivars of adults are being evaluated at the Ivy Farm continuously," he notes. "Not all adult forms are good shrubs, so properly evaluating a cultivar is essential for successful introduction into the nursery trade, and ultimately into the landscape." All of these ivies are zoned 5-11, 12-1.

Small (under 3 feet)
Hedera helix 'California'
Hedera rhombea 'Crème de Mint'

Medium (3 to 5 feet)
Hedera colchica 'Greenspice'
Hedera helix 'Deep Freeze,' 'Iceberg,' 'Poetica,'
    'Sunspot' ('Golden Wedding')

Large (over 5 feet)
Hedera helix 'Emerald Gem,' 'Garnet,' 'Treetop'

VINES

Vines—plants with long stems that twine, cling, or climb with tendrils—are receiving increased attention for their many landscape uses. Where space is limited they can be used as dividers or barriers for "vertical landscaping." They can screen unsightly views or provide privacy for a patio, porch, or backyard. If a long fence or blank wall (like those along highways) seems too bare or monotonous, vines can give interest to the expanse. They can help to soften sharp architectural features or blend a structure with its surroundings. They can be used to create entrances or private areas, especially if trained over a trellis or an arbor.

Vines can become stabilizing ground covers on steep slopes or where grass is inappropriate or too difficult to mow. If trained on trellises against homes and other buildings, vines can help provide shade in the summer and trap warmth in the winter. Use a hinged trellis that will allow access to the wall behind the vine for cleaning or repairs.

MORNING GLORY

Tips for Selecting and Succeeding with Vines

- Be sure you select the right vine for the right location. Dense vines make good screens; fine-textured vines create artistry against walls; vines with flowers, fruits, or colorful leaves fill the landscape with seasonal interest.
- Be mindful of each vine's growth method—twining, clinging, or climbing—and provide appropriate support. Twining vines in particular may need fairly substantial supports made of sturdy, durable materials. If wire is used, select copper or aluminum that won't rust. If wood is used, buy pressure-treated to make it last longer.
- If vines are to grow in particular directions or form a certain pattern, begin training them while they are small.
- Be sure that vines used for their flowers receive adequate sunlight.
- Vines are generally most successful when planted in moist, well-drained soil with a slightly acid pH, but many vines can adapt to less than ideal conditions.
- Vines can be very low maintenance, but most will benefit from some annual pruning for direction, size control, or to encourage flowering.
- Remember that many vines are vigorous plants, so be prepared to confine them to prevent them from becoming invasive.
- Do not let vines climb trees. Vines can cover branches and become heavy enough to break them. Vines that twine can girdle tree trunks and interfere with growth or cause misshapen trees. Vines can also cover so much of a tree that they may interfere with the tree's ability to photosynthesize (manufacture food). Vines can also cover structural flaws—weak branch attachments, cavities—that can be hazardous, especially if an arborist needs to climb the tree to do pruning or diagnostic work. If a vine has grown up a tree, cut the vine stems near the ground, let the top of the vine die back naturally, then carefully cut or pull the dried stems from the tree. Especially troublesome in this respect is English ivy (*Hedera helix*).

TWINING VINES

At least half of the vines mentioned in this chapter climb by wrapping their stems around or through a support. Without support, they'll grow atop themselves rather than reaching out. From time to time, take the shoots and wind them through the structure you've provided for their support. If you held your finger out in front of a real twiner long enough, it might wrap itself around your finger like a coiled spring. Strangely enough, each twiner has a twining direction—either right to left or left to right (some wisterias go one direction while others go the opposite).

The twining vines in this list have been subdivided into perennials (hardy wood vines that are persistent), annuals (tender vines that need replanting each year), and tropicals (tender vines that you'll probably plant in a container and take in and out each year).

Twining Perennials

Hardy kiwi (*Actinidia arguta*)	3-8, 8-1
Kolomikta vine (*Actinidia kolomikta*)	5-8, 8-4
Five-leaf akebia (*Akebia quinata*)	4-8, 8-1
Dutchman's pipe (*Aristolochia macrophylla*)	5-8, 8-4
Trumpet creeper (*Campsis radicans*)	5-9, 9-5
Bittersweet (*Celastrus scandens*)	3-8, 8-1
Carolina jessamine (*Gelsemium sempervirens*)	7-9, 9-2
Winter jasmine (*Jasminum nudiflorum*)	6-9, 9-6
Goldflame honeysuckle (*Lonicera* × *heckrottii*)	6-9, 9-4
Hall's Japanese honeysuckle (*Lonicera japonica* 'Halliana')	4-11, 12-1
Trumpet honeysuckle (*Lonicera sempervirens*)	4-9, 9-2
Silver lace or China fleece vine (*Polygonum aubertii*)	5-9, 9-3
Japanese wisteria (*Wisteria floribunda*)	5-9, 9-4
American wisteria (*Wisteria frutescens*)	6-9, 9-6
Chinese wisteria (*Wisteria sinensis*)	5-9, 9-5

Twining Annuals

Hyacinth bean (*Dolichos lablab*)
Morning glory (*Ipomoea* hybs. and cvs.)
Moonvine (*Ipomoea alba*)
Cardinal climber (*Ipomoea* × *multifida*)
Cypress vine (*Ipomoea quamoclit*)
Mina (*Mina lobata*)
Tropical passion vine (*Passiflora coccinea*)
Scarlet runner bean (*Phaseolus coccineus*)
Black-eyed Susan vine (*Thunbergia alata*)

Twining Tropicals

Allamanda (*Allamanda cathartica*)
Madeira vine (*Anredera cordifolia*)
Bougainvillea (*Bougainvillea spectabilis*)
Bleeding-heart vine (*Clerodendrum thomsoniae*)
Jasmines (*Jasminum* spp.)
Pink mandevilla (*Mandevilla amabilis*)
Dipladenia or mandevilla (*Mandevilla splendens*)
Chilean jasmine (*Mandevilla suaveolens*)
Bower plant (*Pandorea jasminoides*)
Mexican flame vine (*Senecio confusus*)
Stephanotis (*Stephanotis floribunda*)
Cape honeysuckle (*Tecomaria capensis*)
Confederate or star jasmine (*Trachelospermum jasminoides*)

"Twining vines are great for gardeners who have limited time, or who may be like me and prefer or even demand plants that require minimum care. Once you get them headed in the direction you want them to grow, twining vines require only occasional attention to keep them growing on their support. I plant morning glory and moonvine together and train them onto a vine pole. This combination not only provides vertical interest in my garden but also produces colorful new flowers each morning that yield to the moonvine's showy, fragrant flowers every evening."

Debbie Dillion is a Cooperative Extension agent for environmental horticulture in Leesburg, Virginia.

CLINGING VINES

The clinging vines below grab walls, wood fences, or even tree trunks in one of two ways. Either tendrils with disk-like adhesive tips glue them to their supports, or small aerial roots along the stems attach into holes and crevices of porous or rough-textured surfaces, including tree bark. Trying to pull these plants off can be tough, so plant these vines where you know they won't need to be removed for a long time.

Clinging vines are great for covering low walls, especially ones made from concrete block with no facade. But be careful if you let them grow up the wall of your house; keep their tops in check so you don't have to rip them off the gutter or upper windowsills in a few years. Clinging vines can pull off paint or loose mortar if you tug, and the vines often leave pieces of their adhesive structures clinging to a wall. They can also form such a dense covering that moisture builds up behind the vine and causes wood to rot.

Cross vine (*Bignonia capreolata*)	6-9, 9-5
Trumpet creeper (*Campsis radicans*)	3-8, 8-1
Wintercreeper (*Euonymus fortunei*)	5-9, 9-5
Persian ivy (*Hedera colchica*)	5-11, 12-1
English ivy (*Hedera helix*)	5-11, 12-1
Climbing hydrangea (*Hydrangea anomala* subsp. *petiolaris*)	4-9, 9-1
Virginia creeper (*Parthenocissus quinquefolia*)	5-9, 9-5
Boston Ivy (*Parthenocissus tricuspidata*)	4-8, 8-1
Japanese hydrangea vine (*Schizophragma hydrangeoides*)	6-9, 9-6

"Climbing hydrangea produces its flowers on horizontal shoots. These can be very attractive (adding a three-dimensional aspect that shows off the flowers well and attractively holds snow in the winter), but some people feel the horizontal shoots make the vine look unkept and messy. Such neatniks prune off the horizontal shoots and then ask why the plant doesn't bloom."

R. William Thomas, author of *Ortho's Guide to Vines and Climbers* (Meredith, 1999), is research horticulturist at Longwood Gardens in Kennett Square, Pennsylvania.

VINES WITH TENDRILS

Tendrils are thin, flexible, leafless stems that wrap themselves around almost anything they contact, such as chain-link fences and other plants. Vines that climb with tendrils need a small support around which their tendrils can wind. Tendriled vines can't climb walls unless attached to a support such as fishing line or wire. Many species of clematis wind their leaf stalks like tendrils around supports.

Porcelain vine (*Ampelopsis brevipedunculata*)	5-8, 8-3
Cross vine (*Bignonia capreolata*)	6-9, 9-5
Sweet autumn clematis (*Clematis dioscoreifolia robusta*)	4-9, 9-1
Clematis (*Clematis* x *jackmanii* and cvs.)	3-8, 9-7
Scarlet clematis (*Clematis texensis*)	4-9, 9-1
Virginia creeper (*Parthenocissus quinquefolia*)	5-9, 9-5
Passionflower (*Passiflora caerulea*)	6-9, 9-6
Grapes (*Vitis* spp.)	5-9, 9-1

VINES WITH SHOWY FLOWERS

Vines with showy flowers are the vines gardeners look forward to year after year as their blooms mark another peak in a gardening season. You can often grow several flowering vines together on a trellis or arbor to enjoy more variety as well as a longer show. By far the queen of the vines when it comes to variety—flower sizes, petal arrangements (single or double), colors—is clematis, with many of the clematis flowers transforming into unusual and showy fruits for fall interest.

Many Colors

Clematis (*Clematis* x *jackmanii* and cvs.)	3-8, 9-7

CLEMATIS

White

Sweet autumn clematis (*Clematis dioscoreifolia robusta*)	4-9, 9-1
Virgin's bower (*Clematis virginiana*)	5-9, 9-5
Climbing hydrangea (*Hydrangea anomala* subsp. *petiolaris*)	4-9, 9-1
Winter jasmine (*Jasminum nudiflorum*)	6-9, 9-6
Silver lace vine (*Polygonum aubertii*)	5-9, 9-3
Japanese hydrangea vine (*Schizophragma hydrangeoides*)	6-9, 9-6
American wisteria (*Wisteria frutescens* 'Nivea')	6-9, 9-6
Chinese wisteria (*Wisteria sinensis* 'Alba')	5-9, 9-5

Yellow

Yellow trumpet vine (*Campsis radicans* 'Flava')	3-8, 8-1
Carolina jessamine (*Gelsemium sempervirens*)	7-9, 9-2
Trumpet honeysuckle (*Lonicera sempervirens* 'Sulphurea')	4-9, 9-2

Orange to Red

Cross vine (*Bignonia capreolata*)	6-9, 9-5
Trumpet creeper (*Campsis radicans*)	3-8, 8-1

Pink to Red

Scarlet clematis (*Clematis texensis*)	4-9, 9-1
Japanese hydrangea vine (*Schizophragma hydrangeoides* 'Roseum')	6-9, 9-6

Blue to Purple

Passionflower (*Passiflora caerulea*)	6-9, 9-6
Japanese wisteria (*Wisteria floribunda*)	5-9, 9-4
American wisteria (*Wisteria frutescens*)	6-9, 9-6

Bi-color

Goldflame honeysuckle (*Lonicera* x *heckrottii*)	6-9, 9-4
Trumpet honeysuckle (*Lonicera sempervirens*)	4-9, 9-2

According to the catalog of Roslyn Nursery of Dix Hills, New York, "A real knockout clematis that is the best selling clematis in Europe is *Clematis serratifolia* 'Golden Tiara,' with 3-inch yellow flowers that cover the vine from mid-summer to mid-fall. It's a vigorous grower that will grow in full sun or partial shade."

VINES WITH VARIEGATED FOLIAGE

Variegated foliage is a landscape feature to be used sparingly in a garden because it can quickly be overdone. Like a bright color, variegation draws the eye. Colorful foliage is a nice way to set off a dull area of the garden or to provide a contrast with the dark-green foliage of surrounding plants. The leaves of kolomikta vine are green and white with unusual patches of bright pink. The other vines in this list are popular green ones that also come in variegated forms. A few vines have cultivars with leaves other than green, like the purple-leaf cultivar of Japanese honeysuckle (*Lonicera japonica* 'Purpurea').

Kolomikta vine (*Actinidia kolomikta*)	5-8, 8-4
Wintercreeper (*Euonymus fortunei*)	5-9, 9-5
Algerian ivy (*Hedera canariensis*)	6-11, 12-1
English ivy (*Hedera helix*)	5-11, 12-1

SPRING-FLOWERING VINES

In the spring, though most attention goes to flowering trees and shrubs (dogwoods, redbuds, spireas, forsythia) and bulbs (crocus, daffodils), there are vines that can make a major landscape splash. Locate spring-flowering vines where they don't compete with, or aren't overshadowed by, the landscape's other flowering plants. Vines that bloom in spring on old wood (the buds are formed the previous summer) should be pruned within a week or two after they bloom. Silver lace vine and others that bloom in late summer or fall on new growth should be pruned in later winter or early spring, before the flower buds form.

Cross vine (*Bignonia capreolata*)	6-9, 9-5
Clematis (*Clematis* x *jackmanii* and cvs.)	3-8, 7-9
Carolina jessamine (*Gelsemium sempervirens*)	7-9, 9-2
Goldflame honeysuckle (*Lonicera* x *heckrottii*)	6-9, 9-4
Japanese wisteria (*Wisteria floribunda*)	5-9, 9-4

SUMMER-FLOWERING VINES

Though many plants can be counted on for summer flowers, few can cover a wall or a trellis, or cascade from a container. For those effects, you need a flowering vine. Select a perennial vine if you have a location where each summer you want the vine's particular color and flowering effect. Choose an annual vine if you want to change colors and textures each year. Annual summer-flowering vines can also serve as good and usually fast temporary fillers or screens while perennial vines or other plants get established.

This list of summer-flowering vines is from gardening columnist Kathy Van Mullekom of Newport News, Virginia. She has divided it into perennials and annuals.

Perennials

Five-leaf akebia (*Akebia quinata*)	4-8, 8-1
Cross vine (*Bignonia capreolata*)	6-9, 9-5
Trumpet creeper (*Campsis radicans*)	5-9, 9-5
Clematis (*Clematis* x *jackmanii* and cvs.)	3-8, 9-7
Sweet autumn clematis (*Clematis dioscoreifolia robusta*)	4-9, 9-1
Climbing hydrangea (*Hydrangea anomala* subsp. *petiolaris*)	4-9, 9-1
Goldflame honeysuckle (*Lonicera* x *heckrottii*)	6-9, 9-4
Japanese honeysuckle (*Lonicera japonica*)	4-11, 12-1
Trumpet honeysuckle (*Lonicera sempervirens*)	4-9, 9-2
Passionflower (*Passiflora caerulea*)	6-9, 9-6
Japanese hydrangea vine (*Schizophragma hydrangeoides*)	6-9, 9-6
American wisteria (*Wisteria frutescens*)	6-9, 9-6

Annuals

Allamanda (*Allamanda cathartica*)
Dutchman's pipe (*Aristolochia littoralis*)
Love-in-a-puff (*Cardiospermum halicacabum*)
Bleeding-heart vine (*Clerodendrum thomsoniae*)
Cup-and-saucer vine (*Cobaea scandens*)
Purple hyacinth bean (*Lablab purpureus*)
Firecracker vine (*Ipomoea lobata*)
Morning glory (*Ipomoea purpurea*)
Cypress vine (*Ipomoea quamoclit*)
Sweet pea (*Lathyrus odoratus*)
Scarlet runner bean (*Phaseolus coccineus*)
Black-eyed Susan vine (*Thunbergia alata*)
Climbing nasturtium (*Tropaeolum* spp.)

"Vines give vertical vistas to gardens, especially when you've gardened every square inch of horizontal space. The smallness of an urban garden forced me to turn to vines for more gardening interest. After one summer I was hooked, caught up in the twists and turns of vine tendrils. My husband likes to joke, telling people to rescue us if they see vines crawling across our front door and down the chimney. Seriously, summer-flowering vines give my garden a tropical touch, their flowers spiraling upward to touch the heavens. When choosing vines for your garden, plant the aggressive ones in pots or be prepared to tame their rambunctious personality. Small trees can act as temporary trellises for vines, but avoid letting the vine cover too much of the tree's canopy or it will interfere with the tree's ability to manufacture food."

Kathy Van Mullekom is the gardening columnist for the *Daily Press* newspaper and for *Hampton Roads Gardening & Home* magazine (www.hrgardening.com) in Newport News, Virginia.

VINES WITH FALL INTEREST

Anytime you can choose a plant that has more than one season of peak interest, do it. Vines with showy berries or seed pods, leaves that turn color in the fall, or bark that is colored or exfoliating (peeling) give the garden year-round appeal. Though most of us think of fall color as coming from trees, one of the first plants to turn color in the fall is Virginia creeper, followed a month or so later by its relative, Boston ivy. Both are deciduous, and before their leaves drop, they put on a beautiful show that can rival the brightest of fall-colored trees.

Fall Flowers
Scarlet clematis (*Clematis texensis*)	4-9, 9-1
Virgin's bower, woodbine (*Clematis virginiana*)	5-9, 9-5

Showy Fruit or Pods
Hardy kiwi (*Actinidia* spp.)	3-8, 8-1
Porcelain vine (*Ampelopsis brevipedunculata*)	5-8, 8-3
Trumpet creeper (*Campsis radicans*)	5-9, 9-5
Chinese bittersweet (*Celastrus orbiculatus*)	4-8, 8-1
American bittersweet (*Celastrus scandens*)	3-8, 8-1
Clematis (*Clematis* x *jackmanii* and cvs.)	3-8, 9-7
Honeysuckles (*Lonicera* spp.)	6-9, 9-4
Grapes (*Vitis* spp.)	5-9, 9-1
Wisterias (*Wisteria* spp.)	5-9, 9-5

Colorful Leaves
Virginia creeper (*Parthenocissus quinquefolia*)—red	5-9, 9-5
Boston ivy (*Parthenocissus tricuspidata*)—red	4-8, 8-1
Grapes (*Vitis* spp.)—yellow	5-9, 9-1

BOSTON IVY

Showy Bark
Climbing hydrangea (*Hydrangea anomala* subsp. *petiolaris*)	4-9, 9-1

EVERGREEN VINES

If you need the screening effect of a vine year round, you may want to select a vine that is semi to fully evergreen so that even in the winter your screen will be effective. If a vine is located near a building or area where solar heating is desired in the winter, use only vines that are deciduous, not evergreen.

Five-leaf akebia (*Akebia quinata*)	4-8, 8-1
Porcelain vine (*Ampelopsis brevipedunculata*)	5-8, 8-3

Cross vine (*Bignonia capreolata*)	6-9, 9-6
Wintercreeper (*Euonymus fortunei*)	5-9, 9-5
English ivy (*Hedera helix*)	5-11, 12-1
Trumpet honeysuckle (*Lonicera sempervirens*)	4-9, 9-2

VINES WITH FRAGRANT FLOWERS

Nothing is nicer than to walk through the garden and smell a fragrant flower in bloom. A few vines offer flowers that are not only showy, but also fragrant. Position fragrant vines on trellises near windows that are open during the spring and summer to enjoy this often overlooked bonus.

Sweet autumn clematis (*Clematis dioscoreifolia robusta*)	4-9, 9-1
Wood-vamp or climbing hydrangea (*Decumaria barbara*)	6-9, 9-5
Carolina jessamine (*Gelsemium sempervirens*)	7-9, 9-2
Climbing hydrangea (*Hydrangea anomala* subsp. *paniculata*)	4-9, 9-1
Goldflame honeysuckle (*Lonicera* x *heckrottii*)	6-9, 9-4
Japanese honeysuckle (*Lonicera japonica*)	4-11, 12-1
Passionflower (*Passiflora caerulea*)	6-9, 9-5
Silver lace vine (*Polygonum aubertii*)	5-9, 9-3
Japanese wisteria (*Wisteria floribunda*)	5-9, 9-4

"Although I don't grow native exclusively—far from it—I will always pick a native over an exotic if I can. Among honeysuckles, it's a no-brainer. The Japanese honeysuckle is a rampant weed at our weekend home in Virginia's Northern Neck (vying with English ivy for Most Evil Plant), capable of pulling good-sized saplings to the ground. I grow the native carmine-flowered coral honeysuckle (*Lonicera semper-virens*) on a trellis where I can see it from our sunroom and deck. It draws hummingbirds more reliably than a feeder, blooms all year, and produces translucent red berries. It's scentless, however. If you insist on fragrance, try the apparently noninvasive hybrid goldflame honeysuckle (*Lonicera* x *heckrottii*). Deep pink outside and gold inside, it has an aroma that reminds me of Old Spice, and it blooms throughout the year. It can develop a tangle of woody stems, but they're a great place for birds to nest."

Kathleen Fisher, who gardens in Alexandria and Reedville, Virginia, is the author of numerous gardening books and for ten years was the editor of the American Horticultural Society's magazine, *The American Gardener*.

VINES THAT TOLERATE SHADE

Though most vines grow best in full sun, several will tolerate shade. These vines will do well on arbors shaded by large trees, or on the northeast side of your house. For those that have showy flowers, try to give them partial sun during the afternoon.

Kiwis (*Actinidia* spp.)	3-8, 8-1
Five-leaf akebia (*Akebia quinata*)	4-8, 8-1
Dutchman's pipe (*Aristolochia macrophylla*)	5-8, 8-4
American bittersweet (*Celastrus scandens*)	3-8, 8-1
Clematis (*Clematis* x *jackmanii*)	3-8, 9-7
Wintercreeper (*Euonymus fortunei*)	5-9, 9-5
Carolina jessamine (*Gelsemium sempervirens*)	7-9, 9-2
English ivy (*Hedera helix*)	5-11, 12-1
Climbing hydrangea (*Hydrangea anomala* subsp. *petiolaris*)	4-9, 9-1
Honeysuckles (*Lonicera* spp.)	4-9, 9-2
Virginia creeper (*Parthenocissus quinquefolia*)	5-9, 9-5
Boston ivy (*Parthenocissus tricuspidata*)	4-8, 8-1
Silver lace vine (*Polygonum aubertii*)	5-9, 9-3

Grapes (*Vitus* spp.)   5-9, 9-1
Wisterias (*Wisteria* spp.)   5-9, 9-5

VINES FOR ALKALINE CONDITIONS

If you garden where the soil or water has a pH level that is more than 7.0, and you don't want to continually add compost, peat moss, and soil acidifiers to reverse the alkalinity, try any of the vines in this list. All are suitable for alkaline conditions.

Porcelain vine (*Ampelopsis brevipedunculata*)	5-8, 8-3
Dutchman's pipe (*Aristolochia durior*)	5-8, 8-4
Cross vine (*Bignonia capreolata*)	6-9, 9-6
Trumpet creeper (*Campsis radicans*)	5-9, 9-5
Scarlet clematis (*Clematis texensis*)	4-9, 9-1
Virginia creeper (*Parthenocissus quinquefolia*)	5-9, 9-5
Boston ivy (*Parthenocissus tricuspidata*)	4-8, 8-1
Passionflower (*Passiflora caerulea*)	6-9, 9-5
Silver lace vine (*Polygonum aubertii*)	5-9, 9-3

PASSIONFLOWER

VINES FOR HOT, DRY SITES

There always seem to be spots that are a bit drier or hotter than others. These areas may be in full sun all day, which can be a plus for excellent flower production. Or they may be drier because of sandy soil or a slight elevation that causes fast drainage of rain or irrigation water. Or they may be in areas where irrigation isn't possible or practical. Incorporating organic matter into the soil will certainly help, but it's also nice to be able to select plants that you know are tough.

Perennials

Kiwis (*Actinidia* spp.)	3-8, 8-1
Five-leaf akebia (*Akebia quinata*)	4-8, 8-1
Porcelain vine (*Ampelopsis brevipedunculata*)	5-8, 8-3
Dutchman's pipe (*Aristolochia macrophylla*)	5-8, 8-4
Cross vine (*Bignonia capreolata*)	6-9, 9-6
Trumpet creeper (*Campsis radicans*)	5-9, 9-5
American bittersweet (*Celastrus scandens*)	3-8, 8-1
Scarlet clematis (*Clematis texensis*)	4-9, 9-1
Carolina jessamine (*Gelsemium sempervirens*)	7-9, 9-2
English ivy (*Hedera helix*)	5-11, 12-1
Japanese honeysuckle (*Lonicera japonica* 'Halliana')	4-11, 12-1
Trumpet honeysuckle (*Lonicera sempervirens*)	4-9, 9-2
Virginia creeper (*Parthenocissus tricuspidata*)	4-8, 8-1
Boston ivy (*Parthenocissus quinquefolia*)	5-9, 9-5
Passionflower (*Passiflora caerulea*)	6-9, 9-6
Silver lace vine (*Polygonum aubertii*)	5-9, 9-3
Japanese hydrangea vine (*Schizophragma hydrangeoides*)	6-9, 9-6
Wisterias (*Wisteria* spp.)	5-9, 9-5

CAROLINA
JESSAMINE

Annuals

Love-in-a-puff (*Cardiospermum halicacabum*)
Firecracker vine (*Ipomoea lobata*)
Cypress vine (*Ipomoea quamoclit*)
Morning glory (*Ipomoea purpurea*)
Hyacinth bean (*Lablab purpureus*)
Moonseed (*Menispermum canadense*)

VINES FOR MOIST, SOGGY SITES

Most vines prefer a soil that is moist yet drains well, but the vines on this list are distinguished by their ability to grow on soil that would be considered soggy, at least for a time. In fact, these vines can also withstand water puddling around their roots for a few days during heavy nor'easters.

Cross vine (*Bignonia capreolata*)	6-9, 9-5
Trumpet creeper (*Campsis radicans*)	5-9, 9-5
Virgin's bower (*Clematis virginiana*)	5-9, 9-5
Carolina jessamine (*Gelsemium sempervirens*)	7-9, 9-2
English ivy (*Hedera helix*)	5-11, 12-1
Boston ivy (*Parthenocissus quinquefolia*)	5-9, 9-5
Virginia creeper (*Parthenocissus tricuspidata*)	4-8, 8-1

GROUND COVERS

Any plant that is low growing, spreads fairly quickly, and forms a relatively dense mat over the ground can be thought of as a ground cover—a landscape catch-all category that can include perennials, vines, and low shrubs. Though Americans seem to have a love affair with turf grasses—one that seems obsessive to gardeners in many other parts of the world—more people are beginning to appreciate the (usually) reduced maintenance and wide variety of habits, shapes, and colors provided by ground covers. They function similarly to mulches: they shade the soil, keeping it cool and moist in the summer; they protect plant roots and stems from cultivation and mowing damage; and they compete with and suppress weeds.

There certainly are reasons and areas in which to continue to use turf grasses, especially where there is high foot traffic. But ground covers can be better than turf in areas that are difficult to maintain or where the environment works against turf. Use them in hard-to-mow areas—steep slopes, medians, townhouse yards, and where lots of trees and shrubs create a dizzying slalom course if mowed.

Use ground covers where shade is dense—under large or low-branched trees or on the north side of buildings—where turf thins out and weeds move in. Plant ground covers under shrubs and tall perennials. Use them instead of mulch where tree roots have surfaced and make mowing dangerous (to you and the tree). Use them where it is too wet or too dry for turf to grow well. Most ground covers aren't nearly as water dependent as highly maintained turf grasses.

Tips for Selecting and Succeeding with Ground Covers

- Select the right ground cover for the right location. Consider soil type, moisture level, light intensity, and aesthetic effects.
- Prepare beds before planting rather than just digging isolated planting holes. Till or turn the soil, incorporate organic matter if needed, and add any amendments that a soil test might recommend. Eliminate any perennial weeds (Bermuda grass, nutsedge) before you plant.
- Use proper spacing. Spacing depends on growth rate, plant size, and how quickly you want the soil covered.
- Plant in staggered, not straight rows. This assures quicker coverage and less soil erosion if you're planting on a slope.
- Mulch well between plants. Don't allow weeds to become established because they'll compete for space, light, water, and nutrients. Pull weeds when they're small, or spray carefully with a contact or systemic herbicide. Also consider applying a ground-cover-compatible preemergent herbicide atop the mulch to kill weeds whose seeds blow in or are dropped by birds.
- Water as needed the first year after planting to get your ground covers well established and to encourage rapid spread.

THE MOST COMMON GROUND COVERS

Here are the plants that most people in the New York and Mid-Atlantic area include on their list of ground covers if you ask them to name the most reliable, most available ones. You will find many different cultivars available, offering a great diversity of habit, leaf size and color, and even flower colors (ajuga, liriope, sedum, periwinkle), though few of these plants are grown mainly for their flowering effect.

DAYLILY

Ajuga or bugleweed (*Ajuga reptans*)	3-9, 9-1
Wintercreeper (*Euonymus fortunei*)	5-9, 9-5
English ivy (*Hedera helix*)	5-11, 12-1
Liriope or lilyturf (*Liriope muscari*)	6-11, 12-1
Mondo grass or dwarf lilyturf (*Ophiopogon japonicus*)	6-11, 12-1
Pachysandra or Japanese spurge (*Pachysandra terminalis*)	4-8, 8-1
Sedum or stonecrop (*Sedum* spp.)	4-9, 9-1
Common periwinkle (*Vinca minor*)	4-9, 9-1

GROUND COVERS FOR FULL SUN

When you choose a ground cover for a spot that gets lots of sun, you probably could grow grass there but choose not to. Beds of ground cover help delineate the boundaries of a landscape and add interest and variety to a garden design. They also reduce the amount of time spent mowing. The plants listed here are perennials, durable shrubs, and ornamental grasses. You will find a representative sample of low, creeping junipers widely used as ground covers; there are dozens of named varieties with varied colors and growth habits. Also mentioned are bamboos—be sure to select low-growing, noninvasive species.

Ground covers in full sun must be tough enough to stand up to summer heat and humidity without thinning out. The following will thrive if they're in well-drained soil. Poor drainage will quickly doom many of these plants.

Prostrate abelia (*Abelia* × *grandiflora* 'Prostrata')	5-9, 12-6
Ajuga (*Ajuga reptans*)	3-9, 9-1
Bearberry (*Arctostaphylos uva-ursi*)	5-8, 8-4
Heather (*Calluna vulgaris*)	5-7, 7-5
Barberry cotoneaster (*Cotoneaster dammeri*)	6-8, 8-6
Rockspray cotoneaster (*Cotoneaster horizontalis*)	5-7, 7-4
Willowleaf cotoneaster (*Cotoneaster salicifolius* 'Repens')	6-8, 8-6
Bath's Pink dianthus (*Dianthus gratianopolitanus* 'Bath's Pink')	7-10, 10-7
Wintercreeper (*Euonymus fortunei*)	5-9, 9-5
Low, clumping bamboos (*Fargesia spathacea, Pleioblastus pygmaea*)	5-9, 9-4
English ivy (*Hedera helix*)	5-11, 12-1
Daylily (*Hemerocallis* spp., hybs., and cvs.)	3-11, 12-1
Chameleon plant (*Houttuynia cordata*)	6-11, 12-6
St. John's wort (*Hypericum calycinum*)	5-9, 9-4
Liriopes (*Liriope muscari, L. spicata*)	6-11, 12-1
Shore juniper (*Juniperus conferta* 'Blue Pacific,' 'Emerald Sea')	5-9, 9-1
Creeping juniper (*Juniperus horizontalis* 'Bar Harbor,' 'Blue Rug')	3-9, 9-1
Dwarf Japanese-garden juniper (*Juniperus procumbens* 'Nana')	3-9, 9-1
Eulalia, Japanese silver or maiden grass (*Miscanthus sinensis*)	4-9, 9-1
Fountain grass (*Pennisetum* spp.)	6-9, 9-6
Ribbon grass (*Phalaris arundinacea picta*)	4-9, 9-3
Phlox (*Phlox subulata*)	3-8, 8-1
Potentilla (*Potentilla fruticosa*)	3-7, 7-1
Cinquefoil (*Potentilla tridentata*)	2-8, 8-1
Sedums (*Sedum* spp.)	4-9, 9-1
Creeping thymes (*Thymus* cvs.)	5-9, 9-4

GROUND COVERS FOR SUN OR SHADE

Landscapes often have areas that transition from sun to shade over the course of the day, so it's nice to find ground covers that will tolerate this change in light conditions. These plants will also be more tolerant as trees above them grow larger and the shade beneath them becomes denser, or more open as the lower limbs of the trees are removed. Jim Bruce, owner of Hanover Farms, a wholesale ground-cover nursery in Rockville,

Virginia, provided this list of adaptable ground covers. "These are pretty standard and relatively easy to grow, so they should be reasonably available and successful for most people," he notes. Jim also advises, "Ferns make an especially interesting sun/shade ground cover because they are unexpected. Two that are suitable are in the list, and with modest moisture and light conditions are good choices."

Two of the plants on this list—English ivy (*Hedera helix*) and Virginia creeper (*Parthenocissus quinquefolia*)—are vines that should be restricted from growing up trees.

Bishop's weed (*Aegopodium podagraria*)	4-9, 9-3
Ajuga (*Ajuga reptans*)	3-9, 9-1
Bearberry (*Arctostaphylos uva-ursi*)	2-6, 6-1
Hay-scented fern (*Dennstaedtia punctilobula*)	4-8, 8-1
Wintercreeper (*Euonymus fortunei*)	5-9, 9-5
English ivy (*Hedera helix*)	5-11, 12-1
Liriope or lilyturf (*Liriope muscari*)	6-11, 12-1
Spreading lilyturf (*Liriope spicata*)	6-11, 12-1
Ostrich fern (*Matteuccia struthiopteris*)	3-8, 8-1
Virginia creeper (*Parthenocissus quinquefolia*)	5-9, 9-5

GROUND COVERS FOR LIGHT SHADE

Shade is a delight in the summer garden. It can enhance and extend the variety of colors and textures. The following are good choices for areas in the light shade of pines or around large trees whose lower limbs are way overhead. Ground covers planted in the shade should be well spaced to assure good air circulation that will help to reduce insect and disease problems.

Bishop's weed (*Aegopodium podagraria*)	4-9, 9-1
Ajuga (*Ajuga reptans*)	3-9, 9-1
Bearberry (*Arctostaphylos uva-ursi*)	2-6, 6-1
Wild ginger (*Asarum* spp.)	4-8, 8-1
Astilbe (*Astilbe* spp. and cvs.)	3-8, 8-2
Plumbago or leadwort (*Ceratostigma plumbaginoides*)	6-9, 9-1
Barrenwort (*Epimedium* spp.)	5-9, 9-3
Creeping wintergreen (*Gaultheria procumbens*)	3-8, 8-1
Box huckleberry (*Gaylussacia brachycera*)	3-7, 7-1
English ivy (*Hedera helix*)	5-11, 12-1
Lenten rose (*Helleborus orientalis*)	4-9, 9-1
Coral bells (*Heuchera* spp. and cvs.)	3-8, 8-1
Hostas (*Hosta* spp., hybs., and cvs.)	4-9, 9-1
Crested iris (*Iris cristata*)	4-8, 8-1
Yellow archangel (*Lamiastrum galeobdolon*)	4-8, 8-1
Deadnettle (*Lamium maculatum*)	4-8, 8-1
Dwarf drooping leucothoe (*Leucothoe fontanesiana* 'Nana')	5-8, 8-5
Liriopes (*Liriope muscari, L. spicata*)	6-11, 12-1
Creeping Jenny (*Lysimachia nummularia*)	4-8, 8-2
Mazus (*Mazus reptans*)	5-8, 8-4
Siberian carpet grass (*Microbiota decussata*)	3-8, 8-1
Partridge berry (*Mitchella repens*)	4-9, 9-2
Mondo grass (*Ophiopogon japonicus*)	6-11, 12-1
Alleghany spurge (*Pachysandra procumbens*)	6-9, 9-6
Pachysandra (*Pachysandra terminalis*)	4-8, 8-1
Woodland phlox (*Phlox divaricata*)	4-8, 8-1
Gumpo azaleas (*Rhododendron* 'Gumpo')	7-9, 9-7

Strawberry geranium (*Saxifraga stolonifera*)	6-9, 9-6
Foam flower (*Tiarella cordifolia*)	3-7, 7-1
Greater periwinkle (*Vinca major*)	7-11, 12-7
Common periwinkle (*Vinca minor*)	4-9, 9-1
Barren strawberry (*Waldsteinia ternata*)	5-9, 9-4

"One of the good things about the liriope is that it can live in shade whether the ground is moist or dry."
   Jim Willmott is the Camden County agricultural agent for Rutgers Cooperative Extension in Clementon, New Jersey.

GROUND COVERS FOR DEEP SHADE

People tend to panic when all sign of green disappears from beneath the dense shade of trees such as Norway and sugar maples. Often these people fight for years to try to establish grass, and when that fails, they go looking for something, anything else that is green. Some of the ground covers in this list can survive in the shade under decks. They'll grow under shade trees if the root competition isn't too severe and if provided with ample water and fertilizer.

Also, for a deep-shade ground cover, don't ignore moss. Mosses often take over in shady, moist, acid soils and can be quite handsome if you pull out competing grass or weeds and let the moss form a thick carpet. If you already have a spot where you've been fighting moss, relax and see what it will do if encouraged. You can make buttermilk and moss mixtures that help establish more moss; consult a book on moss growing.

Another option for deep shade is to mulch. Use the leaves of the trees that have created the dense shade, or use a mulch that blends with that used in the rest of your landscape. By planting a few deep-shade ferns or very early spring-flowering bulbs in that mulch, you can bring a lot of interest to that shady spot.

Wild ginger (*Asarum canadense*)	4-8, 8-1
Japanese painted fern (*Athyrium niponicum* 'Pictum')	5-8, 8-2
Lily-of-the-valley (*Convallaria majalis*)	4-9, 9-1
Sweet woodruff (*Galium odoratum*)	5-8, 8-5
English ivy (*Hedera helix*)	5-11, 12-1
Foam bells (*Heucherella* hybs.)	3-8, 8-1
Crested iris (*Iris cristata*)	4-8, 8-1
Yellow archangel (*Lamiastrum galeobdolon*)	4-8, 8-1
Partridge berry (*Mitchella repens*)	4-9, 9-2
Black mondo grass (*Ophiopogon planiscapus* 'Arabicus')	6-11, 12-1
Alleghany spurge (*Pachysandra procumbens*)	6-9, 9-6
Pachysandra (*Pachysandra terminalis*)	4-8, 8-1
Sweet box (*Sarcococca hookeriana* var. *humilis*)	6-9, 9-6
Foam flower (*Tiarella cordifolia*)	3-7, 7-1
Common periwinkle (*Vinca minor*)	4-9, 9-1
Wood violets (*Viola odorata*)	7-9, 9-7

HERBS FOR GROUND COVERS

In these complex times, a simple aromatherapy landscape feature can be comforting," observes garden writer and former Norfolk Botanical Garden horticulturist Carol Chewning from Virginia Beach, Virginia, who provided this list. "Okay, so mint usually gets bad press about its ramblings through the garden," she notes, "but in the right area it is a powerfully scented and energizing ground cover." Carol also recommends the many cultivars of thyme that are available and that offer a myriad of color and texture options. An additional benefit of an herb ground cover is fragrance. "The rewards for seeking out herbal ground covers and experimenting with them are worth the effort," Carol advises.

Perennials

Lady's mantle (*Alchemilla vulgaris*)	4-7, 7-1
Beach wormwood (*Artemisia stelleriana*)	3-7, 7-1
Roman chamomile (*Chamaemelum nobile*)	6-9, 9-6
Alpine strawberry (*Fragaria vesca*)	5-9, 9-1
Sweet woodruff (*Galium odoratum*)	5-8, 8-5
Creeping Jenny (*Lysimachia nummularia* 'Aurea')	4-8, 8-2
English pennyroyal (*Mentha pulegium*)	7-9, 9-6
Corsican mint (*Mentha requienii*)	6-9, 9-6
Golden creeping oregano (*Origanum vulgare* 'Aureum')	5-9, 9-4
Grey santolina (*Santolina chamaecyparissus*)	6-9, 9-6
Creeping germander (*Teucrium chamaedrys prostratum*)	5-9, 9-5
Cat thyme (*Teucrium marum*)	5-9, 9-5
Caraway thyme (*Thymus herba-barona*)	5-9, 9-1
Creeping white thyme (*Thymus praecox* subsp. *articus* 'Albus')	5-9, 9-1
Creeping thyme (*Thymus serpyllum*)	5-9, 9-1
Lemon thyme (*Thymus* x *citriodorus*)	6-9, 9-5
English thyme (*Thymus vulgaris*)	4-9, 9-1

PENNYROYAL

Annuals, Biennials, or Tender Perennials

Dwarf curry plant (*Helichrysum italicum* var. 'Nana')	7-11, 12-1
Aztec sweet herb (*Lippia dulcis*)	8-11, 12-1
Spicy globe basil (*Ocimum basilicum*)	9-11, 12-1
Curly parsley (*Petroselinum crispum*)	7-11, 12-1
Salad burnet (*Poterium sanguisorba*)	9-11, 12-1
Silver tansy (*Tanacetum niveum*)	4-8, 8-1

GROUND COVERS FOR DRY CONDITIONS

Dry sites occur in a landscape for various reasons. The soil may be sandy and drain quickly. The roots of large trees may grow through the soil and absorb most of the available water. The area may be beyond the reach of any irrigation system, or landscape watering may be banned during a summer drought. The plants in this list will tolerate dry conditions, but you'll get the best results if you water them deeply on a regular basis for the first year after they're set out. Then mulch to conserve whatever moisture is available in your dry soil.

Prostrate abelia (*Abelia* x *grandiflora* 'Prostrata')	5-9, 12-6
Bishop's weed (*Aegopodium podagraria*)	4-9, 9-1
Northern sea oats (*Chasmanthium latifolium*)	5-9, 9-3
Crown vetch (*Coronilla varia*)	4-9, 9-1
Carolina jessamine (*Gelsemium sempervirens*)	7-9, 9-2
Daylily (*Hemerocallis* spp., hybs., and cvs.)	3-11, 12-1
St. John's wort (*Hypericum calycinum*)	5-9, 9-4
Dwarf yaupon holly (*Ilex vomitoria* 'Nana')	7-10, 12-7
Low junipers (*Juniperus communis, J. conferta, J. horizontalis*)	3-9, 9-1
Hidcote lavender (*Lavandula angustifolia* 'Hidcote')	5-8, 8-1
Japanese honeysuckle (*Lonicera japonica*)	4-11, 12-1
Dwarf nandina (*Nandina domestica* 'Harbor Dwarf,' 'Nana')	6-11, 12-4
Evening primrose (*Oenothera speciosa*)	5-8, 8-4
Ribbon grass (*Phalaris arundinacea* 'Picta')	4-9, 9-3
Dwarf Indian hawthorn (*Rhaphiolepis indica* 'Nana')	7-11, 12-7
Sedum (*Sedum* spp.)	4-9, 9-1

CREEPING
THYME

Creeping thyme (*Thymus* spp.)	5-9, 9-4
Yucca or Adam's needle (*Yucca filamentosa*)	5-11, 12-5

GROUND COVERS FOR WET CONDITIONS

Wet areas may be depressions where water drains after a rainstorm, or they may be areas with clay soils that hold lots of water (but which conversely can be extremely dry when it doesn't rain). Wet areas may be tiny spots at the base of downspouts, or large boggy areas along bodies of water. Regardless, here is a sampling of ground covers that aren't averse to having wet feet.

Japanese sweet flag (*Acorus gramineus*)	4-11, 12-1
Bishop's weed (*Aegopodium podagraria*)	4-9, 9-1
Ajuga (*Ajuga reptans*)	3-9, 9-1
Lady's mantle (*Alchemilla mollis*)	4-7, 7-1
Meadow anemone (*Anemone canadensis*)	3-8, 8-1
Ferns (*Athyrium* spp., *Osmunda* spp.)	4-9, 9-1
Siberian bugloss (*Brunnera macrophylla*)	3-7, 7-1
Sedges (*Carex* spp.)	7-9, 9-7
Plumbago (*Ceratostigma plumbaginoides*)	6-9, 9-1
Turtlehead (*Chelone obliqua*)	5-9, 9-3
Green and gold (*Chrysogonum virginianum*)	5-8, 8-3
Bleeding-hearts (*Dicentra spectabilis*)	3-9, 9-1
Horsetail (*Equisetum hyemale*)	3-11, 12-1
Wintercreeper (*Euonymus fortunei*)	5-9, 9-5
Daylily (*Hemerocallis* spp., hybs., and cvs.)	3-11, 12-1
Hostas (*Hosta* spp., hybs., and cvs.)	4-9, 9-1
Chameleon plant (*Houttuynia cordata*)	6-11, 12-6
Iris (*Iris* spp., hybs., and cvs.)	4-8, 8-1
Spotted deadnettle (*Lamium maculatum* 'Variegatum')	4-8, 8-1
Liriopes (*Liriope* spp.)	4-8, 8-1
Creeping Jenny (*Lysimachia nummularia*)	4-8, 8-2
Primroses (*Primula* spp.)	3-8, 8-1
Lungwort (*Pulmonaria* spp.)	4-8, 8-1
Strawberry geranium (*Saxifraga stolonifera*)	6-9, 9-6
Foam flower (*Tiarella cordifolia*)	3-7, 7-1
Globeflower (*Trollius* x *cultorum*)	5-8, 8-5
Common periwinkle (*Vinca minor*)	4-9, 9-1
Violets (*Viola* spp.)	7-9, 9-7
Yellowroot (*Xanthorhiza simplicissima*)	3-9, 9-1

GROUND COVERS FOR CLAY SOIL

If you've got soil from which bricks could be made, don't despair. As you begin working compost and other organic matter into sections to improve the soil, use the following ground covers that are tolerant of clay soil. These plants can then serve as a nursery from which you can transplant or propagate additional ground covers once you've improved the condition of your soil. Junipers need ground that drains fairly well, so plant them high or on small berms. Many ornamental grasses will tolerate clay soils where turf grasses would struggle.

Bishop's weed (*Aegopodium podagraria*)	4-9, 9-1
Ajuga (*Ajuga reptans*)	3-9, 9-1
Wintercreeper (*Euonymus fortunei*)	5-9, 9-5
Daylily (*Hemerocallis* spp., hybs., and cvs.)	3-11, 12-1
Hostas (*Hosta* spp., hybs., and cvs.)	4-9, 9-1

Chameleon plant (*Houttuynia cordata*)	6-11, 12-6
Junipers (*Juniperus* spp.)	3-9, 9-1
Japanese honeysuckle (*Lonicera japonica*)	4-11, 12-1
Eulalia or silver grass (*Miscanthus* spp.)	4-9, 9-1
Pachysandra (*Pachysandra terminalis*)	4-8, 8-1
Virginia creeper (*Parthenocissus tricuspidata*)	4-8, 8-2
Boston ivy (*Parthenocissus quinquefolia*)	5-9, 9-5
Fragrant sumac (*Rhus aromatica*)	4-9, 9-3

"Plants that can be a nuisance in really good soil, like Boston ivy or chameleon plant, are great in a soil where very little else will grow. In a poor soil location, these plants will keep in bounds and behave themselves!"
   Susan DeBolt is an environmental horticulture agent for Virginia Cooperative Extension in Manassas, Virginia.

GROUND COVERS TO STABILIZE SLOPES

Mowing grass on a slope can be a dangerous struggle that can be avoided by planting ground covers. Plants for this special situation must transplant easily, cover quickly, and send roots, stolons, or rhizomes into the soil for stability. Many wood shrubs with prostrate stems work well in these situations but will be more expensive and slower to cover than many of the vine-type ground covers. Beware, however, that these plants may become invasive, so be sure to monitor their growth. Some of the prettiest ground covers for slopes are the carpet roses that have been appearing over the last few years.

Ajuga (*Ajuga reptans*)	3-9, 9-1
Five-leaf akebia (*Akebia grandiflora*)	4-8, 8-3
Bearberry (*Arctostaphylos uva-ursi*)	5-8, 8-4
Pygmy bamboo (*Arundinaria pygmaea*)	5-9, 9-5
Cross vine (*Bignonia capreolata*)	6-9, 9-5
Crown vetch (*Coronilla varia*)	4-9, 9-1
Creeping cotoneasters (*Cotoneaster* spp.)	5-7, 7-4
Wintercreeper (*Euonymus fortunei*)	5-9, 9-5
Carolina jessamine (*Gelsemium sempervirens*)	7-9, 9-2
English ivy (*Hedera helix*)	5-11, 12-1
Daylily (*Hemerocallis* spp., hybs., and cvs.)	3-11, 12-1
Chameleon plant (*Houttuynia cordata*)	6-11, 12-6
St. John's wort (*Hypericum calycinum*)	5-9, 9-4
Evergreen candytuft (*Iberis sempervirens*)	5-9, 9-5
Creeping junipers (*Juniperus* spp.)	3-9, 9-1
Liriopes (*Liriope* spp.)	6-11, 12-1
Japanese honeysuckle (*Lonicera japonica*)	4-11, 12-1
Pachysandra (*Pachysandra terminalis*)	4-8, 8-1
Virginia creeper (*Parthenocissus quinquefolia*)	5-9, 9-5
Ribbon grass (*Phalaris arundinacea* 'Picta')	4-9, 9-3
Fragrant sumac (*Rhus aromatica*)	4-9, 9-3
Carpet and ground cover roses (*Rosa* spp.)	4-9, 9-3
Lavender cotton (*Santolina chamaecyparissus*)	6-9, 9-6
Creeping thyme (*Thymus serpyllum*)	5-9, 9-1
Common periwinkle (*Vinca minor*)	4-9, 9-1

A MIXED SELECTION OF GROUND COVERS

Sometimes it's hard to keep each plant in a neat category. Some don't want to be just ferns, just ornamental grasses, or just perennials. Here is a mixed selection of plants from many categories that work well in areas where you want a substitute for turf grass. This list is from horticulturist Michele Reichert-Kiss of Perennial Farm in Glen Arm, Maryland.

Northern maidenhair fern (*Adiantum pedatum*)	3-8, 8-1
Lady's mantle (*Alchemilla mollis*)	4-7, 7-1
Native ginger (*Asarum canadense*)	2-8, 8-1
Chinese astilbe (*Astilbe chinensis* 'Pumila')	3-8, 8-2
Japanese painted fern (*Athyrium niponicum* 'Pictum')	5-8, 8-2
Siberian bugloss (*Brunnera macropyhlla*)	3-7, 7-1
Sedge (*Carex* spp.)	5-9, 9-3
Plumbago (*Ceratostigma plumbaginoides*)	6-9, 9-1
Northern sea oats (*Chasmanthium latifolium*)	5-9, 9-3
Lily-of-the-valley (*Convallaria majalis*)	4-9, 9-1
Hardy ice plant (*Delosperma nubigerum*)	6-9, 9-6
Hay-scented fern (*Dennstaedtia punctilobula*)	4-8, 8-1
Barrenwort (*Epimedium* spp.)	5-9, 9-3
Sweet woodruff (*Galium odoratum*)	5-8, 8-5
Bigroot geranium (*Geranium macrorrhizum*)	4-8, 8-1
Daylily (*Hemerocallis* spp., hybs., and cvs.)	3-11, 12-1
Coral bells (*Heuchera* spp.)	3-8, 8-1
Hosta (*Hosta* hybs. and cvs.)	4-9, 9-2
St. John's wort (*Hypericum calycinum*)	5-9, 9-4
Deadnettle (*Lamiastrum galeobdolon*)	4-8, 8-1
Mazus (*Mazus reptans*)	5-8, 8-4
Virginia bluebells (*Mertensia virginica*)	3-7, 7-1
Flame grass (*Miscanthus purpurescens*)	6-9, 9-3
Silver banner grass (*Miscanthus sacchariflorus*)	6-9, 9-3
Silver variegated maiden grass (*Miscanthus sinensis* 'Morning Light')	6-9, 9-3
Dwarf fountain grass (*Pennisetum alopecuroides* 'Hameln')	6-9, 9-6
Russian sage (*Perovskia atriplicifolia*)	6-9, 9-6
Creeping phlox (*Phlox stolonifera*)	4-8, 8-1
Lungwort (*Pulmonaria* spp. and cvs.)	4-8, 8-3
Irish moss (*Sagina subulata*)	4-7, 7-1
Sweetbox (*Sarcococca hookeriana* var. *humilis*)	6-9, 9-5
Sedum (*Sedum* spp. and cvs.)	4-9, 9-1
Lambs' ears (*Stachys* spp. and cvs.)	4-8, 8-1
Foam flower (*Tiarella cordifolia* and cvs.)	3-8, 7-1

WILD
GINGER

"When considering what plant to use as a ground cover, you should try not to limit yourself to the typical choices of pachysandra and liriope. It is always important to keep in mind the effect you are going for such as height, screening, blooms, etc. Many plants that you typically may not think of can be used successfully as ground covers such as one my favorites, silver variegated maiden grass."

Margaret "Michele" Reichert-Kiss of Perennial Farm, a wholesale nursery in Glen Arm, Maryland, is a certified professional horticulturist who specializes in perennials.

GROUND COVERS FOR CREVICES

One of the most enduring looks in a garden is the aged, settled-in effect given to a stepping path or patio by little plants creeping and clumping in the seams and cracks. The following are a few ground covers well suited to planting in such spaces. If you're building a new patio, consider leaving a few cutouts for these low-growing creepers. For more ideas, see the list of ground covers that can tolerate foot traffic; use the smallest cultivars you can find—new ones are added every year. You might even tuck in a few crocus or dwarf daffodil bulbs for some early spring interest and color.

Woolly yarrow (*Achillea tomentosa*)	4-8, 8-2
Ajuga (*Ajuga reptans*)	3-9, 9-1
Rock cress (*Arabis procurrens*)	4-8, 8-1
Sandwort (*Arenaria verna*)	4-7, 7-1
Bergenia (*Bergenia* 'Baby Doll')	4-8, 8-1
Roman chamomile (*Chamaemelum nobile*)	6-9, 9-6
Moonbeam coreopsis (*Coreopsis* 'Moonbeam')	4-9, 9-1
Barrenwort (*Epimedium* x *youngianum* 'Niveum')	5-9, 9-3
Miniature euonymus (*Euonymus fortunei* 'Minima')	5-9, 9-5
Sweet woodruff (*Galium odoratum*)	5-8, 8-5
Sun rose (*Helianthemum* cvs.)	5-8, 8-5
Candytuft (*Iberis sempervirens*)	5-9, 9-3
Black mondo grass (*Ophiopogon planiscapus* 'Arabicus')	6-11, 12-1
Dwarf mondo grass (*Ophiopogon japonicus* 'Nana')	6-11, 12-1
Creeping phlox (*Phlox* spp.)	4-8, 8-1
Cinquefoil (*Potentilla tridentata*)	2-8, 8-1
Lungwort (*Pulmonaria* cvs.)	5-8, 8-5
Scotch moss (*Sagina subulata*)	4-7, 7-1
Sedums (*Sedum* spp.)	4-9, 9-1
Hens and chicks (*Sempervivum* cvs.)	4-8, 8-1
Lambs' ears (*Stachys byzantina*)	4-8, 8-1
Creeping thyme (*Thymus* spp.)	5-9, 9-4
Harebell speedwell (*Veronica prostrata*)	5-8, 8-3
Creeping speedwell (*Veronica repens*)	3-8, 8-1
Barren strawberry (*Waldsteinia ternata*)	5-9, 9-4

> "Plantings in connection with stepping stones provide an opportunity for intimate gardening; one tends to walk more slowly in such situations, looking down as one goes. There is the chance for both flower interest and textural contrasts."
>
> **William Frederick** from Hockessin, Delaware, is a landscape architect and author of *The Exuberant Garden and the Controlling Hand*.

GROUND COVERS THAT TOLERATE FOOT TRAFFIC

One of the major reasons that people resist replacing turf grasses with ground covers is because they think that the only way they can walk through them is atop stepping stones. For many of the more fragile ground covers that's true, but there are some that tolerate light, even moderate foot traffic. A company in Oregon has recently introduced a brand of ground covers called STEPABLES™ for use between stepping stones and as a lawn substitute (see www.UnderAFootplants.com). An added bonus with many of these plants is that when they're stepped on, they release a pleasant fragrance.

CREEPING JENNY

Occasional or Light Foot Traffic

Rock cress (*Arabis alpina*)	4-8, 8-1
Common thrift (*Armeria maritima*)	3-9, 9-1
Snow in summer (*Cerastium tomentosum*)	3-7, 7-1
Creeping Jenny (*Lysimachia nummularia*)	4-8, 8-2
Moss pink (*Phlox subulata*)	3-8, 8-1
Creeping thymes (*Thymus serpyllum*)	5-9, 9-4
Common periwinkle (*Vinca minor*)	4-9, 9-1

Light to Moderate Foot Traffic

Ajuga (*Ajuga reptans*)	3-9, 9-1
Chamomile (*Chamaemelum nobile*)	6-9, 9-6
Mock strawberry (*Duchesnea indica*)	5-9, 9-5
Ground ivy (*Glechoma hederacea*)	4-9, 9-1
Blue Rug juniper (*Juniperus horizontalis* 'Blue Rug')	3-9, 9-1
Miniature moneywort (*Lysimachia japonica* 'Minutissima')	5-9, 9-4
Mazus (*Mazus reptans*)	5-8, 8-4
Scotch moss (*Sagina subulata*)	4-7, 7-1
Sedums (*Sedum* spp.)	4-9, 9-1
Speedwell (*Veronica repens*)	3-8, 8-1

IVY AS GROUND COVER

The genus *Hedera* has long been known for providing good evergreen ground covers. However, ivy has also been labeled an aggressive overtaking nuisance. Typical English ivy is fast growing and can become a pest, but most often the wrong cultivar was selected for the site. Tolerant of most soil with good drainage, especially in areas with root competition, the *Hedera* has a vast number of cultivars that, when properly placed, can add a wonderful array of colors and textures to the landscape. The following is a list of *Hedera* species and cultivars and their relative growth rates that Richard Davis of the Ivy Farm prepared to help improve the image of this bad boy of the landscape. All of these ivies are cold hardy and heat tolerant throughout most of the New York and Mid-Atlantic region. Those marked with an asterisk (*) are sun-tolerant.

Slow—less than 18 inches per year
Hedera colchica 'Dentata Variegata'
Hedera helix 'Adam,' 'Asterisks,' 'Calico,' 'Little Diamond,' 'Midget,' 'Minty,' 'Spetchley'

Medium—18 inches to 3 feet per year
Hedera helix 'Baltica'*, 'Buttercup,' 'California'*, 'Duckfoot,' 'Glacier,' 'Gold Child,' 'Gold Heart,' 'Ivalace,' 'Misty,' 'Ritterkreuz,' 'Sulphur Heart,' 'Zebra'
Hedera hibernica 'Deltoidea' ('Sweetheart')
Hedera rhombea 'Variegata'

Fast—3 to 5 feet per year
Hedera colchica 'Marburg'
Hedera helix 'Gold Craft,' 'Gold Dust,' 'Mandas Crested'*, 'Thorndale'*, 'Wilson's'*, 'Wingertsberg'*, 'Woerner'*
*Hedera hibernica**

"Hundreds of ivy cultivars provide a multitude of selections for all different sites in the landscape. Stressing proper plant for appropriate site will not only create less maintenance headaches, but a more satisfying end result will be accomplished. Growth rates will vary with light (more sun means less growth), soil (better drainage means more growth), water (don't overwater, especially when it's hot), and nutrient availability (a little fertilizer goes a long way)."

Richard Davis and his wife, Meriwether Payne, own the Ivy Farm in Locustville, Virginia, a wholesale nursery specializing in ground cover and shrub ivies, perennials, and ornamental grasses.

PERENNIALS

Just as shrubs can be viewed as the woody plant backbones of design, perennials can be viewed as their equivalents in herbaceous plants. Select any location, use, or time of year, and you'll find a perennial whose flowers can brighten up your garden or landscape. We take for granted that when they die down and disappear below ground, they'll pop back up next year to be bigger and more floriferous than before. In broad horticultural terms, perennials are plants that live three or more years, distinguishing them from annuals (one year) and biennials (two years). Though that term would apply to all trees and shrubs, and many vines and ground covers as well, here it is restricted to herbaceous plants—ones with fleshy rather than woody stems. Their roots are what sustain them each year, storing food that will provide energy for buds to break and send new stems, leaves, and flowers above ground. Perennials have cycled in and out of prominence for color in gardens and landscapes, often seeming to be overshadowed by the faster and longer lasting seasonal color provided by annuals. But where annuals need yearly replanting, perennials will be back year after year, with limited maintenance.

With perennials, as with other plant categories, many new cultivars are introduced each year. Some may prove better than the straight species or other cultivars, and some may be inferior, introduced before they've been in the landscape long enough, and under varied enough climatic conditions and cultural regimes, to really test their worth. Some perennials just seem to live longer than others, or have fewer pest problems or cultural demands, but anything that gives you multiple years of enjoyment is probably worth planting. Some you'll fall in love with and want every cultivar you can obtain. Our devotion to perennials is attested to by the numerous societies that exist for individual perennials, most notably the daylilies, hostas, and iris.

The trick with perennials is to blend ones that bloom at different times of the year, or mix them with annuals, bulbs, ornamental grasses, and low flowering shrubs to assure that your garden or landscape always has something in bloom.

Tips for Selecting and Succeeding with Perennials

- Select the right perennial for the right location. As versatile as this group of plants is, some only do well in full sun; others if planted in full sun will struggle and die.
- Coordinate times of bloom, heights, and flower and leaf colors. It helps to map out your perennial beds on paper to assure garden harmony and succession.
- Plant at any time of the year when the ground can be worked. In the warmer parts of our region that's year-round, but farther north, planting may come to a halt from November to March or April, especially where the ground freezes.
- Buy quality plants. Some of the bargains that may tempt you may be poorly rooted or of inferior size and may struggle without special care.
- Prepare expansive planting beds or holes to assure that the roots of your perennials will quickly establish and begin absorbing water and nutrients. Work compost into entire beds but not into individual planting holes. To ensure good root growth, water regularly for several weeks after planting if rainfall is limited.
- Keep your perennials mulched to prevent competition from weeds. Herbicides can be difficult to use in perennial beds due to the diversity of plants you may select, so read labels carefully.
- Limit nitrogen fertilization to avoid making your plants overly green (too fast growing and succulent). A slowly decomposing layer of compost is usually all that is needed.

- As your perennials grow and expand, don't be afraid to divide them (consult a reference book for the preferred method). Discard roots or stems with evidence of disease or insects. Replant the rest, or share with neighbors and friends.
- Monitor closely for pests, especially leaf diseases and sucking insects. Inspect buds closely, and look underneath leaves. If control methods are needed, select the one—mechanical, biological, or chemical—that is most effective for the problem and compatible with your method of gardening.

PERENNIALS FOR BEGINNERS

Beginners as well as old-time gardeners like to find plants that are just downright easy to grow. Easy-care plants are especially useful if you are new to an area or have a peculiar site in your landscape. This list of easy perennials comes from Mark Viette of Andrea Viette Farm and Nursery in Fishersville, Virginia, who says these will grow even if you have a purple thumb.

Hoffnung yarrow (*Achillea millefolium* 'Hoffnung')	3-9, 9-1
Bishop's weed (*Aegopodium podagraria*)	4-9, 9-3
Blue-star (*Amsonia tabernaemontana*)	3-9, 9-1
Grape-leaf anemone (*Anemone vitifolia* 'Robustissima')	5-8, 8-3
Southernwood (*Artemisia abrotanum*)	5-8, 8-4
New England aster (*Aster novae-angliae* 'Hella Lacy')	4-8, 8-3
Pumila astilbe (*Astilbe chinensis* 'Pumila')	4-8, 8-1
Wild indigo (*Baptisia australis*)	3-9, 9-1
Snowbank boltonia (*Boltonia asteroides* 'Snowbank')	4-9, 9-1
Plumbago (*Ceratostigma plumbaginoides*)	6-9, 9-1
Bugbane (*Cimicifuga racemosa*)	3-8, 8-1
Pinks (*Dianthus deltoides* 'Alba' and 'Brilliant')	3-10, 10-1
Bleeding-heart (*Dicentra spectabilis*)	3-9, 9-1
White bleeding-heart (*Dicentra spectabilis* 'Alba')	3-9, 9-1
Barrenwort (*Epimedium pinnatum*)	5-9, 9-3
White ageratum (*Eupatorium coelestinum* 'Album')	3-7, 7-1
Purple Joe Pye weed (*Eupatorium purpureum* 'Atropurpureum')	3-9, 9-1
Wild strawberry (*Fragaria* 'Pink Panda')	5-9, 9-5
Johnson's Blue hardy geranium (*Geranium ibericum* 'Johnson's Blue')	4-8, 8-1
Hardy geranium (*Geranium wlassovianum*)	4-8, 8-1
False sunflowers (*Heliopsis helianthoides* 'Gold Greenheart,' 'Goldfeather,' 'Hohlspiegel')	4-9, 9-1
Daylily (*Hemerocallis* spp., hybs., and cvs.)	3-11, 12-1
Chameleon plant (*Houttuynia cordata*)	6-11, 12-6
Flore Plena iris (*Iris pseudacorus* 'Flore Plena')	5-8, 8-3
Switzerland shasta daisy (*Leucanthemum maximum* 'Switzerland')	3-8, 8-1
May Queen ox-eye daisy (*Leucanthemum vulgare* 'May Queen')	3-8, 8-1
Gooseneck loosestrife (*Lysimachia clethroides*)	4-9, 9-4
Youngii-lapsley evening primrose (*Oenothera fruticosa* 'Youngii-lapsley')	4-8, 8-1
Evening primrose (*Oenothera speciosa*)	5-8, 8-4
Blue Ridge phlox (*Phlox stolonifera* 'Blue Ridge')	4-8, 8-1
Obedient plant (*Physostegia virginiana*)	4-8, 8-1
Variegated Solomon's seal (*Polygonatum odoratum* 'Variegatum')	4-8, 8-1
Goldsturm rudbeckia (*Rudbeckia fulgida* 'Goldsturm')	4-9, 9-1
Herbstsonne rudbeckia (*Rudbeckia nitida* 'Herbstsonne')	3-7, 7-1
Coneflower (*Rudbeckia subtomentosa*)	4-7, 7-1
Rubra Plena soapwort (*Saponaria officinalis* 'Rubra Plena')	3-9, 9-1
Autumn Joy sedum (*Sedum acre* 'Autumn Joy')	4-9, 9-3
John Creech sedum (*Sedum sieboldii* 'John Creech')	4-9, 9-3
Silver Carpet lambs' ears (*Stachys lanata* 'Silver Carpet')	4-8, 8-1
Comfrey (*Symphytum grandiflorum*)	3-9, 9-1

ASTER

Tansy or painted daisy (*Tanacetum vulgare*)	4-8, 8-1
Germander (*Teucrium chamaedrys*)	5-9, 9-5
Green heliotrope (*Valeriana officinalis*)	4-9, 9-1
White speedwell (*Veronica virginica* 'Alba')	3-8, 8-1
Barren strawberry (*Waldsteinia ternata*)	3-8, 8-1

GUERILLA PERENNIALS

Holly Scoggins, assistant professor of horticulture at Virginia Tech, put together this list of what she calls "guerilla perennials." Gardeners are supposed to be patient sorts, but alas, sometimes we want speedy results. With proper bed preparation (good drainage, lots of organic matter, and a good dose of superphosphate), a border including these plants will come as close to instant gratification as one can get in the realm of perennial gardening. Expect these perennials to be substantial the first year, gonzo the second year, and by the third year, pack your bags or find the dividing spade.

Sun

Yarrow (*Achillea millefolium* 'Paprika')	3-9, 9-1
Powis Castle artemisia (*Artemisia* x 'Powis Castle')	7-9, 9-6
Climbing aster (*Aster carolinianus*)	5-8, 8-5
Calico aster (*Aster lateriflorus* 'Lady in Black')	4-8, 8-4
Leadwort or plumbago (*Ceratostigma plumbaginoides*)	6-9, 9-1
Willowleaf sunflower (*Helianthus salicifolius*)	6-9, 9-5
Sunflower heliopsis (*Heliopsis helianthoides* 'Summer Sun')	4-9, 9-1
Common rose mallow (*Hibiscus moscheutos*)	5-11, 12-1
Japanese aster (*Kalimeris pinnatifida*)	6-8, 8-6
Bush clover (*Lespedeza thunbergii* cvs.)	6-8, 8-1
Gooseneck loosestrife (*Lysimachia clethroides*)	4-9, 9-4
Giant Chinese silver grass (*Miscanthus floridulus*)	6-9, 9-3
Siberian catnip (*Nepeta sibirica*)	3-8, 8-1
Moss phlox (*Phlox subulata*)	3-8, 8-1
Obedient plant (*Physostegia virginiana*)	4-8, 8-1
Cutleaf coneflower (*Rudbeckia nitida* 'Herbsonne')	3-7, 7-1
Three-lobed coneflower (*Rudbeckia triloba*)	4-7, 7-1

Shade

Variegated bishop's weed (*Aegopodium podagraria* 'Variegatum')	4-9, 9-3
Ajuga or bugleweed (*Ajuga reptans* 'Caitlin's Giant')	3-9, 9-1
Grape-leaf anemone (*Anemone vitifolia*)	5-9, 9-3
Sum and Substance hosta (*Hosta* 'Sum and Substance')	4-9, 9-2
Yellow archangel (*Lamiastrum galeobdolon*)	4-8, 8-1
Creeping Jenny (*Lysimachia nummularia* 'Aurea')	4-8, 8-2
Ostrich fern (*Matteuccia struthiopteris*)	3-8, 8-1

"I've always had to do blitz gardening for the short-term. I'm on my fourth home garden in the last eleven years and, as a result, have always looked for plants that go gangbusters. I hope to stay put here in Blacksburg for quite a while, a wonderful opportunity to indulge in the more restrained genera such as *Arisaemas, Epimediums,* and *Asarums.*"

Holly Scoggins is an assistant professor of horticulture at Virginia Tech in Blacksburg, Virginia.

PERENNIAL OF THE YEAR

The Perennial Plant Association, an organization of commercial growers, developed its Plant of the Year program to promote the use of perennials. Each year the members cast their votes for outstanding perennials with the following criteria: the plant is suitable for a wide range of climate types, has low maintenance needs, is easily propagated (true from seed or vegetative means), and exhibits multi-seasonal interest. All of these ten outstanding perennials should do well in a sunny location in most New York and Mid-Atlantic gardens. For more information on the PPA or their Plant of the Year program, see their website: www.perennialplant.org.

1992—*Coreopsis verticillata* 'Moonbeam' (coreopsis)	4-9, 9-1
1993—*Veronica* 'Sunny Border Blue' (speedwell)	3-8, 8-1
1994—*Astilbe* 'Sprite' (astilbe)	4-8, 8-1
1995—*Perovskia atriplicifolia* (Russian sage)	6-9, 9-6
1996—*Penstemon digitalis* 'Husker's Red' (beard-tongue)	2-8, 8-1
1997—*Salvia* 'May Night' (salvia)	5-9, 9-5
1998—*Echinacea purpurea* 'Magnus' (purple coneflower)	4-8, 8-1
1999—*Rudbeckia fulgida* var. *sullivanti* 'Goldstrum' (rudbeckia)	4-9, 9-1
2000—*Scabiosa columbaria* 'Butterfly Blue' (pincushion flower)	4-9, 9-1
2001—*Calamagrostis acutiflora* 'Karl Foerster' (Karl Foerster's feather reed grass)	6-9, 9-3

PERENNIALS FOR FULL SUN

Perennials that love the sun are some of the showiest and toughest of the garden. Many hail from our roadsides and prairies where the hot sun and drought have yielded do-or-die plants. Others, such as lilies, are simply the greatest indulgences of the flower garden; they are sturdy plants, but their bounteous blooms are rarely found outside lovingly tended plots. The sun's intensity varies from the southeastern coastal tip of Virginia to the mid-sections of Pennsylvania and New York, meaning that some perennials that like full sun in New York City might look bleached or brown-edged by August in Richmond. Soil conditions also affect tolerance to sun; plants can usually take more sun in fertile, moist soil.

This list is from Ray Mims and Joe Luebke, head gardeners at the National Cathedral in Washington, D.C. More perennials for the sun can be found in plant and seed catalogs, but this list represents perennials that have held up well in the intense sun that shines on our nation's capital.

Yarrow (*Achillea* spp.)	3-9, 9-1
Anise hyssop (*Agastache foeniculum*)	6-11, 12-6
Blue-star flower (*Amsonia tabernaemontana, A. orientalis*)	3-9, 9-1
Wormwood (*Artemisia* x 'Powis Castle')	7-9, 9-6
Swamp milkweed (*Asclepias incarnata* 'Soul Mate')	3-8, 8-1
Butterfly weed (*Asclepias tuberosa*)	4-9, 9-3
Hella Lacy aster (*Aster novae-angliae* 'Hella Lacy')	4-8, 8-3
Tatarian aster (*Aster tataricus*)	4-8, 8-3
Wild indigo (*Baptisia australis*)	3-9, 9-1
Boltonia (*Boltonia asteroides*)	4-9, 9-1
Bachelor's buttons (*Centaurea cyanus*)	3-8, 8-1
Mountain bluet (*Centaurea montana*)	3-8, 8-1
Chrysanthemum (*Chrysanthemum* 'Ryan's Pink')	5-9, 9-3
Montbretia (*Crocosmia* 'Lucifer')	6-9, 9-3
Pink (*Dianthus gratianopolitanus* 'Bath's Pink')	3-9, 9-1
Coneflower (*Echinacea purpurea, E. tennesseensis*)	4-8, 8-1
Sea holly (*Eryngium* spp.)	5-8, 8-4
Joe Pye weed (*Eupatorium purpureum*)	3-9, 9-1
Swamp sunflower (*Helianthus angustifolius*)	6-9, 9-6
Daylily (*Hemerocallis* spp., hybs., and cvs.)	3-11, 12-1
Iris (*Iris* spp., hybs,. and cvs.)	3-9, 9-1

BLACK-EYED
SUSAN

Red-hot poker (*Kniphofia* cvs.)	6-9, 9-4
Bee balm (*Monarda* 'Cambridge Scarlet')	4-9, 9-3
Evening primrose or sundrops (*Oenothera missouriensis, O. fruticosa*)	4-8, 8-1
Beard-tongue (*Penstemon ovatus*)	6-9, 9-6
Russian sage (*Perovskia atriplicifolia*)	6-9, 9-6
Fleeceflower (*Persicaria afinis* 'Darjeeling Red')	3-8, 8-1
Phlox (*Phlox divaricata, P. paniculata, P. stolonifera*)	4-8, 8-1
Alpha phlox (*Phlox maculata* 'Alpha')	5-8, 8-5
Black-eyed Susan (*Rudbeckia hirta*)	4-9, 9-1
Autumn sage (*Salvia greggii* 'Dark Dancer,' 'Cherry Red')	7-9, 9-7
Salvia (*Salvia guaranitica* 'Argentina Skies,' 'Black and Blue')	7-9, 9-7
Indigo Spires sage (*Salvia* 'Indigo Spires')	7-9, 9-7
Bog sage (*Salvia uliginosa*)	7-9, 9-7
Goldenrod (*Solidago rugosa* 'Fire Works')	5-9, 9-1
Rose verbena (*Verbena canadensis*)	4-7, 7-1
Mullein (*Verbascum* 'Southern Charm,' 'Cotswold Queen,' 'Helen Johnson')	5-9, 9-5

"When we were asked to choose our favorite full-sun perennials, it sounded easy. But as we remembered plants we have, plants we've seen, and plants we covet, it became quite difficult to whittle our list down to a manageable size. We pick what has performed well for us in our harsh summer climate. We also choose plants that are either an outstanding one-season perennial or something that adds interest for more than one season. We have completely ignored ornamental grasses and foliage plants, which are both 'must haves' in any garden."

Ray Mims (left) and Joe Luebke (right) are head gardeners at the National Cathedral in Washington, D.C. The 57-acre property includes the 5-acre Olmsted Woodlands and the 3-acre Bishop's Garden.

SHADE-TOLERANT PERENNIALS

The shade garden can take many forms, from an extensive woodland garden on the north side of a house, to a tiny spot tucked beneath a shrub. All too often these shady areas are looked upon as obstacles to overcome instead of exciting opportunities. The fabulous array of plants offered by the world's temperate woodlands gives more diversity than the most knowledgeable plants person could hope to master.

With proper plant selection, a shady spot can be a subdued and peaceful retreat, especially during the summer, or it can be a riot of color. Combining and contrasting heights, bloom periods, and especially foliage color and texture will lead to a distinctive and beautiful shade garden. But keep in mind the plant's cultural requirements. A moisture-craving plant will never thrive when competing with shallow tree roots, nor will a plant prone to root rot last long in a perpetually dank spot. This list of shade-tolerant perennials from Mark Weathington of the Norfolk, Virginia, Botanical Garden is a sampling of some of the more common and the lesser known.

Lady's mantle (*Alchemilla mollis*)	4-7, 7-1
Chinese anemone (*Anemone hupehensis*)	3-8, 8-1
Columbine (*Aquilegia canadensis*)	3-8, 8-1
Japanese cobra lily (*Arisaema sikokianum*)	5-9, 9-1
Greater masterwort (*Astrantia major*)	5-8, 8-5
Bergenia (*Bergenia purpurescens*)	3-8, 8-1
Japanese ground orchid (*Bletilla striata*)	5-8, 8-5
Siberian bugloss (*Brunnera macrophylla*)	3-8, 8-1
Fairies' thimbles (*Campanula cochleariifolia*)	5-7, 7-5
Bowles' golden sedge (*Carex elata* 'Aurea')	5-9, 9-4

Bugbane (*Cimicifuga* spp.)	4-8, 8-1
Lily-of-the-valley (*Convallaria majalis*)	4-9, 9-1
Bunchberry (*Cornus canadensis*)	2-7, 7-1
Evergreen corydalis (*Corydalis cheilanthifolia*)	5-7, 7-5
Showy bleeding-heart (*Dicentra spectabilis*)	4-9, 9-1
Evergreen Solomon's seal (*Disporopsis pernyi*)	6-9, 9-6
Barrenworts (*Epimedium* spp.)	5-9, 9-5
Cushion spurge (*Euphorbia polychroma*)	5-9, 9-5
Japanese meadowsweet (*Filipendula purpurea*)	5-9, 9-5
Willow gentian (*Gentiana asclepiadea*)	6-9, 9-6
Himalayan geranium (*Geranium wallichianum*)	5-8, 8-5
Purple hellebore (*Helleborus purpurescens*)	5-8, 8-5
Coral bells (*Heuchera sanguinea*)	4-8, 8-1
Crested iris (*Iris cristata*)	4-8, 8-1
Turkscap lily (*Lilium superbum*)	4-8, 8-1
Golden creeping Jenny (*Lysimachia nummularia* 'Aurea')	4-8, 8-1
Mazus (*Mazus reptans*)	5-8, 8-4
Navelwort (*Omphalodes cappadocica*)	6-8, 8-6
Allegheny spurge (*Pachysandra procumbens*)	6-9, 9-5
Japanese primrose (*Primula japonica*)	4-8, 8-1
Buckeye leaf rodgersia (*Rodgersia aesculifolia*)	5-8, 8-5
False Solomon's seal (*Smilacina racemosa*)	4-9, 9-1
Indian pink (*Spigelia marilandica*)	7-9, 9-7
Celandine poppy (*Stylophorum diphyllum*)	6-9, 9-6
Lavender mist (*Thalictrum rochebruneanum*)	5-9, 9-4
Toad lily (*Tricyrtis hirta*)	4-9, 9-1
Purple trillium (*Trillium erectum*)	4-9, 9-1
Chinese globeflower (*Trollius chinensis*)	4-8, 8-1
Vancouveria (*Vancouveria hexandra*)	5-8, 8-5
Bird's-foot violet (*Viola pedata*)	4-8, 8-1

"A good deal of the information we have on shade tolerance has come from British gardeners. In the New York and Mid-Atlantic area, we often have much hotter and brighter conditions than in England, so we can often grow their full-sun plants in the shade."

Mark Weathington is the supervising horticulturist for the Norfolk Botanical Garden, Norfolk, Virginia.

PERENNIALS FOR MOIST SITES

This list of moisture-tolerant plants combines suggestions from numerous wholesale and retail growers, including Andrea Viette Farm of Fishersville, Virginia, Sandy's Plants of Mechanicsville, Virginia, Riverbend Nurseries of Riner, Virginia, and the Perennial Farm of Glen Arm, Maryland. Many of the plants on this list could also be classified as wildflowers, but many growers of perennials now include them among their offerings. Those marked with an asterisk (*) will tolerate wet, boggy soils.

Monkshood (*Aconitum carmichaelii*)	3-7, 7-1
Mexican hyssop (*Agastache cana*)	6-11, 12-6
Lady's mantle (*Alchemilla mollis*)	4-7, 7-1
Jack-in-the-pulpit (*Arisaema dracontium*, *A. triphyllum*)	3-7, 7-1

Lords and ladies (*Arum italicum*)	6-9, 9-6
Goatsbeard (*Aruncus dioicus*)	3-7, 7-1
Milkweed (*Asclepias incarnata*)	3-8, 8-1
Butterfly weed (*Asclepias tuberosa*)	4-9, 9-3
Astilbe (*Astilbe* cvs.)	3-8, 8-2
Bergenia (*Bergenia cordifolia*)	4-8, 8-1
Marsh marigold (*Caltha palustris*)*	3-7, 8-1
Quamash (*Camassia esculenta, C. leichtlinii*)	4-11, 12-1
Bellflower (*Campanula glomerata*)	3-8, 8-1
Turtlehead (*Chelone glabra, C. lyonii*)*	4-9, 9-3
Bugbane (*Cimicifuga racemosa*)	3-8, 8-1
Coreopsis or tickseed (*Coreopsis grandiflora, C. verticillata*)	4-9, 9-1
Umbrella plant (*Darmera peltata*)*	5-9, 9-5
Bleeding-heart (*Dicentra* spp.)	4-8, 8-1
Foxglove (*Digitalis purpurea*)	4-8, 8-1
Umbrella leaf (*Diphylleia cymosa*)	7-10, 10-7
Shooting star (*Dodecatheon meadia*)	4-8, 8-1
Joe Pye weed (*Eupatorium* spp. and cvs.)*	3-9, 9-1
Meadowsweet (*Filipendula* spp.)*	3-9, 9-1
Wandflower (*Galax urceolata*)	5-8, 8-5
Hardy sunflower (*Helianthus* spp.)	5-9, 9-3
Hellebore (*Helleborus* spp.)	4-8, 8-1
Daylily (*Hemerocallis* spp., hybs., and cvs.)	3-11, 12-1
Hostas (*Hosta* spp., hybs., and cvs.)*	4-9, 9-2
Chameleon plant (*Houttuynia cordata*)	6-11, 12-6
Japanese iris (*Iris ensata*)*	3-9, 9-1
Louisiana iris (*Iris louisiana*)	6-9, 9-5
Yellow flag iris (*Iris pseudacorus*)*	5-8, 8-3
Siberian iris (*Iris sibirica*)	3-9, 9-1
Blue flag iris (*Iris versicolor*)	3-9, 9-1
Gayfeather (*Liatris spicata*)	4-9, 9-1
Senecio (*Ligularia* spp.)	4-8, 8-1
Cardinal flower (*Lobelia cardinalis*)*	4-8, 8-1
Loosestrife (*Lysimachia* spp.)	4-8, 8-3
Mazus (*Mazus reptans*)	5-8, 8-4
Virginia bluebells (*Mertensia virginica*)*	3-7, 7-1
Monkey flower (*Mimulus ringens*)	6-9, 9-4
Bee balm (*Monarda didyma*)*	4-9, 9-1
Forget-me-not (*Myosotis palustris*)*	5-9, 9-5
Fleeceflower (*Persicaria* spp.)	3-8, 8-1
Woodland phlox (*Phlox divaricata*)	4-8, 8-1
Obedient plant (*Physostegia virginiana*)	4-8, 8-1
Balloon flower (*Platycodon grandiflorus*)	4-8, 8-1
Jacob's ladder (*Polemonium caeruleum*)	4-8, 8-3
Solomon's seal (*Polygonatum* spp.)	4-8, 8-1
Primrose (*Primula* spp.)*	3-8, 8-1
Rodgersia (*Rodgersia* spp.)*	5-8, 8-4
Black-eyed Susan (*Rudbeckia* spp.)	4-9, 9-1
Meadow rue (*Thalictrum* spp.)	5-9, 9-5
Foam flower (*Tiarella cordifolia*)	3-7, 7-1
Spiderwort (*Tradescantia andersoniana* hybs. and cvs.)	5-9, 9-4
Globeflower (*Trollius* spp.)*	5-8, 8-5
Heliotrope (*Valeriana officinalis*)	5-8, 8-1
Ironweed (*Vernonia noveboracensis*)*	5-9, 9-4

Controversy exists over purple loosestrife (*Lythrum salicaria*), which grows well in moist or boggy conditions but can be extremely invasive. Many growers recommend not growing the straight species, which is banned as a noxious weed in Pennsylvania and Virginia. Instead, they recommend growing one of the sterile cultivars such as 'Morden Gleam,' 'Morden Pink,' or 'Robert.'

PERENNIALS FOR HOT, DRY SITES

Some flower beds, often beside a street or driveway, are hot, dry places. They're often locations where you need and want color but are not sure what flowers will thrive in such hot spots. Plant, mulch and water these perennials in, then walk away and let them amaze passers-by with their ability to tolerate one of the most inhospitable of all landscape situations. Check the light requirements of these plants, because the majority of them are full-sun to partial-shade plants. Some, however, like barrenwort (*Epimedium*) and ironweed (*Vernonia*), need to be located in partial to full shade or they won't be able to tolerate the dryness.

"Many of these are native plants," comments Mike Andruczyk, curator of plants for the Norfolk Botanical Garden. "Be forewarned," he cautions, because "some are very aggressive. But if you're stuck with this type of site, these are plants on which you can depend."

Yarrow (*Achillea* spp.)	3-9, 9-1
Madwort (*Alyssum montanum*)	4-9, 9-1
Mt. Atlas daisy (*Anacyclus pyrethrum* var. *depressus*)	6-8, 8-6
Pasqueflower (*Anemone pulsatilla*)	5-8, 8-5
Marguerite (*Anthemis tinctoria*)	3-7, 7-1
Sea thrift (*Armeria maritima*)	3-9, 9-1
Wormwood (*Artemisia schmidtiana*)	5-8, 8-4
Butterfly weed (*Asclepias tuberosa*)	4-9, 9-3
Asters (*Aster* spp.)	4-8, 8-1
False indigo (*Baptisia australis*)	3-9, 9-1
Poppy mallow (*Callirhoe involucrata*)	4-6, 6-1
Cupid's dart (*Catananche caerulea*)	3-8, 8-1
Mountain bluet (*Centaurea montana*)	3-8, 8-1
Snow in summer (*Cerastium tomentosum*)	3-7, 7-1
Hairy golden aster (*Chrysopsis villosa*)	4-10, 9-2
Coreopsis or tickseed (*Coreopsis* spp.)	4-9, 9-1
Ice plant (*Delosperma* spp.)	6-9, 9-6
Purple coneflower (*Echinacea purpurea*)	4-8, 8-1
Barrenwort (*Epimedium* spp.)	5-9, 9-5
Hardy ageratum (*Eupatorium coelestinum*)	3-9, 9-1
Blanket flower (*Gaillardia* spp.)	3-8, 8-1
Gaura (*Gaura lindheimeri*)	6-9, 9-6
Swamp sunflower (*Helianthus simulans*)	6-9, 9-4
False sunflower (*Heliopsis helianthoides*)	4-9, 9-1
Daylily (*Hemerocallis* spp., hybs., and cvs.)	3-11, 12-1
Candytuft (*Iberis sempervirens*)	5-9, 9-3
Lavender (*Lavandula* spp.)	5-8, 8-1
Gayfeather (*Liatris spicata*)	4-9, 9-1
Catmint (*Nepeta* x *faassenii*)	4-8, 8-1
Evening primrose or sundrops (*Oenothera* spp.)	4-8, 8-1
Cactus (*Opuntia* spp.)	6-10, 12-1
Iceland poppy (*Papaver nudicaule*)	2-8, 8-1
Oriental poppy (*Papaver orientale*)	4-9, 9-1

Russian sage (*Perovskia atriplicifolia*)	6-9, 9-6
Orange coneflower (*Rudbeckia fulgida*)	4-9, 9-1
Sage (*Salvia* × *superba*)	5-9, 9-5
Lavender cotton (*Santolina chamaecyparissus*)	6-9, 9-4
Sedum or stonecrop (*Sedum spectabile*)	4-9, 9-1
Hens and chicks (*Sempervivum* spp. and cvs.)	4-8, 8-1
Goldenrod (*Solidago* spp.)	5-9, 9-1
Lambs' ears (*Stachys byzantina*)	4-8, 8-1
Stokes' aster (*Stokesia laevis*)	5-9, 9-5
Clump verbena (*Verbena canadensis*)	4-7, 7-1
Ironweed (*Vernonia fasciculata*)	5-9, 9-4
Speedwell (*Veronica incana*)	3-8, 8-1

"There are many great herbaceous perennials available and the choices increase dramatically each year. Careful selection will give the garden a succession of flowering all season, but don't overlook perennials that have good foliage characteristics. Some of my favorites for dry conditions include candytuft, purple coneflower, ice plant, lambs' ears, pasqueflower, sedum, and sea thrift."
 Scott Clark is a nursery specialist for Cornell Cooperative Extension in Suffolk County, Long Island.

PERENNIALS FOR CLAY SOIL

When planting perennials into heavy clay soil, mix bark or compost into the entire planting area before planting. The soil will still be heavy, but as long as it doesn't stay wet all the time, these perennials should do well. Start with these if you're working on the site of a new home or building where the topsoil has been scraped away and you're challenged to plant in the underlying subsoil. As you build your soil, you can add more variety. If your clay stays wet for a long time after a rain, see the list of perennials for moist sites.

Bear's breeches (*Acanthus spinosus*)	5-9, 9-5
Lady's mantle (*Alchemilla* spp.)	4-7, 7-1
Marguerite (*Anthemis tinctoria*)	3-7, 7-1
Lords and ladies (*Arum italicum*)	6-9, 9-6
Goatsbeard (*Aruncus dioicus*)	3-7, 7-1
Wild ginger (*Asarum canadensis*)	2-8, 8-1
Milkweed (*Asclepias incarnata*)	3-8, 8-1
Blackberry lily (*Belamcanda chinensis*)	5-9, 9-3
Bergenia (*Bergenia cordifolia*)	4-8, 8-1
Boltonia (*Boltonia asteroides*)	4-9, 9-1
Siberian bugloss (*Brunnera macrophylla*)	3-7, 7-1
Carpathian bellflower (*Campanula carpatica*)	4-7, 7-1
Red valerian (*Centranthus ruber*)	5-8, 8-1
Green and gold (*Chrysogonum virginianum*)	5-8, 8-3
Lily-of-the-valley (*Convallaria majalis*)	4-9, 9-1
Delphinium (*Delphinium exaltatum*)	3-8, 8-1
Purple coneflower (*Echinacea purpurea*)	4-8, 8-1
Barrenwort (*Epimedium* spp.)	5-9, 9-5
Joe Pye weed (*Eupatorium* spp.)	3-9, 9-1
Hardy geranium (*Geranium* spp., hybs., and cvs.)	5-9, 9-4
Hellebore (*Helleborus* spp.)	4-8, 8-1
Daylily (*Hemerocallis* spp., hybs., and cvs.)	3-11, 12-1
Hosta (*Hosta* hybs. and cvs.)	4-9, 9-2
German bearded iris (*Iris germanica*)	3-9, 9-1
Spotted deadnettle (*Lamium maculatum*)	4-8, 8-1
Shasta daisy (*Leucanthemum* × *superbum*)	5-8, 8-3

Flax (*Linum perenne*)	5-8, 8-4
Peony (*Paeonia* cvs.)	4-8, 8-1
Obedient plant (*Physostegia virginiana*)	4-8, 8-1
Solomon's seal (*Polygonatum* spp.)	4-8, 8-1
Self-heal (*Prunella vulgaris*)	5-8, 8-5
Rodgersia (*Rodgersia henricii*)	5-8, 8-5
Black-eyed Susan (*Rudbeckia hirta*)	3-7, 7-1
Goldenrod (*Solidago* spp.)	5-9, 9-1
Brazilian verbena (*Verbena bonariensis*)	4-11, 12-7

PERENNIALS FOR ALKALINE SOIL

Although most of the soils in our region have pH levels that are moderately acid (6.0 to 6.5), there are pockets where the pH is above 7.0. If you live in one of these alkaline areas, the easiest garden strategy is to use plants that tolerate an alkaline pH level. This list will give you a partial shopping list, but always check with local sources for other plants that may also do well.

COLUMBINE

Columbine (*Aquilegia canadensis*)	3-8, 8-1
Hardy begonia (*Begonia grandis*)	6-9, 9-1
Bergenia (*Bergenia cordifolia*)	4-8, 8-1
Cornflower, bachelor's buttons (*Centaurea* spp.)	3-8, 8-1
Red valerian (*Centranthus ruber*)	5-8, 8-1
Leadwort or plumbago (*Ceratostigma plumbaginoides*)	6-9, 9-1
Lance-leaf coreopsis (*Coreopsis lanceolata*)	4-9, 9-1
Delphiniums (*Delphinium exaltatum, D. grandiflorum*)	3-8, 8-1
Pinks (*Dianthus* spp.)	3-9, 9-1
Bleeding-heart (*Dicentra* spp.)	4-8, 8-1
Gas plant (*Dictamnus albus*)	3-8, 8-1
Purple coneflower (*Echinacea purpurea*)	4-8, 8-1
Globe thistle (*Echinops* spp.)	5-9, 9-3
Hardy geraniums (*Geranium* spp.)	5-9, 9-4
Baby's breath (*Gypsophila* spp.)	4-9, 9-2
Candytuft (*Iberis sempervirens*)	5-9, 9-3
Shasta daisy (*Leucanthemum × superbum*)	5-8, 8-3
Spider lily (*Lycoris radiata*)	7-10, 10-7
Peony (*Paeonia* cvs.)	4-8, 8-1
Creeping phlox (*Phlox subulata*)	3-8, 8-1
Primrose (*Primula* spp.)	3-8, 8-1
Pincushion flower (*Scabiosa* spp.)	4-9, 9-1

SPRING-BLOOMING PERENNIALS

As the temperatures slowly warm up in February and March and the early spring-flowering bulbs start to shake off winter, the spring-flowering perennials begin to appear as well. Lenten roses are the earliest spring harbingers in this list of perennials that will give you flowers through May, when the summer-blooming perennials appear.

Yarrow (*Achillea* spp.)	3-9, 9-1
Columbine (*Aquilegia* spp.)	3-8, 8-1
Sea thrift (*Armeria maritima*)	3-9, 9-1
Astilbes (*Astilbe* spp.)	4-8, 8-1
False indigo (*Baptisia australis*)	3-9, 9-1
Bergenia (*Bergenia cordifolia*)	4-8, 8-1
Siberian bugloss (*Brunnera macrophylla*)	3-7, 7-1

Red valerian (*Centranthus ruber*)	5-8, 8-1
Lily-of-the-valley (*Convallaria majalis*)	4-9, 9-1
Pinks (*Dianthus* spp.)	3-9, 9-1
Gas plant (*Dictamnus albus*)	3-8, 8-1
Bleeding-heart (*Dicentra spectabilis*)	3-9, 9-1
Barrenwort (*Epimedium* spp.)	5-9, 9-3
Sweet woodruff (*Galium odoratum*)	5-8, 8-5
Lenten rose (*Helleborus orientalis*)	4-8, 8-1
Coral bells (*Heuchera* spp.)	4-8, 8-1
Foam bells (*Heucherella* spp.)	3-8, 8-1
Candytuft (*Iberis sempervirens*)	5-9, 9-3
Iris (*Iris* spp.)	3-9, 9-1
Yellow archangel (*Lamiastrum galeobdolon*)	4-8, 8-1
Spotted deadnettle (*Lamium maculatum*)	4-8, 8-1
Shasta daisy (*Leucanthemum* x *superbum*)	5-8, 8-3
Mazus (*Mazus reptans*)	5-8, 8-4
Virginia bluebells (*Mertensia virginica*)	3-7, 7-1
Forget-me-not (*Myosotis palustris*)	5-9, 9-5
Peony (*Paeonia* cvs.)	4-8, 8-1
Iceland poppy (*Papaver nudicaule*)	2-8, 8-1
Phlox (*Phlox stolonifera*, *P. subulata*)	4-8, 8-1
Solomon's seal (*Polygonatum* spp.)	4-8, 8-1
Lungwort (*Pulmonaria* spp.)	4-8, 8-1
Foam flower (*Tiarella cordifolia*)	3-7, 7-1
Globeflower (*Trollius* spp.)	5-8, 8-5
Verbena (*Verbena canadensis*)	4-7, 7-1
Violets (*Viola* spp.)	4-8, 8-1

FALL-BLOOMING PERENNIALS

Most perennials bloom in the spring and summer, but fall is a great time to enjoy the garden. Nature often puts on its most spectacular display in the New York and Mid-Atlantic region in the fall. Sure, dogwoods and azaleas are pretty in the spring, but nothing beats the combination of brilliant foliage, yellow and purple flowers, and brightly colored fruit that we find during the fall. At one time gardeners were limited to mums and ornamental cabbage and kale for fall accents, but now there are many great perennials available to gardeners for fall bloom.

This list is from Susan Barton, a horticulturist with the University of Delaware in Newark, who advises: "Take time to extend your gardening season with this list of great plants that provide interest from flowers, fruit, and foliage well into the fall."

Blue-star flower (*Amsonia hubrectii*)	5-9, 9-3
Dwarf aster (*Aster dumosus*)	4-8, 8-1
Frikart's aster (*Aster* x *frikartii*)	5-8, 8-5
New England aster (*Aster novae-angliae*)	4-8, 8-3
New York aster (*Aster novi-belgii*)	4-8, 8-1
Blackberry lily (*Belamcanda chinensis*)	5-9, 9-3
White boltonia (*Boltonia asteroides*)	4-9, 9-1
Blue mist (*Caryopteris* x *clandonensis*)	6-9, 9-2
Turtlehead (*Chelone glabra*)	4-8, 8-3
Hybrid red chrysanthemum (*Chrysanthemum rubellum*)	5-9, 9-3
Hairy golden aster (*Chrysopsis villosa*)	4-10, 9-2
Snakeroot (*Cimicifuga racemosa*)	3-8, 8-1
Joe Pye weed (*Eupatorium maculatum*)	3-9, 9-1

Hardy sunflower (*Helianthus angustifolius*)	6-9, 9-4
Foam bells (*Heucherella tiarelloides*)	5-8, 8-3
Autumn lycoris (*Lycoris squamigera*)	6-11, 12-6
Gooseneck loosestrife (*Lysimachia clethroides*)	4-8, 8-1
Ornamental oregano (*Origanum laevigatum*)	7-11, 12-7
Obedient plant (*Physostegia virginiana*)	4-8, 8-1
Tuberose (*Polianthes tuberosa*)	7-11. 12-7
Pincushion flower (*Scabiosa caucasica*)	4-9, 9-1
Sedum or stonecrop (*Sedum* × 'Autumn Joy')	4-9, 9-3
Goldenrod (*Solidago rugosa*)	5-9, 9-1
Toad lily (*Tricyrtis hirta*)	4-9, 9-1

PERENNIALS FOR A LONG SEASON OF BLOOM

When you compare perennials to annuals, you find there is a compromise. Perennials come back every year, but annuals bloom longer. Some perennials, however, come close to combining the best of both because they bloom so long. With many of these plants, if you trim away the old flowers (deadhead), you will encourage better and longer flowering. Many of these long bloomers also have flowers that dry naturally, providing either fall and winter garden interest, or material for dried arrangements. Also consider ornamental grasses; many of the wispy grass flowers remain until beaten down by winter rain or snow.

Bloom 2 to 3 months

Bear's breeches (*Acanthus spinosis*)	5-9, 9-5
Yarrow (*Achillea* spp.)	3-9, 9-1
Monkshood (*Aconitum* spp.)	3-7, 7-1
Columbine (*Aquilegia* spp.)	3-8, 8-1
Sea thrift (*Armeria maritima*)	3-9, 9-1
Masterwort (*Astrantia* spp.)	4-7, 7-1
Hardy begonia (*Begonia grandis*)	6-9, 9-1
Boltonia (*Boltonia asteroides*)	4-9, 9-1
Siberian bugloss (*Brunnera macrophylla*)	3-7, 7-1
Carpathian bellflower (*Campanula carpatica, C. glomerata*)	4-7, 7-1
Blue mist (*Caryopteris* × *clandonensis*)	6-9, 9-3
Cornflower or bachelor's buttons (*Centaurea* spp.)	3-8, 8-1
Red valerian (*Centranthus ruber*)	5-8, 8-1
Plumbago (*Ceratostigma plumbaginoides*)	6-9, 9-1
Coreopsis or tickseed (*Coreopsis lanceolata, C. grandiflora*)	4-9, 9-1
Purple coneflower (*Echinacea purpurea*)	4-8, 8-1
Globe thistle (*Echinops ritro*)	5-9, 9-4
Joe Pye weed (*Eupatorium* spp.)	3-9, 9-1
Baby's breath (*Gypsophila paniculata*)	4-9, 9-2
Sun rose (*Helianthemum* cvs.)	6-8, 8-5
Hardy sunflower (*Helianthus* spp.)	6-9, 9-4
False sunflower (*Heliopsis helianthoides*)	4-9, 9-1
Hellebore (*Helleborus* spp.)	4-8, 8-1
Candytuft (*Iberis sempervirens*)	5-9, 9-3
Sunray flower (*Inula magnifica*)	5-8, 8-5
Red-hot poker (*Kniphofia* spp.)	6-9, 9-4
Spotted deadnettle (*Lamium maculatum*)	4-8, 8-1
Cardinal flower (*Lobelia cardinalis*)	4-8, 8-1
Gooseneck loosestrife (*Lysimachia clethroides*)	4-8, 8-1
Loosestrife (*Lythrum* cvs.)	4-9, 9-1
Bee balm (*Monarda didyma*)	4-9, 9-1
Evening primrose (*Oenothera* spp.)	5-9, 8-4

RED-HOT
POKER

Hardy oxalis (*Oxalis crassipes*)	3-8, 8-1
Patrinia (*Patrinia scabiosaefolia*)	5-8, 8-5
Meadow phlox (*Phlox maculata*)	5-8, 8-4
Garden phlox (*Phlox paniculata*)	4-8, 8-1
Obedient plant (*Physostegia virginiana*)	4-8, 8-1
Balloon flower (*Platycodon grandiflorus*)	4-9, 9-1
Sage (*Salvia nemerosa*)	5-9, 9-4
Checker mallow (*Sidalcea* spp.)	6-8, 8-5
Golden Fleece goldenrod (*Solidago sphacelata* 'Golden Fleece')	5-9, 9-1
Stokes' aster (*Stokesia laevis*)	5-9, 9-5
Comfrey (*Symphytum grandiflorum*)	5-9 9-5
Spiderwort (*Tradescantia andersoniana*)	5-9, 9-4
Garden heliotrope (*Valeriana officinalis*)	5-8, 8-5
Speedwell (*Veronica* spp.)	4-8, 8-1

Bloom 3 to 5 months

Mexican hyssop (*Agastache cana*)	6-11, 12-6
Marguerite (*Anthemis tinctoria*)	3-7, 7-1
Butterfly weed (*Asclepias tuberosa*)	4-9, 9-1
Frikart's aster (*Aster frikartii*)	5-8, 8-5
Green and gold (*Chrysogonum virginianum*)	5-8, 8-3
Coreopsis (*Coreopsis verticillata*)	4-9, 9-1
Yellow bleeding-heart (*Corydalis* spp.)	6-8, 8-4
Ice plant (*Delosperma* spp.)	6-10, 10-8
Bleeding-heart (*Dicentra eximia*)	4-8, 8-1
Blanket flower (*Gaillardia* x *grandiflora*)	3-8, 8-1
Gaura (*Gaura lindheimeri*)	6-9, 9-6
Hardy geraniums (*Geranium* spp.)	5-9, 9-4
Daylily (*Hemerocallis* cvs.)	3-11, 12-1
Coral bells (*Heuchera* spp.)	4-8, 8-1
Shasta daisy (*Leucanthemum* x *superbum*)	5-8, 8-3
Patrinia (*Patrinia scabiosaefolia*)	5-8, 8-4
Russian sage (*Perovskia atriplicifolia*)	6-9, 9-6
Goldsturm rudbeckia (*Rudbeckia fulgida* 'Goldsturm')	4-9, 9-1
Rudbeckia (*Rudbeckia speciosa*)	4-9, 9-1
Soapwort (*Saponaria officinalis*)	3-9, 9-1
Pincushion flower (*Scabiosa columbaria*)	3-8, 8-1
Sedum (*Sedum* 'Autumn Joy,' 'Brilliant')	4-9, 9-1
Vervain (*Verbena* spp.)	4-7, 7-1
Wild violet (*Viola labradorica*)	2-8, 8-1

LOW-PEST PERENNIALS

For those who wish to limit pest control efforts in their gardens, here are some perennials that rarely have serious attacks. Part of reducing pest problems is to select the right perennials for the right locations, so keep in mind that this list is for sunny, well-drained sites. Ethel Dutky, who compiled this list, has been the director of the Maryland Plant Diagnostic Laboratory since 1979, and she covers all diseases on all crops for the Cooperative Extension Service with the University of Maryland in College Park. "The more I think about it," she says, "the more I think that lacking pests is a silly reason to grow a plant. In fact, I tend to grow the ones that have more pests or interesting pests." Ethel notes that no plant is truly free of pests or diseases, but the perennials in her list have few problems.

Bear's breeches (*Acanthus* spp.)	5-9, 9-5
Lady's mantle (*Alchemilla mollis*)	3-9, 9-1
Blue-star flower (*Amsonia tabernaemontana*)	3-9, 9-1
Japanese anemone (*Anemone* x *hybrida*)	4-8, 8-1
Hardy orchid (*Bletilla striata*)	5-8, 8-2
Bluebeard (*Caryopteris clandonensis*)	6-9, 9-6
Plumbago or leadwort (*Ceratostigma plumbagnoides*)	6-9, 9-1
Coreopsis or tickseed (*Coreopsis verticillata* 'Moonbeam' and 'Zagreb')	4-9, 9-1
Bleeding-heart (*Dicentra eximia*)	4-8, 8-1
Purple coneflower (*Echinacea purpurea*)	4-8, 8-1
Barrenwort (*Epimedium* spp.)	5-9, 9-5
Gaura (*Gaura lindheimeri*)	6-9, 9-6
Siberian iris (*Iris sibirica*)	3-9, 9-1
Red-hot poker (*Kniphofia* cvs.)	6-9, 9-4
Russian sage (*Perovskia atriplicifolia*)	6-9, 9-6
Goldsturm rudbeckia (*Rudbeckia fulgida* 'Goldstrum')	4-9, 9-1
Autumn Joy sedum (*Sedum spectabile* 'Autumn Joy')	4-9, 9-1
Vera Jameson sedum (*Sedum* x 'Vera Jameson')	4-9, 9-3
Spiderwort (*Tradescantia andersoniana*)	5-9, 9-4

PERENNIALS FOR CUT FLOWERS

Veteran gardeners cut just about anything that will last indoors for at least a day. Use your imagination and mix these perennials with ferns, herbs, hostas, ivies, evergreen shrubs, or unusual tree branches to give additional interest to your fresh-cut arrangements. Also use the leaves of perennials that are silver like *Artemisia* and *Stachys*, or that are variegated like *Ajuga*, *Heuchera*, *Houttuynia*, *Iris*, *Salvia*, *Sedum*, and *Vinca*. Many perennials also can be used dried; some that are good for this purpose are marked with an asterisk (*). Some, such as wild indigo (*Baptisia australis*), also have interesting pods.

Yarrows (*Achillea* spp.)*	3-9, 9-1
Monkshood (*Aconitum carmichaelii*)	3-7, 7-1
Lady's mantle (*Alchemilla mollis*)*	4-7, 7-1
Ornamental onions (*Allium* spp.)	5-8, 8-4
Golden marguerite (*Anthemis tinctoria*)	3-7, 7-1
Columbine (*Aquilegia* spp.)	3-8, 8-1
Sea thrift (*Armeria maritima*)	3-9, 9-1
Butterfly weed (*Asclepias tuberosa*)	4-9, 9-3
Asters (*Aster* spp.)	4-8, 8-1
Astilbe (*Astilbe* cvs.)*	4-8, 8-1
Wild indigo (*Baptisia australis*)*	3-9, 9-1
Blackberry lily (*Belamcanda chinensis*)	5-9, 9-3
Bergenia (*Bergenia cordifolia*)	4-8, 8-1
Boltonia (*Boltonia asteroides*)	4-9, 9-1
Bellflower (*Campanula* cvs.)	3-8, 8-1
Bachelor's buttons (*Centaurea cyanus*)*	3-8, 8-1
Red valerian (*Centranthus ruber*)	5-8, 8-1
Chrysanthemums (*Chrysanthemum* spp.)	3-9, 9-1
Lily-of-the-valley (*Convallaria majalis*)*	4-9, 9-1
Coreopsis (*Coreopsis* spp.)	4-9, 9-1
Montbretia (*Crocosmia* cvs.)	6-9, 9-3
Delphinium (*Delphinium* spp.)*	3-8, 8-1
Cushion mum (*Dendrathema zawadskii*)	3-9, 9-1
Pinks (*Dianthus* spp.)	3-9, 9-1
Bleeding-heart (*Dicentra* spp.)	4-8, 8-1

DIANTHUS

Foxglove (*Digitalis* spp.)	4-8, 8-1
Leopard's bane (*Doronicum orientale*)	5-8, 8-5
Purple coneflower (*Echinacea purpurea*)*	4-8, 8-1
Globe thistle (*Echinops* spp.)*	5-9, 9-4
Joe Pye weed (*Eupatorium maculatum*)*	3-9, 9-1
Blanket flower (*Gaillardia* x *grandiflora*)	3-8, 8-1
Gaura (*Gaura lindheimeri*)	5-9, 9-6
Baby's breath (*Gypsophila paniculata*)*	4-9, 9-2
Hardy sunflower (*Helianthus* spp.)	6-9, 9-4
False sunflower (*Heliopsis scabra*)	4-9, 9-1
Hellebores (*Helleborus* spp.)	4-8, 8-1
Coral bells (*Heuchera* spp.)*	4-8, 8-1
Iris (*Iris* spp.)	3-9, 9-1
Red-hot poker (*Kniphofia* cvs.)	6-9, 9-4
Lavender (*Lavandula* spp.)*	5-8, 8-1
Shasta daisy (*Leucanthemum* x *superbum*)	5-8, 8-3
Gayfeather (*Liatris spicata*)*	4-9, 9-1
Lilies (*Lilium* spp., hybs., and cvs.)	4-8, 8-1
Cardinal flower (*Lobelia cardinalis*)	4-8, 8-1
Catchfly (*Lychnis coronaria*)	4-8, 8-1
Gooseneck loosestrife (*Lysimachia clethroides*)	4-9, 9-4
Plume poppy (*Macleaya cordata*)*	4-9, 9-1
Bee balm (*Monarda didyma*)	4-9, 9-1
Peony (*Paeonia* cvs.)	4-8, 8-1
Patrinia (*Patrinia scabiosaefolia*)	5-8, 8-5
Beard-tongue (*Penstemon digitalis*)*	2-8, 8-1
Russian sage (*Perovskia atriplicifolia*)*	6-9, 9-6
Meadow phlox (*Phlox maculata*)	5-8, 8-4
Garden phlox (*Phlox paniculata*)	4-8, 8-1
Obedient plant (*Physostegia virginiana*)	4-8, 8-1
Balloon flower (*Platycodon grandiflorus*)	4-9, 9-1
Primroses (*Primula* spp.)	3-8, 8-1
Black-eyed Susan, Rudbeckia (*Rudbeckia* spp.)*	3-8, 8-1
Salvias (*Salvia* spp.)*	6-9, 9-5
Pincushion flower (*Scabiosa* spp.)*	4-9, 9-1
Sedum (*Sedum spectabile* cvs.)*	4-9, 9-4
Goldenrod (*Solidago* spp.)*	5-9, 9-1
Stokes' aster (*Stokesia laevis*)	5-9, 9-5
Painted daisy (*Tanacetum coccineum*)	4-8, 8-1
Meadow rue (*Thalictrum* spp.)	5-9, 9-5
False lupine (*Thermopsis lanceolata*)	6-9, 9-3
Vervain (*Verbena canadensis*)	4-7, 7-1
Speedwell (*Veronica* spp.)	4-8, 8-1
Violets (*Viola* spp.)	2-8, 8-1

PERENNIALS WITH EVERGREEN FOLIAGE

One of the negatives of many perennials is that when they die back during the dormant season (winter for most, summer for a few), the ground is bare. That means that something else interesting needs to be going on nearby to compensate, or that the perennial must be in a place where the bare ground doesn't matter. One solution to this bareness is to plant evergreen perennials such as hellebores. Another is to mix perennials with alternating seasons such as hostas and arums; the hostas die back in fall about the time the arums pop up for winter. Daffodils with this combination also contribute to a greener late winter and early spring look. The farther north you go, the less likely that some of these plants will stay truly evergreen, but even if they're only semi-green (at least through the fall), that still keeps an area from having a prolonged void. Another way to fill in around perennials whose foliage doesn't last is to combine them with evergreen ferns, ground covers, or low evergreen shrubs.

Ajuga (*Ajuga reptans*)	3-9, 9-1
Bearberry (*Arctostaphylos uva-ursi*)	2-6, 6-1
Sea thrift (*Armeria maritima*)	3-9, 9-1
Wild gingers (*Asarum* spp.)	2-8, 8-1
Bergenia (*Bergenia cordifolia*)	4-8, 8-1
Pinks (*Dianthus* spp.)	3-9, 9-1
Hellebore (*Helleborus* spp.)	4-8, 8-1
Coral bells (*Heuchera* cvs.)	4-8, 8-1
Candytuft (*Iberis sempervirens*)	5-9, 9-3
Lavender (*Lavandula* spp.)	5-8, 8-5
Bitter root (*Lewisia cotyledon*)	6-8, 8-6
Phlox (*Phlox divaricata, P. stolonifera, P. subulata*)	4-8, 8-1
Strawberry geranium (*Saxifraga* spp.)	6-9, 9-6
Sedum (*Sedum* some spp. and cvs.)	4-9, 9-3
Hens and chicks (*Sempervivum* spp.)	4-8, 8-1
Lambs' ear (*Stachys byzantina*)	4-8, 8-1
Stokes' aster (*Stokesia laevis*)	5-9, 9-5

CANDY-
TUFT

FRAGRANT PERENNIALS

Fragrance in a garden is valued by almost everyone, with the possible exception of those who may be allergic. Locate fragrant perennials near areas that are frequented, or use them in arrangements to give a special touch when bringing in the outdoors. Not all species or cultivars of these plants will necessarily have fragrant flowers, so if possible, select when they're in bloom to be sure they are indeed fragrant. For perennials with fragrant leaves, it is rare that the fragrance not exist in all species and cultivars, but again, use your nose to double check—just crush a leaf and sniff! Also, don't forget the culinary and medicinal herbs; many easily double as ground covers and perennials.

Fragrant Flowers

Doll's eyes (*Actaea pachypoda*)	4-9, 9-1
Ornamental onion (*Allium* spp.)	5-8, 8-5
Ice Ballet swamp milkweed (*Asclepias incarnata* 'Ice Ballet')	3-8, 8-1
Butterfly weed (*Asclepias tuberosa*)	4-9, 9-3
Bridal Veil astilbe (*Astilbe* 'Bridal Veil')	3-8, 8-2
Red valerian (*Centranthus ruber*)	5-8, 8-1
Lily-of-the-valley (*Convallaria majalis*)	4-9, 9-1
Pinks (*Dianthus* spp.)	3-9, 9-1
Frosty Fire pink (*Dianthus amurensis* 'Frosty Fire')	3-9, 9-1
Old Spice pink (*Dianthus gratianopolitanus* 'Old Spice')	3-9, 9-1
Variegated pink fleece flower (*Fallopia japonica* 'Variegata')	5-9, 9-5
Sweet woodruff (*Galium odoratum*)	5-8, 8-5
Lemon daylily (*Hemerocallis flava*)	3-11, 12-1
Hyperion daylily (*Hemerocallis* 'Hyperion')	3-11, 12-1
Honeybells and Royal Standard hosta (*Hosta* 'Honeybells' and 'Royal Standard')	4-9, 9-1
August lily hosta (*Hosta plantaginea*)	4-9, 9-2
Sweet iris (*Iris pallida* 'Aurea-Variegata')	5-9, 9-5
False lily-of-the-valley (*Maianthemum canadense*)	4-7, 7-1
Partridge berry (*Mitchella repens*)	4-9, 9-1
Peony (*Paeonia* cvs.)	4-8, 8-1
Phlox (*Phlox divaricata, P. stolonifera*)	4-8, 8-1

Chadd's Ford hardy orchid (*Spiranthes cernua* 'Chadd's Ford')	7-9, 9-7
Pink Bouquet foam flower (*Tiarella* 'Pink Bouquet')	3-7, 7-1

Fragrant Foliage

Yarrow (*Achillea* cvs.)	3-9, 9-1
Mexican hyssop (*Agastache* spp. and cvs.)	6-11, 12-6
Fragrant false indigo (*Amorpha canescens, A. nana*)	2-6, 6-1
Marguerite (*Anthemis tinctoria*)	3-7, 7-1
Wormwood (*Artemisia* spp. and cvs.)	4-8, 8-1
Wild geranium (*Geranium* spp., hybs., and cvs.)	4-8, 8-1
Chameleon plant (*Houttuynia cordata*)	6-11, 12-6
Lavender (*Lavandula* spp.)	5-8, 8-1
Bee balm (*Monarda didyma*)	4-9, 9-3
Russian sage (*Perovskia atriplicifolia*)	6-9, 9-6
Santolina (*Santolina incana, S. virens*)	6-9, 9-6

"I like to use lavender in landscape designs for the wonderful gray-green foliage as well as the delightful fragrance both foliage and flowers give. The gray-green foliage softens the hot reds and yellows and brightens up the blues and whites of other perennials. Best of all are the varieties of fragrance that each cultivar has. Be sure to sniff each plant before you buy it to be sure it has fragrance you desire."

Ginny Rosenkranz is a Cooperative Extension agent for commercial horticulture on the Eastern Shore of Maryland.

DAYLILIES—EARLY, MIDSEASON, AND LATE

Daylilies mean summer color!" say Richard and Rikki Sterrett, daylily growers and owners of Sterrett Gardens in Craddockville, on Virginia's eastern shore. The Sterretts, who compiled this list, advise gardeners to select daylilies that have different seasons of bloom and repeat habit, "so your perennial borders can have color throughout the summer. Visiting a local daylily grower will help you select daylilies that will do well in your area."

Thumb through the catalogs of many daylily growers in our region and you'll note many decisions you need to make when selecting daylilies. During what part of the growing season do you want them to bloom? Do you want them to rebloom (bloom more than once) or do you want extended bloom (for more than sixteen hours)? Do you want those gorgeous flowers to also be fragrant? Do you want multiple colors or color patterns? Do you want dramatic tall ones or petite dwarf or miniature ones? Do you want them to have leaves that disappear during the winter (dormant), or that persist for part of the fall or winter (semi-evergreen), or for most or all of the winter (evergreen)?

Most daylilies prefer a full-sun location, though shade can be beneficial in very hot locations and generally reduces blooming only slightly. Many will tolerate soil moisture extremes, and they are a good perennial for a site exposed to salty conditions—be it salt spray or occasional saline water over their roots. The Behmke Nurseries of Beltsville and Largo, Maryland, recommend deep watering once per week in the absence of rain, especially during bud formation and flowering.

Many daylilies grow and multiply very rapidly, meaning you can divide them for planting in additional locations in your landscape, or you can share them with friends. Be careful: this group of perennials can really get you hooked and might even get you into your garden playing bee as you try to hybridize your own new cultivars.

Early Bloomers

Always Afternoon, Charles Johnston, Chorus Line, Condilla, Elegant Candy, Happy Returns, Lemon Lollypop, Little Grapette, Malaysian Monarch, Scarlet Orbit, Siloam Amazing Grace, Siloam Double Classic

Midseason Bloomers

Barbara Mitchell, Beautiful Edgings, Mary's Gold, Mountain Violet, Orange Velvet, Pardon Me, Pink Monday, Ruffled Apricot, Scatterbrain, Spider Miracle, Strawberry Candy, White Lemonade

Late Bloomers

Bountiful Valley, Catherine Folker, Catherine Neal, El Desperado, Flameburst, Jersey Spider, Krakatoa Lava, Madame Ruby, Sandra Elizabeth, Siloam Jerome Pillow, Sweet Sugar Candy, Vera Bigalow

REGION-THREE DAYLILY FAVORITES

Region Three of the American Hemerocallis Society (AHS) covers Delaware, the District of Columbia, Maryland, New Jersey, Pennsylvania, Virginia, and West Virginia. Within the region there are thirty-six AHS display gardens, some at public gardens and some at private homes. (For more information, try www.daylilies.org.) In their 1999 popularity poll the members selected the following as their favorite daylily cultivars (in descending order of vote).

Strawberry Candy	Ruby Spider	Orange Velvet
Custard Candy	Dragon's Eye	Daring Dilemma
Janice Brown	Bill Norris	Moonlit Masquerade
Barbara Mitchell	Wedding Band	Jolyene Nichole
Paper Butterfly	Always Afternoon	Canadian Border Patrol

MOST POPULAR HOSTAS

Shade-loving hosta species, hybrids, and cultivars number in the thousands, from dwarfs to large, almost shrub-like plants. Once you select the size hosta you want, you have an amazing range of greens from which to pick—pale lime, deep forest greens, striking blue-greens, and more. Couple that with many beautiful variegation patterns—white, cream, or yellow mixed into various portions of the leaves—and you're assured of finding a hosta for any garden or landscape use. Moreover, many cultivars have very showy flowers that hang on spikes that rise above the leaf clusters. Color range is limited—whites and light to medium purples—but some have the added bonus of a very pleasant fragrance.

Patrick Sarisky, who owns Eminence Meadows, a perennials nursery in Summit, New York, provided this list, which shows the poll results when members of the American Hosta Society (www.hosta.org) were asked to pick their favorites. They appear in descending order of vote. All of these cultivars are suited to the New York and Mid-Atlantic region.

Sagae; Sum and Substance (1st-place tie)	Blue Angel	Regal Splendor
	Fragrant Bouquet	Elegans
Pauls Glory	Krossa Regal	On Stage
Patriot	Guacamole	Whirlwind
Great Expectations	Halcyon	Tokudama Aureonebulosa
Gold Standard	Love Pat	Striptease
Aureomarginata	Sun Power	Inniswood
June	Frances Williams	Tokudama Flavocircinalis

"Missing from the American Hosta Society popularity poll results, but in my opinion deserving to be on the list, are the golden giant 'Solar Flare,' recently introduced from Japan, and the tiny gold-centered 'Cat's Eyes.' The most important step in planting hostas is the addition of rich organic material to the growing site. This will insure healthy strong growth and moisture retention in the soil."

Patrick Sarisky is a horticulturist/sculptor who owns Eminence Meadows, a perennials nursery in Summit, New York, in the northern Catskill Mountains.

DEPENDABLE REBLOOMING IRISES

Irises that rebloom in late summer and autumn are relatively new to the gardening world, but iris hybridizers have developed some excellent bearded iris cultivars that often produce a second and sometimes even a third burst of bloom. Most of these are tall bearded irises, but there are also some intermediate and dwarf reblooming iris cultivars, as you'll see in this list from Clarence Mahan, president of the American Iris Society. Reblooming irises require the same minimal requirements as other bearded iris: full sun, good drainage, and weekly watering if it does not rain. Sometimes it takes a year or two for these irises to get established and start to produce stalks in autumn. They usually produce their second set of flowers when evenings start to get cooler, and they are more likely to rebloom in milder winter climate areas. Bloom color is indicated in the list.

Standard Dwarf Bearded Reblooming Irises
Autumn Maple, pinkish orange
Baby Blessed, yellow
Baby Prince, purple
Dark Crystal, dark wine
Glitter Bit, gold and violet
Hot, yellow and reddish brown
Plum Wine, red-violet
Smell the Roses, purple

Intermediate Bearded Reblooming Irises
Blessed Again, yellow
I Bless, white
Low Ho Silver, white
Midsummer's Night Dream, purple

Miniature Tall Bearded Reblooming Irises
Lady Emma, muted yellow

Tall Bearded Reblooming Irises
Autumn Bugler, white and rosy lavender
Autumn Circus, white and purple
Autumn Tryst, lavender and white
Buckwheat, yellow
Clarence, white and violet
Coral Charmer, pink

Corn Harvest, yellow
Earl of Essex, white and violet
Eternal Bliss, white shaded violet
Feedback, purple
Gideon Victorious, reddish brown
Harvest of Memories, yellow
I Do, white
Immortality, white
Jean Guymer, peach
Jennifer Rebecca, pinkish rose
Late Lilac, lilac
Matrix, creamy yellow
Northward Ho, white and purple
Perfume Counter, purple
Pink Attraction, pink
Queen Dorothy, white and violet
Renown, oyster white
Rosalie Figge, deep purple
Silver Dividends, white
Sunny Disposition, yellow
Unchained Melody, white
Violet Music, medium violet
Violet Returns, deep violet
Witch of Endor, rust
Zurich, white

The American Iris Society (www.irises.org) has divided the irises most often used as garden perennials into three main groups:

BEARDED IRIS—those with thick, bushy "beards" on each of the lower petals or "falls"
ARIL IRIS—Near-East iris not commonly grown in our region
BEARDLESS IRIS—including the commonly grown siberian, Japanese, and native Louisiana iris

JAPANESE IRISES

Hundreds of good Japanese iris cultivars are available to the gardener, but the buyer must beware! Some nurseries obtain stock of this spectacularly beautiful perennial from unscrupulous overseas wholesale dealers who provide inferior and misnamed cultivars. Remember also that Japanese irises come in many shades and patterns of white, pink, and violet, but there is no such thing as a red or yellow Japanese iris. Some Japanese irises are "singles" with three falls (lower petals) and three standards (upper petals). Some are "doubles" with six falls but no standards. Some have more than six falls and are called multipetal cultivars. Clarence Mahan, president of the American Iris Society, provided this list, which includes bloom color.

JAPANESE IRIS

Three Falls (singles)
Asahimaru, maroon
Bellender Blue, dark blue-violet
Enduring Pink Frost, white and pink
Japanese Pinwheel, red-violet
Joy Peters, pink
Kalamazoo, blue-violet and white
Kozasa Gawa, light and dark lavender
Maine Chance, white
Mystic Buddah, wine red and white
Prairie Twilight, lavender
Reisyun, pink
Rose Frappe, red-violet and white
Rose Queen, rose
The Great Mogul, maroon
Trance, light violet
Yamataikoku, red-violet

Six Falls (doubles)
Anytus, white
Caprician Butterfly, white and purple
Cascade Crest, blue and white
Crystal Halo, purple and white
Dancing Waves, white and dark violet
Diomedes, two-toned blue-violet

Edge of Frost, red-violet
Electric Rays, violet
Freckled Geisha, white and red-violet
Frilled Enchantment, white and red-violet
Galatea Marx, flax blue
Hegira, white and deep blue violet
Hidenishiki, red-violet
Mai Ogi, red-violet
Michio, blue-violet
Mystic Buddah, wine red and white
Oriental Eyes, light violet and purple
Raspberry Glow, bitone violet
Reign of Glory, blue-violet and white
Southern Son, blue-violet
Strut and Flourish, dark and light violet
Warai Hotei, blue-violet and dark purple

Multipetal Japanese Irises
Chidori, white and blue-lilac
Koshui no Asa, blue
Nemurijishi, white and light blue
Oriental Bouquet, light blue-violet
Purple Plus, blue-violet
Ushio-no-Kemuri, blue-violet and white

"Japanese irises like rich acid soil, and a lot of water, especially in spring. Lime is fatal to these irises, so do not plant them next to cement or mortar. Divide these irises at least every four years, and unless they are growing on the edge of a pond, lake, or stream, do not plant them back where they were previously growing."

Clarence Mahan, president of the American Iris Society, lives in McLean, Virginia.

LOUISIANA IRISES

Louisiana irises, found growing naturally in the hot and humid swamps of Louisiana, make excellent additions to water gardens and even adapt to drier perennial gardens. Some are hardy all the way up to Canada's zone 4! They are also the only group of irises that includes the color red. Louisiana irises produce beautiful flowers in brilliant hues and color patterns. Flower arrangers have discovered that they make excellent specimens for flower arrangements and can last for up to a week after being cut. Iris expert Bill Smoot of Portsmouth, Virginia, provided this list of cultivars recommended by irisarians on a Louisiana iris discussion group (www.tropica.com, "LAIRIS").

Black Gamecock, dark blue-black
Blue Duke, navy blue
Cajun Sunrise, orange-red
Clyde Redmond, cornflower blue
Dixie Deb, sulfur yellow
Full Eclipse, velvety purple
Geisha Eyes, dark violet-blue
Godzilla, very dark violet
Hurricane Party, red violet
Jazz Hot, velvet red and yellow

Koorawatha, golden yellow
Obvious Heir, white
Princess Leia, cyclamen purple with white rim
Red Echo, scarlet red
Rokki, cream chartreuse
Rokki Rockwell, golden yellow
Sinfonetta, bluebird blue
Stop and Go, shrimp rose
Vermillion Treasure, violet red
Waverly Pink, pink and rose

ROSES

Few garden or landscape plants can match the rose when it comes to flower color, variety of flower shape and configuration, and fragrance. You can select an appropriate rose for any garden use imaginable ranging from a showy specimen to a utilitarian hedge, or from a miniature rose or small tree rose in a container to one of the large sprawling roses that makes a dramatic sweep as a ground cover. If you want the showiest of the roses in your garden—the hybrid teas, grandifloras, and floribundas—you must be prepared to give them the care they require. They represent three of the ten classes of modern roses, roses that date forward from 1867 (the universally accepted date of the first hybrid tea rose). The problem with many of the modern roses is that inbreeding has often lead to delicate, disease- and insect-susceptible plants whose flowers may have little or no fragrance.

Roses that belong to a classification that existed before 1867 are called old garden, antique, old-fashioned, or grandma's roses. There are fifteen classes of these roses that include the wild species roses, the highly fragrant damask roses, the ever-blooming China roses, and the repeat-blooming Portland roses. These older roses, in which there has been increased interest in recent years, generally require far less monitoring and care than the modern roses, and are much more pest resistant and fragrant.

But to relegate all roses from any class to the high-maintenance category would be unfair. From the wonderful old garden rugosas to the modern ground cover or carpet roses, plenty of roses exist for those who want to enjoy them but not be enslaved by them.

Many of the modern roses featured in these lists were All-American Rose Selections (AARS, started in 1938), having been evaluated for two years for fifteen traits including disease resistance, hardiness, color, and novelty. These evaluations are conducted across the country, with many AARS display gardens scattered throughout the New York and Mid-Atlantic area. To locate the AARS garden nearest you, check their website at www.rose.org.

Tips for Selecting and Succeeding with Roses

- Select the right rose for the right location. Most roses need to be in full sun or receive at least six hours of direct sun per day. They also need a fertile soil that possesses both good drainage and good moisture retention.
- Roses should be located where air circulation is good to help keep the foliage dry and reduce leaf spot diseases.
- Check local sources—local rose societies, Cooperative Extension Services, garden centers, botanical gardens, AARS display gardens, American Rose Society (www.ars.org)—to find out which species and cultivars best tolerate the conditions in your area.
- Whenever possible buy top-grade roses. Whether dormant and bare root or containerized and actively growing, look for stems or canes that are smooth and plump, never dried out or shriveled looking. If you need help locating a source for a particular species or cultivar, order the "Combined Rose List," a 198-page list of all roses known to be in commerce worldwide (Peter Schneider, P.O. Box 677, Mantua, OH 44255; www.combinedroselist.com).

- If possible, plant the modern roses together in beds so that maintenance is easier. Only amend the planting soil if the roses are in a bed together—do not amend if planting them individually.
- For grafted or budded roses, be sure when you plant to keep the bud union (the knob or crook in the stem) at least one inch about the soil level. If you bury the union, you may lose the desired cultivar that has been attached to the roots of a seedling rose.
- Keep roses well mulched and watered during the growing season to reduce stress and encourage flowers. To reduce disease problems, use a soaker hose or drip irrigation to water the roots, not the stems and leaves. One way to fertilize your roses is to "fertigate": inject the fertilizer into the water line.
- Fertilize your roses according to rose type and frequency of bloom. Repeat-blooming roses require more fertilizer than those that only bloom once each season. In the warmer areas of our region, many one-time-only bloomers may actually bloom twice per year, in the spring and again in the fall.
- Different types of roses require different types of pruning at different times of the year. When you select roses, learn what is appropriate for each type.
- To keep the plants looking attractive and to encourage additional flowers, regularly cut roses for flower arrangements, or deadhead them (remove spent flowers). Cut above an outward facing leaf that has five leaflets (individual segments making up a whole leaf).
- Monitor, monitor, monitor by knowing what rose pests look like. Diseases like black spot, rust and powdery mildew, and insects like aphids, thrips, spider mites, borers, and Japanese beetles, can easily get ahead of you and ruin the appearance of your roses. Learn the life cycles of these pests so that you know when they may occur and can therefore select the most appropriate biological, cultural, or chemical control measures (integrated pest management). If you don't have the time for this level of maintenance, select roses that are more disease and insect resistant.
- Depending on the severity of your winters, use appropriate protection: soil, leaf, compost, or mulch mounds; rose caps, bushel baskets, or tar paper or burlap covers for the rose canes (stems).

LOW-PEST ROSES

Finding roses that require little maintenance because they are relatively pest and chemical free isn't that difficult. Many of the species roses that we see growing wild—whether native or introduced—are a great place to start. But steer clear of one introduced (non-native) rose, the multiflora rose (*Rosa multiflora*), which has become an invasive pest, outcompeting indigenous plants.

Lady Banks rose (*Rosa banksiae*)
Cabbage rose (*Rosa centifolia*)
Swamp rose (*Rosa palustris*)
Rugosa rose (*Rosa rugosa*)

Scotch or burnet rose (*Rosa spinosissima*)
Virginia rose (*Rosa virginiana*)
Memorial rose (*Rosa wichuraiana*)

ROSES THAT RESIST BLACK SPOT

Even with the fussier modern roses, there are cultivars with considerable resistance to perhaps the biggest rose-leaf spoiler—black spot. This list of black-spot-resistant roses comes from Deborah Smith-Fiola and can be found in her manual *Pest Resistant Ornamental Plants*. Deborah is an associate professor and extension agent with Rutgers Cooperative Extension in Toms River, New Jersey. "Planting a plant that is prone to insects and diseases is a commitment to future high-maintenance tasks and costs, including pesticide maintenance," she cautions. "Instead, investigate the use of inherently pest-resistant plants, as well as pest-resistant varieties and cultivars. The purchase cost of a resistant variety will more than pay for itself by unneeded future maintenance fees. Established sites can be relandscaped to substitute a resistant variety for a desired yet susceptible plant."

Hybrid Tea
Carla
Cayenne
Charlotte Armstrong
Chrysler Imperial
Duet
Electron
First Prize
Forty-Niner
Granada
Miss All-American Beauty
Mister Lincoln
Olympiad
Pascali
Peace
Pink Peace
Portrait
Pristine
Proud Land
Smooth Lady
Sutter's Gold

Tiffany
Tropicana

Floribunda and Grandiflora
Angel Face
Betty Prior
Carousel
Cathedral
Europeana
Fashion
First Edition
Gene Boerner
Goldilocks
Impatient
Ivory Fashion
Love
Mirandy
Montezuma
Pink Parfait
Prominent
Queen Elizabeth

Razzle-Dazzle
Red Gold
Rose Parade
Sonia
Sunsprite

Shrub
All that Jazz
Carefree Wonder

Hybrid Rugosa
Charles Albanel
Henry Hudson
Jens Munk

Miniature
Baby Betsy McCall
Gourmet Popcorn
Little Artist
Rainbow's End
Rose Gilardi

MODERN ROSES WITH GREAT FLOWERS

Two Virginians from different climate zones—William Blevins of Manassas and Howard Jones of Virginia Beach—made the recommendations that make up this list of roses with great flowers. These rose cultivars range from ones just introduced, to cultivars that have been around for seventy-five years. If you're connected to the Internet and want more information about a rose—color, class, height, fragrance—check www.everyrose.com, which has information on almost 7,000 cultivars.

Hybrid Tea

Alabama	deep pink/white blend
Andrea Stelzer	light pink
Artistry	orange blend
Bride's Dream	light pink
Carla	orange pink
Century Two	medium pink
Chicago Peace	pink blend
Crystalline	white
Dainty Bess	soft rose pink
Double Delight	red/white blend
Dublin	raspberry red
Elina	light yellow
Elizabeth Taylor	deep rose pink
First Prize	pink blend
Fragrant Cloud	orange red
Gemini	coral/pink blend
Helen Naudé	white blend
Jema	apricot blend
Keepsake	pink blend
Louise Estes	pink blend

Marijke Koopman	deep medium pink	Iceberg	white
Milestone	red blend	Illumination	apricot blend
Mister Lincoln	dark red	Impatient	orange red
Moonstone	white blend	Kanegem	orange red
Mother's Value	carmine red	Playboy	red/orange blend
Olympiad	medium red	Playgirl	hot magenta pink
Paradise	mauve blend	Redgold	red/yellow blend
Peace	yellow blend	Royal Occasion	orange red
Portrait	pink blend	Sexy Rexy	medium pink
Pristine	white blend	Sheila's Perfume	red/yellow blend
Suffolk	white /pink edge	Showbiz	medium red
Swarthmore	deep pink blend	Summer Fashion	yellow blend
Thriller	pink/white blend	Sun Flare	medium yellow
Tiffany	pink blend	Sunsilk	medium yellow
Touch of Class	orange pink blend	Sunsprite	deep yellow
Valencia	apricot blend	Traumerei	orange blend
Veterans Honor	red	Vera Dalton	medium pink

Floribunda

Grandiflora

Angel Face	deep purple	Fame!	deep pink
Bill Warriner	orange pink blend	Gold Medal	medium yellow blend
Bridal Pink	medium pink	Magic Lantern	orange blend
Cherish	orange pink	Pink Parfait	medium pink blend
Destiny	pink/white blend	Queen Elizabeth	medium pink
Dicky	orange pink	Rejoice	pink blend
Europeana	dark red	Sonia	coral pink
French Lace	white	Tournament of Roses	russet pink
Golden Holstein	deep yellow		

"I have been growing replacement roses in fiber pots for seven to eight years, and keep them in pots for their first growing season (eight to nine months) before planting them in the ground. They get off to an excellent start this way and are then ready to compete with the plants already in an existing bed." (For a more detailed discussion see "Container Planting for Roses" on the American Rose Society's website—www.ars.org/experts/jones-pots.html.)

Howard Jones is an American Rose Society consulting rosarian and an accredited horticulture judge from Virginia Beach, Virginia.

MINIATURE ROSES

Miniature or dwarf roses are a class of modern roses that, with the exception of the miniature cascading and climbing roses, grow no taller than 18 inches. All parts of miniature roses are proportionately smaller, making them ideal for small niches in the garden, for low borders and edging, or for growing in containers. Less care is needed in planting them because most are rooted from cuttings (they're not budded or grafted, except for those trained as tree roses). The Maryland Cooperative Extension recommends the following cultivars for the New York and Mid-Atlantic region.

Red and Red Blends

Baby Masquerade
Beauty Secret
Dwarf King
Little Artist
Magic Carrousel
Midget

Red Cascade
Red Gilardi
Red Imp
Scarlet Gem
Starina
Tom Thumb

Pink and Pink Blends
Baby Betsy McCall
Baby Darling
Bo-Peep
Chipper
Judy Fisher
Minnie Pearl
Opal Jewell
Pacesetter
Patty Lou
Pixie Rose
Rosa Rouletti
Sweet Fairy
Tinker Bell

Yellow and Yellow Blends
Baby Gold Star
Bit-O-Sunshine
Ella Mae
Party Girl
Pixie Gold
Rise-N-Shine

White
Cinderella
Easter Morning
Gourmet Popcorn
Pixie
Twinkles

RUGOSA ROSES

Rugosa or saltspray roses can grow along Atlantic beaches and bays and tolerate wind-borne salt. Catch the wonderful fragrance of one and your mind runs to sand dunes and crashing waves. Rugosa roses rarely have any pest problems, and they produce not only some of the most fragrant of flowers, but also some of the largest, showiest, and most vitamin-C-packed hips (the fruit of the rose). After the first frost, rugosa leaves put on a fall color display that is rare for roses, usually in combinations of yellow, orange, red, and/or purple. A wonderful reference book is *Rosa Rugosa* by Suzanne Verrier.

While there are over 200 known hybrids and cultivars, the following are the most readily available (many others can be ordered from mail-order catalogs). This list includes flower type and color.

Alba	single, white
Blanc Double De Coubert	double, white
F. J. Grootendorst	small clusters, crimson
Fru Dagmar Hastrup	single, pale pink
Hansa	double, dark magenta
Linda Campbell	clusters, double, scarlet red
Marie Bugnet	double, white
Mont Blanc	semi-double, white
Snow Owl	single, white
Therese Bugnet	double, pink
Topaz Jewel	semi-double, light yellow

 In their garden fact-sheet, Waterloo Gardens of Exton and Devon, Pennsylvania, calls rugosa roses "macho" roses because they require little or no spraying or watering and will tolerate seashore soil that may be bad and dry.

CLIMBING ROSES

Roses that climb don't have tendrils or aerial roots as do many climbing vines, nor are they able to twine around supports. Climbing roses produce long stems or canes that if given adequate support—a trellis or an arbor—can be trained to grow upright, often creating a very colorful, and often fragrant, outdoor room or enclosure. Some climbing roses are everblooming while others just bloom once at the beginning of the season. Ramblers are climbers with very pliable canes.

Large Flowered

America	orange pink
Don Juan	dark red
Golden Showers	medium yellow
Handel	red blend
Royal Sunset	apricot

Repeat Bloomers

Altissimo	dark red
America	orange pink
Crimson Glory Climber	dark red
Don Juan	dark red
Dublin Bay	dark red
Fourth of July	semi-double red blend
Golden Showers	deep yellow
Handel	pink/white blend
High Hopes	medium pink
New Dawn	light pink
Red Fountain	dark red
Royal Sunset	apricot

ROSES THAT MAKE GOOD HEDGES

When a hedge is planted in the landscape, it's usually for some utilitarian purpose—to screen an objectionable view or object, to create privacy, to control traffic, or to divert the wind. But who says a hedge has to be just green leaves? Why not create a hedge from roses to add wonderful color? If you use the rugosas, you'll add delightful fragrance as well to your functional planting. As with most hedges, pruning will be needed in the spring and fall; not only will this control the size of your hedge, but it will also encourage more flowers. This list of roses for hedges is divided into height categories, and it indicates rose type.

Medium (3 to 6 feet)	Class
Carefree Wonder	Shrub
Eutin	Floribunda
F.J. Grootendorst	Hybrid rugosa
Pink Grootendorst	Hybrid rugosa
Rosa rugosa 'Alba'	Species
Rosa rugosa 'Rubra'	Species
Simplicity	Floribunda
Stretch Johnson	Shrub
Topaz Jewel	Hybrid rugosa

Large (6 feet and taller)	Class
Carefree Beauty	Shrub
Cocktail	Shrub
Flutterbye	Shrub
Linda Campbell	Hybrid rugosa
Long Tall Sally	Shrub
Nicole	Floribunda
O'Neal's Bequest	Shrub
Queen Elizabeth	Grandiflora
Sally Holmes	Shrub
Tabris	Floribunda

ROSES TO USE AS GROUND COVER

Roses with long stems or canes that will trail over the ground can be used to cover flat areas or slopes. How much prettier to see a blooming rose on a hill too steep to mow than a collection of weeds. If you have low rock walls, or an area that is terraced, these roses are good to plant for overhanging and softening harsh divides.

Just about every class of rose—miniature, climber and rambler, rugosa, polyantha, species—contains cultivars that grow low (no more than 2 to 3 feet) and can be used as ground covers. But hit the browse button and look under ground covers at the www.everyrose.com website and it becomes obvious that the shrub roses contain the greatest number of cultivars. Within that class are two modern groups with many cultivars that are well suited to most conditions in the New York and Mid-Atlantic region.

Flower Carpet: Apple Blossom, Pink, Red, White, Yellow
Meidiland: Alba, Fire, Flamingo, Fuchsia, Ice, Magic, Mystic, Pearl, Pink, Red, Scarlet, White

FRAGRANT ROSES

For those of us who love to stick our noses into flowers, one of the biggest disappointments is to sniff a beautiful rose only to find it has no fragrance. The following list from Howard Jones and William Blevins describes the scent of these fragrant roses, be it a classic rose smell, or something with a hint of citrus, clove, or even honeysuckle.

Cultivar	Fragrance
Ain't She Sweet	heavy rose
Arlene Francis	sweet licorice
Angel Face	strong citrus
Barbra Streisand	strong rose and citrus
Chrysler Imperial	heavy damask
Crimson Glory	strong damask
Dolly Parton	heavy clove
Double Delight	strong spicy rose
Fair Bianca	strong myrrh
Fragrant Cloud	strong spicy rose
Fragrant Hour	strong spice and fruit
Fragrant Plum	strong fruity
Full Sail	heavy honeysuckle
Granada	strong rose and spice
Iceberg	strong honey
Intrigue	strong citrus
Judy Garland	strong apple and rose
Just Joey	strong fruity
Lemon Spice	heavy citrus
Margaret Merrill	rich citrus and spice
Medallion	sweet licorice
Mirandy	strong rose
Miss All-American Beauty	heavy rose
Mister Lincoln	heavy damask
New Zealand	strong honeysuckle
Oklahoma	heavy rose
Papa Meilland	very heavy damask
Perfume Delight	strong rose
Pink Peace	strong rose
Portrait	sweet, fruity
Roseanne	sweet damask

Royal Amethyst	strong, fruity
Scentimental	strong sweet spice
Secret	strong sweet and spicy
Sheila's Perfume	strong rose and fruit
Stainless Steel	strong rose
Sunsilk	strong sweet licorice
Sutter's Gold	strong spice
Sweet Surrender	heavy tea rose
The McCartney Rose	rich fruity
Tiffany	strong fruity
White Christmas	very sweet rose

"Modern roses are often compared to old-garden and pre-1900 roses and considered sub-par in fragrance—a statement unfairly supported by myth and repetition. In fact, modern roses are just as fragrant as their predecessors, if not more so."

William Blevins, from Manassas, Virginia, is an American Rose Society consulting rosarian and accredited life judge who has a great website at www.wildbillsroses.com.

ROSES TO GROW IN CONTAINERS

If you don't have a large yard in which to garden, yet would like to grow a rose or two, don't despair! Roses can be grown successfully in containers if they're given plenty of sunlight and their potting substrate is carefully monitored so they don't dry out. They'll also need to be fertilized more frequently than roses grown in the ground. Roses ranging from miniatures to large shrubs can all be used. Rosarian William Blevins, who provided this list, advises: "If you plan to grow a rose in a container, for a deck, patio, or balcony, be sure to use a large enough container—one that is at least 5 to 7 gallons."

Cultivar	Class
Angel Face	Floribunda
Baby Love	Miniature Shrub
Carefree Delight	Shrub
Child's Play	Miniature
George Burns	Floribunda
Giggles	Miniature
Incognito	Miniature
Knock Out	Shrub
Pillow Fight	Shrub
Playgirl	Floribunda
Rockin' Robin	Shrub
Showbiz	Floribunda

ORNAMENTAL GRASSES

Grass to most people conjures up an image of their yard and a lot of maintenance—mowing, edging, controlling weeds. But one type of grass generally requires little maintenance and can dramatically enhance your landscape. For lack of a better term, we call them ornamental grasses—grasses used for their aesthetic and design contribution to a landscape. Much of the interest in ornamental grasses was created by landscape architects at Oehme, van Sweden and Associates of Washington, D.C., who have demonstrated how well ornamental grasses can be used in anything from small home gardens to large commercial or public landscapes.

Use ornamental grasses much as you would shrubs—as hedges, screens, specimens, borders. Their foliage comes in a wide variety of colors, and their flowers (inflorescence) and seedheads can range from totally inconspicuous to very striking and dramatic, especially in the winter. A unique feature of the ornamental grasses is the motion they bring to a garden. Some of the grasses wave gracefully in a breeze; others shiver or quake.

Ornamental grasses, once established, require little special care. Few are very site specific, and most require little supplemental watering, pest control, or other maintenance. They're good to use for "water wise" gardens, or for sustainable landscaping—landscaping needing minimal human input or intervention.

Included among the ornamental grasses are a few plants that taxonomically are not true grasses but are grass-like: sedges (*Carex*), mondo grass (*Ophiopogon*), blue-eyed grass (*Sisyrinchium*). All have foliage similar to the true grasses and therefore have been added to some of the lists.

GIANT
REED GRASS

Tips for Selecting and Succeeding with Ornamental Grasses
- Select the right ornamental grass for the right location. Most ornamental grasses grow best in full sun, although there are some exceptions, and they prefer moist, well-drained soil.
- Avoid applying much supplemental fertilizer, especially if your ornamental grasses are in mulched beds where adequate nutrients will be available from decomposing organic matter.
- Irrigate newly planted grasses to help establish their roots, but do not overwater them. Use drip irrigation if possible to keep the foliage dry—this will reduce pest problems.
- Mulch to control weeds. Remember that ornamental grasses are still grasses and will be injured by most grass herbicides.
- Do a bit of clean-up by removing the previous year's dead leaves early each spring.

ORNAMENTAL GRASSES THAT COMMAND ATTENTION

Some of the most spectacular plants that you can use as specimens—plants that are used to command attention—can be found in the ornamental grasses. Their specimen use may come from their size, unusual foliage, lovely flowers or plumes, or a wonderful combination of these features.

Giant reed grass (*Arundo donax*)   6-11, 12-1
Pampas grass (*Cortaderia selloana* and cvs.)   7-10, 10-7

Variegated orchard grass (*Dactylis glomerata* 'Variegata')	5-9, 9-5
Japanese blood grass (*Imperata cylindrica* 'Red Baron')	4-9, 9-1
Corkscrew rush (*Juncus effusus spiralis*)	6-9, 9-6
Eulalia or Japanese silver grass (*Miscanthus sinensis* and cvs.)	4-9, 9-1
Tall purple moor grass (*Molinia* spp. and cvs.)	5-9, 9-4
Switch grass (*Panicum virgatum* and cvs.)	5-9, 9-4
Fountain grass (*Pennisetum* spp. and cvs.)	6-9, 9-6
Ravennae grass (*Saccharum ravennae*)	6-9, 9-6
Indian grass (*Sorghastrum nutans*)	5-8, 8-5

"As I drive through the metropolitan areas of Virginia, Maryland, and Pennsylvania, I see more and more ornamental grasses used in commercial, residential, and institutional plantings. Golf courses are also using grasses around the clubhouse and on the course. It is only recently that grasses have become popular. When our nursery started growing ornamental grasses in the early sixties, fellow nurserymen thought I was crazy. They didn't see what I saw—a group of plants which provided a completely different texture than plants commonly in use, which changed with the seasons, and which were relatively maintenance free, besides producing beautiful flowers (plumes)."

Richard A. Simon is the retired president of Bluemount Nurseries, Inc., in Monkton, Maryland.

ORNAMENTAL GRASSES FOR SCREENING

Generally speaking, screening plants are tall, but today people want to screen anything which hints of ugliness, be it a neighbor's garage, compost pile, dog kennel, driveway, or outdoor light fixture. Norm Hooven, who grows ornamental grasses at his Limerock Ornamental Grasses nursery in Port Matilda, Pennsylvania, compiled this list of grasses for screening. Norm's list indicates the height of the foliage; flowering will add to that. The foliage of Karl Foerster feather reed grass, for example, will be 3 to 4 feet in height, but the plant can attain 6 feet during flowering; since it is a cool-season grass and blooms in early summer, its height for screening is effective when outdoor activity is at its greatest. However, growing conditions and siting affect height, as does the hardiness zone. Keep in mind that these same grasses (most of which are clumping) also work well as backgrounds to show off lower shrubs and perennials.

Foliage Height: 2 to 3 feet

Blue oat grass (*Helictotrichon sempervirens*)	5-8, 8-1
Japanese silver grass (*Miscanthus sinensis* 'Little Kitten,' 'Nippon,' 'Yaka Jima,' 'Yaku Shima')	4-9, 9-1
Tall purple moor grass (*Molinia litorialis* 'Karl Foerster,' 'Sky Racer,' 'Staeffa,' 'Transparent,' 'Windspiel')	5-9, 9-4
Fountain grass (*Pennisetum alopecuroides*)	6-9, 9-6
Japanese themeda (*Themeda triandra japonica*)	6-9, 9-6

Foliage Height: 3 to 4 feet

Karl Foerster feather reed grass (*Calamagrostis* X *acutiflora* 'Karl Foerster')	6-9, 9-3
Northern sea oats (*Chasmanthium latifolium*)	5-9, 9-3
Flame grass (*Miscanthus purpurescens*)	4-9, 9-1
Japanese silver grass (*Miscanthus sinensis* 'Arabesque,' 'Ferner Osten,' 'Kirk Alexander,' 'Kleine Silberspinne,' 'Rigoletto,' 'Undine')	4-9, 9-1
Switch grass (*Panicum virgatum* 'Dallas Blue,' 'Heavy Metal,' 'Hanse Herms,' 'Prairie Sky,' 'Rehbraun')	5-9, 9-4
Japanese fountain grass (*Pennisetum japonicum*)	6-9, 9-6
Indian grass (*Sorghastrum nutans* 'Sioux Blue')	5-8, 8-5
Silver spike grass (*Spodiopogon sibericus*)	4-9, 9-1

Foliage Height: 5 to 6 feet

Japanese silver grass (*Miscanthus sinensis* 'Adagio,' 'Dixieland,' 'Flamingo,' 'Morning Light,' 'November Sunset,' 'White Kascade,' 'Zwergzebra')	4-9, 9-1
Zebra grass (*Miscanthus sinensis* 'Zebrinus')	4-9, 9-1
Cloud Nine switch grass (*Panicum virgatum* 'Cloud Nine')	5-9, 9-4
Ravennae grass (*Saccharum ravennae*)	6-9, 9-6

Foliage Height: 7 feet plus

Giant reed (*Arundo donax*)	6-11, 12-1
Variegated giant reed (*Arundo donax variegata*)	6-11, 12-1
Giant miscanthus (*Miscanthus floridulus*)	6-9, 9-6
Giant Chinese silver grass (*Miscanthus giganteus*)	4-9, 9-1
Japanese silver grass (*Miscanthus sinensis* 'Central Park,' 'Cosmopolitan,' 'Emerald Shadow,' 'Grosse Fontaine,' 'Strictus')	4-9, 9-1
Goliath Japanese silver grass (*Miscanthus sinensis* 'Goliath')	4-9, 9-1
Silver Tower Japanese silver grass (*Miscanthus sinensis* 'Silberturm')	4-9, 9-1

"Most descriptions of grasses in the popular literature of today are described at their full height, which includes the flowers. This will add at least 1 to 2 feet to the plant, and even more in some newer varieties of *Miscanthus* (for shorter grasses it makes little difference). The flowering phase is such a transient feature that to use it in making a decision for height and screening purposes decreases one's choices in some cases. Therefore, I continually recommend using only the effective foliage height when choosing what to use. Then the client won't be disappointed when the 4-foot plant they thought would cover the garbage can only accentuates the crinkled lid and half-dented body they thought would be hidden because a foot of the plant is flower stem and flower!"

Norm Hooven grows one of the largest commercial collections of ornamental grasses in the United States at his Limerock Ornamental Grasses nursery in Port Matilda, Pennsylvania.

SHADE-TOLERANT ORNAMENTAL GRASSES

Shade is a relative term. The shade pattern under the open canopy of a honeylocust tree is considered light, dappled, or bright partial shade, whereas the shade under a sugar maple tree would be considered dense or heavy shade. Though most grasses prefer full-sun conditions, these grasses will tolerate more shade than most. A few, marked with an asterisk (*) in this list, actually prefer some shade.

BLUE-EYED
GRASS

Yellow foxtail (*Alopecurus pratensis* 'Aureovariegatus')	5-8, 8-5
Bulbous oat grass (*Arrhenatherum elatius bulbosum* 'Variegatum')	5-8, 8-5
Quaking grass or trembling hearts (*Briza media*)	4-10, 10-1
Karl Foerster feather reed grass (*Calamagrostis* × *acutiflora* 'Karl Foerster')	6-9, 9-3
Sedges (*Carex* spp.)*	6-9, 9-5
Northern sea oats (*Chasmanthium latifolium*)	5-9, 9-8
Tufted hair grass (*Deschampsia cespitosa* and cvs.)	5-9, 9-4
Golden variegated Japanese forest grass (*Hakonechloa macra* 'Aureola')*	5-9, 9-5
Variegated velvet grass (*Holcus mollis* 'Albovariegatus')	5-9, 9-5
Japanese blood grass (*Imperata cylindrica* 'Red Baron')*	4-9, 9-1
Woodrush (*Luzula nivea*, *L. sylvatica*)*	4-9, 9-1
Golden grass (*Milium effusum* 'Aureum')	6-9, 9-6
Maiden grass (*Miscanthus sinensis* 'Gracillimus')	4-9, 9-1
Striped eulalia grass (*Miscanthus sinensis* 'Variegatus')	4-9, 9-1
Tall purple moor grass (*Molinia caerulea* and cvs.)	5-9, 9-4
Ebony Knight mondo grass (*Ophiopogon planiscapus* 'Ebony Knight')	6-11, 12-1
Oriental fountain grass (*Pennisetum orientale*)	7-9, 9-7
Feesey's ribbon grass (*Phalaris arundinacea* 'Feesey')	4-9, 9-1

Yellow ribbon grass (*Phalaris arundinacea luteo* 'Picta')	4-9, 9-1
Blue moor grass (*Sesleria autumnalis*)	5-8, 8-5
Blue-eyed grass (*Sisyrinchium angustifolium*)	5-, 8-5
Prairie cord grass (*Spartina pectinata aureomarginata*)	4-7, 7-1

ORNAMENTAL GRASSES FOR WET SITES

Most ornamental grasses are like turf grasses, preferring to grow in soil that has adequate moisture yet is well drained. As with any group of plants, however, there are species that are more tolerant of extremes, and within the ornamental grasses and grass-like plants there are plenty of choices if you have an area that is damp or wet most of the time.

Sweet flag (*Acorus gramineus* and cvs.)	4-11, 12-1
Foxtail grass (*Alopecurus pratensis*)	5-8, 8-5
Giant reed grass (*Arundo donax*)	6-1, 12-1
Karl Foerster feather reed grass (*Calamagrostis* × *acutiflora* 'Karl Foerster')	6-9, 9-3
Sedges (*Carex* spp.)	6-9, 9-5
Northern sea oats (*Chasmanthium latifolium*)	5-9, 9-3
Tufted hair grass (*Deschampsia cespitosa*)	5-9, 9-4
Cotton grass (*Eriophorum angustifolium*)	4-7, 7-1
Reed manna grass (*Glyceria maxima* 'Variegata')	5-9, 9-3
Rushes (*Juncus* spp.)	6-9, 9-6
Woodrushes (*Luzula* spp.)	4-9, 9-1
Giant miscanthus (*Miscanthus floridulus*)	4-9, 9-1
Eulalia or Japanese silver grass (*Miscanthus sinensis* and cvs.)	4-9, 9-1
Tall purple moor grass (*Molinia caerulea* and cvs.)	5-9, 9-4
Switch grass (*Panicum virgatum* and cvs.)	5-9, 9-4
Fountain grass (*Pennisetum* spp.)	6-9, 9-6
Feesey's ribbon grass (*Phalaris arundinacea* 'Feesey')	4-9, 9-3
Yellow ribbon grass (*Phalaris arundinacea luteo picta*)	4-9, 9-3
Reed grass (*Phragmites australis*)	5-9, 9-3
Ravennae grass (*Saccharum ravennae*)	6-9, 9-6
Prairie cord grass (*Spartina pectinata aureomarginata*)	4-7, 7-1

RUSH

ORNAMENTAL GRASSES FOR DRY SITES OR DROUGHT

Because parts of our region frequently suffer through droughty summers with limited rainfall, often causing cities and towns to restrict landscape irrigation, plants that tolerate limited soil moisture are becoming more sought after. Many of the cool-season turf grasses go dormant when irrigation must be limited, but many of the ornamental grasses can survive and look good under dry or droughty conditions. The grasses in this list are also good for the low-water landscaping concept called xeriscaping.

Bluestem (*Andropogon gerardii*)	2-7, 7-1
Bulbous oat grass (*Arrhenatherum elatius bulbosum*)	5-8, 8-5
Giant reed grass (*Arundo donax*)	6-11, 12-1
Sideoats grama grass (*Bouteloua curtipendula*)	5-9, 9-5
Mosquito grass (*Bouteloua gracilis*)	5-9, 9-5
Karl Foerster feather reed grass (*Calamagrostis* × *acutiflora* 'Karl Foerster')	5-9, 9-3
Northern sea oats (*Chasmanthium latifolium*)	5-9, 9-3
Pampas grass (*Cortaderia selloana* and cvs.)	7-10, 10-7
European dune grass (*Elymus arenarius*)	4-9, 9-1
Blue fescues (*Festuca amethystina, F. cinerea, F. glauca, F. mairei, F. muelleri, F. ovina*)	4-8, 8-1
Blue oat grass (*Helictotrichon sempervirens*)	5-8, 8-1

SWITCH
GRASS

Blue hair grass (*Koeleria glauca*)	6-9, 9-6
Eulalia or Japanese silver grass (*Miscanthus sinensis* and cvs.)	4-9, 9-1
Switch grass (*Panicum* spp. and cvs.)	5-9, 9-4
Fountain grass (*Pennisetum alopecuroides* and cvs.)	6-9, 9-6
Ribbon grass (*Phalaris arundinacea* and cvs.)	4-9, 9-1
Ravennae grass (*Saccharum ravennae*)	6-9, 9-6
Little bluestem (*Schizachyrium scoparium*)	5-9, 9-5
Autumn moor grass (*Sesleria autumnalis*)	5-8, 8-5
Indian grass (*Sorghastrum nutans*)	5-8, 8-5
Prairie dropseed (*Sporobolus heterolepis*)	3-9, 9-1

ORNAMENTAL GRASSES FOR CLAY SOIL

No ornamental grass wants to grow in soil that compresses nicely into bricks, but a few will take the generally least desirable type of soil—heavy clay—where moisture over the course of the year can range from soggy and saturated to utterly bone dry. Whenever possible, try to improve a heavy clay soil before planting, but should this be impossible, try one of these very tolerant plants.

Karl Foerster feather reed grass (*Calamagrostis* x *acutiflora* 'Karl Foerster')	5-9, 9-3
Tufted hair grass (*Deschampsia cespitosa*)	5-9, 9-3
European dune grass (*Elymus arenarius*)	4-9, 9-1
Reed manna grass (*Glyceria maxima*)	5-9, 9-3
Eulalia or Japanese silver grass (*Miscanthus sinensis* and cvs.)	4-9, 9-1
Ribbon grass (*Phalaris arundinacea*)	4-9, 9-1

AGGRESSIVE ORNAMENTAL GRASSES

Norm Hooven, the owner of Limerock Ornamental Grasses in Port Matilda, Pennsylvania, compiled this list of mobile grasses. Some of these grasses are slower to invade than others, but since all move from where they are originally planted, they are considered aggressive. "Small Japanese silver grass grows moderately slowly in poor soil, but if the soil is moist, watch out," Norm cautions. Variegated blue sedge is quick spreading even in partial shade, he notes, and cotton grass spreads quickly in moist soils. Ribbon grass, prairie cord grass, and yellow variegated reed grass spread quickly. Less aggressive are giant reed, variegated Japanese sedge, creeping broad-leaved sedge, reed manna grass, Shogun oriental fountain grass, and Feesey's ribbon grass.

Allow adequate room for these grasses to spread, or plant them in bottomless containers to inhibit their walk in the landscape.

Giant reed (*Arundo donax*)	6-11, 12-1
Variegated giant reed (*Arundo donax* 'Variegata')	6-11, 12-1
Formosan reed grass (*Arundo formosana*)	6-11, 12-1
Plini's reed grass (*Arundo pliniani*)	6-11, 12-1
Variegated blue sedge (*Carex glauca variegata*)	6-9, 9-5
Variegated Japanese sedge (*Carex morrowii* 'Ice Dance,' 'Silver Sceptre')	6-9, 9-5
Black blooming sedge (*Carex nigra*)	6-9, 9-5
Island Brocade creeping broad-leaved sedge (*Carex siderosticha* 'Island Brocade')	6-9, 9-5
Creeping variegated broad-leaved sedge (*Carex siderosticha variegata*)	6-9, 9-5
Cotton grass (*Eriophorum angustifolium*)	4-7, 7-1
Variegated reed manna grass (*Glyceria maxima variegata*)	5-9, 9-3
Japanese forest grass (*Hakonechloa macra*)	5-9, 9-5
White variegated Japanese forest grass (*Hakonechloa macra albo-striata*)	5-9, 9-5
Golden variegated Japanese forest grass (*Hakonechloa macra* 'Aureola')	5-9, 9-5
Red Baron Japanese blood grass (*Imperata cylindrica* 'Red Baron')	4-9, 9-1
European dune grass (*Leymus arenarius*)	4-9, 9-1
Blue Dune European dune grass (*Leymus arenarius* 'Blue Dune')	4-9, 9-1

Small Japanese silver grass (*Miscanthus oligostachys*)	6-9, 9-6
Running fountain grass or pasture fountain grass (*Pennisetum incomptum*)	6-9, 9-6
Shogun oriental fountain grass (*Pennisetum orientale* 'Shogun')	6-9, 9-6
Yellow ribbon grass (*Phalaris arundinacea luteo-picta*)	4-9, 9-3
Ribbon grass (*Phalaris arundinacea picta*)	4-9, 9-3
Feesey's ribbon grass (*Phalaris arundinacea picta* 'Feesey')	4-9, 9-1
Yellow variegated reed grass (*Phragmites australis aurea*)	5-9, 9-5
Candy Stripe reed grass (*Phragmites australis* 'Candy Stripe')	5-9, 9-5
Prairie cord grass (*Spartina pectinata aureomarginata*)	4-7, 7-1

> **"Running fountain grass or pasture fountain grass (*Pennisetum incomptum*) is great for that wavy, pasture effect. Island Brocade creeping variegated broad-leaved sedge (*Carex siderosticha*) has trailing stems. Ribbon grass (*Phalaris arundinacea picta*) tolerates bright shade and poor soil but is quick to spread. Yellow variegated reed grass (*Phragmites australis aurea*) is fast but has great color."**
> **Norm Hooven is the owner of Limerock Ornamental Grasses in Port Matilda, Pennsylvania.**

ORNAMENTAL GRASSES FOR SPRING AND SUMMER FLOWERS

The flowers, plumes, or inflorescences of ornamental grasses lend a different textural appearance to a landscape. Some are thin and wispy while others are heavy and dense. Some look like feathers or bottlebrushes while others look like they'd be great for dusting the furniture. These flowers or seedheads may stick only a few inches above the foliage or may soar several feet above, often doubling the plant's height when in bloom. As for colors—from creams and tans to pinks and purples—many have lovely hues when the flowers are fresh, and many are likewise wonderful as dried seedheads. Those marked with an asterisk (*) in this list are especially good for fresh or dried arrangements.

FEATHER REED GRASS

Spring Inflorescence

Quaking grass or trembling hearts (*Briza media*)*	4-10, 10-1
Star sedge (*Carex grayii*)	6-9, 9-6
Drooping or weeping sedge (*Carex pendula*)	6-9, 9-6
Tufted hair grass (*Deschampsia cespitosa* and cvs.)*	5-9, 9-4
Blue fescues (*Festuca* spp.)	4-8, 8-1
Blue oat grass (*Helictotrichon sempervirens*)	4-9, 9-1
Blue hair grass (*Koeleria glauca*)	6-9, 9-6
Woodrushes (*Luzula* spp. and cvs.)	4-9, 9-1

Summer Inflorescence

Karl Foerster feather reed grass (*Calamagrostis* x *acutiflora* 'Karl Foerster')*	5-9, 9-3
Northern sea oats (*Chasmanthium latifolium*)*	5-9, 9-3
Pampas grass (*Cortaderia selloana* and cvs.)	7-10, 10-7
Sand love grass (*Eragrostis trichoides*)	5-9, 9-5
Eulalia or Japanese silver grass (*Miscanthus sinensis* 'Arabesque,' 'Malepartus,' 'Silberfeder,' 'Yaku Jima')*	4-9, 9-1
Tall purple moor grass (*Molinia caerulea* and cvs.)	5-9, 9-4
Switch grass (*Panicum virgatum* 'Rehbraun' and 'Rotstrahlbusch')	5-9, 9-4
Fountain grass (*Pennisetum alopecuroides* and cvs.)	6-9, 9-6
Oriental fountain grass (*Pennisetum orientale*)	7-9, 9-7
Indian grass (*Sorghastrum nutans*)*	5-8, 8-5
Feather grass (*Stipa capillata*)	7-10, 10-7
Japanese themeda (*Themeda triandra japonica*)*	6-9, 9-6

COLORFUL ORNAMENTAL GRASSES

Many are the colors of the grasses, not just green. In addition to a subtle range of green hues, there are many variegated patterns and entirely different foliage colors from which to select. Try using ornamental grasses with colorful foliage as stand-alone specimens, as a complement or contrast with other landscape plants, or to bring added color to an area that may be just too green. Norm Hooven of Limerock Ornamental Grasses in Port Matilda, Pennsylvania, who provided this list, notes that no true red grasses are perennial in the New York and Mid-Atlantic region. The ones listed here have varying degrees of red on the leaf blades, enough to give them a red appearance but not strongly so.

White Variegated

Bulbous oat grass (*Arrhenatherum elatius bulbosum* 'Variegatum')	5-8, 8-5
Variegated giant reed (*Arundo donax variegata*)	6-11, 12-1
Overdam feather reed grass (*Calamagrostis acutiflora* 'Overdam')	6-9, 9-6
Frosted Curls New England hair sedge (*Carex comans* 'Frosted Curls')	7-9, 9-7
Variegated Japanese sedge (*Carex morrowii* 'Ice Dance,' 'Silver Sceptre')	5-9, 9-5
Variegated Japanese sedge (*Carex morrowii variegata*)	5-9, 9-5
Ice Fountain palm sedge (*Carex muskingumensis* 'Ice Fountain')	3-8, 8-1
Creeping variegated broad-leaved sedge (*Carex siderosticha variegata*)	6-9, 9-6
White variegated Japanese forest grass (*Hakonechloa macra albo-striata*)	5-9, 9-5
Variegated velvet grass (*Holcus mollis* 'Albovariegatus')	5-9, 9-5
Variegated Japanese silver grass (*Miscanthus sinensis* 'Cabaret,' 'Cosmopolitan,' 'Dixieland,' 'Rigoletto,' 'Silberpfeil,' 'Variegatus')	4-9, 9-1
Ribbon grass (*Phalaris arundinacea picta*)	4-9, 9-3
Candy Stripe common reed grass (*Phragmites australis* 'Candy Stripe')	4-9, 9-1

Yellow

Golden sedge (*Carex elata* 'Bowles Golden')	5-9, 9-5
Knightshaye golden sedge (*Carex elata* 'Knightshaye')	5-9, 9-6
Golden millet (*Milium effusum aureum*)	6-9, 9-6

Yellow Variegated

Yellow foxtail (*Alopecurus pratensis aureus*)	5-8, 8-5
Gold fountain sedge (*Carex dolichostachya* 'Gold Fountain')	7-9, 9-7
Evergold variegated Japanese sedge (*Carex hachijoensis* 'Evergold')	6-9, 9-6
Gold Band variegated Japanese sedge (*Carex morrowii* 'Gold Band')	5-9, 9-5
Variegated palm sedge (*Carex muskingumensis*)	3-8, 8-1
Island Brocade broad-leaved sedge (*Carex siderosticha* 'Island Brocade')	6-9, 9-6
Variegated reed manna grass (*Glyceria maxima variegata*)	5-9, 9-2
Yellow variegated Japanese forest grass (*Hakonechloa macra* 'Aureola')	5-9, 9-5
Eulalia or Japanese silver grass (*Miscanthus sinensis* 'Goldfeder,' 'Hinjo,' 'Kirk Alexander,' 'Little Nickey,' 'Little Dot,' 'Zebrinus,' 'Zwergzebra')	4-9, 9-1
Porcupine Japanese silver grass (*Miscanthus sinensis strictus*)	4-9, 9-1
Yellow ribbon grass (*Phalaris arundinacea luteo-picta*)	4-9, 9-3
Yellow variegated common reed grass (*Phragmites australis aurea*)	4-9, 9-1
Prairie cord grass (*Spartina pectinata aureomarginata*)	4-7, 7-1

Blue

Magellan wheatgrass (*Agropyron magellanicus*)	5-9, 9-5
Sentinal big bluestem (*Andropogon gerardii* 'Sentinal')	2-7, 7-1
Burton's blue carex (*Carex* 'Burton's Blue')	5-9, 9-5
Blue sedge (*Carex glauca*)	5-9, 9-5
Black blooming sedge (*Carex nigra*)	4-8, 8-1
Large blue fescue (*Festuca amethystina* 'Bronzeglanz,' 'Klose')	4-8, 8-1
Blue fescue (*Festuca glauca* 'Blaufink,' 'Blaufuchs,' 'Elijah Blue,' 'Harz,' 'Sea Urchin')	4-8, 8-1

Gray fescue (*Festuca glauca* 'Blausilber,' 'Solling,' 'Silver Lining')	4-8, 8-1
Blue oat grass (*Helictotrichon sempervirens*)	4-9, 9-1
Sapphire Blue oat grass (*Helictotrichon sempervirens* 'Saphiresprudel')	4-9, 9-1
Large blue hair grass (*Koeleria glauca*)	6-9, 9-6
European dune grass (*Leymus arenarius*)	4-9, 9-1
Blue Dune European dune grass (*Leymus arenarius* 'Blue Dune')	4-9, 9-1
Switch grass (*Panicum virgatum* 'Cloud Nine,' 'Dallas Blue,' 'Heavy Metal,' 'Prairie Sky')	5-9, 9-4
The Blue little bluestem (*Schizachryium scoparium* 'The Blue')	5-9, 9-5

Copper

Leather-leaf sedge (*Carex buchananii*)	6-9, 9-6
Orange-colored sedge (*Carex flagellifera*)	7-9, 9-7
Brown sedge (*Carex petriei*)	7-9, 9-7

Black

Black mondo grass (*Ophiopogon planiscapus niger*)	6-10, 10-6

Red/Purple

Red Baron Japanese blood grass (*Imperata cylindrica* 'Red Baron')	4-9, 9-1
Switch grass (*Panicum virgatum* 'Hanse Herms,' 'Rotstrahlbusch,' 'Rehbraun,' 'Shenandoah')	5-9, 9-4

EVERGREEN ORNAMENTAL GRASSES

Perhaps surprisingly, some ornamental grasses are evergreen rather than deciduous. Among them are several species and cultivars of sedge. A few of those are included in this list, as are several blue fescues.

Leather-leaf sedge (*Carex buchananii*)	6-9, 9-6
New England hair sedge (*Carex comans*)	6-9, 9-6
Kaga Nishiki sedge (*Carex dolichostachya* 'Kaga Nishiki')	6-9, 9-6
Ice Dance sedge (*Carex morrowii* 'Ice Dance')	6-9, 9-6
Drooping sedge (*Carex pendula*)	6-9, 9-6
Pampas grass (*Cortaderia selloana* and cvs.)	7-10, 10-7
Tufted hair grass (*Deschampsia cespitosa* and cvs.)	5-9, 9-4
Large blue fescue (*Festuca amethystina*)	4-8, 8-1
Blue fescue (*Festuca glauca*)	4-8, 8-1
Maire's fescue (*Festuca mairei*)	5-10, 10-1
Compact blue oat grass (*Helictotrichon sempervirens* 'Saphirsprudel')	4-9, 9-1
Snowy woodrush (*Luzula nivea*)	4-9, 9-1
Formosan miscanthus (*Miscanthus sinensis transmorrisonensis*)	4-9, 9-1
Black mondo grass (*Ophiopogon planiscapus* 'Ebkinzam')	6-10, 10-6
Autumn moor grass (*Sesleria autumnalis*)	5-8, 8-5

FERNS

Mention ferns and certain images usually appear: a woodland, a cool quiet retreat, or a place where sunlight may be limited, but where many shades of green, and textures of leaves, create a setting that is very unique. Of course the younger gardeners in the family may have a different image, one where snakes, spiders, bugs, and dinosaurs are slithering, creeping, and stomping about.

Ferns, with their graceful fronds, can serve as magnificent specimens to create garden focal points, or as backgrounds to enhance the appearance of flowering annuals and perennials. Their diversity—from low-growing ground covers to tall feathery hedges—lets you design them into many landscape types and situations. Though they lack flowers and the palette of color that most other landscape plant groups offer, fern lovers are quick to point out that this often underused group of plants does provide color choices. You can select from soft pale greens to glossy dark greens, and can find a fair amount of silver, gold, and burgundy coming from new fronds, stems, variegation patterns, or fall color.

If you like to use native plants in your landscape you'll find many to select from within the ferns. Try the beautiful fan-shaped maidenhair fern, the tall ostrich fern, the cinnamon fern whose fronds are dotted with loads of brown spores, or the Christmas fern with rich green evergreen fronds. Mix these and introduced species of ferns with bulbs and shade-loving perennials such as astilbe, columbine, and hostas, or with woodland wildflowers such as violets and trilliums.

Tips for Selecting and Succeeding with Ferns
- Select the right fern for the right location. Most ferns prefer to grow in conditions similar to the woods or forests that are their native habitats. In general, use them in shady areas where the soil is rich and moist and has lots of organic matter (decaying leaves from overhead trees, compost you've added, or mulch).
- Most ferns prefer an acid soil, though some prefer or will tolerate moderate alkalinity.
- Ferns need good soil moisture and good soil drainage. In the woods, many grow on or near rocks that seem to preserve moisture and keep an area cooler in the summer.
- Siting ferns near bodies of water (a small constructed pond, natural swamp, bog, or stream) can help keep the air humid and reduce dehydration of the fronds.
- Established ferns can tolerate periodic dry spells, but don't locate them where drought is the norm.
- While evergreen ferns are the most tolerant of low light levels, most ferns grow best in open, light, or dappled but not deep shade.
- Allow falling tree leaves, decomposing mulch, or incorporated compost to supply nutrients to your ferns. If supplemental fertilizer is needed, use a slow-release commercial product, or preferably just add more organic matter (fish emulsion, rotted manure).
- If ferns are in a windy area, provide some form of windbreak or screen to prevent dehydration and breakage of tall or brittle fronds.
- Avoid cultivating or digging around the roots of ferns. Ferns grow from horizontal stems, called rhizomes, that can easily be damaged.
- If properly sited and planted, ferns have few pest problems. Keep away debris that might harbor pests such as slugs and snails.

FERNS FOR BEGINNERS

People often think that unless dense, moist woods surround their homes, they can't grow ferns. Ferns, however, are a widely varied group of plants, being found from the Arctic to the tropics, from swamps to deserts. If you've never tried them before, observe which ferns are growing naturally in your area or in neighboring gardens and consider incorporating some of those in your landscape, or choose something from this list. "Ferns are a satisfying endeavor," says Kathleen Winer of the Merrifield Garden Center in Fairfax, Virginia, who helped compile this list. "Rewarding success and ease of achievement are obtainable with these beginner's ferns," she notes.

Fern expert Nancy Swell of Richmond, Virginia, suggests adding a few sandstone or granite rocks for those that like acid soils (such as deer, holly, cinnamon, royal, Christmas, New York), and adding limestone or even cement rubble for those that prefer alkalinity (such as maidenhair, bladder, broad buckler, interrupted), to create a unique microclimate where ferns will flourish.

Maidenhair fern (*Adiantum pedatum*)	3-8, 8-1
Lady fern (*Athyrium filix-femina* 'Vernoniae Cristatum')	5-9, 9-1
Deer fern (*Blechnum spicant*)	5-8, 8-4
Japanese holly fern (*Cyrtomium falcatum*)	6-10, 10-6
Bladder ferns (*Cystopteris* spp.)	4-8, 8-1
Toothed wood fern (*Dryopteris carthusiana*)	6-8, 8-6
Broad buckler fern (*Dryopteris dilatata*)	5-8, 8-5
Autumn fern (*Dryopteris erythrosora*)	6-9, 9-6
Spiny wood fern (*Dryopteris expansa*)	4-8, 8-1
Male fern (*Dryopteris filix-mas*)	4-8, 8-1
Goldie's fern (*Dryopteris goldieana*)	6-8, 8-6
Leatherwood fern (*Dryopteris marginalis*)	3-8, 8-1
Ostrich fern (*Matteuccia struthiopteris*)	3-8, 8-1
Cinnamon fern (*Osmunda cinnamomea*)	4-8, 8-1
Interrupted fern (*Osmunda claytoniana*)	4-8, 8-1
Royal fern (*Osmunda regalis*)	4-9, 9-1
Christmas fern (*Polystichum acrostichoides*)	3-8, 8-1
Soft shield fern (*Polystichum setiferum*)	6-9, 9-6
New York fern (*Thelypteris noveboracensis*)	2-8, 8-1

TALL FERNS

For a tropical look in a New York or Mid-Atlantic garden, try some of the tall ferns. Growing thirty inches and taller, these few quickly conceal the raw appearance of a new garden. Their vertical fronds lift the eye, while forming a soft backdrop to lower-growing hostas, impatiens, or other colorful plants. Use them in shady areas as you might use tall ornamental grasses in sunny areas.

ROYAL
FERN

Log fern (*Dryopteris celsa*)	6-8, 8-6
Goldie's fern (*Dryopteris goldieana*)	6-8, 8-6
Ostrich fern (*Matteuccia struthiopteris*)	3-8, 8-1
Cinnamon fern (*Osmunda cinnamomea*)	4-8, 8-1
Interrupted fern (*Osmunda claytoniana*)	4-8, 8-1
Royal fern (*Osmunda regalis*)	4-9, 9-1
Marsh fern (*Thelypteris palustris*)	5-8, 8-3

FERNS THAT TOLERATE SOGGY SITES

The classic fern habitat is a soil that is moist and rich in decaying organic matter like leaf mold, which explains why the native habitat of so many ferns is the woods. Fortunately, a few species of ferns will also grow in outright wet or soggy sites. Ferns that tolerate wet feet are excellent for low lots, sites that get soggy after heavy rains, or that are at the edge of a lake or stream where the waterline may occasionally reach them. For some of these water lovers, drought is the kiss of death, at least for the current year's fronds.

Walking fern (*Asplenium rhizophyllum*)	5-9, 9-8
Lady fern (*Athyrium filix-femina*)	4-9, 9-1
Japanese painted fern (*Athyrium niponicum* 'Pictum')	5-8, 8-2
Silvery glade fern (*Athyrium thelypterioides*)	4-8, 8-1
Toothed wood fern (*Dryopteris carthusiana*)	6-8, 8-6
Broad swamp fern (*Dryopteris clintoniana*)	5-8, 8-4
Climbing fern (*Lygodium palmatum*)	7-10, 10-7
Ostrich fern (*Matteuccia struthiopteris*)	3-8, 8-1
Sensitive fern (*Onoclea sensibilis*)	4-9, 9-1
Interrupted fern (*Osmunda claytonia*)	4-8, 8-1
Royal fern (*Osmunda regalis*)	4-9, 9-1
New York fern (*Thelypteris noveboracensis*)	2-8, 8-1
Marsh fern (*Thelypteris palustris*)	5-8, 8-3
Chain fern (*Woodwardia areolata*)	2-8, 8-1
Virginia chain fern (*Woodwardia virginica*)	6-8, 8-5

 In the catalog of Wild Earth Native Plant Nursery of Freehold, New Jersey, Rich Pillar says that the ostrich fern "may innocently sit for two or three years and then begin to spread by underground rhizomes. Then there is no turning back. Good for those who want to harvest fiddleheads in the spring."

FERNS FOR DRY SITES

There is a fern for almost any location in the garden, including dry ground. This is especially comforting if you have sandy soil that is prone to dry out even if you try incorporating organic matter into the entire planting area in order to retain more moisture. The following ferns stand a good chance of surviving stressful conditions, but try to provide supplemental irrigation until they're established in your garden.

MALE FERN

Maidenhair fern (*Adiantum pedatum*)	3-8, 8-1
Ebony spleenwort (*Asplenium platyneuron*)	3-9, 9-1
Bladder fern (*Cystopteris bulbifera*)	4-8, 8-1
Hay-scented fern (*Dennstaedtia punctilobula*)	4-8, 8-1
Male fern (*Dryopteris filix-mas*)	4-8, 8-1
Fancy fern (*Dryopteris intermedia*)	4-9, 9-1
Leatherwood fern (*Dryopteris marginalis*)	3-8, 8-1
Cinnamon fern (*Osmunda cinnamomea*)	4-8, 8-1
Interrupted fern (*Osmunda claytoniana*)	4-8, 8-1
Royal fern (*Osmunda regalis*)	4-9, 9-1
Southern beech fern (*Phegopteris hexagonoptera*)	3-8, 8-1
Christmas fern (*Polystichum acrostichoides*)	3-8, 8-1
Blunt-lobed woodsia fern (*Woodsia obtusa*)	4-7, 7-1

FERNS FOR DEEP SHADE

Most ferns prefer to grow in the dappled or open shade of tall trees, or on the north side of walls, fences, and buildings. No ferns really thrive in deep shade, but the woodland ferns and those that are evergreen will tolerate the lowest light levels of any ferns. Try these ferns if you have areas with very deep shade, particularly if there is adequate soil moisture.

Walking fern (*Asplenium rhizophyllum*)	5-9, 9-3
Deer fern (*Blechnum spicant*)	5-8, 8-4

Japanese holly fern (*Cyrtomium falcatum*)	6-10, 10-6
Leatherwood fern (*Dryopteris marginalis*)	3-8, 8-1
Oak fern (*Gymnocarpium dryopteris*)	4-8, 8-1
Cinnamon fern (*Osmunda cinnamomea*)	4-8, 8-1
Beech ferns (*Phegopteris* spp.)	4-6, 6-1
Christmas fern (*Polystichum acrostichoides*)	3-8, 8-1
Chain fern (*Woodwardia areolata*)	2-8, 8-1

FERNS THAT TOLERATE SOME SUN

Since most ferns prefer to grow in at least partial shade, a list of ferns for sun may seem a contradiction. If you have no shade but still want to try some ferns, start with these that will be the most sun tolerant. Remember that if you stretch the limits of a fern by locating it in the sun, the soil should have excellent water-holding capacity, and you may have to irrigate frequently to minimize hot summer stress. According to fern expert John Mickel, retired from the New York City Botanical Garden, a fern should be considered sun tolerant if it can withstand the sun in dry or at least average conditions, rather than if supplemented with lots of water.

EBONY
SPLEENWORT

Lady fern (*Athyrium filix-femina*)	4-9, 9-1
Ebony spleenwort (*Asplenium platyneuron*)	3-9, 9-1
Japanese painted fern (*Athyrium niponicum* 'Pictum')	4-9, 9-1
Hay-scented fern (*Dennstaedtia punctilobula*)	4-8, 8-1
Ostrich fern (*Matteuccia struthiopteris*)	3-8, 8-1
Sensitive fern (*Onoclea sensibilis*)	4-9, 9-1
Cinnamon fern (*Osmunda cinnamomea*)	4-8, 8-1
Interrupted fern (*Osmunda claytonia*)	5-8, 8-4
Royal fern (*Osmunda regalis*)	4-9, 9-1
Christmas fern (*Polystichum acrostichoides*)	3-8, 8-1
Chain fern (*Woodwardia areolata*)	2-8, 8-1
Virginia chain fern (*Woodwardia virginica*)	6-8, 8-6

FERNS FOR ALKALINE SOIL

Though most of the garden soils in our region are slightly acid, areas of alkaline soil (pH levels above 7) can be found. Many of the ferns on this list are so adaptable that they will grow in soils with a fairly wide pH range. If you live in a limestone area, use ferns that like alkaline conditions rather than trying to acidify your soil with large amounts of organic matter and sulfur.

Maidenhair fern (*Adiantum pedatum*)	3-8, 8-1
Spleenwort ferns (*Asplenium* spp.)	3-9, 9-1
Walking fern (*Asplenium rhizophyllum*)	5-9, 9-5
Bladder fern (*Cystopteris bulbifera*)	4-8, 8-1
Glade fern (*Diplazium pycnocarpon*)	4-8, 8-1
Broad buckler fern (*Dryopteris dilatata*)	5-8, 8-5
Spiny wood fern (*Dryopteris expansa*)	4-8, 8-1
Leatherwood fern (*Dryopteris marginalis*)	3-8, 8-1
Limestone oak fern (*Gymnocarpium robertianum*)	3-7, 7-1
Ostrich fern (*Matteuccia struthiopteris*)	3-8, 8-1
Interrupted fern (*Osmunda claytoniana*)	5-8, 8-4
Purple cliffbrake (*Pellaea atropurpurea*)	5-9, 9-4
Hart's tongue fern (*Phyllitis scolopendrium*)	5-9, 9-5
Hard shield fern (*Polystichum aculeatum*)	3-6, 6-1
Marsh fern (*Thelypteris palustris*)	5-8, 8-3

FERNS FOR VERY ACID SOIL

If you live in an area where azaleas, rhododendrons, mountain laurel, blueberries, and heath and heather thrive, such as the Pine Barrens in New Jersey, your soil is probably fairly acid, and so the following ferns may be wonderful companions for these plants. An acid soil can be made more alkaline by adding crushed limestone, ground shells from oysters harvested from the Atlantic Ocean and Chesapeake Bay, or pulverized cement rubble.

Ebony spleenwort (*Asplenium platyneuron*)	3-9, 9-1
Deer fern (*Blechnum spicant*)	5-8, 8-4
Holly ferns (*Cyrtomium* spp.)	6-10, 10-6
Hay-scented fern (*Dennstaedtia punctilobula*)	4-8, 8-1
Mountain wood fern (*Dryopteris campyloptera*)	6-8, 8-6
Southern maidenhair fern (*Dryopteris ludoviciana*)	6-8, 8-6
Oak fern (*Gymnocarpium dryopteris*)	4-8, 8-1
Cinnamon fern (*Osmunda cinnamomea*)	4-8, 8-1
Royal fern (*Osmunda regalis*)	4-9, 9-4
Watt beech fern (*Phegopteris connectilis*)	4-6, 6-1
Shield ferns (*Polystichum* spp.)	3-8, 8-1
Christmas fern (*Polystichum acrostichoides*)	3-8, 8-1
New York fern (*Thelypteris noveboracensis*)	2-8, 8-1
Blunt-lobed woodsia fern (*Woodsia obtusa*)	4-7, 7-1
Chain ferns (*Woodwardia* spp.)	6-8, 8-5

EVERGREEN FERNS

Evergreen ferns are definitely more evergreen the farther south one goes, and although they may not be as pristine as they were during the peak growing season, they are nevertheless a welcome sight in the winter. When mixed with other winter delights like Lenten rose, evergreen ferns will keep a woodland garden alive with a quiet midwinter beauty that is one of the pleasures of New York and Mid-Atlantic gardening. Evergreen ferns are also a great backdrop for spring-flowering bulbs.

This list is from Nancy Swell of Swell Azaleas in Richmond, Virginia. Nancy, a member of the American Fern Society, notes that most *Polystichum* species are evergreen, and any that are available are worth trying.

Ebony spleenwort (*Asplenium platyneuron*)	3-9, 9-1
Maidenhair spleenwort (*Asplenium trichomanes*)	5-8, 8-3
Deer fern (*Blechnum spicant*)	5-8, 8-4
Japanese holly fern (*Cyrtomium falcatum*)	6-10, 10-6
Crested wood fern (*Dryopteris cristata*)	3-7, 7-3
Autumn fern (*Dryopteris erythrosora*)	6-9, 9-6
Fancy fern (*Dryopteris intermedia*)	4-9, 9-1
Leatherwood fern (*Dryopteris marginalis*)	2-8, 8-1
Christmas fern (*Polystichum acrostichoides*)	3-8, 8-1
Braun's holly fern (*Polystichum braunii*)	3-6, 8-1
Makino's holly fern (*Polystichum makinoi*)	3-8, 8-1
Japanese tassel fern (*Polystichum polyblepharum*)	5-8, 8-3
Tagawa's holly fern (*Polystichum tagawanum*)	4-8, 8-4

"Autumn fern is my favorite of all the evergreen ferns. The young foliage is coppery colored before changing to a deep green. It is the most evergreen fern I know. I have picked it in March for flower arrangements."

Nancy Swell of Swell Azaleas in Richmond, Virginia, is a member of the American Fern Society, the British Pteridological Society, and the Hardy Fern Foundation.

COLORFUL FERNS

Ferns with colorful foliage contrast beautifully with the deeper green of mondo grass or other ferns. Japanese painted fern combines silver, green, and burgundy to give a very striking appearance. Royal and autumn ferns rise from the ground each spring with a beautiful reddish cast that turns to green as the leaves mature. The fronds of Christmas fern and Braun's holly fern unfurl with a beautiful silvery flush that matures to a rich, deep green. Cinnamon and royal ferns change from green to yellow in the fall.

Japanese painted fern (*Athyrium niponicum* 'Pictum')	5-8, 8-2
Autumn fern (*Dryopteris erythrosora*)	6-9, 9-6
Cinnamon fern (*Osmunda cinnamomea*)	4-8, 8-1
Royal fern (*Osmunda regalis*)	4-9, 9-1
Braun's holly fern (*Polystichum braunii*)	3-6, 8-1

FERNS FOR ROCK WALLS

If you're about to build a rock wall, leave a few pockets between the rocks for ferns and trailing plants such as woodland phlox for shade or sedum for sun. The best time to plant is when you're actually building the wall; you can tuck the roots in to be sure they're in good contact with the soil behind the wall. For an existing wall, use a butter knife to dig out a spot between rocks and to maneuver the soil.

For Moist Rock Walls

Ebony spleenwort (*Asplenium platyneuron*)	3-9, 9-1
Walking fern (*Asplenium rhizophyllum*)	5-9, 9-5
Maidenhair spleenwort (*Asplenium trichomanes*)	4-8, 8-1
Hairy lip fern (*Cheilanthes lanosa*)	6-9, 9-6
Bladder fern (*Cystopteris bulbifera*)	4-8, 8-1
Brittle fern (*Cystopteris fragilis*)	4-8, 8-1
Hart's tongue fern (*Phyllitis scolopendrium*)	5-9, 9-5
Blunt-lobed woodsia fern (*Woodsia obtusa*)	4-7, 7-1

For Dry Rock Walls

Purple cliffbrake (*Pellaea atropurpurea*)	5-9, 9-4

FERNS FOR GROUND COVER

A few ferns are small, like the rainbow moss fern, which is 3 to 5 inches tall. Others send out underground stems or rhizomes that produce expanding clumps of fronds around the original plant. You can use rhizomatous ferns, which aren't good for confined spaces, as ground covers that will spread fairly quickly to provide easy maintenance. The native walking fern is so named because the leaf tips actually root when they touch the soil, producing new plants. Ground-cover ferns are nice garden plants because there are always new plants to dig and give away to friends.

Walking fern (*Asplenium rhizophyllum*)	5-9, 9-5
Lady fern (*Athyrium filix-femina*)	4-9, 9-1
Bladder fern (*Cystopteris bulbifera*)	4-8, 8-1
Hay-scented fern (*Dennstaedtia punctilobula*)	4-8, 8-1
Sensitive fern (*Onoclea sensibilis*)	4-9, 9-1
New York fern (*Thelypteris noveboracensis*)	2-8, 8-1
Marsh fern (*Thelypteris palustris*)	5-8, 8-3
Virginia chain fern (*Woodwardia virginica*)	6-8, 8-5

VIRGINIA
CHAIN FERN

BULBS

Bulbs, those odd-shaped structures with a brown covering, hold surprises in store for those who aren't familiar with them. Not only can you select bulbs that will flower during almost the entire year, especially in the warmer parts of the New York and Mid-Atlantic region, but many of those flowers have fragrances that saturate the air. Real show-stoppers are bulbs that combine wonderful flowers with unusually colored leaves, like the hardy cyclamen (*Cyclamen hederifolium*), which have heart-shaped, light- and dark-green patterned leaves. The leaves of the Greigii tulips (*Tulipa greigii*) are mottled or striped with purples and browns.

The term "bulb" is used loosely here to include not only the "true bulbs"—those with large fleshy leaves surrounding a bud and vertical stem piece (like a daffodil or onion)—but also other types of underground storage stems and roots. These bulb relatives are corms (crocus and gladiolus), tubers (anemone and tuberous begonias), tuberous roots (dahlias), and rhizomes (iris and lily-of-the-valley).

One of the best landscape features of bulbs is their mixability. They're great combined with ground covers, perennials, wildflowers, annuals, and other bulbs, and under trees and shrubs. Most of the good mail-order bulb catalogs have lists of companion plants—those with which to mix and match your bulbs. Bulbs are also great for naturalizing or giving color to a less highly maintained, more natural-looking area.

Tips for Selecting and Succeeding with Bulbs

- Select the right bulb for the right location. Most bulbs prefer full sun. A few will tolerate shade.
- Buy the biggest bulbs you can afford to get the biggest, earliest flowers. Smaller-sized bulbs are less expensive and are great for naturalizing but are slower to produce a dramatic effect.
- Buy only bulbs that are solid and that show no signs of mold, mildew, or rot diseases.
- If you buy species bulbs, be sure they are nursery-grown, not collected from the wild.
- Plant bulbs as soon as possible after buying them, or store them in a cool, dry, well-ventilated area.
- Prepare the beds, unless planting a very large area. Follow instructions about planting depth—usually three to four times the height of the bulb. Deep planting helps to naturalize and perennialize bulbs, especially tulips.
- Plant bulbs in random patterns with varied spacing. Don't plant them in equally spaced straight lines so they look like soldiers marching to your front door. Make them look natural, not formal.
- Keep your bulbs growing by providing fertilizer (with more nitrogen than old recommendations used to call for). Let the leaves stay attached until they die back; this ensures that sugars made by the leaves will be stored in the bulbs. Hide fading daffodil leaves by interplanting with perennials such as hostas or daylilies that emerge as the daffodil leaves die back.
- Some bulbs are yummy to animals (crocus, tulips), while some are poisonous or seldom consumed (daffodils, hyacinths). For those that might be munched, plant them in wire cages or in pockets of finely crushed gravel, or dip them in chemical repellants. Planting among woody shrub ground covers like cotoneasters and junipers will also help foil rodents.
- Watch your timing. In the New York and Mid-Atlantic region, plant spring-flowering bulbs in the fall to be sure they have time to establish roots that can absorb the water they'll need for their spring flowers and leaves to develop.

SPRING-FLOWERING BULBS

Daffodils, tulips, and hyacinths come to mind most often when people think about spring-flowering bulbs. But to put added interest in your garden, and to fill more little niches, microclimates, or design needs, consider some of the other bulbs in this list. These bulbs start flowering when the late winter or early spring scillas, spring colchicum, and Kaufmanniana tulips leave off, and they flower until the late spring or early summer lilies start. Paul Blom of Blom's Bulbs in West Chester, Pennsylvania, helped organize this list in the order of bloom period (approximately March to May).

FRITILLARY

Star-of-Bethlehem (*Ornithogalum nutans*)	5-10, 12-7
Fosteriana tulips (*Tulipa* hybs. and cvs.)	3-8, 8-1
Hyacinths (*Hyacinthus orientalis*)	5-9, 9-1
Starflower (*Ipheion uniflorum*)	6-9, 9-6
Greek windflower (*Anemone blanda*)	4-8, 8-1
Greigii tulips (*Tulipa greigii*)	3-9, 9-1
Snowflake (*Leucojum vernum*)	4-8, 8-1
Grape hyacinth (*Muscari* spp.)	3-8, 8-1
Single early tulips (*Tulipa* hybs. and cvs.)	3-9, 9-1
Double early tulips (*Tulipa* hybs. and cvs.)	3-9, 9-1
Trumpet, tazetta, and split corona daffodils (*Narcissus* spp., hybs., and cvs.)	3-9, 9-1
Darwin hybrid tulips (*Tulipa* hybs. and cvs.)	3-9, 9-1
Triumph tulips (*Tulipa* hybs. and cvs.)	3-9, 9-1
Crown imperial fritillary (*Fritillaria imperialis*)	5-9, 9-4
Silver bells (*Corydalis solida*)	5-7, 7-3
Dwarf fritillary (*Fritillaria* spp.)	3-8, 8-1
Oxalis (*Oxalis* spp.)	7-9, 9-7
Jonquilla and poeticus daffodils (*Narcissus* spp., hybs., and cvs.)	3-9, 9-1
Fringed, parrot, and late tulips (*Tulipa* hybs. and cvs.)	3-9, 9-1
Spanish bluebells (*Hyacinthoides hispanica*)	5-8, 8-4
Ornamental onion (*Allium* spp.)	5-8, 8-4
Quamash or wild hyacinth (*Camassia cusickii*)	3-11, 12-1
Triteleia (*Triteleia* spp.)	4-9, 9-1
Lilies (*Lilium* spp.)	4-7, 7-1

DAFFODILS

According to Brent and Becky Heath, third-generation bulb producers in Gloucester, Virginia, "Daffodils are the most cost-effective, pest-free perennial plants available." Here are the Heaths' favorites. In their very educational catalog, you will find not only detailed descriptions of these and several hundred other daffodil species and cultivars, but also lists of other bulbs, perennials, annuals, and flowering shrubs that are good companion plants. If you ever have a chance to visit their farm, especially in the spring, your eyes (and nose) will be treated to an incredible feast.

This list includes information about flower type, color, and bloom period.

Early

Bridal Crown	double; white and saffron
Little Beauty	trumpet; white with yellow cup
Rijnveld's Early Sensation	trumpet; yellow
The Alliance	single; yellow

Early Midseason

Abba	double; white with orange center
Avalanche	multiflowered; white
Tracey	single; white
Jetfire	single; yellow with orange cup

Jumblie   multiflowered; yellow

Midseason
Accent   large cup; white with pink cup
Quail   multiflowered; bronzy yellow
Stint   multiflowered; yellow
Sweetness   multiflowered; golden yellow
Virginia Sunrise   large cup; white with orange cup

Late Midseason
Curlew   multiflowered; yellow to ivory
Fruit Cup   multiflowered; white and yellow
Ice Wings   multiflowered; ivory white
Misty Glen   large cup; white
Sir Winston Churchill   double; white with orange specks
Tahiti   double; yellow with red segments

Late
Sun Disc   multiflowered; yellow
Camelot   large cup; yellow
Fragrant Rose   large cup; white with pink cup; fragrant
Intrigue   multiflowered; yellow with white cup

"Rodents don't like daffodil bulbs because they are poisonous to them. If you have trouble with voles eating your other bulbs, dump a handful of sharp gravel into the planting hole. Dig the hole big enough so an inch or so of gravel completely surrounds the bulb on the bottom, sides, and tops. Voles don't seem to like the rocks and will look elsewhere for a meal."

Brent and Becky Heath are owners of Brent and Becky's Bulbs (www.brentandbeckysbulbs.com) in Gloucester, Virginia, and authors of *Daffodils for American Gardens*.

TULIPS

Tulips are a very inexpensive source of garden color coming in almost every color except true blue. Several of the tulips in this list have leaves that are striped, mottled, or a color other than green. Many of these tulips work well not only in the garden but also in containers and window boxes in combinations with daffodils, hyacinths, and other bulbs. Also, many tulips are good for forcing. This list is from Brent and Becky Heath, of Brent and Becky's Bulbs in Gloucester, Virginia, who like to think of tulips as the colorful peacocks and parrots of the bulb world.

Early
Ancilla   single; rose red and pink with white center
Juan   single; orange with yellow base
Mickey Mouse   single; dark yellow with red flames
Monsella   double; yellow with red flames

Midseason
Daydream   single; yellow to apricot
Burgundy Lace   single; wine red, fringed
Prinses Irene   single; orange with purple flames
Toronto   single; red with yellow heart

TULIP

| Tulipa bakeri 'Lilac Wonder' | single; lilac pink, yellow heart |
| White Triumphator | single; ivory |

Late

Blushing Lady	single; orange and yellow with rose flames
Carmine Parrot	single; carmine and cherry red with blue heart
Greenland	single; dusky rose with green flames
Lilac Perfection	double; lilac with white heart

SUMMER-FLOWERING BULBS

The array of flowers available to us during the summer is staggering. Don't limit yourself to annuals and perennials for super displays, but find spots for some of these wonderful summer-flowering bulbs as well. These are listed in approximate order of bloom, starting in about May in the warmest part of our region, and continuing into August and September. Bulbs that are not hardy enough for your zone can be treated as annuals, or try a warm south- or west-facing protected niche. Mulch them well and they may overwinter.

Mariposa lily (*Calochortus venustus*)	6-10, 10-1
Greek windflower (*Anemone blanda*)	5-8, 8-1
Golden stars (*Bloomeria crocea*)	5-9, 9-1
Lily-of-the-valley (*Convallaria majalis*)	5-10, 10-1
Asiatic lily (*Lilium* spp.)	4-8, 8-1
Triplet lily (*Triteleia laxa*)	5-9, 9-1
Hardy gloxinia (*Incarvillea delaveyi*)	6-10, 10-1
Poppy anemone (*Anemone coronaria*)	7-10, 10-1
Chinese ground orchid (*Bletilla striata*)	7-10, 10-1
Lilies (*Lilium* spp.)	3-8, 8-1
Harlequin flower (*Sparaxis tricolor*)	7-10, 10-1
Peruvian lily (*Alstroemeria aurantiaca*)	6-10, 10-1
Canna (*Canna hybrida*)	7-10, 10-1
Shamrock (*Oxalis* spp.)	7-10, 10-1
Blazing star (*Liatris spicata*)	3-10, 10-1
Oriental lily (*Lilium* hybs.)	4-8, 8-1
Crinum lily (*Crinum* spp.)	7-10, 10-1
Montbretia (*Crocosmia* x *crocosmiiflora*)	6-10, 10-1
Pineapple lily (*Eucomis comosa*)	7-10, 10-1
Summer hyacinth (*Galtonia candicans*)	5-10, 10-1
Rain lily (*Zephyranthes* spp.)	7-10, 10-1
Kaffir lily (*Schizostylis coccinea*)	5-10, 10-1

In the catalog of K. Van Bourgondien, a bulb company in Babylon, New York, that goes back more than 200 years, Debbie Van Bourgondien (known to many as "The Bulb Lady") says, "Oriental lilies are one of the most beautiful of all lilies and their fragrance permeates the garden air. These are the lilies that florists favor for summer bouquets and bridal centerpieces. Blooming later in the season than most other lilies, these exotic beauties are truly spectacular in color and flower size."

TENDER BULBS TO PROTECT IN WINTER

Some summer-flowering bulbs aren't hardy but are worth planting (especially in movable containers) and digging up in the winter. This list of bulbs is organized by bloom period, from early to late summer.

Siam tulip (*Curcuma alismatifolia*)
Glory lily (*Gloriosa superba*)
Upright elephant's ears (*Alocasia* spp.)
Caladiums or angel wings (*Caladium hortulanum*)
Elephant's ears (*Colocasia esculenta*)
Dahlias (*Dahlia hybrida*)
Gladiolus (*Gladiolus* spp.)
Blood lily (*Scadoxus multiflorus*)
Mexican shellflower (*Tigridia pavonia*)
Tritonia (*Tritonia crocata*)
Ginger lily (*Hedychium* spp.)
Amazon lily (*Eucharis amazonica*)
Naked lady (*Amaryllis belladonna*)
Tuberose (*Polianthes tuberosa*)
Calla lilies (*Zantedeschia* spp.)

DAHLIA

BULBS FOR FALL AND WINTER FLOWERS

Fewer bulbs are available for flowering in fall and winter than during the spring and summer. Those that are, however, provide us with flowers during a time of year when we often think we can only rely on fall-flowering perennials and the fall colors of deciduous trees, shrubs, and vines. The bulbs listed here (in order of bloom period) pick up in September when the summer-flowering bulbs are finished, and they continue into early spring with the first of the tulips.

Colchicum (*Colchicum* spp.)	4-9, 9-1
Crocus (*Crocus* spp.)	3-8, 8-1
Hardy cyclamen (*Cyclamen* spp.)	5-9, 9-1
Autumn daffodil (*Sternbergia lutea*)	7-9, 9-6
Autumn zephyr lily (*Zephyranthes candida*)	7-10, 10-1
Surprise lily (*Lycoris squamigera*)	6-11, 12-6
Winter aconite (*Eranthis hyemalis*)	4-9, 9-1
Snowdrop (*Galanthus nivalis*)	3-9, 9-1
Striped squill (*Puschkinia scilloides*)	3-9, 9-1
Scilla and bluebells (*Scilla* spp.)	5-8, 8-4
Dwarf iris (*Iris reticulata*)	5-8, 8-1
Kaufmanniana tulips (*Tulipa kaufmanniana*)	3-9, 9-1
Spring colchicum (*Bulbocodium vernum*)	3-9, 9-1
Chionodoxa or glory of the snow (*Chionodoxa luciliae*)	3-9, 9-1

SNOWDROP

BULBS FOR SHADE

Some bulbs are tolerant of light to medium shade. A few, like lily-of-the-valley and the native fawn and trout lilies, actually prefer to be grown in the shade, as do some of the tender summer bulbs like caladiums and elephant's ears. Plants marked with an asterisk (*) in this list will tolerate the most shade.

Greek windflower (*Anemone blanda*)	4-8, 8-1
St. Bernard's lily (*Anthericum liliago*)	7-9, 9-7
Hardy begonia (*Begonia evansiana*)	6-9, 9-6
Blackberry lily (*Belamcanda chinensis*)	5-9, 9-3
Chinese ground orchids (*Bletilla striata*)	5-8, 8-2

Golden stars (*Bloomeria crocea*)	5-9, 9-1
Spring meadow saffron (*Bulbocodium vernum*)	3-9, 9-1
Glory of the snow (*Chionodoxa* spp.)	3-9, 9-1
Colchicum (*Colchicum* spp.)	4-9, 9-1
Lily-of-the-valley (*Convallaria majalis*)*	4-9, 9-1
Montbretia (*Crocosmia* x *crocosmiiflora*)	6-9, 9-3
Crocus (*Crocus* spp.)	3-8, 8-1
Winter aconite (*Eranthis* spp.)*	4-9, 9-1
Fawn and trout lilies (*Erythronium* spp.)*	3-9, 9-1
Fritillary (*Fritillaria* spp.)	5-9, 9-4
Common snowdrop (*Galanthus nivalis*)*	3-9, 9-1
Spanish bluebells (*Hyacinthoides hispanica*)	4-9, 9-1
Spring starflower (*Ipheion uniflorum*)	6-9, 9-6
Netted iris (*Iris reticulata*)	5-8, 8-4
Snowflakes (*Leucojum* spp.)	4-8, 8-1
Blazing star (*Liatris spicata*)	4-9, 9-1
Lilies (*Lilium* spp.)	4-7, 7-1
Hardy amaryllis (*Lycoris squamigera*)	6-10, 10-1
Grape hyacinth (*Muscari* spp.)	3-8, 8-1
Daffodils (*Narcissus* cvs.)	3-8, 8-1
Nodding star-of-Bethlehem (*Ornithogalum nutans*)	6-10, 10-1
Oxalis (*Oxalis* spp.)*	6-10, 10-1
St. Bruno's lily (*Paradisea liliastrum*)	7-9, 9-7
Striped squill (*Puschkinia scilloides*)	3-9, 9-1
Scilla and bluebells (*Scilla* spp.)*	5-8, 8-3
Autumn daffodil (*Sternbergia lutea*)	7-9, 9-6

BULBS FOR NATURALIZING

If you have a lawn area where you'd like to add a bit of color (from other than dandelions), many bulbs, particularly those blooming March through May, can be scattered, planted, and allowed to propagate and spread naturally. To succeed at naturalizing bulbs in a lawn, you can't mow the grass until after the bulb foliage dies back, allowing the leaves to manufacture and store food in the bulb for flowering the following year.

DAFFODIL

Anemone (*Anemone* spp.)	4-8, 8-1
Golden stars (*Bloomeria crocea*)	5-9, 9-1
Glory of the snow (*Chionodoxa* spp.)	3-9, 9-1
Colchicum (*Colchicum* spp.)	4-9, 9-1
Montbretia (*Crocosmia* x *crocosmiiflora*)	6-9, 9-6
Crocus (*Crocus* spp.)	3-8, 8-1
Winter aconite (*Eranthis hyemalis*)	4-9, 9-1
Common snowdrop (*Galanthus nivalis*)	3-9, 9-1
Spanish bluebells (*Hyacinthoides hispanica*)	4-9, 9-1
Starflower (*Ipheion uniflorum*)	6-9, 9-6
Snowflakes (*Leucojum* spp.)	4-8, 8-1
Blazing star (*Liatris spicata*)	4-9, 9-1
Hardy amaryllis (*Lycoris squamigera*)	6-11, 12-6
Grape hyacinth (*Muscari* spp.)	3-8, 8-1
Daffodils (*Narcissus* spp. and cvs.)	3-8, 8-1
Star-of-Bethlehem (*Ornithogalum* spp.)	6-10, 10-1
Oxalis (*Oxalis* spp.)	6-10, 10-1
Striped squill (*Puschkinia scilloides*)	3-9, 9-1
Scilla (*Scilla* spp.)	5-8, 8-3
Autumn daffodil (*Sternbergia lutea*)	7-9, 9-6

In *The Exuberant Garden and the Controlling Hand*, a wonderful book full of plant lists and design information, landscape architect William Frederick of Hockessin, Delaware, says: "Bulbs for naturalizing do best where grass roots are less vigorous and mat-like (fescues are ideal) and where they receive an annual feeding."

BULBS THAT TOLERATE MOIST CONDITIONS

Few bulbs will grow in areas with really dry soils, or in boggy or swampy areas. If the large underground fleshy storage leaves of a bulb sit in poorly drained soil, they will quickly rot. However, if you have an area that puddles temporarily after a rain, that has a bit more clay in it, or that is moister than surrounding areas because of shade, the following bulbs will tolerate a moister soil than most. In addition, many of the tender summer bulbs will tolerate moister areas, including caladiums, calla lilies, canna lilies, elephant's ears, and rain lilies.

Wood anemone (*Anemone* spp.)	4-8, 8-1
Crinum lily (*Crinum* spp.)	7-11, 12-6
Winter aconite (*Eranthis hyemalis*)	4-9, 9-1
Fawn and trout lilies (*Erythronium* spp.)	3-9, 9-1
Snowdrops (*Galanthus* spp.)	3-9, 9-1
Snowflakes (*Leucojum* spp.)	4-9, 9-1
Oriental lilies (*Lilium* hybs.)	6-9, 9-6

BULBS FOR FRAGRANCE

An easy way to add fragrance to your garden year in and year out is to select bulbs that bloom at different seasons. Plant them near areas that you frequent, and then stand back for some of the easiest fragrance treats you could ever imagine. Some, like lily-of-the-valley, make great cut flowers, and many, like hyacinths and the miniature daffodils, are wonderful to pot in fall, chill in the refrigerator or cold frame, and then force into early bloom and fragrance indoors. Daffodil and tulip cultivars are grouped separately in this list because so many are available.

Acidantheras (*Acidanthera bicolor*)	7-10, 10-7
Lily-of-the-valley (*Convallaria majalis*)	5-10, 10-1
Crinum lily (*Crinum* spp.)	7-10, 10-6
Winter aconite (*Eranthis* spp.)	4-9, 9-1
Pineapple lily (*Eucomis comosa*)	7-10, 10-4
Snowdrop (*Galanthus nivalis*)	3-8, 8-1
Summer hyacinth (*Galtonia candicans*)	5-10, 10-4
Hyacinth (*Hyacinthus orientalis*)	4-8, 8-1
Netted iris (*Iris reticulata*)	5-10, 10-1
Oriental lilies (*Lilium* hybs. and cvs.)	4-8, 8-1
Grape hyacinth (*Muscari* spp.)	4-9, 9-1

Daffodils
Abba
Avalanche
Bell Song
Bridal Crown
Canaliculatus
Canarybird
Carlton
Fragrant Rose
Fruit Cup

Geranium
Golden Dawn
Honolulu
Ice Wings
Kidling
Minnow
New-Baby
Pappy George
Pencrebar
Petrel

Punchline
Sailboat
Sir Winston Churchill
Stratosphere
Sundial
Sweetness
Thalia
Tripartite

Tulips
Angelique
Apricot Beauty
Ballerine

Bellona
Christmas Marvel
Generaal de Wet
Golden Melody

High Society
Hohango Ad Rem
Monte Carlo

"A move is afoot to recoup floral fragrances. Professional and amateur gardeners alike are viewing flowers with an eye to the nose. Unfortunately, fragrance too often has been lost in the modern shuffle as hybridizers and gardeners focus on other important flower characteristics such as color, flower size, flowering times and duration, and disease-resistance. Tulips that are fragrant in the garden often lose their fragrance when cut, so they are often better forced indoors in pots."

Sally Ferguson works for the Netherlands Flower Bulb Information Center in Brooklyn, New York. Their website (www.bulb.com) is an excellent source for bulb information.

ANNUALS

There's no easier, faster, and generally more economical way to add color to your spring, summer, or fall garden than by planting annuals, plants often referred to by the nursery industry as bedding plants. Annuals, as distinguished from other color-providing plants such as perennials and bulbs, are plants that germinate, flower, set seed, and die in one season in a garden. Annuals are what rescue us when we find garden spots where plants have died or where color is lacking. Just plug in a few annuals and the landscape seems complete.

Mention annuals and most people think of commonly planted summer annuals such as petunias and marigolds. These are tender annuals whose seeds require warm soil in order to germinate. We can also transplant tender annuals to our gardens as seedlings or bedding plants during the spring, once we're past the average time when the last frost usually occurs. There are half-hardy or winter annuals that can tolerate from light frost to what is commonly called a killing frost, one that would kill tender annuals. Pansies and snapdragons are examples of half-hardy annuals that, particularly in the warmer areas of the New York and Mid-Atlantic region, can be planted for color in fall and in spring. In some cases they can be planted even during the winter; they may occasionally look frozen but will often recover.

A few annuals have seeds that overwinter in the ground, ready to germinate the following spring. These plants, like cleome (spider lily), often pleasantly surprise people by reseeding in place year after year, behaving more like perennials than annuals. A few biennials (canterbury bells, stock) and some perennials (dahlias, dusty miller, forget-me-not, four o'clocks) are often treated as annuals and are included in some of these lists.

One thing that's very exciting about annuals is the large number of new choices (including new genera, not just new species or cultivars) that have been added over the past few years. Through plant explorations and breeding, this group of landscape plants always has lots of new faces and surprises from which to select each year.

Tips for Selecting and Succeeding with Annuals

- Select the right annual for the right location. Keep tall annuals to the back of a border, or in the center of a bed accessible from all sides, grading down to low-growing annuals around the edge. Combinations of annuals look good if viewed up close, but if your annuals will be seen mainly from a distance, try massing just one type or color.
- Have a purpose for planting annuals in your garden, whether for aesthetics, a quick ground cover, a cut-flower source, or some other use.
- Annuals can be used anywhere. If you have no ground area in which to plant, try containers, window boxes, and hanging baskets.
- Keep the color scheme simple. More than three colors in one spot may look too busy. Warm colors (yellow, orange, red) draw attention and create excitement, while cool colors (green, blue, purple) tend to recede and have a calming effect. White and gray go with everything and can help unify various parts of a garden.
- Buy annuals when the temperature is appropriate for planting them. Buying frost-sensitive plants too early may necessitate replanting. Select plants with healthy leaves. Don't buy plants that are too compact, too spindly, or bloomed out. Select plants that are insect and disease free. Don't bring home plants with aphids, white flies, spider mites, or other insects common on annuals. Peek under plant leaves and

look at the buds where many of these pests congregate or hide. Be sure that plants haven't developed root rot from excessive watering (to check, slip the plant from its container; look for white roots and be sure the potting substrate has an earthy smell).

- Plant on a cloudy or overcast day, or late in the day, to help acclimate plants going into full sun. Mark the planting spots (use spray paint, a spot of lime or flour, or a plant label), and position plants in those spots so adjustments can be made before planting. If multiple rows of annuals will be planted, stagger or offset the plants. Don't plant in straight lines in both directions—coverage won't be as good and lines can be too obvious.

- Water plants before removing them from their containers to ensure that their root balls are moist and to make removal from containers easier. Carefully remove plants from their containers unless you are planting individual peat pots. For peat pots, remove the top half of the pot prior to planting to ensure good root penetration into the surrounding soil.

To figure out how many plants to buy or how many to set into a particular planting area, first calculate the number of square feet in the area. Then multiply the number of square feet by the "plants per square foot factor," which is determined by the plant's spread or spacing requirement—usually stated on a garden-center tag or in a plant reference book. Once you know the spacing requirement of a plant, you can use the following formula to determine the number of plants for your site.

Spacing requirement	Plants per square foot
4 inches	9 plants
6 inches	4 plants
8 inches	2.3 plants
10 inches	1.4 plants
12 inches	1 plant

ANNUALS FOR BEGINNERS

Some plants are easier than others to grow, especially for people who feel they have a black rather than a green thumb. With a well-prepared soil, a thin layer of mulch, and a bit of organic or slow-release nitrogen fertilizer at planting, the following annuals should give confidence to even the most hesitant beginner.

SNAPDRAGON

Snapdragons (*Antirrhinum majus*)
Wax-leafed begonia (*Begonia* x *semperflorens-cultorum*)
Madagascar periwinkle (*Catharanthus roseus*)
Coleus (*Coleus* x *hybridus*)
Sweet William (*Dianthus barbatus*)
Globe amaranth (*Gomphrena globosa*)
Impatiens (*Impatiens walleriana*)
Lantana (*Lantana* spp.)
Medallion plant (*Melampodium paludosum*)
Pentas (*Pentas lanceolata*)
Petunias (*Petunia* x *hybrida*)
Rose moss (*Portulaca grandiflora*)
Verbena (*Verbena* x *hybrida*)
Pansies (*Viola* x *wittrockiana*)
Narrowleaf zinnia (*Zinnia angustifolia*)

GUERILLA ANNUALS

Holly Scoggins, the Virginia Tech assistant professor of horticulture who compiled this list, uses the term "guerilla plants" for these fast-establishing annuals and tender perennials that are treated as annuals in our region. "All of these will, by the end of the growing season, take up significant space—either vertically or horizontally," Holly promises. "Perfect for the barren landscape of a newly built house, or any other space you'd like to stuff chock-full of flowers and colorful foliage, they all should be grown in full sun." Few plants can be installed and expected to take off faster than these. You can use them in an area where slower-growing plants are getting established, or you may want to use them repeatedly in areas that nothing else colors and covers as well.

Wheat celosia (*Celosia spicata* 'Flamingo Purple')
Yellow cosmos (*Cosmos sulfureus*)
Sweet potato vine (*Ipomoea batatas* 'Margarita,' 'Blackie')
Spanish flag (*Ipomoea lobata*)
Purple hyacinth bean (*Lablab purpureus*)
Four o'clocks (*Mirabilis jalapa*)
Purple Wave petunia (*Petunia* 'Purple Wave')
Annual black-eyed Susan (*Rudbeckia hirta* 'Indian Summer')
Velvet or Mexican bush sage (*Salvia leucantha*)
Scarlet sage (*Salvia splendens*)
Persian shield (*Strobilanthes dyerianus*)
Black-eyed Susan vine (*Thunbergia alata*)
Mexican sunflower (*Tithonia rotundifolia*)

ANNUALS THAT BEAT THE HEAT

Gardeners who have mainly shade often envy gardeners who have nothing but unshaded sunny areas, but hot sunny areas necessitate either really tough plants or lots of mulch and irrigation. Heat may be due to summer's high temperatures, or it may be because a planting site is surrounded by hot paving or reflective surfaces. In these tough areas, the annuals in this list may wilt during the heat of the day, but you can go away for a week-long vacation without worrying that you'll return to nothing more than crispy, crunchy flowers.

This list is from Peggy Singlemann, horticulture manager for the Maymont Foundation in Richmond, Virginia. "Caring for a public garden with no automatic irrigation has forced me to rely on annuals that will perform well despite the temperature," she says. "Each of these plants has been researched and trialed before being placed in the garden. Finding where a plant originates from is helpful to determine its heat/drought tolerance."

Musk mallow (*Abelmoschus moschatus*)
Floss flower, blue ageratum (*Ageratum houstonianum*)
Joseph's coat (*Alternanthera ficoidea*)
Borage (*Borago officinalis*)
Dwarf canna (tuber) (*Canna* × *generalis* 'Tropical Rose')
Madagascar periwinkle (*Catharanthus roseus*)
Crested celosia (*Celosia argentea* var. *cristata*)
Plumed celosia (*Celosia argentea* var. *plumosa*)
Spider flower (*Cleome hassleriana*)
Cosmos (*Cosmos bipinnatus*)
Yellow cosmos (*Cosmos sulfureus*)
Mexican heather (*Cuphea hyssopifolia*)
Angels' trumpets (*Datura metel*)

Snow on the mountain (*Euphorbia marginata*)
Blue daze (*Evolvulus glomeratus*)
Blanket flower (*Gaillardia pulchella*)
Gazania (*Gazania rigens*)
Globe amaranth (*Gomphrena globosa*)
Sunflower (*Helianthus annuus*)
Sweet potato vine (*Ipomoea batatas* 'Blackie,' 'Margarita')
Cardinal vine (*Ipomoea coccinea*)
Spanish flag (*Ipomoea lobata*)
Purple hyacinth bean (*Lablab purpureus*)
Medallion plant (*Melampodium paludosum*)
Dwarf flowering tobacco (*Nicotiana alata*)
Flowering tobacco (*Nicotiana* × *sanderae* 'Domino Series')

Nodding flowering tobacco (*Nicotiana sylvestris*)
Cup flower (*Nierembergia caerulea*)
Geranium (*Pelargonium* x *hortorum*)
Pentas (*Pentas lanceolata*)
Petunia (*Petunia* x *hybrida*)
Cape leadwort (*Plumbago auriculata*)
Rose moss (*Portulaca grandiflora*)
Castor bean (*Ricinus communis*)
Black-eyed Susan (*Rudbeckia hirta*)
Texas sage (*Salvia coccinea* 'Lady in Red')
Mealycup sage (*Salvia farinacea*)

Scarlet sage (*Salvia splendens*)
Creeping zinnia (*Sanvitalia procumbens*)
Dusty miller (*Senecio cineraria*)
African marigold (*Tagetes erecta*)
French marigold (*Tagetes patula*)
Signet marigold (*Tagetes tenuifolia*)
Mexican sunflower (*Tithonia rotundifolia*)
Verbena (*Verbena* hybs.)
Zinnia (*Zinnia elegans*)
Mexican zinnia (*Zinnia haageana*)

"Experiment with textures and color combinations. Consider plants for just their foliage and blend in tropicals (*Mandevilla, Crossandra, Brugmansia*) to add a lush look to the landscape. Find a corner in your garden where you can trial new annuals and go beyond the old tried and true!"
Peggy Singlemann is the horticulture manager for the Maymont Foundation in Richmond, Virginia.

ANNUALS FOR HOT SPOTS

Barbara Bromely, Mercer County horticulturist for the Rutgers Cooperative Extension in Trenton, New Jersey, provided this list. In one of her on-line fact sheets (www.princetonol.com/groups/mg/bbfactsheets. html), she says that annuals tolerant of hot summer temperatures are "useful for bed planting in street dividers, in exposed containers, by parking lots, and in other hot locations. Some, like wax begonias, tolerate heat better if their roots are kept cooler by mulching." Plants that are marked with an asterisk (*) in this list will also tolerate very dry conditions.

Love-lies-bleeding (*Amaranthus caudatus*)*
Joseph's coat amaranthus (*Amaranthus tricolor*)*
Wax-leafed begonia (*Begonia* x *semperflorens-cultorum*)*
Ornamental pepper (*Capsicum annuum*)*
Madagascar periwinkle (*Catharanthus roseus*)*
Cockscomb (*Celosia cristata*)*
Plume celosia (*Celosia plumosa*)*
Spider flower (*Cleome hassleriana*)
Dwarf morning glory (*Convolvulus tricolor*)*
Annual coreopsis (*Coreopsis tinctoria*)*
Yellow cosmos (*Cosmos sulfureus*)
Firecracker plant (*Cuphea ignea*)
Dahlia (*Dahlia* hybs.)
Dahlberg daisy (*Dyssodia tenuiloba*)
California poppy (*Eschscholzia californica*)
Snow on the mountain (*Euphorbia marginata*)*
Blanket flower (*Gaillardia pulchella*)
Gerbera or Transvaal daisy (*Gerbera jamesonii*)
Globe amaranth (*Gomphrena globosa*)*
Sunflowers (*Helianthus* spp.)*
Kochia or burning bush (*Kochia scoparia*)*
Prairie gentian (*Lisianthus grandiflorum*)
Medallion plant (*Melampodium paludosum*)

PETUNIA

Four o'clocks (*Mirabilis jalapa*)*
Nicotiana or flowering tobacco (*Nicotiana alata*)
Cup flower (*Nierembergia hippomanica*)
Petunia (*Petunia* hybs.)
Rose moss (*Portulaca grandiflora*)*
Castor bean (*Ricinus communis*)
Gloriosa daisy (*Rudbeckia hirta*)

Salvia, sage (*Salvia* spp.)*
Creeping zinnia (*Sanvitalia procumbens*)*
Pincushion flower (*Scabiosa atropurpurea*)
Triploid marigold (*Tagetes erecta* x *patula*)
Mexican sunflower (*Tithonia rotundifolia*)*
Verbena (*Verbena* hybs.)
Zinnia (*Zinnia elegans*)

ANNUALS FOR SHADE

Shade in a garden may vary from light shade where sun occurs four to six hours of the day, to deep shade where no direct sunlight ever penetrates. Try the following alone or in combination with perennials and flowering shrubs that also like shade.

Light to Medium or Partial Shade
Floss flower (*Ageratum houstonianum*)
Alkanet (*Anchusa capensis*)
Snapdragon (*Antirrhinum majus*)
Sapphire flower (*Browallia speciosa*)
Caladium (*Caladium* x *hortulanum*)
Canterbury bells (*Campanula medium*)
Ornamental peppers (*Capsicum annuum*)
Madagascar periwinkle (*Catharanthus roseus*)
Godetia or farewell-to-spring (*Clarkia* hybs.)
Spider flower (*Cleome hassleriana*)
Coleus (*Coleus* x *hybridus*)
Mexican heather (*Cuphea hyssopifolia*)
Dahlia (*Dahlia* hybs.)
Sweet William, dianthus (*Dianthus* spp.)
Balsam (*Impatiens balsamina*)
Impatiens (*Impatiens walleriana*)
Lobelia (*Lobelia erinus*)
Sweet alyssum (*Lobularia maritima*)
Stock (*Matthiola incana*)
Monkey flower (*Mimulus* hybs.)
Forget-me-not (*Myosotis sylvatica*)

Baby blue-eyes (*Nemophila menziesii*)
Flowering tobacco or nicotiana (*Nicotiana alata*)
Blue cup flower (*Nierembergia hippomanica* var. *violacea*)
Annual phlox (*Phlox drummondiii*)
Mignonette (*Reseda odorata*)
Scarlet sage or salvia (*Salvia splendens*)
Dusty miller (*Senecio cineraria*)
Black-eyed Susan vine (*Thunbergia alata*)
Nasturtium (*Tropaeolum majus*)
Pansy (*Viola* x *wittrockiana*)

Light to Deep Shade
Wax begonia (*Begonia* x *semperflorens-cultorum*)
Sapphire flowers (*Browallia* spp.)
Coleus (*Coleus* x *hybridus*)
Fuchsia (*Fuchsia* spp.)
Impatiens (*Impatiens walleriana*)
Lobelia (*Lobelia erinus*)
Mimulus or monkey flower (*Mimulus* x *hybridus*)
Torenia or wishbone flower (*Torenia fournieri*)

ALL-AMERICAN SELECTIONS

The All-American Selection (AAS) designation that you see on many seed packets and plant labels is a prestigious award. The AAS organization was founded in 1932 to test new cultivars of annual flowers and vegetables grown from seed. These new cultivars are trialed in test and display gardens across the United States. AAS annual flower winners may display improvements in characteristics such as compactness, heat and drought tolerance, or disease resistance, or they may have a new or improved flower color. To find the AAS garden nearest you, check the website: www.all-americaselections.org.

This list is from master gardener Gloria Winiker, who for fifteen years has managed the All-American Selection trials at Virginia Tech's Hampton Roads Agricultural Research and Extension Center in Virginia Beach. These AAS winners have performed well in the lower Mid-Atlantic region. "Over the years the list of winners has become quite long, but there are standout plants, both dependable as well as beautiful, which I call The Best of the Best. In addition, one herb—'Siam Queen' basil—and one summer-flowering bulb—'Tropical Rose' canna—have been excellent.

Cockscomb (*Celosia cristata* 'Prestige Scarlet')
Sweet William (*Dianthus barbatus* 'Telstar Picotee,' 'Ideal Violet')
Blanket flower (*Gaillardia pulchella* 'Red Plume')
Baby's breath (*Gypsophila repens* 'Gypsy')
Impatiens (*Impatiens hawkeri* 'New Guinea Tango')
Cup flower (*Nierembergia hippomanica* 'Mont Blanc')
Cape daisy (*Osteospermum compositae* 'Passion Mix')
Geranium (*Pelargonium* x *hortorum* 'Freckles')
Rose moss or portulaca (*Portulaca grandiflora* 'Sun Dial Peach')
Gloriosa daisy (*Rudbeckia hirta* 'Indian Summer')
Salvia or sage (*Salvia farinacea* 'Strata')
Wishbone flower (*Torenia fournieri* 'Clown Mix')
Verbena (*Verbena tenuisecta* 'Imagination')
Pansy (*Viola* x 'Maxim Marina')
Zinnia (*Zinnia elegans* 'Scarlet Splendor')
Hybrid zinnia (*Zinnia angustifolia* x *elegans* 'Profusion Orange,' 'Profusion Cherry')

ANNUALS FOR CLAY SOIL

Though it is always desirable to plant annuals into soil that is high in organic matter, or to which compost or other organic matter has been added, sometimes it is impractical to improve a site prior to planting. In a case like that there are some really adaptable annuals that can tolerate a less-than-desirable soil texture. One thing that will help is to plant shallow and mulch generously.

Musk mallow (*Abelmoschus moschatus*)
Love-lies-bleeding (*Amaranthus caudatus*)
Yellow cosmos (*Cosmos sulfureus*)
Globe amaranth (*Gomphrena globosa*)
Sunflower (*Helianthus annuus*)
Moonvine (*Ipomoea alba*)
Morning glory (*Ipomoea purpurea*)
Cypress vine (*Ipomoea quamoclit*)

COSMOS

ANNUALS THAT TOLERATE ALKALINE SOIL

If the soil in your area is naturally alkaline, or you're planting in an area where alkaline water is used for irrigation, or a rock mulch such as limestone is applied, the following annuals will tolerate the higher pH without their leaves yellowing excessively.

Bachelor's buttons (*Centaurea cyanus*)
Spider flower (*Cleome hassleriana*)
Larkspur (*Consolida* spp.)
Calliopsis (*Coreopsis tinctoria*)
Cosmos (*Cosmos bipinnatus*)
Yellow cosmos (*Cosmos sulfureus*)
Dianthus, sweet William (*Dianthus* spp.)
Dahlberg daisy (*Dyssodia tenuiloba*)
California poppy (*Eschscholzia californica*)
Lisianthus (*Eustoma grandiflorum*)
Indian blanket (*Gaillardia pulchella*)
Globe amaranth (*Gomphrena globosa*)
Strawflowers (*Helichrysum bracteatum*)
Scarlet flax (*Linum grandiflorum*)

Sweet alyssum (*Lobularia maritima*)
Money plant (*Lunaria annua*)
Stocks (*Matthiola incana*)
Medallion plant (*Melampodium paludosum*)
Love-in-a-mist (*Nigella damascena*)
Drummond phlox (*Phlox drummondii*)
Gloriosa daisy (*Rudbeckia hirta*)
Scabiosa, pincushion flower (*Scabiosa atropurpurea*)
Mexican sunflower (*Tithonia rotundifolia*)
Narrowleaf zinnia (*Zinnia angustifolia*)
Zinnias (*Zinnia elegans*)
Chippendale zinnia (*Zinnia haageana*)

ANNUALS THAT RESIST ROOT ROT

Root rot is a soil-borne disease that tends to occur on plants growing in soils that remain wet for prolonged periods, either due to poor drainage or excessively frequent irrigation or rainfall. *Phytophthora*, the main pathogen that causes this disease, has swimming, motile spores that attack a wide variety of plants, including annuals, perennials, and woody species. Symptoms include yellowing, wilting, general decline or rapid collapse, and death. "In order to identify bedding plants that might resist this disease, we inoculated the soil of over forty popular bedding plant species or cultivars with the *Phytophthora* fungus," reports Tom Banko, associate professor of horticulture at Virginia Tech's Hampton Roads Agricultural Research and Extension Center in Virginia Beach. "Annuals were then planted out into beds and irrigated frequently to maintain moist conditions. The plants were evaluated through the growing season for disease symptoms and growth. This list represents plants that were resistant or tolerant of the root-rot disease and performed well in the landscape. Two perennials, black-eyed Susan (*Rudbeckia hirta*) and salvia (*Salvia farinacea*) also performed well."

Floss flower (*Ageratum houstonianum*)
Celosia (*Celosia argentea*)
Dahlia (*Dahlia coccinea*)
Prairie gentian, lisianthus (*Eustoma grandiflorum*)
Alyssum (*Lobularia maritima*)
Flowering tobacco (*Nicotiana* x *sanderae*)
Geranium (*Pelargonium* x *hortorum*)

Petunia (*Petunia* x *hybrida*)
Rose moss (*Portulaca grandiflora*)
Scarlet salvia (*Salvia coccinea*)
African marigold (*Tagetes erecta*)
French marigold (*Tagetes patula*)
Zinnia (*Zinnia angustifolia*)

ANNUALS FOR WET SITES

A number of annuals tolerate damp conditions. This list will help you select annuals that can tolerate a slightly moist soil or an area with low spots or slow drainage.

Caladiums (*Caladium* x *hortulanum*)
Madagascar periwinkle (*Catharanthus roseus*)
Cleome or spider flower (*Cleome hassleriana*)
Coleus (*Coleus* x *hybridus*)
Persian violet (*Exacum affine*)
Mallows (*Hibiscus* spp.)
Impatiens (*Impatiens walleriana*)

Meadow foam (*Limnanthes douglasii*)
Mimulus or monkey flower (*Mimulus* x *hybridus*)
Forget-me-not (*Myosotis sylvatica*)
Castor bean (*Ricinus communis*)
Torenia or wishbone flower (*Torenia fournieri*)
Pansy (*Viola* x *wittrockiana*)

ANNUALS WITH COLORFUL FOLIAGE

Don't think the only way to get a striking display of color is with flowers. The following annuals are as striking as their flowering counterparts, and they create a refreshing surprise in a bed otherwise filled with flowers. Use the silvery leaves of dusty miller as a background for or contrast to bright orange or yellow marigolds.

Copperleaf (*Alternanthera ficoidea*)
Joseph's Coat amaranthus (*Amaranthus tricolor*)
Wax-leafed begonia (*Begonia* x *semperflorens-cultorum*)
Swiss chard (*Beta vulgaris*)
Ornamental cabbage and kale (*Brassica oleracea*)
Caladium (*Caladium* x *hortulanum*)
Coleus (*Coleus* x *hybridus*)
Snow on the mountain (*Euphorbia marginata*)
Ornamental fennel (*Foeniculum vulgare* 'Redform')
Mallow (*Hibiscus acetosella*)

Polka-dot plant (*Hypoestes sanguinolenta*)
New Guinea impatiens (*Impatiens* x 'New Guinea')
Morning glories (*Ipomoea* spp.)
Beefsteak plant (*Iresine herbstii*)
Kochia (*Kochia scoparia*)
Basil (*Ocimum basilicum*)
Perilla (*Perilla frutescens*)
Castor bean (*Ricinus communis*)
Dusty miller (*Senecio cineraria*)
Holy thistle (*Silybum marianum*)
Irish lace marigold (*Tagetes filifolium*)

"Many of the herbs, particularly the many new types of basils that love hot weather, have leaves ranging from yellow to burgundy and purple. These plants serve not only as interesting contrast to annual flowers but can also be used in cooking and for making great vinegars."
   Barbara Brawley is a Virginia Beach, Virginia, master gardener and a member of the Herb Society of America.

FRAGRANT ANNUALS

The annuals in this list have scents that reach out to you. Their alluring perfumes float across the yard when the air is warm and bring back experiences locked in memory. Plant fragrant annuals near outdoor sitting areas and by your front door. Some annuals, like moonvine and petunias, are most fragrant at night. Not all petunias are fragrant, so sniff and compare before you buy.

For Spring Fragrance
Sweet William (*Dianthus barbatus*)
Pinks (*Dianthus* spp.)
Heliotrope (*Heliotropium peruvianum*)
Sweet peas (*Lathyrus odoratus*)
Sweet alyssum (*Lobularia maritima*)
Stock (*Matthiola incana*)
Petunias (*Petunia* x *hybrida*)

For Summer Fragrance
Swan River daisy (*Brachyscome iberidifolia*)
Moonvine (*Ipomoea alba*)
Four o'clocks (*Mirabilis jalapa*)
Flowering tobacco (*Nicotiana alata*)
Nodding flowering tobacco (*Nicotiana sylvestris*)
Petunias (*Petunia* x *hybrida*)
Mignonette (*Reseda odorata*)

ANNUALS FOR CUTTING

It's always nice to be able to walk out to your garden to cut flowers for your house or office, for a friend, or for a variety of other reasons. Some people plant cut flower gardens in secluded areas of their yards, while others just cut from annuals used as part of their gardens and landscapes. Either way, be sure to include a few of the plants in this list from garden writer Liz Ball so you can take the beautiful color and diversity of summer annuals with you anywhere. For a real treat, include annuals that have a wonderful fragrance as well. Those marked with an asterisk (*) in this list are also good as dried flowers.

Floss flower (*Ageratum houstonianum*)
Love-lies-bleeding (*Amaranthus caudatus*)
False bishop's weed, lace flower (*Ammi majus*)
Windflowers (*Anemone* spp.)
Dill (*Anethum graveolens*)
Snapdragon (*Antirrhinum majus*)
Asters (*Aster* spp. and hybs.)
Calendula (*Calendula* spp.)
China aster (*Callistephus chinensis*)
Bellflowers (*Campanula* spp.)
Cockspur (*Celosia argentea* var. *cristata*)*
Bachelor's buttons, cornflowers (*Centaurea cyanus*)
Spider flower (*Cleome hassleriana*)
Larkspur (*Consolida ambigua*)
Cosmos, Klondike (*Cosmos* spp.)
Dahlias (*Dahlia* spp.)
Dianthus, sweet William, pinks (*Dianthus* spp.)
Sun marigold (*Dimorphotheca sinnuata*)
Snow on the mountain (*Euphorbia marginata*)
Blanket flower (*Gaillardia pulchella*)

Transvaal daisy (*Gerbera jamesonii*)
Cranesbill (*Geranium* spp.)
Globe amaranth (*Gomphrena globosa*)*
Annual baby's breath (*Gypsophila paniculata*)
Sunflowers (*Helianthus* spp.)
Everlasting, strawflower (*Helichrysum* spp.)*
Sweet pea (*Lathyrus odoratus*)
Statice (*Limonium* spp.)*
Toadflax (*Linaria maroccana*)
Stock (*Matthiola* spp.)
Bells of Ireland (*Moluccella laevis*)
Flowering tobacco (*Nicotiana* spp.)
Love-in-a-mist (*Nigella damascena*)
Poppies (*Papaver* spp.)
Phlox (*Phlox drummondii*)
Painted tongue (*Salpiglossis* spp.)
Mealycup sage (*Salvia farinacea*)
Red salvia (*Salvia splendens*)
Pincushion flower (*Scabiosa* spp.)
Butterfly flower (*Schizanthus* x *wisetonensis*)
Marigolds (*Tagetes* spp.)

Mexican sunflower (*Tithonia rotundifolia*)
Nasturtiums (*Tropaeolum majus*)
Verbena (*Verbena* spp.)

Pansy (*Viola* x *wittrockiana*)
Zinnias (*Zinnia* spp.)

"It's always a tough decision whether to cut flowers for indoors or leave them on display outdoors in the garden. Establishing a separate production garden dedicated to growing flowers to be cut for arrangements and crafts allows you to have your flowers and pick them too!"
Liz Ball of Springfield, Pennsylvania, is the author of Smith & Hawken's *Composting* and *The Philadelphia Garden Book* (Cool Springs Press).

TROPICALS FOR THE LANDSCAPE

Gardening with tropical plants—either in pots or in the ground for summer bedding—is an exciting new trend. For a touch of *tropicalismo* in your garden and containers, try some of the easy to grow, highly satisfactory plants in this list from Brian O'Neil, owner of Southern Meadows Landscaping of Virginia Beach, Virginia. They revel in a steamy growing season, but their fast growth justifies the purchase price wherever these plants aren't hardy. (Some can be brought indoors for the winter and then set out again when temperatures are warm enough. Some you will have to treat as annuals.)

Included is a group of tropicals with a spiky, linear texture that can be attention-grabbers as a centerpiece in containers, or a foil to the more relaxed, billowy form of other plants. They provide architectural drama with their long, strap-like leaves, some highlighted with colored foliage and others with spectacular flowers.

Foliage
Giant alocasia, upright elephant's ear (*Alocasia macrorrhiza*)
Australian tree fern (*Alsophila australis*)
Fancy-leaved caladium (*Caladium* x *hortulanum*)
Taro or dasheen (*Colocasia esculenta* 'Illustris,' 'Black Magic')
Giant dracaena, cabbage palm (*Cordyline australis* 'Albertii,' 'Atropurpurea')
Dumb cane (*Dieffenbachia maculata*)
Rubber plant (*Ficus elastica*)
White polka-dot plant (*Hypoestes phyllostachya*)
Sweet potato vine (*Ipomoea batatas* 'Blackie,' 'Margarita,' 'Tricolor')
Bananas (*Musa* spp.)
Purple fountain grass (*Pennisetum setaceum rubrum*)
Swedish ivy mint (*Plectranthus argentatus*)
Coleus (*Solenostemon scutellarioides*)
Persian shield (*Strobilanthes dyerianus*)
Purple heart (*Tradescantia pallida* 'Purple Heart')

Flowers
Angelonia (*Angelonia angustifolia*)
Angels' trumpets (*Brugmansia* x *candida*)
Canna lily (*Canna* spp.)
Cigar plant (*Cuphea ignea*)
Lantana (*Lantana camara*, *L. montevidensis*)
Mandevilla (*Mandevilla* x *amoena* 'Alice du Pont')
Cape leadwort (*Plumbago auriculata*)
Hardy blue petunia (*Ruellia malacosperma*)
Peace lily (*Spathiphyllum* spp.)
Cape primrose (*Streptocarpus saxorum*)
Princess flower (*Tibouchina urvilleana*)

Spikes

Japanese sweet flag (*Acorus gramineus* 'Variegatus,' 'Ogon')
Bromeliads (*Aechmea, Guzmania, Neoregelia, Nidularium, Vriesea*)
Lily of the Nile (*Agapanthus* cvs.)
Agaves (*Agave* spp.)
Giant dracaena, cabbage palm (*Cordyline australis* 'Albertii,' 'Atropurpurea')
Crinum lily (*Crinum zeylanicum*)
Flax lily (*Dianella tasmanica*)
Rainbow plant (*Dracaena marginata* 'Tricolor')
Ginger lilies (*Hedychium* spp. and hybs.)
Red yucca (*Hesperaloe parviflora*)
Variegated Japanese iris (*Iris ensata variegata*)
New Zealand flax (*Phormium tenax* and hybs.)
Adam's needle (*Yucca filamentosa* 'Gold Edge,' 'Garland Gold,' 'Variegata')

"Lately I've become enamored of plants with dark foliage—anything from crimson-red or purple to chocolate or black will do. Some of the best foliage tropicals for this effect are 'Purple Heart' tradescantia, 'Blackie' sweet potato vine, and Persian shield. Purple foliage and orange flowers make a spectacular combination that is definitely not for the faint of heart."

Brian O'Neil, owner of Southern Meadows Landscaping of Virginia Beach, Virginia, usually wins a landscape design award at the Virginia Flower and Garden Show, often incorporating tropicals into his designs.

ANNUALS THAT BLOOM FROM SPRING TO FROST

If you're looking for annuals that you can set out right after the last frost in spring and that will bloom until the first frost of fall, choose from this list. They are generally the ones that will flower through the summer, and with renewed vigor when the nights begin to cool down in the fall. This list is divided into two groups. The first contains annuals that continue to bloom without deadheading or flower removal, making them low maintenance. The next group will bloom from spring until frost provided you deadhead them. Deadheading is removing the dead flowers from plants. Because annuals live only one year, they are internally programmed to produce seed for survival. As long as you keep removing the faded flowers, most annuals will continue to produce more flowers in an effort to make seeds. Some annuals, such as ageratum, alyssum, begonias, impatiens, lobelia, salvia, and vinca, have flowers that fall cleanly from the plant and don't need deadheading.

These Bloom Unaided

Floss flower (*Ageratum houstonianum*)
Wax-leafed begonia (*Begonia* X *semperflorens-cultorum*)
New Guinea impatiens (*Impatiens* X 'New Guinea')
Impatiens (*Impatiens walleriana*)
Moonvine (*Ipomoea alba*)
Morning glory (*Ipomoea tricolor*)
Lantana (*Lantana* spp.)
Pentas (*Pentas lanceolata*)
Narrowleaf zinnia (*Zinnia angustifolia*)

Deadheading Needed

Calendula or pot marigold (*Calendula officinalis*)
Spider flower (*Cleome hassleriana*)

Calliopsis (*Coreopsis tinctoria*)
Cosmos (*Cosmos bipinnatus*)
Yellow cosmos (*Cosmos sulfureus*)
Dahlia (*Dahlia* X *hybrida*)
China pink (*Dianthus chinensis*)
Blanket flower (*Gaillardia pulchella*)
Multibranched sunflowers (*Helianthus annuus*)
Floribunda and multibloom geraniums (*Pelargonium* X *hortorum*)
Petunias (*Petunia* X *hybrida*)
Blue salvia (*Salvia farinacea*)
Scarlet sage (*Salvia splendens*)
African marigolds (*Tagetes erecta*)
Mexican sunflower (*Tithonia rotundifolia*)
Zinnias (*Zinnia elegans*)

ANNUALS FOR FALL BLOOM

As master gardener Gloria Winiker of Virginia Beach, Virginia, is quick to point out, when the days begin to shorten and the temperatures drop, many annuals look downright ratty and need to be pulled and composted. You can assure yourself of fall flower color if you include a few of the annuals in this list when you do your spring purchasing and planting.

CHRYSANTHEMUM

Floss flower (*Ageratum houstonianum*)
Wax-leafed begonia (*Begonia* x *semperflorens-cultorum*)
Ornamental pepper (*Capsicum annuum*)
Annual chrysanthemum (*Chrysanthemum* spp.)
Dahlia (*Dahlia* x *hybrida*)
Globe amaranth (*Gomphrena globosa*)
Sweet alyssum (*Lobularia maritima*)
Medallion plant (*Melampodium paludosum*)
Flowering tobacco (*Nicotiana alata*)
Cup flower (*Nierembergia hippomanica*)
Geraniums (*Pelargonium* x *hortorum*)
Petunias (*Petunia* x *hybrida*)
Scarlet sage (*Salvia splendens*)
Marigolds (*Tagetes* spp.)

ANNUALS THAT BLOOM INTO WINTER

For those of us in the warmer portions of the New York and Mid-Atlantic region, late fall and early winter don't mean just perennials like asters, chrysanthemums, and goldenrods. Several annuals are hardy enough to flower on into winter when it's mild. This list is from master gardener Gloria Winiker of Virginia Beach, Virginia, who advises: "The trick to having annual flowers in the fall and winter is to remember to sow the seed during the summer when we all seem to get distracted by vacations and other more interesting activities." Some of these plants take a fair amount of frost, and some may even bounce back after a light dusting of snow.

Snapdragon (*Antirrhinum majus*)
Ornamental cabbage and kale (*Brassica oleracea*)
Pot marigold or calendula (*Calendula officinalis*)
Chinese forget-me-not (*Cynoglossum amabile*)
Sweet pea (*Lathyrus odoratus*)
Sweet alyssum (*Lobularia maritima*)
Stocks (*Matthiola incana* 'Annua')
Pansy (*Viola* hybs. and cvs.)

PANSY

HARDY ANNUALS FOR THE EARLIEST SPRING BLOOM

When you're out in your garden planting bulbs for spring bloom, remember to sow some of these hardy annuals that will bloom right along with the daffodils and tulips. You can sow these annuals directly into your garden in soil with a colder temperature than the summer annuals will tolerate.

Bachelor's buttons (*Centaurea cyanus*)
Chinese forget-me-not (*Cynoglossum amabile*)
Larkspur (*Delphinium consolida*)
California poppy (*Eschscholzia californica*)
Annual baby's breath (*Gypsophila elegans*)
Annual candytuft (*Iberis umbellata*)

Sweet pea (*Lathyrus odorata*)
Sweet alyssum (*Lobularia maritima*)
Bells of Ireland (*Moluccella laevis*)
Baby blue-eyes (*Nemophila menziesii*)
Love-in-a-mist (*Nigella damascena*)
Annual phlox (*Phlox drummondii*)

ANNUAL VINES

Annual vines grow incredibly fast, with the bonus of flowering that goes on for months. They're not just inexpensive landscape oddities but can be used to quickly cover a problem slope, frame a door or window if given a string on which to climb, cover a compost pile as it decomposes, or climb up the supports of a hanging basket. Because they bloom so long and most can be started from seed, they are a very inexpensive way to add more color to trellises, fences, and arbors. Children (and the child in all of us) love them too, because their fast growth (especially the luffa, which gives you gourd sponges for scrubbing) satisfies a child's relative inability to wait. Grow them singly or twined together for a mosaic look.

SWEET
PEA

Twining snapdragon (*Asarina* spp.)
Love-in-a-puff (*Cardiospermum halicacabum*)
Cup and saucer vine (*Cobaea scandens*)
Chilean glory vine (*Eccremocarpus* spp.)
Morning glories (*Ipomoea* spp.)
White moonvine (*Ipomoea alba*)
Spanish flag (*Ipomoea lobata*)
Cardinal climber (*Ipomoea* x *multifida*)
Cypress vine (*Ipomoea quamoclit*)
Purple hyacinth bean (*Lablab purpureus*)
Sweet pea (*Lathyrus odoratus*)
Luffa gourd (*Luffa aegyptiaca*)
Bitter melon (*Momordica charantia*)
Climbing nasturtium (*Nasturtium majus, N. peregrinum*)
Tropical passion vine (*Passiflora coccinea*)
Scarlet runner bean (*Phaseolus coccineus*)
Purple bell vine (*Rhodochiton* spp.)
Black-eyed Susan vine (*Thunbergia alata*)

ANNUALS FOR CONTAINERS

Container gardening allows a gardener to easily control most of the factors that influence plant growth: soil, water, fertilizer, sun exposure, and growing environment. Use the largest pot possible—drainage holes are a must—and a sterile commercial-grade potting substrate to which you add a timed-release fertilizer formulated for blooming plants. Pack the pot full of plants! For a pot with a 20-inch diameter, add a one-gallon plant that has drama, such as a geranium or a dracaena; then add at least eight to ten plants from 4-inch pots. Include some with upright or spreading growth, and some that are trailing. Using perennials such as ivy or vinca keeps you from replanting all the plants every year. Including an annual or perennial herb, such as basil, parsley, oregano, or thyme, spices up your kitchen. Annuals grown for their dramatic foliage, like sun coleus, copper plant, and cordyline, mix well with other colorful plants in contrasting or monochromatic color schemes. If using a clay pot, seal it with roofing compound or terra-cotta sealer and water your container garden every day.

Janel Leatherman, manager of the Farmers' Market in Virginia Beach, Virginia, provided this list. "Most blooming plants on this list deadhead themselves," she notes. "I deadhead geraniums once a week and let the other blossoms fall where they may. Selfishly, I can put my colorful container gardens where I see them, where I spend time, or where there is a vacant space in my garden. Container gardening with annuals isn't forever, so I repeat my successes and add a few new combinations each season."

Copper plant (*Acalypha* spp.)
Joseph's coat amaranthus (*Amaranthus tricolor*)
Asparagus fern (*Asparagus plumosus*)
Wax-leafed begonia (*Begonia* x *semperflorens-cultorum*)
Caladium (*Caladium* x *hortulanum*)
Spider plant (*Chlorophytum comosum*)

Sun coleus (*Coleus* x *hybridus*)
Cordyline (*Cordyline* 'Red Sister')
Mexican heather (*Cuphea hyssopifolia*)
Dracaena spike (*Dracaena marginata* 'Tricolor')
Blue daze (*Evolvulus glomeratus* 'Blue Daze')
Purple velvet (*Gynura aurantiaca*)
Licorice plant (*Helichrysum petiolare* 'Limelight')

Heliotrope (*Heliotropium arborescens*)
Hibiscus (*Hibiscus rosa-sinensis*)
New Guinea impatiens (*Impatiens* x *hybridus*)
Impatiens, Busy Lizzie (*Impatiens walleriana*)
Sweet potato vine (*Ipomoea batatas* 'Blackie,' 'Margarita')
Lobelia (*Lobelia erinus*)
Sweet alyssum (*Lobularia maritima*)
Prayer plant (*Maranta leuconeura*)
Nemesia (*Nemesia strumosa*)
Geranium (*Pelargonium* spp.)

New Zealand flax (*Phormium tenax*)
Variegated creeping Charlie (*Plectranthus coleoides*)
Fan-flower (*Scaveola aemula* 'Blue Wonder,' 'Petite Wonder')
Dusty miller (*Senecio cineraria*)
Purple heart (*Tradescantia pallida* 'Purple Heart')
Bacopa (*Sutera cordata* 'Snowstorm,' 'Snowflake')
Persian shield (*Strobilanthes dyerianus*)
Pinwheel zinnia (*Zinnia angustifolia*)

"I have container gardened successfully for over twenty years in climates ranging from sunny, hot, dry southwestern New Mexico, to unpredictable, hot, windy Kansas and Missouri, to my current hot, humid Norfolk, Virginia. I am a lazy, selfish gardener, and when I container garden with annuals I, proudly, can maintain those qualities. There is no weeding, very little disease or insect problems, and because I use timed-release fertilizer mixed into the substrate at planting time, the fertilizing takes care of itself."

Janel Leatherman is the manager of the Farmers' Market in Virginia Beach, Virginia; through her business Zinnia Productions, she specializes in writing, speaking, and consulting about horticulture and gardening.

ANNUALS FOR HANGING BASKETS

Gardening in the air" is what horticulturist Dwayne Jones calls growing annuals in hanging baskets. Dwayne, a horticulturist for the city of Waynesboro, Virginia, provided this list of plants that you are bound to notice even if you're zipping down the street in your car, not just sitting on your deck or patio. The same advice given for growing annuals in containers should be followed. According to Dwayne, "Colorful hanging baskets are one of the hottest trends in gardening today, although growing them is one of the biggest challenges gardeners face. Wind, heat, root competition, lack of water, and a minimal soil volume all create a tough environment for most plants. Proper plant selection is the best insurance that you will have an attractive, healthy hanging basket all summer."

Dragon Wing begonia (*Begonia* x *tuber-hybrida* 'Dragon Wing')
Golden Eye bidens (*Biden ferulifera* 'Golden Eye')
Blue Million Bells (*Calibrachoa* x *hybrida* 'Million Bells Trailing Blue')
Apricot Beauty cockscomb (*Celosia argentea* var. *plumosa* 'Apricot Beauty')
New Look cockscomb (*Celosia argentea* var. *plumosa* 'New Look')
Prestige Scarlet cockscomb (*Celosia cristata* 'Prestige Scarlet')
Inky Fingers coleus (*Coleus* x *hybridus* 'Inky Fingers')
Red Trailer coleus (*Coleus* x *hybridus* 'Red Trailer')
Dwarf globe amaranth (*Gomphrena globosa* 'Gnome Purple')
Limelight licorice plant (*Helichrysum petiolare* 'Limelight')
Antigua impatiens (*Impatiens* x *hawkeri* 'Antigua')
Black sweet potato vine (*Ipomoea batatas* 'Blackie')
Yellow sweet potato vine (*Ipomoea batatas* 'Sulfur' and 'Margarita')
Pink Frost sweet potato vine (*Ipomoea batatas* 'Pink Frost')
Palace Blue lobelia (*Lobelia erinus* 'Palace Blue')
Blizzard White geranium (*Pelargonium* x *hortorum* 'Blizzard White')
Sophie Cascade geranium (*Pelargonium* x *hortorum* 'Sophie Cascade')
Cranberry Punch star flower (*Penta lanceolata* 'Cranberry Punch')

Purple Wave petunia (*Petunia* x *hybrida* 'Purple Wave')
Supercascade White petunia (*Petunia* x *hybrida* 'Supercascade White')
Dwarf Toto rudbeckia (*Rudbeckia hirta* 'Toto')
New Blue Wonder scaveola (*Scaveola aemula* 'New Blue Wonder')
Purple heart (*Tradescantia pallida*)
Silver Dust dusty miller (*Senecio cineraria* 'Silver Dust')
Brazilian verbena (*Verbena bonariensis*)
Peruvian verbena (*Verbena peruviana*)
Imagination verbena (*Verbena tenuisecta* 'Imagination')
Soft Pink verbena (*Verbena* x *hybrida* 'Soft Tapien Pink')
Profusion Orange zinnia (*Zinnia angustifolia* x *elegans* 'Profusion Orange')

WATER GARDENS

Water in a garden has a magical calming and refreshing effect. While it would be nice to have a stream or large pond in every garden, even the smallest of landscapes can have water in a container or tiny pond. Though professional designers may be needed to install a large formal water garden, most backyard gardeners can design and build an informal one, given the numerous kits, books, and instructional videos that are available. Be sure not to make your water garden an isolated feature in your landscape. Blend it in with its surroundings (use complementary flower colors or leaf textures) to give the feel that it naturally belongs in your garden, or on your deck or patio.

WATER LILY

According to Laurie Fox, horticulture associate at Virginia Tech's Hampton Roads Agricultural Research and Extension Center in Virginia Beach, Virginia, "Aesthetically, water gardens are popular because they are soothing and add sound, movement, reflection, and depth to a landscape as well as attracting wildlife. Instead of remodeling or taking an expensive vacation, many homeowners are improving their landscapes and creating mini vacation spots right in their own yards. Economically, water gardens increase residential, commercial, and public property values."

Tips for Selecting Water Gardening Plants

- Select the right water garden plant for the right location. Some water garden plants belong in wet soil on the edge of the water, some in shallow water, and some in the deeper center water. When selecting water lilies, be aware that some are hardy and others tropical, some need full sun and some will tolerate partial shade. If you're new to water gardens, start with hardy species.
- Every pond needs submerged plants that help trap debris in their leaves. They also compete with algae for dissolved nutrients in the water, and thereby help to keep the pond's water clear.
- Many water garden plants have fast growth rates, so often only one or two are needed to start. If certain plants begin to multiply rapidly, thin them out and compost the extras or give them to a friend to help them start a water garden. A good balance to strive for is one-third open water to two-thirds plant-covered surface.
- Plant your water garden plants in containers in heavy garden soil; do not use lightweight commercial potting soils that will float to the water's surface.
- Periodically remove yellowing leaves and spent flowers to avoid debris buildup, and keep weeds pulled.
- Water garden plants need to be periodically fertilized with fertilizers specially formulated for water gardens, and they need to be monitored for pest problems.
- In the colder sections of our region, even hardy water garden plants may need to be brought indoors in the winter. To keep the water in your water garden from freezing, use a stock tank de-icer.
- Add goldfish and koi to your water garden, not only for color and movement, but to stir up the pond bottom as they search for food, to eat mosquito larvae, and as biological controls against insects.

Use the cold and heat zones as a guide but not an absolute. Considerable disagreement exists among the various books and water plant catalogs for many of these plants. Perhaps as they become more widely used the zone ratings will become more uniform. If in doubt as to winter hardiness, treat the plant as a tropical.

SUN-TOLERANT HARDY AQUATIC PLANTS

Keith Folsom of Springdale Water Gardens and Springdale Aquatic Nursery and Supply in Greenville, Virginia, compiled this list. Water gardens perform at their peak when located in full sun, though most experience at least partial shade. While acting as an essential cooling mechanism for the water, the aquatic plants ravenously gorge themselves on the heat of the sun. This in turn promotes lush growth that shades and filters the water, resulting in a balanced ecosystem.

Plant into quality clay-loam topsoil that provides anchoring and nutrition for the rapid growth. Bog plants that are planted in the margins of the pond or grown in containers (not in a true bog) mask the borders of the water garden, softening the harsh stonework. Water lilies and lotus provide the most dramatic display in the water garden while cooling the water most efficiently.

Sweetflag, variegated (*Acorus calamus* 'Variegatus')	4-11, 12-1
Flowering rush (*Butomus umbellatus*)	5-11, 12-1
Dwarf bamboo (*Dulichium arundinaceum*)	5-9, 9-1
Hair grass (*Eleocharis acicularis*)	6-11, 12-4
Spike rush (*Eleocharis montevidensis*)	6-11, 12-4
Water chestnut (*Eleocharis tuberosa*)	7-11, 12-4
Cotton grass (*Eriophorum angustifolium*)	6-11, 12-4
Variegated manna grass (*Glyceria spectabilis variegata*)	5-9, 9-4
Pennywort (*Hydrocotyle verticillata*)	5-11, 12-7
Louisiana iris (*Iris* hybs. and cvs.)	6-11, 12-4
Blue flag iris (*Iris versicolor*)	4-11, 8-4
Southern blue flag (*Iris virginica*)	5-8, 8-1
Variegated common rush (*Juncus effusus* 'Gold Strike')	3-8, 8-1
Corkscrew rush (*Juncus effusus* 'Spiralis')	3-8, 8-1
Cardinal flower (*Lobelia cardinalis*)	4-8, 8-1
Primrose creeper (*Ludwigia repens*)	5-11, 12-7
Creeping mazus (*Mazus reptans*)	5-8, 8-4
Water clover (*Marsilea mutica*)	6-11, 12-4
Aquatic mint (*Mentha aquatica*)	6-9, 9-6
Bog bean (*Menyanthes trifoliata*)	3-7, 7-1
Monkey flower (*Mimulus ringens*)	3-7, 7-1
Water forget-me-not (*Myosotis scorpioides*)	5-9, 9-4
Parrot feather (*Myriophyllum aquaticum*)	5-11, 12-7
Watercress (*Nasturtium officinale*)	4-11, 12-1
Lotus (*Nelumbo* hybs. and cvs.)	4-11, 12-1
Hardy water lily (*Nymphaea* hybs. and cvs.)	3-11, 12-1
Water snowflake (*Nymphoides cristata*)	7-10, 12-1
Yellow snowflake (*Nymphoides geminata*)	7-10, 12-1
Water arum (*Peltandra virginica*)	5-9, 9-5
Ribbon grass (*Phalaris arundinacea*)	4-9, 9-1
Pickerel rush (*Pontederia cordata*)	3-11, 12-1
Buttercup (*Ranunculus acris*)	4-8, 8-1
Water crowfoot (*Ranunculus aquatilis*)	5-8, 8-1
Miniature spearwort (*Ranunculus flammula*)	5-9, 9-5
Arrowheads (*Sagittaria australis, S. japonica, S. latifolia*)	5-11, 12-1
Lizard's-tail (*Saururus cernuus*)	4-7, 7-1
White or zebra bulrush (*Scirpus lacustris* subsp. *tabernaemontani*)	5-11, 12-1
Marsh betony (*Stachys palustris*)	7-9, 9-7
Hardy thalia (*Thalia dealbata*)	7-11, 12-1
Graceful cattail (*Typha laxmanni*)	3-11, 12-1
Miniature cattail (*Typha minima*)	3-11, 12-1

"Bog plants should be given ample space for growth, but more importantly, they must be placed at the proper growing depth. Some marginal aquatics do well with wet feet and dry ankles, while others must have the roots constantly submerged. Some of these plants will do quite well as cuttings placed between the stones on the perimeter of the pond. They will root into the silt layer between the rocks and survive the winter even without soil."

Keith Folsom is president of Springdale Water Gardens and Springdale Aquatic Nursery and Supply, Greenville, Virginia, and has worked for twenty years in many aspects of water gardening.

SPRING-FLOWERING AQUATIC PLANTS

Spring is always an exciting time in any garden as the daffodils, tulips, and other spring-flowering bulbs and the early-flowering deciduous shrubs and trees begin to wake the winter landscape. All attention does not have to focus on the land-based garden, however, because the water garden also comes alive in spring, especially with some of the early-blooming aquatics. The first to bloom is the water hawthorn (grown as an annual), sometimes flowering while there is snow still on the ground.

Water hawthorn (*Aponogeton distachyos*)	6-9, 10-1
Marsh marigold (*Caltha palustris*)	2-6, 6-1
Louisiana iris (*Iris* hybs.)	6-11, 12-4
Water iris (*Iris laevigata*)	6-11, 12-4
Yellow flag iris (*Iris pseudacorus*)	4-9, 9-4
Blue flag iris (*Iris versicolor*)	4-11, 8-4
Creeping mazus (*Mazus reptans*)	5-8, 8-4
Water forget-me-not (*Myosotis scorpioides*)	5-9, 9-4
Golden club (*Orontium aquaticum*)	6-10, 10-6
Water crowfoot (*Ranunculus aquatilis*)	5-8, 8-1
Buttercup (*Ranunculus repens*)	3-8, 8-1
Arrowheads (*Sagittaria* spp.)	5-11, 12-1

MARSH MARIGOLD

SUMMER-FLOWERING AQUATIC PLANTS

Summer-flowering aquatic plants can be the most dependable show in the garden. Water lilies, blooming from May through September, and lotus in July and August, give a dazzling display. As dependable as the rain is not, they open and close their flowers daily, giving a non-stop performance. The variety of colors—white, orange, yellow, pink, red—will satisfy any gardener looking for midsummer color. Fertilization is important for enjoying the full potential of water lilies and lotus because they are heavy feeders. Given ample soil and space, they can spread quite well, or they can be confined to the smallest of tub gardens.

"The larger the pot or planting zone, the more robust the plant," advises Keith Folsom, president of Springdale Water Gardens and Springdale Aquatic Nursery and Supply, Greenville, Virginia, who provided this list. "Like many herbaceous perennials, these plants respond well to deadheading, fertilization, and a good, rich soil. Leave a lot of spaces in the water garden for summer-flowering plants; nobody can stop at just one or two."

Flowering rush (*Butomus umbellatus*)	5-11, 12-1
Pennywort (*Hydrocotyle verticillata*)	5-11, 12-7
Cardinal flower (*Lobelia cardinalis*)	4-8, 8-1
Primrose creeper (*Ludwigia repens*)	5-11, 12-7
Creeping mazus (*Mazus reptans*)	5-8, 8-4
Aquatic mint (*Mentha aquatica*)	6-9, 9-6
Bog bean (*Menyanthes trifoliata*)	3-7, 7-1
Monkey flower (*Mimulus ringens*)	3-7, 7-1

Water forget-me-not (*Myosotis scorpioides*)	5-9, 9-4
Lotus (*Nelumbo* hybs. and cvs.)	4-11, 12-1
Hardy water lily (*Nymphaea* hybs. and cvs.)	3-11, 12-1
Pickerel rush (*Pontederia cordata*)	3-11, 12-1
Miniature spearwort (*Ranunculus flammula*)	5-9, 9-5
Japanese double arrowhead (*Sagittaria japonica flore-plena*)	5-11, 12-1
Arrowhead (*Sagittaria latifolia*)	5-11, 12-1
Lizard's-tail (*Saururus cernuus*)	4-7, 7-1
Marsh betony (*Stachys palustris*)	7-9, 9-7
Hardy thalia (*Thalia dealbata*)	7-11, 12-1

FALL-FLOWERING AQUATIC PLANTS

Finding plants that flower in the fall can be a challenge for any land-based or water garden. Fortunately, a number of aquatic plants that start blooming during the summer will continue well into the fall, helping to maintain the appeal of the water garden as temperatures and deciduous leaves begin to drop.

Cardinal flower (*Lobelia cardinalis*)	4-8, 8-1
Water forget-me-not (*Myosotis scorpioides*)	5-9, 9-4
Lotus (*Nelumbo* hybs. and cvs.)	4-11, 12-1
Hardy water lily (*Nymphaea* hybs. and cvs.)	3-11, 12-1
Water snowflake (*Nymphoides cristata*)	7-10, 12-1
Yellow snowflake (*Nymphoides geminata*)	7-10, 12-1
Floating heart (*Nymphoides peltata*)	6-11, 12-1
Pickerel rush (*Pontederia cordata*)	3-11, 12-1
Arrowhead (*Sagittaria latifolia*)	5-11, 12-1
Marsh betony (*Stachys palustris*)	7-9, 9-7

CARDINAL
FLOWER

SURFACE-COVERING AQUATIC PLANTS

No water garden is complete without surface-covering aquatic plants, which are the cooling system of the pond, the main contributors to good water quality. The most recognizable are the water lilies and lotus. Their beauty is complemented by the various textures, leaf sizes, and colors of the many other aquatic plants that send runners to the pond surface. These other aquatics have their roots anchored in soil, but their stems spread to the surface, covering and cooling the water. The size and appearance of the flowers of these other surface-covering aquatic plants may be in sharp contrast to the coarse-textured lotus and water lilies as they intermingle with them.

Water hawthorn (*Aponogeton distachyos*)	6-9, 10-1
Floating fern (*Ceratopteris pteridoides*)	6-11, 12-1
Water poppy (*Hydrocleys nymphoides*)	5-11, 12-1
Pennywort (*Hydrocotyle verticillata*)	5-11, 10-1
Primrose creeper (*Ludwigia repens*)	5-11, 11-1
Creeping Jenny (*Lysimachia nummularia*)	3-8, 8-1
Four-leaf water clover (*Marsilea mutica*)	6-11, 12-1
Bog bean (*Menyanthes trifoliata*)	3-7, 7-1
Parrot feather (*Myriophyllum aquaticum*)	5-11, 12-1
Miniature parrot feather (*Myriophyllum proserpinacoides*)	9-11, 12-1
Watercress (*Nasturtium officinale*)	4-11, 12-1
Lotus (*Nelumbo* hybs. and cvs.)	4-11, 12-1
Hardy water lily (*Nymphaea* hybs. and cvs.)	4-11, 12-1
Water snowflake (*Nymphoides cristata*)	7-11, 12-1
Yellow snowflake (*Nymphoides geminata*)	7-11, 12-1
Floating heart (*Nymphoides peltata*)	6-11, 12-1

CAUTION: Check with local, state, and federal officials before using water hyacinth (*Eichhornia crassipes*) or water lettuce (*Pistia stratiotes*). They are outlawed in some states due to their invasive nature. If you do plant them, never throw extra plants into open bodies of water where they may multiply and become noxious weeds.

"Unfortunately, I built a pond before I did all the research I needed to do to write a water gardening book. If I had to do it over, here are some things I would do differently: Don't build shelves—place plant containers on bricks to elevate them. Dig a sump hole—it makes a good place to keep your pump and is a place where you can scoot all the final residue when you clean your pond. Consider some professional help for stone laying—big stones, artfully laid, spell the difference between a so-so pond and a great pond."
    Kathleen Fisher, former editor of *The American Gardener*, is the author of *The Complete Guide to Water Gardens* (Creative Homeowner Press).

GROUND-COVERING AQUATIC PLANTS

The key to using aquatic plants that have a ground-covering nature is to realize that they may require a bit of extra maintenance to keep them from spreading too far or too fast. Many of these plants are very versatile, able to grow in sun or shade.

Hair grass (*Eleocharis acicularis*)	6-11, 12-4
Horsetail (*Equisetum hyemale*)	3-11, 12-1
Horsetail, miniature (*Equisetum scirpoides*)	5-11, 12-1
Variegated manna grass (*Glyceria spectabilis* 'Variegata')	5-9, 9-4
Pennywort (*Hydrocotyle verticillata*)	5-11, 10-1
Variegated water clover (*Marsilea mutica* 'Variegata')	6-11, 12-1
Creeping mazus (*Mazus reptans*)	5-8, 8-4
Aquatic mint (*Mentha aquatica*)	6-9, 9-6
Monkey flower (*Mimulus ringens*)	3-7, 7-1
Water forget-me-not (*Myosotis scorpioides*)	5-9, 9-4
Water crowfoot (*Ranunculus aquatilis*)	5-8, 8-1
Miniature spearwort (*Ranunculus flammula*)	5-9, 9-1
Buttercup (*Ranunculus repens*)	3-8, 8-1
Miniature cattail (*Typha minima*)	3-11, 12-1

"I enjoy using bog plants in patio containers because I do not have to water them during the dry months. I begin by planting combinations of bog plants in a small pot and then place that pot into a large container without drainage holes. The larger pot is then filled with water and I usually don't have to water the rest of the summer. My favorite combinations are *Canna* and *Lysimachia* 'Aurea'; *Equisetum hyemale* and *Lysimachia* 'Aurea'; *Acorus calamus* 'Variegatus' and *Mazus reptans* 'Alba'; *Eupatorium* and *Ajuga*; *Panicum* 'Heavy Metal' and *Ajuga*; *Juncus* 'Spiralis' and *Lysimachia* 'Aurea.'"
    Sandy McDougle is the owner of Sandy's Plants, Inc., a retail and wholesale perennial nursery in Mechanicsville, Virginia.

GRASS-LIKE AQUATIC PLANTS

Textural differences can be as important in a water garden as in any garden. While the best-known aquatic plants, water lilies and lotus, have large round leaves, the various hardy aquatic grasses, rushes, and horsetails have very linear, often very long leaves that may project well above the water surface. Use them as interesting specimens, or as wonderful backgrounds, particularly for the flowering aquatic plants.

CATTAIL

Flowering rush (*Butomus umbellatus*)	5-11, 12-1
Dwarf bamboo (*Dulichium arundinaceum*)	5-9, 9-1
Hair grass (*Eleocharis acicularis*)	6-11, 12-4
Water chestnut (*Eleocharis dulcis*)	9-11, 12-9
Spike rush (*Eleocharis montevidensis*)	6-11, 12-6
Horsetail (*Equisetum hyemale*)	3-11, 12-1
Miniature horsetail (*Equisetum scirpoides*)	5-11, 12-1
Variegated manna grass (*Glyceria spectabilis* 'Variegata')	5-9, 9-4
Ribbon grass (*Phalaris arundinacea*)	4-9, 9-1
White or zebra bulrush (*Scirpus lacustris* subsp. *tabernaemontani*)	5-11, 12-1
Narrowleaf cattail (*Typha angustifolia*)	2-11, 12-1
Miniature cattail (*Typha minima*)	3-11, 12-1
Wild rice (*Zizania latifolia*)	5-10, 10-1

SPECIALS LISTS AND GARDENS

Most of this book has been organized by plant category—trees, shrubs, vines, etc. In this chapter, however, many of the plant categories have been pooled for special situations. Here you will find lists of award-winning plants, native plants, seashore plants, edible plants, invasives, plants that attract or resist certain wildlife, and plants that may adversely affect human health. Once you select plants of interest from these lists, you can double check their environmental requirements by consulting the index for the other lists on which they appear, or consult one of the many plant reference books that are available.

PENNSYLVANIA GOLD-MEDAL TREES, SHRUBS, AND VINES

For the Pennsylvania Horticultural Society's Gold Medal Award program, a working committee meets twice yearly to evaluate and select winners from trees, shrubs, and vines nominated by anyone who loves woody plants—home gardeners, garden designers, horticulturists, landscape architects, nursery growers. The criteria are cold hardiness for zones 5-7, disease and insect resistance, ease of care, landscape durability, and beauty. Here are the PHS Gold Medalist species and cultivars from the program's beginning through 2001.

Nordman fir (*Abies nordmanniana*)
Trident maple (*Acer buergerianum*)
Paperbark maple (*Acer griseum*)
Cutleaf Japanese maple (*Acer palmatum* var. *dissectum* 'Tamukeyama')
Japanese maple (*Acer palmatum* 'Waterfall')
Three-flowered maple (*Acer triflorum*)
Bottlebrush buckeye (*Aesculus parviflora*)
Red buckeye (*Aesculus pavia*)
Red chokeberry (*Aronia arbutifolia* 'Brilliantissima')
River birch (*Betula nigra* 'Heritage')
Boxwood (*Buxus* 'Green Velvet')
Purple beautyberry (*Callicarpa dichotoma*)
Japanese plum yew (*Cephalotaxus harringtonia* 'Prostrata')
Yellowwood (*Cladrastis kentukea*)
Clematis (*Clematis viticella* 'Betty Corning')
Summersweet (*Clethra alnifolia* 'Hummingbird,' 'Ruby Spice')

Kousa dogwood (*Cornus kousa* x *C. florida* 'Rutban,' 'Rutlan')
Cornelian cherry dogwood (*Cornus mas* 'Golden Glory')
Red osier dogwood (*Cornus sericea* 'Silver and Gold')
Hawthorn (*Crataegus viridis* 'Winter King')
Japanese cedar (*Cryptomeria japonica* 'Yoshino')
Caucasian daphne (*Daphne caucasica*)
Slender deutzia (*Deutzia gracilis* 'Nikko')
Enkianthus (*Enkianthus perulatus* 'J. L. Pennock')
Dwarf fothergilla (*Fothergilla gardenii* 'Blue Mist')
Silverbell (*Halesia diptera* var. *magniflora*)
Chinese witch hazel (*Hamamelis mollis* 'Pallida')
Witch hazel (*Hamamelis* x *intermedia* 'Diane')
English ivy (*Hedera helix* 'Buttercup')
Seven-son flower (*Heptacodium miconioides*)
Rose of Sharon (*Hibiscus syriacus* 'Diana')
Smooth hydrangea (*Hydrangea arborescens* 'Annabelle')
Bigleaf hydrangea (*Hydrangea macrophylla* 'Blue Billow')
Oakleaf hydrangea (*Hydrangea quercifolia* 'Snow Queen')
Inkberry holly (*Ilex glabra* 'Densa')
American holly (*Ilex opaca*)
Winterberry (*Ilex* 'Harvest Red,' 'Sparkleberry')
Blue holly (*Ilex* x *meserveae* 'Mesid')
Winterberry (*Ilex verticillata* 'Scarlett O'Hara,' 'Winter Red')
Sweetspire (*Itea virginica* 'Henry's Garnet')
Eastern red cedar (*Juniperus virginiana* 'Corcorcor')
Golden-rain tree (*Koelreuteria paniculata* 'Rose Lantern')
Southern magnolia (*Magnolia grandiflora* 'Edith Bogue')
Yellow magnolia (*Magnolia* 'Elizabeth')
Galaxy magnolia (*Magnolia* 'Galaxy')
Centennial magnolia (*Magnolia kobus* var. *stellata* 'Centennial')
Leatherleaf mahonia (*Mahonia bealei*)
Crabapple (*Malus* 'Donald Wyman,' 'Jewelberry')
Dawn redwood (*Metasequoia glyptostroboides*)
Persian ironwood (*Parrotia persica*)
Oriental spruce (*Picea orientalis*)
Flowering cherry (*Prunus* 'Hally Jolivette,' 'Okame')
White oak (*Quercus alba*)
Japanese umbrella pine (*Sciadopitys verticillata*)
Hydrangea vine (*Schizophragma hydrangeoides* 'Moonlight')
Japanese stewartia (*Stewartia pseudocamellia* var. *koreana*)
Meyer lilac (*Syringa meyeri* 'Palibin')
Japanese tree lilac (*Syringa reticulata* 'Ivory Silk')
Giant arborvitae (*Thuja* 'Green Giant')
Linden viburnum (*Viburnum dilatatum* 'Erie')
Possumhaw (*Viburnum nudum* 'Winterthur')
Doublefile viburnum (*Viburnum plicatum* f. *tomentosum* 'Shasta')
Burkwood viburnum (*Viburnum* x *burkwoodii* 'Conoy,' 'Mohawk')
Viburnum (*Viburnum* 'Eskimo')
Weigela (*Weigela florida* 'Alexandra')
Japanese zelkova (*Zelkova serrata* 'Green Vase')

"The winterberry hollies are a favorite of mine. They are beautiful in the landscape, with the red berries produced by the female plants attracting many colorful birds. Winterberries like wet sites. When I run across these natives on a hike or hunt, I'm almost sure to find a stream or pond, and therefore wildlife, nearby. Three of these hollies have been selected as Gold Medal Plants by the Pennsylvania Horticultural Society."

   Joseph Ziccardi is Gold Medal Plant coordinator for the Pennsylvania Horticultural Society, and operations and production assistant for the annual Philadelphia Flower Show.

DELAWARE PLANTS OF THE YEAR

Each year two plants, one woody and one herbaceous, are selected as the Delaware Nursery and Landscape Association's Plants of the Year. Criteria include: cold hardy in zones 7b-6b, few disease and insect problems, non-invasive, adapted to a variety of landscape uses, possessing horticultural assets such as flower, fruit, leaf, habit, and structure, attractive to wildlife, currently under-used in Delaware landscapes, and readily available from Delaware growers, nurseries, and garden centers.

Woody	Herbaceous
1995	
Sweet-bay magnolia (*Magnolia virginiana*)	Coreopsis (*Coreopsis verticillata* 'Moonbeam')
1996	
Possumhaw (*Viburnum nudum* 'Winterthur')	Purple coneflower (*Echinacea purpurea* 'Bright Star')
1997	
Summersweet (*Clethra alnifolia* 'Hummingbird')	Switch grass (*Panicum virgatum* 'Heavy Metal')
1998	
Fothergilla (*Fothergilla gardenii*)	Blue star (*Amsonia tabernaemontana*)
1999	
Winterberry (*Ilex verticillata* 'Sparkleberry')	Gaura (*Gaura lindheimeri* 'Whirling Butterflies')
2000	
Nandina or heavenly bamboo (*Nandina domestica*)	Goldenrod (*Solidago rugosa* 'Fireworks')
2001	
Oakleaf hydrangea (*Hydrangea quercifolia*)	Sedum (*Sedum* 'Matrona')

"*Viburnum nudum* 'Winterthur' is a little known but garden worthy plant with a local connection. It fits into landscapes easily with its relatively small 6-foot stature. I use it mostly in masses with a drift of perennials in the foreground in front of its glossy leaves. This viburnum's reddish-purple fall color combined with dwarf asters and 'Matrona' sedum create a spectacular garden that's nearly trouble free."

   Naomi McCafferty owns Farm Meadows Nursery in Hockessin, Delaware, and is chair of the Delaware Nursery and Landscape Association's Plant of the Year committee.

LONG ISLAND GOLD-MEDALISTS

In bestowing their Gold Medal Plant Award, the Long Island Horticultural Society looks for outstanding plants that are grown locally and adapted to Long Island conditions and the climate effects of being surrounded by the waters of Long Island Sound and the Atlantic Ocean. Here are the recent winners.

2000

Fothergilla (*Fothergilla gardenii*)
Japanese stewartia (*Stewartia pseudocamellia*)

Russian arborvitae (*Microbiota decussata*)
Buttercup witch hazel (*Corylopsis pauciflora*)

2001

Black-eyed Susan (*Rubeckia nitida* 'Autumn Sun' or 'Herbsonne')
Lace shrub or cutleaf stephanandra (*Stephanandra incisa* 'Crispa')

Japanese plum yew (*Cephalotaxus harringtonia* 'Duke Gardens')
Barrenwort (*Epimedium × perralchicum* 'Frohnleiten')

"**The Russian arborvitae and Japanese plum yew are not just your mother's evergreens. Enough blue rug juniper! These plants prove you can have hard-working and elegant conifers.**"
Darrell Trout is former director of the Garden Writers Association of America, and author of two Country Home Books: *Country Garden Planner* and *Kitchen Garden Planner*.

NATIVE PLANTS

The New York and Mid-Atlantic region is fortunate to have many wonderful native plants, especially trees such as red maples, river birches, and the flowering dogwood. Native plants are plants that are indigenous to a region—living, growing, and reproducing naturally in that environment. Geographic ranges can be debated, but the plants included on these lists are native to at least a large part, if not all of our region. Do not confuse *native* plants with *naturalized* plants. Naturalized plants are non-native, imported, or exotic plants that may have escaped cultivation in gardens and landscapes and now freely populate uncultivated areas such as meadows, pastures, and woodlands. English ivy, multiflora rose, purple loosestrife, and Norway maple have all escaped the garden and are now naturalized.

Are native plants better than non-natives? It all comes down to "right plant, right location." Heritage goes out the window if a plant can't establish and grow within a site's conditions, especially in our urban areas. If the soil, water patterns, or light intensities have been altered so that no native will grow well (as happens with flowering dogwood and eastern white pine), then try a non-native.

The argument that natives have fewer pest problems isn't necessarily true if you look at the past devastation of the American chestnut and the American elm by fungal diseases, the current plague on oaks by gypsy moths, on flowering dogwood by *Discula* anthracnose, or on Canadian hemlocks by woolly adelgid. The pests of our natives are often non-native (imported) pests; with world commerce flourishing, it is impossible to keep introduced pests outside our borders. Use natives whenever and wherever you can, but realize their limitations, and plant accordingly.

The list of native trees comes from horticulturist Ed Milhous of Haymarket, Virginia; the shrubs list is the work of John Wise, horticulturist for the Lewis Ginter Botanical Garden in Richmond, Virginia; Barry Glick, owner of Sunshine Farm and Gardens Nursery in Renick, West Virginia, compiled the perennials.

Trees and shrubs marked with an asterisk (*) in this list are evergreen.

NEW JERSEY
TEA

Native Trees

Red or swamp maple (*Acer rubrum*)
Red buckeye (*Aesculus pavia*)
Serviceberry, shadblow (*Amelanchier arborea*)
Pawpaw (*Asimina triloba*)
River birch (*Betula nigra*)
Hornbeam, blue beech (*Carpinus caroliniana*)
Bitternut hickory (*Carya cordiformis*)

Pignut hickory (*Carya glabra*)
Shellbark hickory (*Carya laciniosa*)
Shagbark hickory (*Carya ovata*)
Mockernut hickory (*Carya tomentosa*)
American chestnut (*Castanea dentata*)
Chinkapin (*Castanea pumila*)
Hackberry (*Celtis occidentalis*)
Eastern redbud (*Cercis canadensis*)

Atlantic white cedar (*Chamaecyparis thyoides*)*
White fringe tree (*Chionanthus virginicus*)
Pagoda dogwood (*Cornus alternifolia*)
Flowering dogwood (*Cornus florida*)
Green hawthorn (*Crataegus viridis*)
Common persimmon (*Diospyros virginiana*)
American beech (*Fagus grandifolia*)
White ash (*Fraxinus americana*)
Green ash (*Fraxinus pennsylvanica*)
Honeylocust (*Gleditsia triacanthos*)
Carolina silverbell (*Halesia carolina*)
American holly (*Ilex opaca*)*
Black walnut (*Juglans nigra*)
Eastern red cedar (*Juniperus virginiana*)*
Sweetgum (*Liquidambar styraciflua*)
Tulip tree (*Liriodendron tulipifera*)
Cucumber tree (*Magnolia acuminata*)
Southern magnolia (*Magnolia grandiflora*)*
Bigleaf magnolia (*Magnolia macrophylla*)
Umbrella magnolia (*Magnolia tripetala*)
Sweet-bay magnolia (*Magnolia virginiana*)
Black gum, tupelo (*Nyssa sylvatica*)
Hop hornbeam (*Ostrya virginiana*)
Sourwood (*Oxydendrum arboreum*)
Shortleaf pine (*Pinus echinata*)*
Eastern white pine (*Pinus strobus*)*
Loblolly pine (*Pinus taeda*)*
Virginia pine (*Pinus virginiana*)*
American sycamore (*Platanus occidentalis*)
American plum (*Prunus americana*)
White oak (*Quercus alba*)
Swamp white oak (*Quercus bicolor*)
Scarlet oak (*Quercus coccinea*)
Southern red oak, Spanish oak (*Quercus falcata*)
Laurel oak (*Quercus hemisphaerica*)
Shingle oak (*Quercus imbricaria*)
Overcup oak (*Quercus lyrata*)
Blackjack oak (*Quercus marilandica*)
Swamp chestnut oak (*Quercus michauxii*)
Chinkapin oak (*Quercus muehlenbergii*)
Water oak (*Quercus nigra*)
Cherrybark oak (*Quercus pagodifolia*)
Pin oak (*Quercus palustris*)
Willow oak (*Quercus phellos*)
Chestnut oak (*Quercus prinus*)
Northern red oak (*Quercus rubra*)
Post oak (*Quercus stellata*)
Black oak (*Quercus velutina*)
Live oak (*Quercus virginiana*)*
Pussy willow (*Salix discolor*)
Black willow (*Salix nigra*)
Sassafras (*Sassafras albidum*)
American snowbell (*Styrax americanus*)
Pond cypress (*Taxodium ascendens*)

Bald cypress (*Taxodium distichum*)
American arborvitae, white cedar (*Thuja occidentalis*)*
American linden, basswood (*Tilia americana*)
Slippery elm (*Ulmus rubra*)

Native Shrubs
Bottlebrush buckeye (*Aesculus parviflora*)
Red chokeberry (*Aronia arbutifolia*)
American beautyberry (*Callicarpa americana*)
Sweetshrub (*Calycanthus floridus*)
New Jersey tea (*Ceanothus americanus*)
Buttonbush (*Cephalanthus occidentalis*)
Leatherleaf (*Chamaedaphne calyculata*)*
Sweet pepperbush (*Clethra alnifolia*)
Pagoda dogwood (*Cornus alternifolia*)
Silky dogwood (*Cornus amomum*)
Gray dogwood (*Cornus racemosa*)
Red osier dogwood (*Cornus sericea*)
Strawberry bush (*Euonymus americana*)
Fothergilla (*Fothergilla gardenii*)
Witch hazel (*Hamamelis virginiana*)
Smooth hydrangea (*Hydrangea arborescens*)
Oakleaf hydrangea (*Hydrangea quercifolia*)
Shrubby St. John's wort (*Hypericum prolificum*)
Possumhaw (*Ilex decidua*)
Inkberry (*Ilex glabra*)*
Winterberry (*Ilex verticillata*)
Virginia sweetspire (*Itea virginica*)
Common juniper (*Juniperus communis*)*
Creeping juniper (*Juniperus horizontalis*)*
Mountain laurel (*Kalmia latifolia*)*
Sand myrtle (*Leiophyllum buxifolium*)
Coast leucothoe (*Leucothoe axillaris*)*
Drooping leucothoe (*Leucothoe fontanesiana*)*
Fetterbush leucothoe (*Leucothoe racemosa*)
Spice bush (*Lindera benzoin*)
Wax myrtle (*Myrica cerifera*)*
Bayberry (*Myrica pensylvanica*)*
Fetterbush, mountain pieris (*Pieris floribunda*)*
Potentilla, bush cinquefoil (*Potentilla fruticosa*)
Sweet azalea (*Rhododendron arborescens*)
Coast azalea (*Rhododendron atlanticum*)
Cumberland azalea (*Rhododendron bakeri*)
Flame azalea (*Rhododendron calendulaceum*)
Rhodora (*Rhododendron canadense*)
Catawba rhododendron (*Rhododendron catawbiense*)*
Rosebay rhododendron (*Rhododendron maximum*)*
Pinxterbloom azalea (*Rhododendron periclymenoides*)
Pinkshell azalea (*Rhododendron vaseyi*)
Swamp azalea (*Rhododendron viscosum*)
Shining sumac (*Rhus copallina*)

Staghorn sumac (*Rhus typhina*)
Virginia rose (*Rosa virginiana*)
Elderberry (*Sambucus canadensis*)
Highbush blueberry (*Vaccinium corymbosum*)
Maple-leaf viburnum (*Viburnum acerifolium*)
Witherod viburnum (*Viburnum cassinoides*)
Arrowwood viburnum (*Viburnum dentatum*)
Nannyberry (*Viburnum lentago*)
Blackhaw viburnum (*Viburnum prunifolium*)
American cranberry-bush viburnum (*Viburnum trilobum*)
Dusty zenobia (*Zenobia pulverulenta*)

Native Vines
Cross vine (*Bignonia capreolata*)
Trumpet vine (*Campsis radicans*)
Virgin's bower (*Clematis virginiana*)
Climbing hydrangea (*Decumaria barbara*)
Trumpet honeysuckle (*Lonicera sempervirens*)
Virginia creeper (*Parthenocissus quinquefolia*)
American wisteria (*Wisteria frutescens*)

Native Ground Covers
Bearberry (*Arctostaphylos uva-ursi*)
Bunchberry (*Cornus canadensis*)
Partridge berry (*Mitchella repens*)
Alleghany pachysandra (*Pachysandra procumbens*)
Canby paxistima (*Paxistima canbyi*)
Fragrant sumac (*Rhus aromatica*)

Native Perennials and Wildflowers
FOR SUNNY LOCATIONS
Yarrow (*Achillea* spp.)
Agave (*Agave virginica*)
Blue-star (*Amsonia tabernaemontana*)
Swamp milkweed (*Asclepias incarnata*)
Butterfly weed (*Asclepias tuberosa*)
Asters (*Aster carolinianus, A. dumosus, A. novae-angliae, A. novi-belgii*)
Wild indigo (*Baptisia australis*)
Boltonia (*Boltonia asteroides*)
Wine cups (*Callirhoe alcaeoides*)
Quamash (*Camassia leichtlinii*)
Tickseed (*Coreopsis tripteris, C. verticillata, C. zampfir*)
Coneflower (*Echinacea purpurea*)
Joe Pye weed (*Eupatorium fistulosum*)
Swamp sunflower (*Helianthus angustifolius*)
Crested iris (*Iris cristata*)
Gayfeather (*Liatris spicata*)
American Turk's cap lily (*Lilium superbum*)
Bee balm (*Monarda didyma*)
Evening primrose (*Oenothera fruticosa, O. speciosa*)

Beardtongue (*Penstemon digitalis*)
Phlox (*Phlox amoena, P. divaricata, P. paniculata, P. pilosa, P. stolonifera, P. subulata*)
Rudbeckia or black-eyed Susan (*Rudbeckia fulgida, R. laciniata, R. maxima*)
Goldenrod (*Solidago caesia, S. rigida, S. rugosa, S. sphacelata*)
Stokes' aster (*Stokesia laevis*)
False lupine (*Thermopsis lanceolata*)
Rose verbena (*Verbena canadensis*)
Ironweed (*Vernonia fasciculata*)

FOR SHADE AND WOODLANDS
Doll's eyes (*Actaea pachypoda*)
Rue anemone (*Anemonella thalictroides*)
Columbine (*Aquilegia canadensis*)
Jack-in-the-pulpit (*Arisaema triphyllum*)
Wild ginger (*Asarum canadense*)
False indigo (*Baptisia pendula*)
Blue cohosh (*Caulophyllum thalictroides*)
Turtlehead (*Chelone glabra, C. lyonii*)
Bugbane (*Cimicifuga racemosa*)
Spring beauty (*Claytonia virginica*)
Clinton's lily (*Clintonia umbellulata*)
Wild bleeding-heart (*Dicentra eximia*)
Shooting star (*Dodecatheon meadia*)
Trout lily, dog's-tooth violet (*Erythronium americanum*)
Joe Pye weed (*Eupatorium fistulosum, E. maculatum*)
Hardy geranium (*Geranium maculatum*)
Rattlesnake orchid (*Goodyera pubescens*)
Liver leaf (*Hepatica acutiloba*)
Coral bells (*Heuchera americana, H. villosa*)
Crested iris (*Iris cristata*)
Cardinal flower (*Lobelia cardinalis, L. siphilitica*)
False lily-of-the-valley (*Maianthemum canadense*)
Meehan's mint (*Meehania cordata*)
Virginia bluebells (*Mertensia virginica*)
Woodland phlox (*Phlox divaricata*)
Obedient plant (*Physostegia virginiana*)
Mayapple (*Podophyllum peltatum*)
Solomon's seal (*Polygonatum biflorum*)
False Solomon's seal (*Smilacina racemosa*)
Golden wood poppy (*Stylophorum diphyllum*)
Foam flower (*Tiarella cordifolia, T. wherryi*)
Spiderwort (*Tradescantia andersoniana, T. virginiana*)
Tassle rue, false bugbane (*Trautvetteria caroliniensis*)
Large merrybells (*Uvularia grandiflora*)
Culver's root (*Veronicastrum virginicum*)
Wild violets (*Viola cucullata, V. labradorica*)

"In their native haunts, many of our abundant wild plants are overlooked for several reasons. They are sometimes lost in a jungle of weeds or stifled by obstacles such as foot traffic, competition from tree roots, or lack of adequate moisture. But give them a nice home with good, rich soils, a little love, attention, and fertilizer, and stand back. Only buy nursery-propagated plants, however, or plants that have been rescued from construction sites or moved with permission from the landowner."

Barry Glick is owner of Sunshine Farm and Gardens Nursery in Renick, West Virginia, and is a regular contributor to many gardening magazines. He edits The Cyber-Plantsman, an Internet magazine for gardeners (www.sunfarm.com).

Native Ferns
Maidenhair fern (*Adiantum pedatum*)
Ebony spleenwort (*Asplenium platyneuron*)
Walking fern (*Asplenium rhizophyllum*)
Lady fern (*Athyrium filix-femina*)
Hay-scented fern (*Dennstaedtia punctilobula*)
Clinton wood fern (*Dryopteris clintoniana*)
Crested wood fern (*Dryopteris cristata*)
Goldie's fern (*Dryopteris goldieana*)
Leatherwood fern (*Dryopteris marginalis*)
New York fern (*Dryopteris noveboracensis*)
Northern beech fern (*Dryopteris phegopteris*)
Ostrich fern (*Matteuccia pennsylvanica*)
Sensitive fern (*Onoclea sensibilis*)
Adder's tongue (*Ophioglossum vulgatum*)
Cinnamon fern (*Osmunda cinnamomea*)
Interrupted fern (*Osmunda claytoniana*)
Royal fern (*Osmunda regalis* var. *spectabilis*)

Hairy purple cliffbrake (*Pellaea atropurpurea*)
Christmas fern (*Polystichum acrostichoides*)
Bracken fern (*Pteridium aquilinum*)
Virginia chain fern (*Woodwardia virginica*)

Native Grasses
Big bluestem (*Andropogon gerardii*)
Broom sedge (*Andropogon virginicus*)
Sideoats grama (*Bouteloua curtipendula*)
Northern sea oats (*Chasmanthium latifolium*)
Tufted hair grass (*Deschampsia cespitosa*)
Sand love grass (*Eragrostis trichoides*)
Plume grass (*Erianthus contortus*)
Switch grass (*Panicum virgatum*)
Little bluestem (*Schizachyrium scoparium*)
Indian grass (*Sorghastrum avenaceum*, *S. nutans*)
Prairie dropseed (*Sporobolus heterolepsis*)
Eastern grama grass (*Tripsicum dactyloides*)

"The use of native plants is not 'your final answer' for a low-maintenance garden. However, many are quite adaptable to climate and soils, and offer a plethora of flowers and fruit."

John Wise is a horticulturist for the Lewis Ginter Botanical Garden in Richmond, Virginia.

INVASIVE NON-NATIVE PLANTS

Many people think that the greatest threat to our native plants is not urbanization, or human vandalism and neglect, or insects and diseases, or the loss of many of our pesticides, but invasive introduced plants. Some of these plants have been brought into this country on purpose by plant collectors, or for food, fiber, medicines, and landscapes. Some have arrived as hitchhikers with other imported items. Thousands of plant species have been brought to the United States during the past four centuries, and most of these plants pose no threat, rarely escaping into natural, uncultivated areas. A few hundred, however, are increasingly troublesome; with no natural controls and no native plants able to out-compete them for habitat, they become invasive. While many of them are considered weeds, many others definitely qualify as garden and landscape plants.

Native plant societies suggest that you answer the following questions as a test for whether to introduce a non-native into your garden.
- Does it naturalize or self-sow its seed?
- Is it a food plant for wildlife?
- Is it a ground cover that can rapidly spread?
- Is it cold and heat hardy, pest free, and tolerant of shade or soil moisture extremes?

- Does it have the ability to suppress the growth of other plants by shading or growing over them, or outcompeting them for water and soil nutrients, or by allelopathy (producing toxins)?

If you answer yes to one or more of these questions, the plant has the potential to become invasive and puts the responsibility on you to prevent its escape from your landscape.

For additional information on invasives, contact your state's department of agriculture or conservation or a native plant society. Also check the USDA Agricultural Research Service's Invaders Database System (http//:invader.dbs.umt.edu/ Noxious_Weeds/).

Invasive Trees and Shrubs
Norway maple (*Acer platanoides*)
Tree of heaven (*Ailanthus altissima*)
Mimosa (*Albizia julibrissin*)
Japanese barberry (*Berberis thunbergii*)
Russian olive (*Elaeagnus angustifolia*)
Autumn olive (*Elaeagnus umbellata*)
Thorny elaeagnus (*Elaeagnus pungens*)
Winged euonymus or burning bush (*Euonymus alatus*)
Tatarian honeysuckle (*Lonicera tatarica*)
White mulberry (*Morus alba*)
Princess or empress tree (*Paulownia tomentosa*)
White poplar (*Populus alba*)

Glossy buckthorn (*Rhamnus frangula*)
Siberian elm (*Ulmus pumila*)

Invasive Vines, Ground Covers, and Perennials
Five-leaf akebia (*Akebia quinata*)
Porcelain berry (*Ampelopsis brevipedunculata*)
Wintercreeper (*Euonymus fortunei*)
English ivy (*Hedera helix*)
Japanese honeysuckle (*Lonicera japonica*)
Purple loosestrife (*Lythrum salicaria, L. virgatum*)
Vinca (*Vinca minor*)
Chinese wisteria (*Wisteria sinensis*)
Japanese wisteria (*Wisteria floribunda*)

CAUTION: Purple loosestrife (*Lythrum salicaria, L. virgatum*) has been declared a noxious weed in Pennsylvania and Virginia. It is illegal to buy, sell, or transport the plant, and technically even to plant it (including any hybrids or cultivars).

EDIBLE LANDSCAPES

Aside from standard fruit (apple, pear, peach, cherry, plum, apricot) and nut (walnut, pecan, filbert, chestnut) trees, several other trees produce less common, but generally no less delicious and nutritious, edible fruit. Many of these trees are ornamental, with showy flowers and fall color in addition to often very showy fruit. Many require far less pest management and directive pruning than standard fruit and nut trees. Some shrubs, vines, and even ground-cover plants likewise put on a show while delighting your taste buds as well. If you have acid soil, don't plant just azaleas and rhododendrons—add some blueberries. You'll find other berry suggestions in the list of edible shrubs and hedges from Rob and Sybil Mays, who own Paradise Nursery in Virginia Beach, Virginia. Also, there's a list of edible flowers from Sandy Lane of Riverbend Nursery in Riner, Virginia.

Trees for Edible Landscapes
Serviceberries, juneberries (*Amelanchier* spp.)
Pawpaw (*Asimina triloba*)
Mayhaw (*Crataegus aestivalis*)
Mediterranean medlar (*Crataegus azarolus*)
Oriental persimmon (*Diospyros kaki*)
Native persimmon (*Diospyros virginiana*)
Goumi (*Elaeagnus multiflora*)
Japanese raisin tree (*Hovenia dulcis*)
Crabapples (*Malus* spp.)
Medlar (*Mespilus germanica*)

Mulberries (*Morus* spp.)
Beach plum (*Prunus maritima*)
Dwarf asian pear (*Prunus pyrifolia*)
Pomegranate (*Punica granatum*)
Mountain ash (*Sorbus aucuparia* and hybs.)
Jujube (*Ziziphus jujuba*)

Shrubs and Hedges for Edible Landscapes
Flowering quince (*Chaenomeles japonica*)
Pineapple guava (*Feijoa sellowiana, Acca sellowiana*)

Fig (*Ficus carica*)
Hybrid bush cherry (*Prunus* x 'Jan,' 'Joel,' 'Joy')
Nanking bush cherry (*Prunus tomentosa*)
Catherina or invicta gooseberry (*Ribes hirtellum*)
Glenndale gooseberry (*Ribes missouriense*
x *R. grossularia*)
Consort black currant (*Ribes nibrum*)
Thornless jostaberry (*Ribes nidigrolaria*)
Cherry Red currant (*Ribes rubrum*)
Bianca white currant (*Ribes rubrum alba*)
American red currant (*Ribes sanguineum*)
Thornless blackberry (*Rubus* 'Arapaho,' 'Kiowa,'
'Navaho')
Raspberry (*Rubus idaeus*)
Elderberry (*Sambucus canadensis*)
Cutleaf elderberry (*Sambucus nigra laciniata*)
Variegated elderberry (*Sambucus nigra variegata*)
Rabbiteye blueberry (*Vaccinium ashei*)
Northern highbush blueberry (*Vaccinium
corymbosum*)

**Ground Covers and Vines for Edible
Landscapes**
Hardy kiwi (*Actinidia arguta* 'Issai')
Hardy red kiwi (*Actinidia purpurea*)
Bearberry (*Arctostaphylos uva-ursi*)
Wintergreen (*Gaultheria procumbens*)
Salal (*Gaultheria shallon*)
Maypop or passionflower (*Passiflora incarnata*)
Vining thornless blackberry (*Rubus* 'Black Satin,'
'Chester,' 'Triple Crown')
Thornless ground-cover raspberry (*Rubus arcticua*
x *R. stellata*)
Ground-cover raspberry (*Rubus calycinoides*)
Ground-cover blueberry (*Vaccinium
angustifolium*)
Cranberry (*Vaccinium macrocarpum*)
Eastern bunch grapes (*Vitis labrusca*)

"Thornless blackberries do not invade the garden like thorny varieties. Vining blackberries form long arching canes suitable for training on a trellis or fence. Delicate pink flowers are followed by brilliant red and black berry clusters. Many varieties show deep burgundy fall and winter color. The new stems on blueberry bushes add lovely color to the winter garden, followed by delicate spring flowers, colorful pink and blue berries, and finally a blaze of autumn foliage. Pruning maintains a dense shape and can be used to create a solid hedge of plants. Rabbiteye blueberries are recommended for the hotter, more humid areas, where they'll have excellent fall colors. Raspberries can be grown as a fruiting hedge. Some support is needed as canes grow and arch. Bush cherries create a frothy display with hundreds of tiny white flowers borne each spring on graceful arching branches, followed in summer by bright red, tart cherries."
     Sybil and Rob Mays are owners of Paradise Nursery (www.paradisenursery.com), a Virginia Beach, Virginia, mail-order nursery specializing in figs and other edible landscaping plants.

Edible Perennial Flowers
Anise hyssop (*Agastache foeniculum*)
Hollyhock (*Alcea rosea*)
Roman chamomile (*Chamaemelum nobile*)
Chrysanthemum (*Chrysanthemum* spp. and cvs.)
Pinks (*Dianthus* spp.)
Sweet woodruff (*Galium odoratum*)

Daylilies (*Hemerocallis* spp. and cvs.)
Lavender (*Lavandula* spp.)
Bee balm (*Monarda* cvs.)
Peony (*Paeonia* cvs.)
Pineapple sage (*Salvia elegans*)
Culinary sage (*Salvia officinalis*)
Wild violets, Johnny-jump-up (*Viola* spp.)

"Eat only flowers that you are sure have been grown without chemicals. Remove pistils and stamens from flowers before eating. Do not eat flowers if you have severe hay fever. Start with small quantities. People can have allergic reactions to flowers just as with any food."
     Sandy Lane is with Riverbend Nursery in Riner, Virginia.

WILDLIFE GARDENS

Planting a wildlife garden is one of the best things you can do to preserve and restore the natural environment, which is something that our highly developed region needs," observes David Mizejewski, who manages the Backyard Wildlife Habitat Program for the National Wildlife Federation in Vienna, Virginia, and who contributed this list of plants for creating a backyard wildlife habitat. "Habitat loss, through development and invasion of exotic species, is the number one reason for the disappearance of wildlife. Noah had to build an ark to save his furred, feathered, and scaled friends—you can plant a garden!"

The best way to garden for wildlife is to re-create the local native plant communities with which wildlife co-evolved. Learn to identify the four elements of habitat—food, water, cover, and places to raise young—in your local woodlands and meadows, then try to replicate them in your garden. If you follow their guidelines, the National Wildlife Federation will recognize your efforts by certifying your yard as an official Backyard Wildlife Habitat.

To create a wildlife-friendly garden or landscape, use plants that are native to the New York and Mid-Atlantic region (avoid commonly available non-native plants with the same genus or common name).

Wildlife-Friendly Trees and Shrubs
Serviceberry (*Amelanchier canadensis*)
River birch (*Betula nigra*)
Hackberry (*Celtis occidentalis*)
Buttonbush (*Cephalanthus occidentalis*)
Eastern redbud (*Cercis canadensis*)
Dogwood (*Cornus amomum, C. florida,*
    C. racemosa, C. stolonifera)
American beech (*Fagus grandifolia*)
Holly (*Ilex glabra, I. opaca, I. verticillata*)
Eastern red cedar (*Juniperus virginiana*)
Spice bush (*Lindera benzoin*)
Red mulberry (*Morus rubra*)
White pine (*Pinus strobus*)
Oak (*Quercus alba, Q. palustris, Q. phellos*)
Elderberry (*Sambucus canadensis*)
Blueberry (*Vaccinium angustifolium,*
    V. corymbosum)
Viburnum (*Viburnum acerifolium, V. dentatum,*
    V. prunifolium)

Wildlife-Friendly Vines and Ground Covers
Bearberry (*Arctostaphylos uva-ursi*)
Wild ginger (*Asarum canadense*)

Trumpet creeper (*Campsis radicans*)
Coral honeysuckle (*Lonicera sempervirens*)
Partridge berry (*Mitchella repens*)
Virginia creeper (*Parthenocissus quinquefolia*)

Wildlife-Friendly Perennials and Grasses
Big bluestem (*Andropogon gerardii*)
Wild columbine (*Aquilegia canadensis*)
Jack-in-the-pulpit (*Arisaema triphyllum*)
Swamp milkweed (*Asclepias incarnata*)
Butterfly weed (*Asclepias tuberosa*)
Aster (*Aster novae-angliae, A. novi-belgii,*
    A. pilosus)
Coreopsis (*Coreopsis lanceolata, C. tripteris,*
    C. verticillata)
Joe Pye weed (*Eupatorium fistulosum*)
Blazing star (*Liatris spicata*)
Cardinal flower (*Lobelia cardinalis*)
Bee balm (*Monarda didyma*)
Mayapple (*Podophyllum peltatum*)
Cutleaf coneflower (*Rudbeckia laciniata*)
Little bluestem (*Schizachyrium scoparium*)
Violets (*Viola papilionacea, V. pedata, V. striata*)

PLANTS THAT ATTRACT BIRDS

The flash of red flitting through the garden, and a wonderfully recognizable song, are enough to get many people to plant a serviceberry or a dogwood, or to delay cutting down a pesky-fruited mulberry or sweetgum or a disease-prone mimosa. These trees provide favorite foods for the male cardinal. Birds are a very special form of wildlife in our gardens and landscapes because of their color, motion, and sound. Some birds help us out by feasting on weeds or undesirable insects, although some also seed pesky plants like mulberries and black cherries, or compete with us for edible goodies like blueberries. Use a diverse plant array that provides both food (fruits or seeds) and shelter for resident and migratory birds.

FRINGE
TREE

Trees

Fir (*Abies* spp.)
Maple (*Acer* spp.)
Mimosa (*Albizia julibrissin*)
Alder (*Alnus* spp.)
Serviceberry (*Amelanchier* spp.)
Birch (*Betula* spp.)
Hickories (*Carya* spp.)
Hackberry (*Celtis occidentalis*)
White fringe tree (*Chionanthus virginicus*)
Flowering dogwood (*Cornus florida*)
Hawthorn (*Crataegus* spp.)
Russian olive (*Elaeagnus angustifolia*)
American beech (*Fagus grandifolia*)
Ash (*Fraxinus* spp.)
American holly (*Ilex opaca*)
Yaupon holly (*Ilex vomitoria*)
Eastern red cedar (*Juniperus virginiana*)
Larch (*Larix* spp.)
Sweetgum (*Liquidambar styraciflua*)
Tulip tree (*Liriodendron tulipifera*)
Crabapple (*Malus* spp.)
Mulberry (*Morus alba*, *M. rubra*)
Black gum (*Nyssa sylvatica*)
Spruce (*Picea* spp.)
Pines (*Pinus* spp.)
Cherries, plums (*Prunus* spp.)
Oaks (*Quercus* spp.)
Sassafras (*Sassafras albidum*)
Mountain ash (*Sorbus* spp.)
Canadian hemlock (*Tsuga canadensis*)

Shrubs

Red chokeberry (*Aronia arbutifolia*)
Japanese barberry (*Berberis thunbergii*)
Butterfly bush (*Buddleia davidii*)
Buttonbush (*Cephalanthus occidentalis*)
Dogwoods (*Cornus* spp.)
American hazel (*Corylus americana*)
Cotoneaster (*Cotoneaster* spp.)
Elaeagnus (*Elaeagnus* spp.)
St. John's wort (*Hypericum* spp.)
Deciduous hollies (*Ilex decidua*, *I. serrata*, *I. verticillata*)
Juniper (*Juniperus* spp.)
Privet (*Ligustrum* spp.)
Spice bush (*Lindera benzoin*)
Honeysuckle (*Lonicera* spp.)
Oregon holly grape (*Mahonia aquifolium*)
Wax myrtle (*Myrica cerifera*)
Bayberry (*Myrica pensylvanica*)
Photinia (*Photinia* spp.)
Bush cherries and plums (*Prunus* spp.)
Pyracantha (*Pyracantha coccinea*)

Sumac (*Rhus* spp.)
Roses (*Rosa palustris*, *R. rugosa*, *R. virginiana*)
Brambles (*Rubus* spp.)
Pussy willow (*Salix discolor*)
Elderberry (*Sambucus racemosa*)
Snowberry (*Symphoricarpos albus*)
Coralberry (*Symphoricarpos orbiculatus*)
Yew (*Taxus* spp.)
American arborvitae (*Thuja occidentalis*)
Blueberry (*Vaccinium* spp.)
Viburnum (*Viburnum* spp.)
Weigela (*Weigela florida*)

Vines and Ground Covers

Ajuga (*Ajuga reptans*)
Trumpet creeper (*Campsis radicans*)
Bittersweet (*Celastrus* spp.)
Honeysuckle (*Lonicera* spp.)
Bunchberry (*Cornus canadensis*)
Virginia strawberry (*Fragaria chiloensis*)
Wintergreen (*Gaultheria procumbens*)
Partridge berry (*Mitchella repens*)
Virginia creeper (*Parthenocissus quinquefolia*)
Grapes (*Vitis* spp.)

Grasses [Annual (A) and Perennial (P)]

Bluestems, broom sedge (*Andropogon* spp.) (P)
Bulbous oat grass (*Arrhenatherum elatius* var. *bulbosum*) (P)
Sideoats grama grass (*Bouteloua* spp.) (P)
Quaking grass (*Briza maxima*) (A)
Pampas grass (*Cortaderia selloana*) (P)
Tufted hair grass (*Deschampsia cespitosa*) (P)
Love grass (*Eragrostis tef*) (A)
Ravennae grass (*Erianthus ravennae*) (P)
Hare's tail grass (*Lagurus ovatus*) (A)
Miscanthus or eulalia grass (*Miscanthus* spp.) (P)
Tall purple moor grass (*Molinia* spp.) (P)
Switch grass (*Panicum* spp.) (P)
Fountain grass (*Pennisetum alopecuroides*, *P. setaceum*) (P)
Plains bristle grass (*Setaria macrostachya*) (A)
Indian grass (*Sorghastrum* spp.) (P)
Dropseed (*Sporobolus* spp.) (P)

Flowers [Annual (A) and Perennial (P)]

Amaranthus (*Amaranthus* spp.) (A)
Snapdragon (*Antirrhinum majus*) (A)
Columbine (*Aquilegia* spp.) (P)
Butterfly weed (*Asclepias tuberosa*) (P)
Aster (*Aster* spp.) (P)
Calendula (*Calendula officinalis*) (A)
Bachelor's buttons (*Centaurea cyanus*) (A)
Chrysanthemums (*Chrysanthemum* spp.) (P)

California poppy (*Eschscholzia californica*) (A)
China aster (*Callistephus chinensis*) (A)
Coreopsis or tickseed (*Coreopsis* spp.) (A, P)
Cosmos (*Cosmos* spp.) (A)
Delphinium (*Delphinium* spp.) (P)
Pinks (*Dianthus* spp.) (A, P)
Foxglove (*Digitalis* spp.) (P)
Purple coneflower (*Echinacea purpurea*) (P)
Globe thistle (*Echinops ritro*) (P)
Sunflower (*Helianthus* spp.) (A, P)
Dame's rocket (*Hesperis matronalis*) (P)
Candytuft (*Iberis* spp.) (A, P)
Balsam (*Impatiens balsamina*) (A)
Sea lavender or statice (*Limonium* spp.) (A, P)
Cardinal flower (*Lobelia cardinalis*) (P)
Lunaria (*Lunaria* spp.) (P)
Stocks (*Matthiola* spp.) (A)

Love-in-a-mist (*Nigella damascena*) (A)
Evening primrose (*Oenothera* spp.) (P)
Wood sorrel or oxalis (*Oxalis* spp.) (P)
Poppies (*Papaver* spp.) (A, P)
Phlox (*Phlox* spp.) (A, P)
Portulaca (*Portulaca grandiflora*) (A)
Primrose (*Primula* spp.) (P)
Mignonette (*Reseda* spp.) (A)
Black-eyed Susan (*Rudbeckia* spp.) (P)
Pincushion flower (*Scabiosa caucasica*) (P)
Sedum (*Sedum spectabile*) (P)
Goldenrod (*Solidago* spp.) (P)
Marigold (*Tagetes* spp.) (A)
Valerian (*Valeriana* spp.) (P)
Zinnia (*Zinnia* spp.) (A)

PLANTS THAT ATTRACT HUMMINGBIRDS

From March to September, almost any New York or Mid-Atlantic garden can be a host to hummingbirds. Hummingbirds feed three to five times per hour, and they are especially attracted by long, thin, tubular flowers that produce nectar at the flower's base even in hot weather or rainstorms. These birds fly mainly to brightly colored flowers, with red preferred, but also yellow, orange, and pink. Even purple and blue flowers, if a good nectar source, will do. The more extended the flowering time of the plants in your garden, the better for attracting hummingbirds and other wildlife. Plant various attracting plants together (shrubs, vines, flowers) to provide a variety of heights and nectars, and also to attract the small insects and spiders that are another important part of the hummingbird's diet.

LUPINES

Trees, Shrubs, and Vines
Glossy abelia (*Abelia* × *grandiflora*)
Buckeyes (*Aesculus* spp.)
Mimosa (*Albizia julibrissin*)
Cross vine (*Bignonia capreolata*)
Butterfly bush (*Buddleia davidii*)
Trumpet creeper (*Campsis radicans*)
Flowering quince (*Chaenomeles* spp.)
Hawthorn (*Crataegus* spp.)
Hardy hibiscus (*Hibiscus moscheutos* and hybs.)
Beautybush (*Kolkwitzia amabilis*)
Tulip tree (*Liriodendron tulipifera*)
Honeysuckles (*Lonicera* spp.)
Azaleas and rhododendrons (*Rhododendron* spp.)
Black locust (*Robinia pseudoacacia*)
Lilac (*Syringa vulgaris*)
Viburnum (*Viburnum* spp.)
Chaste tree (*Vitex agnus-castus*)
Weigela (*Weigela florida*)
Wisteria (*Wisteria* spp.)
Yucca (*Yucca* spp.)

Flowers [Annuals (A) and Perennials (P)]
Monkshood (*Aconitum carmichaelii*) (P)
Mexican hyssop (*Agastache* spp.) (P)
Ajuga (*Ajuga reptans*) (P)
Hollyhock (*Alcea rosea*) (A, P)
Columbine (*Aquilegia* spp.) (P)
Butterfly weed (*Asclepias tuberosa*) (P)
Begonia (*Begonia* spp.) (A, P)
Bellflower (*Campanula* spp.) (P)
Canna (*Canna* hybs.) (A)
Madagascar periwinkle (*Catharanthus roseus*) (A)
Red valerian (*Centranthus ruber*) (P)
Plumbago (*Ceratostigma plumbaginoides*) (P)
Turtlehead (*Chelone obliqua*) (P)
Cleome or spider flower (*Cleome hassleriana*) (A)
Montbretia (*Crocosmia* spp.) (P)
Delphinium or larkspur (*Delphinium* spp.) (P)
Pinks (*Dianthus* spp.) (A, P)
Bleeding-heart (*Dicentra* spp.) (P)
Purple coneflower (*Echinacea purpurea*) (P)
Gaillardia (*Gaillardia* spp.) (A, P)
Daylilies (*Hemerocallis* spp., hybs., and cvs.) (P)

Dame's rocket (*Hesperis matronalis*) (P)
Coral bells (*Heuchera sanguinea*) (P)
Hosta (*Hosta* spp. and hybs.) (P)
Balsam (*Impatiens balsamina*) (A)
Impatiens (*Impatiens walleriana*) (A)
Morning glory (*Ipomoea purpurea*) (A)
Red-hot poker (*Kniphofia* cvs.) (P)
Lantana (*Lantana camara*) (A)
Sweet pea (*Lathyrus odoratus*) (A)
Gayfeather (*Liatris spicata*) (P)
Lilies (*Lilium* spp.) (A, P)
Cardinal flower (*Lobelia cardinalis*) (P)
Lupines (*Lupinus* hybs.) (P)
Catchfly (*Lychnis* spp.) (P)
Bee balm (*Monarda didyma*) (P)

Catmint (*Nepeta* spp.) (P)
Flowering tobacco (*Nicotiana alata*) (A)
Beard-tongue (*Penstemon* spp.) (P)
Petunia (*Petunia* x *hybrida*) (A)
Phlox (*Phlox* spp.) (A, P)
Obedient plant (*Physostegia virginiana*) (P)
Black-eyed Susan (*Rudbeckia* spp.) (P)
Rosemary (*Rosmarinus officinalis*) (P)
Salvia or sage (*Salvia* spp.) (A, P)
Soapwort (*Saponaria officinalis*) (P)
Pincushion flower (*Scabiosa* spp.) (P)
Indian pink (*Spicelia marilandica*) (P)
Torenia (*Torenia fournieri*) (A)
Nasturtium (*Tropaeolum majus*) (A)
Verbena (*Verbena* spp.) (A, P)

PLANTS THAT ATTRACT BUTTERFLIES

A garden alive with butterflies often has more than just nectar-rich flowers for hungry visitors. Butterflies are insects with four separate life stages. Whereas most adults are sustained by "nectar plants," the egg, larva (caterpillar), and pupa (chrysalis) depend on particular "host plants" for survival. These hosts may be nearby trees, shrubs, vines, or grasses. Holly Cruser, who owns Terra Earth-Friendly Designs in Virginia Beach, Virginia, compiled this list of plants that support a complete life cycle for butterflies. "Be sure to plan the garden so there is always something blooming," she advises. "The more masses of color, the better!" Butterflies like their plants in warm, sunny, wind-protected locations. They also need a shallow water source and large, flat areas on which to rest and warm themselves.

Perennial Nectar Plants
Yarrow (*Achillea* spp.)
Chives (*Allium shoenoprasum*)
Swamp milkweed (*Asclepias incarnata*)
Butterfly weed (*Asclepias tuberosa*)
New England aster (*Aster novae-angliae*)
Red valerian (*Centranthus ruber*)
Plumbago (*Ceratostigma plumbaginoides*)
Ox-eye daisy (*Chrysanthemum leucanthemum*)
Threadleaf coreopsis (*Coreopsis verticillata* 'Moonbeam')
Purple coneflower (*Echinacea purpurea*)
Hardy ageratum (*Eupatorium coelestinum*)
Compact Joe Pye weed (*Eupatorium* 'Gateway')
Blanket flower (*Gaillardia* hybs.)
Sunflower (*Helianthus* spp.)
Gayfeather (*Liatris* spp.)
Bee balm (*Monarda* spp.)
Forget-me-not (*Myosotis sylvatica*)
Garden phlox (*Phlox* spp.)
Obedient plant (*Physostegia virginiana*)
Orange coneflower (*Rudbeckia fulgida* 'Goldsturm')
Black-eyed Susan (*Rudbeckia hirta*)

Salvia (*Salvia* x *superba* cvs.)
Sedum (*Sedum spectabile* 'Autumn Joy,' 'Brilliant')
Dwarf goldenrod (*Solidago* 'Laurin,' 'Golden Fleece')
Rough-leaf goldenrod (*Solidago rugosa* 'Fireworks')
Rose verbena (*Verbena canadensis* 'Homestead Series')
New York ironweed (*Vernonia noveboracensis*)
Veronica (*Veronica spicata* cvs.)

Annual Nectar Plants
Ageratum (*Ageratum houstonianum*)
Blood flower (*Asclepias curassavica*)
Cosmos (*Cosmos bipinnatus*, *C. sulfureus*)
Globe amaranth (*Gomphrena globosa* 'Buddy')
Impatiens (*Impatiens walleriana*)
Lantana (*Lantana* spp.)
Star flower (*Pentas lanceolata*)
Petunia (*Petunia* x *hybrida* 'Wave' series)
Cape leadwort (*Plumbago auriculata*)
Primrose (*Primula* spp.)
Salvia (*Salvia* spp.)

French marigold (*Tagetes patula*)
Mexican sunflower (*Tithonia rotundifolia*)
Garden verbena (*Verbena* x *hybrida*)

Pansy (*Viola cornuta*)
Johnny-jump-up (*Viola tricolor*)
Zinnias (*Zinnia* spp.)

Host Plants
Hollyhock (*Alcea rosea*)
Milkweed (*Asclepias* spp.)
Pawpaw (*Asimina* spp.)
Aster (*Aster* spp.)
Hackberry (*Celtis* spp.)
Flowering dogwood (*Cornus florida*)
Tulip tree (*Liriodendron tulipifera*)
Parsley (*Petroselinum crispum*)
Plantain (*Plantago* spp.)
Wild cherry (*Prunus* spp.)
Willow (*Salix* spp.)
Sassafras (*Sassafras albidum*)
Clover (*Trifolium* spp.)
Violet (*Viola* spp.)

Butterflies Attracted
Painted Lady
Monarch
Zebra swallowtail
Pearl crescent
Angelwings, mourning cloak
Spring azure
Tiger swallowtail
Black swallowtail
Buckeye
Red-spotted purple
Viceroy
Spicebush swallowtail
Common sulphur, Eastern-tailed blue
Fritillary

DEER-RESISTANT PLANTS

Only plastic plants and a few cacti are truly deer proof," observes Sandy McDougle, owner of Sandy's Plants, a retail and wholesale ground cover and perennial nursery in Mechanicsville, Virginia. Sandy provided this list of plants that are not preferred by deer. "Deer are less likely to eat aromatic (most, but not all, herbs) or medicinal plants." But keep in mind that if food is in short supply, or preferred plants are unavailable, almost any plant may be browsed. A helpful book on the topic is *Gardening in Deer Country* by New York gardener Karen Hescavage-Bernard, who dealt with this problem as she tried to start a nursery in Croton-on-Hudson. For information about physical barriers and chemical repellents, see Maryland Cooperative Extension Service Bulletin 354, *Controlling Deer Damage in Maryland*, by Jonathan Kays.

CROCUS

Trees
Firs (*Abies* spp.)
Maple (*Acer* spp.)
Serviceberry (*Amelanchier* spp.)
Birch (*Betula* spp.)
Hornbeam (*Carpinus* spp.)
Hickory (*Carya* spp.)
Cedar (*Cedrus* spp.)
Redbud (*Cercis canadensis*)
False cypress (*Chamaecyparis* spp.)
Dogwood (*Cornus* spp.)
Smoke tree (*Cotinus coggygria*)
Hawthorn (*Crataegus* spp.)
Japanese cedar (*Cryptomeria japonica*)
Russian olive (*Elaeagnus angustifolia*)
Beech (*Fagus* spp.)
Ash (*Fraxinus* spp.)
Ginkgo (*Ginkgo biloba*)
Honeylocust (*Gleditsia triacanthos* var. *inermis*)

English holly (*Ilex aquifolium*)
American holly (*Ilex opaca*)
Golden chain tree (*Laburnum* x *watereri*)
Larch (*Larix* spp.)
Sweetgum (*Liquidambar styraciflua*)
Tulip tree (*Liriodendron tulipifera*)
Magnolia (*Magnolia* spp.)
Dawn redwood (*Metasequoia glyptostroboides*)
Mulberries (*Morus* spp.)
Sourwood (*Oxydendrum arboreum*)
Spruce (*Picea* spp.)
Pines (*Pinus* spp.)
London plane tree (*Platanus* x *acerifolia*)
Oak (*Quercus* spp.)
Black locust (*Robinia pseudoacacia*)
Willow (*Salix* spp.)
Sassafras (*Sassafras albidum*)
Canadian hemlock (*Tsuga canadensis*)

Shrubs

Aucuba (*Aucuba japonica*)
Barberry (*Berberis* spp.)
Butterfly bush (*Buddleia davidii*)
Boxwood (*Buxus* spp.)
Sweetshrub (*Calycanthus floridus*)
Bluebeard (*Caryopteris* × *clandonensis*)
Cotoneaster (*Cotoneaster* spp.)
Scotch broom (*Cytisus scoparius*)
Daphne (*Daphne* spp.)
Wintercreeper (*Euonymus fortunei*)
Forsythia (*Forsythia* spp.)
Witch hazel (*Hamamelis* spp.)
Rose of Sharon (*Hibiscus syriacus*)
Hydrangea (*Hydrangea* spp.)
St. John's wort (*Hypericum calycinum*)
Chinese holly (*Ilex cornuta*)
Inkberry (*Ilex glabra*)
Juniper (*Juniperus* spp.)
Mountain laurel (*Kalmia latifolia*)
Globeflower (*Kerria japonica*)
Beautybush (*Kolkwitzia amabilis*)
Leucothoe (*Leucothoe* spp.)
Privet (*Ligustrum* spp.)
Spice bush (*Lindera benzoin*)
Oregon holly grape (*Mahonia aquifolium*)
Bayberry (*Myrica pensylvanica*)
Heavenly bamboo (*Nandina domestica*)
Mountain pieris (*Pieris floribunda*)
Japanese pieris (*Pieris japonica*)
Mock orange (*Philadelphus coronarius*)
Bush cinquefolia (*Potentilla fruticosa*)
Pyracantha (*Pyracantha coccinea*)
Spirea (*Spiraea* spp.)
Snowberry (*Symphoricarpos albus*)
Lilac (*Syringa vulgaris*)
Viburnum (*Viburnum* spp.)
Weigela (*Weigela florida*)

Ground Covers and Vines

Bishop's weed (*Aegopodium podagraria*)
Ajuga (*Ajuga reptans*)
Bearberry (*Arctostaphyllos uva-ursi*)
Cross vine (*Bignonia capreolata*)
Trumpet creeper (*Campsis radicans*)
Bittersweet (*Celastrus scandens*)
Plumbago (*Ceratostigma plumbaginoides*)
Clematis (*Clematis* spp.)
Wintercreeper (*Euonymus fortunei*)
Creeping wintergreen (*Gaultheria procumbens*)
English ivy (*Hedera helix*)
Honeysuckle (*Lonicera* spp.)
Pachysandra (*Pachysandra terminalis*)
Virginia creeper (*Parthenocissus quinquefolia*)

Boston ivy (*Parthenocissus tricuspidata*)
Silver lace vine (*Polygonum aubertii*)
Lavender cotton (*Santolina chamaecyparissus*)
Himalayan sweetbox (*Sarcococca hookeriana* var. *humilis*)
Sedum (*Sedum* spp.)
Hens and chicks (*Sempervivum* spp.)
Vinca (*Vinca major, V. minor*)
Wisteria (*Wisteria* spp.)

Perennials and Wildflowers

Yarrow (*Achillea* spp. and hybs.)
Monkshood (*Aconitum* spp.)
Lady's mantle (*Alchemilla* spp.)
Basket of gold (*Alyssum saxatile*)
Blue-star (*Amsonia* spp.)
Japanese anemone (*Anemone* × *hybrida*)
Columbine (*Aquilegia* spp.)
Rock cress (*Arabis* spp.)
Jack-in-the-pulpit (*Arisaema triphyllum*)
Sea thrift (*Armeria maritima*)
Wormwood (*Artemisia* spp.)
Goatsbeard (*Aruncus* spp.)
Ginger (*Asarum* spp.)
Butterfly weed (*Asclepias tuberosa*)
Aster (*Aster* spp.)
Astilbe (*Astilbe* spp. and cvs.)
False indigo (*Baptisia* spp.)
Saxifrage (*Bergenia cordifolia*)
Boltonia (*Boltonia asteroides*)
Bellflower (*Campanula* spp.)
Bachelor's buttons (*Centaurea* spp.)
Red valerian (*Centranthus ruber*)
Snow in summer (*Cerastium tomentosum*)
Turtlehead (*Chelone* spp.)
Chrysanthemum (*Chrysanthemum* spp.)
Green and gold (*Chrysogonum virginianum*)
Bugbane or snakeroot (*Cimicifuga racemosa*)
Lily-of-the-valley (*Convallaria majalis*)
Tickseed (*Coreopsis* spp.)
Delphinium (*Delphinium* spp.)
Sweet William (*Dianthus* spp.)
Bleeding-heart (*Dicentra eximia, D. spectabilis*)
Foxglove (*Digitalis purpurea*)
Purple coneflower (*Echinacea purpurea*)
Globe thistle (*Echinops ritro*)
Barrenwort (*Epimedium* spp.)
Hardy ageratum (*Eupatorium* spp.)
Spurge (*Euphorbia* spp.)
Meadowsweet (*Filipendula* spp.)
Blanket flower (*Gaillardia* × *grandiflora*)
Sweet woodruff (*Galium odoratum*)
Cranesbill (*Geranium* spp.)
Avens (*Geum* spp.)

Baby's breath (*Gypsophila paniculata*)
Hellebore (*Helleborus* spp.)
Dame's rocket (*Hesperis matronalis*)
Coral bells (*Heuchera* spp. and cvs.)
Candytuft (*Iberis sempervirens*)
Iris (*Iris* spp.)
Golden deadnettle (*Lamiastrum galeobdolon*)
Deadnettle (*Lamium maculatum*)
Lavender (*Lavandula* spp.)
Gayfeather (*Liatris spicata*)
Statice (*Limonium latifolium*)
Toadflax (*Linaria vulgaris*)
Flax (*Linum perenne*)
Rose campion or catchfly (*Lychnis coronaria*)
Loosestrife (*Lysimachia* spp.)
Purple loosestrife (*Lythrum salicaria*)
Bee balm (*Monarda didyma*)
Forget-me-not (*Myosotis palustris*)
Evening primrose (*Oenothera* spp.)
Peony (*Paeonia* cvs.)
Oriental poppy (*Papaver orientale*)
Beard-tongue (*Penstemon* spp.)
Russian sage (*Perovskia atriplicifolia*)
Creeping phlox (*Phlox paniculata*)
Balloon flower (*Platycodon grandiflorus*)
Mayapple (*Podophyllum peltatum*)
Jacob's ladder (*Polemonium* spp.)
Primrose (*Primula* spp.)

Lungwort (*Pulmonaria* cvs.)
Black-eyed Susan (*Rudbeckia* spp.)
Meadow sage (*Salvia* spp.)
Soapwort (*Saponaria* spp.)
Pincushion flower (*Scabiosa* spp.)
Goldenrod (*Solidago* spp.)
Lambs' ears (*Stachys byzantina*)
Stokes' aster (*Stokesia laevis*)
Meadow rue (*Thalictrum* spp.)
Foam flower (*Tiarella cordifolia*)
Spiderwort (*Tradescantia* x *andersoniana*)
Speedwell (*Veronica* spp.)
Thyme (*Thymus* spp.)

Bulbs
Ornamental onion (*Allium* spp.)
Glory of the snow (*Chionodoxa* spp.)
Autumn crocus (*Colchicum* spp.)
Crocus (*Crocus* spp.)
Daffodils and narcissus (*Narcissus* spp.)
Winter aconite (*Eranthis cilicica*)
Fritillary (*Fritillaria* spp.)
Snowdrop (*Galanthus nivalis*)
Snowflake (*Leucojum aestivum*, *L. vernum*)
Grape hyacinth (*Muscari* spp.)
Puschkinia (*Puschkinia scilloides*)
Scilla (*Scilla* spp.)

COASTAL GARDENS

Much of our region is seashore, with hundreds of miles of coastline along the Atlantic Ocean, Chesapeake Bay, and many smaller bays, inlets, and tributaries. Plants for coastal areas must adapt well to sandy soils and strong winds, and be able to tolerate aerial salt spray. Salt deposited on leaves, buds, and twigs desiccates them. Typical symptoms of salt damage are browned margins on leaves, and dead buds and twigs. Symptoms can be most severe on the windward side of the plants, which may brown out completely while the downwind side stays green. Salt can also accumulate in the soil, but that is generally less of a problem than aerial salt.

In a few cases, salt deposition may actually benefit certain plants that are adapted to living along the seashore. In her book *Gardening on the Eastern Seashore*, Marilyn Schmidt mentions that some plants, like roses and the native beach plum, rarely have fungal disease problems on their leaves when salt spray occasionally coats these plants, but that away from the seashore these problems increase. The same has been noted with fungal problems and leaf miners of hollies.

Grouped here are separate lists for trees, shrubs, vines, perennials and ground covers, ornamental grasses, and annuals—all suitable for coastal gardens. Virginia Beach landscape architect Bartow (Pat) Bridges contributed the list of vines that tolerate coastal conditions. Jo Anne Gordon, a horticulturist for the City of Norfolk who lives near Chesapeake Bay, helped compile the list of annuals.

Trees
Amur maple (*Acer ginnala*)
Box elder (*Acer negundo*)
Norway maple (*Acer platanoides*)
Red maple (*Acer rubrum*)
American horse chestnut (*Aesculus hippocastanum*)

Tree of heaven (*Ailanthus altissima*)
Shadblow serviceberry (*Amelanchier canadensis*)
European hornbeam (*Carpinus betulus*)
Hackberry (*Celtis occidentalis*)
Hawthorn (some) (*Crataegus* spp.)
Japanese cedar (*Cryptomeria japonica*)
Leyland cypress (x *Cupressocyparis leylandii*)

Russian olive (*Elaeagnus angustifolia*)
White ash (*Fraxinus americana*)
Ginkgo (*Ginkgo biloba*)
Honeylocust (*Gleditsia triacanthos* var. *inermis*)
Foster's holly (*Ilex* × *attenuata* 'Fosteri')
American holly (*Ilex opaca*)
Black walnut (*Juglans nigra*)
Eastern red cedar (*Juniperus virginiana*)
Golden-rain tree (*Koelreuteria paniculata*)
Sweetgum (*Liquidambar styraciflua*)
Southern magnolia (*Magnolia grandiflora*)
Sweet-bay magnolia (*Magnolia virginiana*)
Mulberries (*Morus alba, M. rubra*)
Black gum (*Nyssa sylvatica*)
White spruce (*Picea glauca*)
Colorado spruce (*Picea pungens*)
Shortleaf pine (*Pinus echinata*)
Austrian pine (*Pinus nigra*)
Scotch pine (*Pinus sylvestris*)
Japanese black pine (*Pinus thunbergiana*)
London plane tree (*Platanus* × *acerifolia*)
White poplar (*Populus alba*)
Amur choke cherry (*Prunus maackii*)
Sargent cherry (*Prunus sargentii*)
Black cherry (*Prunus serotina*)
Callery pear (*Pyrus calleryana*)
White oak (*Quercus alba*)
Blackjack oak (*Quercus marilandica*)
Water oak (*Quercus nigra*)
Willow oak (*Quercus phellos*)
English oak (*Quercus robur*)
Northern red oak (*Quercus rubra*)
Live oak (*Quercus virginiana*)
Black locust (*Robinia pseudoacacia*)
Umbrella pine (*Sciadopitys verticillata*)
Japanese pagoda tree (*Sophora japonica*)
Japanese tree lilac (*Syringa reticulata*)
Bald cypress (*Taxodium distichum*)
Lacebark elm (*Ulmus parvifolia*)

Shrubs
Red chokeberry (*Aronia arbutifolia*)
Saltbush (*Baccharis halimifolia*)
Boxwoods (*Buxus harlandii, B. microphylla*)
Beautyberry (*Callicarpa americana*)
False cypress (*Chamaecyparis* spp.)
Summersweet (*Clethra alnifolia*)
Red osier dogwood (*Cornus sericea*)
Spreading cotoneaster (*Cotoneaster divaricatus*)
Rockspray cotoneaster (*Cotoneaster horizontalis*)
Warminster broom (*Cytisus* × *praecox*)
Scotch broom (*Cytisus scoparius*)
Japanese euonymus (*Euonymus japonicus*)

Gardenia (*Gardenia jasminoides*)
Rose of Sharon (*Hibiscus syriacus*)
House hydrangea (*Hydrangea macrophylla*)
St. John's wort (*Hypericum calycinum*)
Chinese holly (*Ilex cornuta*)
Japanese holly (*Ilex crenata*)
Inkberry (*Ilex glabra*)
Yaupon holly (*Ilex vomitoria*)
Anise (*Illicium floridanum*)
Chinese juniper (*Juniperus chinensis*)
Common juniper (*Juniperus communis*)
Shore juniper (*Juniperus conferta*)
Creeping juniper (*Juniperus horizontalis*)
Amur privet (*Ligustrum amurense*)
California privet (*Ligustrum ovalifolium*)
Tatarian honeysuckle (*Lonicera tatarica*)
Wax myrtle (*Myrica cerifera*)
Bayberry (*Myrica pensylvanica*)
Mock orange (*Philadelphus coronarius*)
Red-tip photinia (*Photinia* × *fraseri*)
Mugo pine (*Pinus mugo*)
Shrubby cinquefoil (*Potentilla fruticosa*)
Purple-leaf sand cherry (*Prunus* × *cistena*)
Cherry laurel (*Prunus laurocerasus*)
Beach plum (*Prunus maritima*)
Pyracantha (*Pyracantha coccinea*)
Staghorn sumac (*Rhus typhina*)
Lady Banks rose (*Rosa banksiae*)
Shining rose (*Rosa nitida*)
Rugosa rose (*Rosa rugosa*)
Scotch rose (*Rosa spinosissima*)
Memorial rose (*Rosa wichuraiana*)
Elderberry (*Sambucus canadensis*)
Spirea (*Spiraea* spp.)
Snowberry (*Symphoricarpos albus*)
Lilac (*Syringa vulgaris*)
Tamarisk (*Tamarix ramosissima*)
Yew (*Taxus* spp.)
Highbush blueberry (*Vaccinium corymbosum*)
Arrowwood (*Viburnum dentatum*)
European cranberry bush viburnum (*Viburnum opulus*)

Vines
Pepper vine (*Ampelopsis arborea*)
Cross vine (*Bignonia capreolata*)
Trumpet creeper (*Campsis radicans*)
Bittersweet (*Celastrus* spp.)
Sweet autumn clematis (*Clematis paniculata*)
Wintercreeper (*Euonymus fortunei*)
Carolina jessamine (*Gelsemium sempervirens*)
Variegated Algerian ivy (*Hedera canariensis* 'Canary Cream')

English ivy (*Hedera helix*)
Climbing hydrangea (*Hydrangea anomala* subsp. *petiolaris*)
Winter jasmine (*Jasminum nudiflorum*)
Hall's honeysuckle (*Lonicera japonica* 'Halliana')
Virginia creeper (*Parthenocissus quinquefolia*)
Passionflower (*Passiflora caerulea*)
Japanese hydrangea vine (*Schizophragma hydrangeoides*)
Chinese wisteria (*Wisteria sinensis*)

Perennials and Ground Covers
Yarrow (*Achillea* spp.)
Basket of gold (*Alyssum saxatile*)
Rock cress (*Arabis caucasica*)
Bearberry (*Arctostaphylos uva-ursi*)
Thrift (*Armeria maritima*)
Wormwood (*Artemisia schmidtiana* 'Silvermound')
Bamboo (*Arundinaria* spp.)
Asters (*Aster* spp.)
Bamboo (*Bambusa* spp.)
Bergenia (*Bergenia cordifolia*)
Heather (*Calluna vulgaris*)
Snow in summer (*Cerastium tomentosum*)
Plumbago (*Ceratostigma plumbaginoides*)
Silver and gold (*Chrysanthemum pacificum*)
Carnation, sweet William (*Dianthus* spp.)
Globe thistle (*Echinops ritro*)
Heath (*Erica* spp.)
Fleabane (*Erigeron* spp.)
Sea holly (*Eryngium* spp.)
Joe Pye weed (*Eupatorium* spp.)
Cushion spurge (*Euphorbia* spp.)
Baby's breath (*Gypsophila* spp.)
Sun rose (*Helianthemum* spp.)
Daylily (*Hemerocallis* spp.)
Coral bells (*Heuchera sanguinuea*)
Evergreen candytuft (*Iberis sempervirens*)
Tall bearded iris (*Iris germanica*)
Red-hot poker, torch lily (*Kniphofia* hybs.)
Ligularia (*Ligularia* spp.)
Sea lavender (*Limonium* spp.)
Liriope (*Liriope muscari*)
Evening primrose, sundrops (*Oenothera* spp.)
Mondo grass (*Ophiopogon japonicus*)
Prickly pear cactus (*Opuntia* spp.)
Beard-tongue (*Penstemon* spp.)
Russian sage (*Perovskia atriplicifolia*)
Creeping phlox (*Phlox subulata*)
Cinquefoil (*Potentilla* spp.)

Pincushion flower (*Scabiosa* spp.)
Stonecrop (*Sedum* spp.)
Hens and chicks (*Sempervivum* spp.)
Lambs' ears (*Stachys* spp.)
Germander (*Teucrium chamaedrys*)
Verbena (*Verbena* spp.)
Speedwell (*Veronica* spp.)
Violets (*Viola* spp.)
Adam's needle (*Yucca filamentosa*)

Ornamental Grasses
Giant reed grass (*Arundo donax*)
Northern sea oats (*Chasmanthium latifolium*)
Pampas grass (*Cortaderia selloana*)
European dune grass (*Elymus arenarius*)
Blue wild rye (*Elymus glaucus*)
Northen pampas grass (*Erianthus ravennae*)
Blue fescue (*Festuca ovina*)
Reed manna grass (*Glyceria maxima*)
Blue oat grass (*Helictotrichon sempervirens*)
Miscanthus, eulalia grass (*Miscanthus* spp.)
Switch grass (*Panicum virgatum*)
Ribbon grass (*Phalaris arundinacea*)
Reed grass (*Phragmites australis*)
Prairie cord grass (*Spartina pectinata*)

Annuals
Ageratum (*Ageratum houstonianum*)
Wax-leafed begonia (*Begonia* × *semperflorens-cultorum*)
Ornamental cabbage (*Brassica* spp.)
Calendula (*Calendula officinalis*)
Calliopsis (*Coreopsis tinctoria*)
Cosmos (*Cosmos bipinnatus*)
Mexican heather (*Cuphea hyssopifolia*)
Lisianthus (*Eustoma grandiflorum*)
Indian blanket (*Gaillardia pulchella*)
Gazania (*Gazania hybrida*)
Sunflowers (*Helianthus annuus*)
Lantana (*Lantana* spp.)
Sweet alyssum (*Lobularia maritima*)
Melampodium (*Melampodium* spp.)
Fancy-leafed geranium (*Pelargonium domesticum*)
Ivy-leafed geranium (*Pelargonium peltatum*)
Petunia (*Petunia purpurea*)
Drummond phlox (*Phlox drummondii*)
Rose moss (*Portulaca olearacea*)
Purslane (*Purslane* cvs.)
Dusty miller (*Senecio cineraria*)
Nasturtium (*Tropaeolum majus*)
Verbena (*Verbena* × *hybrida*)

"When planting at the beach, the soil is so sandy that you really need to add organic matter to the soil to help keep moisture in it."
Bartow (Pat) Bridges is a landscape architect in Virginia Beach, Virginia.

"Dehydration is a big factor on the beach because the wind pulls water from leaves faster than the roots can replace it, especially in dry, sandy soil. The best thing to do is grow your flowers behind a windbreak or on the side of the house away from the ocean-front."
Jo Anne Gordon is a horticulturist for the City of Norfolk, Virginia, and lives near the Chesapeake Bay.

BAYSCAPING WITH NATIVE PLANTS

The term bayscaping refers to the Chesapeake Bay area; however, the low-input landscape principles apply everywhere," explains horticulturist Laurie Fox, who designed and maintains Virginia Tech's Bayscape Garden. "After all, who doesn't want to have a great-looking garden while saving time, energy, money, and protecting their water resources?" Virginia Tech horticulturists use the term bayscaping to describe low-maintenance landscapes that protect the streams, rivers, and waters of the Chesapeake Bay, the world's largest estuary. Native plants are used because they are adapted to local climate and soil types, require minimal water, fertilizer, and pesticides, and provide food and shelter to wildlife. Laurie provided the following lists of trees, shrubs, perennials, and grasses used in the Bayscape Garden project. For more information on bayscape gardening, contact the Alliance for the Chesapeake Bay, P.O. Box 1981, Richmond, VA 23218 (www.acb-online.org).

Bayscape Trees
Serviceberry (*Amelanchier canadensis*)
River birch (*Betula nigra*)
American hornbeam (*Carpinus caroliniana*)
Eastern redbud (*Cercis canadensis*)
White fringe tree (*Chionanthus virginicus*)
Green ash (*Fraxinus pennsylvanica*)
American holly (*Ilex opaca*)
Sweet-bay magnolia (*Magnolia virginiana*)
Longleaf pine (*Pinus palustris*)
Virginia pine (*Pinus virginiana*)
Bald cypress (*Taxodium distichum*)

Bayscape Shrubs
Bog rosemary (*Andromeda polifolia*)
Red chokeberry (*Aronia arbutifolia* 'Autum Magic,' 'Brilliantissima')
Saltbush (*Baccharis halimifolia*)
Beautyberry (*Callicarpa americana*)
Buttonbush (*Cephalanthus occidentalis*)
Silky dogwood (*Cornus amomum*)
Gray dogwood (*Cornus racemosa*)

Scotch broom (*Cytisus scoparius* 'Dorothy Walpole,' 'Moonlight')
Dwarf fothergilla (*Fothergilla gardenii*)
Witch hazel (*Hamamelis* x *intermedia* 'Arnold's Promise')
Winterberry (*Ilex verticillata*)
Sweetspire (*Itea virginica*)
Coastal leucothoe (*Leucothoe axillaris*)
Wax myrtle (*Myrica cerifera*)
Bush cinquefoil (*Potentilla fruticosa* 'Abbotswood,' 'Jackmanii')
Nannyberry (*Viburnum lentago*)
Blackhaw viburnum (*Viburnum prunifolium*)
Dusty zenobia (*Zenobia pulverulenta*)

Bayscape Perennials
Blue-star (*Amsonia tabernaemontana* var. *salicifolia*)
Bearberry (*Arctostaphylos uva-ursi* 'Vancouver Jade')
New York aster (*Aster novi-belgii* 'Winston Churchill,' 'Woods Pink')

Longleaf aster (*Aster oblongifolius* 'Raydon's Favorite')

Turtlehead (*Chelone lyonii*)

Threadleaf coreopsis (*Coreopsis verticillata* 'Moonbeam')

Purple coneflower (*Echinacea purpurea*)

White coneflower (*Echinacea purpurea* 'Alba')

Joe Pye weed (*Eupatorium maculatum* 'Gateway')

Chocolate Joe Pye weed (*Eupatorium rugosum* 'Chocolate')

Gaura (*Gaura lindheimeri* 'Siskiyou Pink')

White cranesbill (*Geranium sanguineum* 'Album')

Pink cranesbill (*Geranium sanguineum* var. *striatum*)

St. John's wort (*Hypericum calycinum*)

Louisiana iris (*Iris louisiana* 'Clara Goula,' 'Full Eclipse')

Cardinal flower (*Lobelia cardinalis* 'Misty Morn,' 'Rose Beacon,' 'Sparkle Divine')

Bee balm (*Monarda didyma* 'Aquarius,' 'Jacob Kline,' 'Prarie Night,' 'Cambridge Scarlet,' 'Marshall's Delight')

Evening primrose (*Oenothera fruticosa* 'Sonnenwende')

Beard-tongue (*Penstemon digitalis* 'Husker Red')

Orange coneflower (*Rudbeckia fulgida* 'Goldstrum')

Black-eyed Susan (*Rudbeckia hirta* 'Indian Summer')

Three-lobed coneflower (*Rudbeckia triloba*)

Perennial salvia or sage (*Salvia* x *superba* 'Blue Queen,' 'Rose Queen,' 'Blue Hill,' 'May Night')

Goldenrod (*Solidago sphacelata* 'Golden Fleece')

Spiderwort (*Tradescantia* x *andersoniana* 'Bilberry Ice')

Bayscape Grasses

Variegated sedge (*Carex morrowii* 'Old Gold')

Rush (*Juncus effusus*)

Corkscrew rush (*Juncus effusus* f. *spiralis*)

Feesey ribbon grass (*Phalaris arundinacea* var. *picta*)

 "What grows on the ocean side compared to the bay side can be very different, due mostly to the influence of the wind. Many plants that are very salt tolerant can grow on the beach provided they receive good protection from ocean winds. Protection can be in the form of a large dune or a building, anything that will divert the wind away from the plant. After a nor'easter, rinse your plants with fresh water to get rid of the accumulated salt, and keep in mind that many plants listed as tolerant of salt in the air will often die if the soil is flooded with saltwater by high tides for any length of time."

George Rosenkranz has owned a successful landscape design business on the Eastern Shore of Maryland for twenty-five years.

PLANTS VS. HUMAN HEALTH

Working in the garden or having plants around is generally viewed as beneficial and is the basis for horticultural therapy. Unfortunately, some plants can cause allergic reactions. Sensitivities vary greatly from person to person, as noted by two prominent plants vs. people conflicts—poison ivy and hayfever. Being aware of the major potential offenders can help you design a garden that will be beneficial to all of your senses, but don't ban plants unless you know they are really causing problems. Chesapeake, Virginia, dermatologist Sam Selden provided the following information about plant-related dermatitis and allergies.

TAMARISK

Contact Dermatitis

Dermatitis (red, itchy, swollen, dry, blistered, crusted, or scabby skin rashes) can be caused by contact with substances (allergens) in plants. There are two basic types of contact dermatitis. One type is *allergic*, which occurs following reexposure to certain allergens. Only people who are allergic to these plants will develop this form of contact dermatitis as their immune system tries to expel the allergen from their skin. The other type is *irritant* contact dermatitis, which does not require previous exposure to the allergen and is not a result of the body's immune reaction. Everyone can develop a reaction to these allergens, though the potential to develop irritant contact dermatitis varies greatly.

PLANTS THAT CAN CAUSE ALLERGIC CONTACT DERMATITIS:
Boxwood, chrysanthemums, English ivy, junipers, kiwi, primrose, St. John's wort, trumpet creeper, poison ivy

PLANTS THAT CAN CAUSE IRRITANT CONTACT DERMATITIS:
Barberry, bulbs (daffodils, hyacinths, tulips), hawthorn, prickly pear (cactus), roses, sharp ornamental grasses

Plant-Related Allergies

The pollen of some plants can cause allergic reactions in people. The actual allergens are proteins. When sensitive people inhale pollen, symptoms such as sneezing, watery eyes, and hives may occur. Some of the most pollen-offensive plants are trees that may begin releasing pollen as early as February in the warmer parts of our region. The biggest offenders are dioecious trees, those that have male and female flowers on separate trees. One way to reduce potentially allergenic pollen is to plant only female trees or female cultivars, since only the males produce pollen. In the list that follows, dioecious trees are marked with an asterisk (*).

TREES THAT CAN CAUSE ALLERGIC REACTIONS:

Beech family—beeches, oaks
Birch family—alders, birches
Cypress family—arborvitaes, cedars, junipers*
Elm family—elms
Horse chestnut family—buckeyes
Maple family—box elders, maples*
Mulberry family—mulberries*, osage oranges*
Olive family—ashes*

Pine family—hemlocks
Quassia family—tree-of-heaven*
Sycamore family—London plane trees, sycamore
Tamarisk family—tamarisks
Taxodium family—bald cypresses
Walnut family—hickories, pecans, walnuts
Willow family—cottonwoods*, poplars*, willows*
Witch hazel family—sweetgums

Wind-borne pollen travels long distances, but the following steps can help to reduce exposure in your immediate vicinity.

- Identify allergenic trees in your landscape.
- With the help of a health care professional, determine which trees are producing the allergens.
- Assess the value of allergenic trees. Choose non-allergenic trees for replacements or new landscaping. Non-allergenic trees generally possess flowers that are showy to attract bird and insect pollinators.
- Minimize personal exposure by avoiding the times of the day when pollen is most abundant—early morning and late afternoon. Also avoid outdoor activities when conditions are dry and windy. Keep windows (house and car) shut during these peak times.
- If allergies are severe, wear gloves, long-sleeved clothing, a hat, and goggles when working outdoors. Surgical masks may also help filter some pollen.
- Shower and wash hair immediately after working outdoors. Also promptly launder clothing. Dry clothing in a clothes dryer. If you hang clothing outside to dry, pollen can accumulate on it and be brought inside.
- Do not use power leaf blowers because they aerosolize large quantities of tree pollen.
- Be aware that pets and other people can also bring pollen inside.

All categories of plants can have allergy-causing properties. For those who suffer, a detailed book that rates the allergy potential of most common landscape plants is *Allergy-Free Gardening* by Thomas L. Ogren (Ten-Speed Press).

"Consider irritant contact dermatitis when you're weeding out plants such as spurges and Queen Anne's lace. Beware that latex gloves provide no protection to poison ivy, and that you must wear heavy plastic or cloth gloves for protection."
Sam Selden is a dermatologist practicing in Chesapeake, Virginia.

RESOURCES

Reference Books

Allergy-Free Gardening by Thomas L. Ogren. Ten-Speed Press, Berkeley, Calif.

Gardening on the Eastern Seashore by R. Marilyn Schmidt. Barnegat Light Press, Barnegat Light, N.J.

Gardening with Native Wildlowers by Samuel R. Jones Jr. and Leonard E. Foote. Timber Press, Portland, Ore.

Heat-Zone Gardening by H. Marc Cathey with Linda Bellamy. Time Life Inc., New York, N.Y.

Herbaceous Perennial Plants by Alan Armitage. Varsity Press, Inc. Athens, Ga.

Hortus III by the L. H. Bailey Hortorium staff, Cornell University, Ithaca, N.Y.

Know It & Grow It by Carl E. Whitcomb. Lacebark, Inc., Stillwater, Okla.

Landscape Plants for Eastern North America by Harrison L. Flint. John Wiley & Sons, New York, N.Y.

Manual of Herbaceous Ornamental Plants by Steven M. Still. Stipes Publishing, Champaign, Ill.

Manual of Woody Landscape Plants by Michael A. Dirr. Stipes Publishing, Champaign, Ill.

Native Treees, Shrubs and Vines for Urban and Rural America by Gary Hightshoe. Van Nostrand Reinhold, New York, N.Y.

Noah's Garden by Sara Stein. Houghlin Mifflin Company, New York, N.Y.

Ornamental Grasses, the Amber Wave by Carole Ottesen. McGraw-Hill, New York, N.Y.

Pest-Resistant Ornamental Plants by Deborah Smith-Fiola. Rutgers Cooperative Extension, Toms River, N.J.

Shrubs and Vines for American Gardens by Donald Wyman. Macmillan, New York, N.Y.

The American Horticultural Society A-Z Encyclopedia of Garden Plants by Christopher Brickell and Judith Zuk (eds). American Horticultural Society, Alexandria, Va.

The Exuberant Garden and the Controlling Hand by William H. Frederick. Little, Brown, Boston, Mass.

The National Wildlife Federations's Guide to Gardening for Wildlife by Craig Tufts and Peter Loewer. Rodale Press, Emmaus, Pa.

The Native Plant Primer by Carol Ottesen. Harmony Books, New York, N.Y.

Trees for American Gardens by Donald Wyman. Macmillan, New York, N.Y.

Two CD-ROMs to use for plant information, pictures, and selection are from Horticopia, Purcellville, Va.: Trees, Shrub and Groundcovers, 2d ed.; Perennials and Annuals, 2d ed.

Mail-Order Sources

Andre Viette Farm & Nursery
PO Box 1109
Fishersville, VA 22939
540-943-2315
www.viette.com
(perennials)

Asiatica
PO Box 270
Lewisberry, PA 17339
717-938-8677
www.asiatica-pa.com
(shade/woodland perennials)

Bloms Bulbs Inc.
1495 Wilmington Pike
West Chester, PA 19382
484-840-0568
www.blomsbulbs.com
(bulbs)

Brent and Becky's Bulbs
7463 Heath Trail
Gloucester, VA 23061
877-661-2852
www.brentandbeckysbulbs.com
(bulbs)

Carlson's Gardens
Box 305-HC 0700
South Salem, NY 10590
914-763-5958
www.carlsonsgardens.com
(azaleas and rhododendrons)

Carroll Gardens
444 East Main Street
Westminster, MD 21157
800-638-6334
www.carrollgardens.com
(shrubs, perennials)

Crownsville Nursery
PO Box 797
Crownsville, MD 21032
410-849-3143
www.crownsvillenursery.com
(shrubs, vines, perennials)

Dismal Swamp Nursery
PO Box 372
Chesapeake, VA 23322-0372
www.dismalswampnursery.com
757-421-3843
(natives and wetland plants)

Edible Landscaping
PO Box 77
Afton, VA 22920-0077
800-524-4156
www.eat-it.com
(edible landscaping plants)

Eminence Meadows
HCR 2, Box 34, Eminence Road
Summit, NY 12175
518-287-1524
www.eminencemeadows.com
(perennials)

Fairweather Gardens
PO Box 330
Greenwich, NJ 08323
856-451-6261
www.fairweathergardens.com
(trees, shrubs, ground covers, perennials, vines)

Hydrangeaplus
Foran, Inc.
269 Dayton Avenue
Manorville, NY 11949
888-642-1333
www.hydrangeaplus.com
(hydrangeas)

K. Van Bourgondien & Sons
PO Box 1000
Babylon, NY 11702-9004
1-800-662-9997
www.dutchbulbs.com
(bulbs, perennials)

Kurt Bluemel, Inc.
2740 Greene Lane
Baldwin, MD 21013
800-248-7584
www.bluemel.com
(bamboo, ornamental grasses)

Lilypons Water Gardens
PO Box 10
6800 Lilypons Road
Buckeystown, MD 21717-0010
1-800-999-5459
www.lilypons.com
(water gardening plants)

Limerock Ornamental Grasses Inc.
70 Sawmill Road
Port Matilda, PA 16870
814-692-2272
(ornamental grasses)

New Gardens
PO Box 357
Greenwich, NJ 08323
856-455-7368
(trees and shrubs)

Paradise Nursery
6385 Blackwater Road
Virginia Beach, VA 23457-1040
757-421-0201
www.paradisenursery.com
(edible landscape plants)

Peekskill Nurseries
PO Box 428
Shrub Oak, NY 10588
914-245-5595
www.peekskillnurseries.com
(evergreen groundcovers)

Pine Knot Farms Perennials
681 Rock Church Road
Clarksville, VA 23927
804-252-1900
www.gloryroad.net/~hellebores
(hellebores)

Rare Find Nursery, Inc.
957 Patterson Road
Jackson, NJ 08527
732-833-0613
(trees, shrubs, rhododendrons)

Roslyn Nursery, Inc.
211 Burrs Lane
Dix Hills, NY 11746
631-643-9347
www.roslynnursery.com
(trees, shrubs, rhododendrons, azaleas)

Seneca Hill Perennials
3712 Country Route 57
Oswego, NY 13126
315-342-5915
www.senecahill.com
(trees, shrubs, perennials)

Smirnow's Son's Peonies
168 Maple Hill Road
Huntington, NY 11743
631-421-0836
(tree peonies)

Springdale Aquatic Nursery & Supply
PO Box 546
340 Old Quarry Lane
Greenville, VA 24440-0546
540-337-1929
www.springdalewatergardens.com
(water gardening plants)

Sterrett Gardens
PO Box 85
Craddockville, VA 23341
757-442-4606
(daylilies)

Sunnyboy Gardens Inc.
3314 Earlysville Road
Earlysville, VA 22936
888-431-0006
www.sunnyboygardens.com
(perennials, herbs)

Sunshine Farm & Gardens
Rt. 5
Renick, WV 24966
304-497-2208
www.sunfarm.com
(perennials, wildflowers, natives)

The Magic Garden
358 Benjamin Hill Road
Newfield, NY 14867
607-564-9055
www.magicgardenplants.com
(perennials)

Wild Earth Native Plant Nursery
PO Box 7258
Freehold, NJ 07728
732-308-9777
(perennials, ferns, ornamental grasses, vines, shrubs)

Windrose
1093 Mill Road
Pen Argyl, PA 18072-9670
610-588-1037
www.windrosenursery.com
(trees, shrubs, vines, perennials)

Woodside Nursery
327 Beebe Run Road
Bridgeton, NJ 08302
856-451-2162
www.woodsidenursery.com

Extension Websites

Delaware Cooperative Extension (University of Delaware)
bluehen.ags.udel.edu/deces
Maryland Cooperative Extension (University of Maryland)
www.agnr.umd.edu/CES
New Jersey—Rutgers Cooperative Extension
www.rce.rutgers.edu
New York—Cornell Cooperative Extension
www.cce.cornell.edu
Penn State Cooperative Extension
www.extension.psu.edu
Virginia Cooperative Extension, Virginia Tech
www.ext.vt.edu
West Virginia University Cooperative Extension
www.wvu.edu/~exten

INDEX

Celtis laevigata, 14

Celtis occidentalis, 14, 15, 18, 27, 28, 29, 30, 34, 35, 159, 165, 166, 171

Centaurea, 94, 96, 170

Centaurea cyanus, 88, 98, 141, 143, 146, 166

Centaurea montana, 88, 92

Centranthus ruber, 93, 94, 95, 96, 98, 100, 167, 168, 170

Cephalanthus occidentalis, 41, 54, 57, 62, 64, 160, 165, 166, 174

Cephalotaxus harringtonia, 46, 156, 159

Cerastium tomentosum, 83, 92, 170, 173

Ceratopteris pteridoides, 153

Ceratostigma plumbaginoides, 77, 80, 82, 86, 87, 94, 96, 98, 167, 168, 170, 173

Cercidiphyllum japonicum, 10, 14, 15, 22, 35, 38

Cercis canadensis, 14, 17, 20, 21, 28, 29, 30, 33, 159, 165, 169, 174

Cercis canadensis alba, 19

Cercis chinensis, 20, 26

Cercis mexicana, 17

Cercis reniformis, 7

Chaenomeles, 167

Chaenomeles japonica, 48, 163

Chaenomeles speciosa, 49, 52, 61, 63

Chain fern (Woodwardia), 126

Chain fern (Woodwardia areolata), 124, 125

Chamaecyparis, 21, 33, 36, 47, 169, 172

Chamaecyparis lawsoniana, 56

Chamaecyparis nootkatensis, 2

Chamaecyparis obtusa, 10, 32, 37, 42, 56

Chamaecyparis pisifera, 45, 56

Chamaecyparis thyoides, 26, 27, 37, 160

Chamaedaphne calyculata, 160

Chamaemelum nobile, 79, 83, 84, 164

Chameleon plant (Houttuynia cordata), 76, 80, 81, 86, 91, 101

Chamomile (Chamaemelum nobile), 84

Chasmanthium latifolium, 79, 82, 115, 116, 117, 119, 162, 173

Chaste tree (Vitex agnus-castus), 19, 54, 55, 57, 61, 63, 64, 65, 167

Checker mallow (Sidalcea), 97

Cheilanthes lanosa, 127

Chelone, 170

Chelone glabra, 91, 95, 161

Chelone lyonii, 91, 161, 175

Chelone obliqua, 80, 167

Cherry (Prunus), 13, 21, 35, 37, 166

Cherry (Prunus serrulata), 20

Cherry red currant (Ribes rubrum), 164

Cherry laurel (Prunus laurocerasus), 46, 47, 48, 53, 172

Cherry plum (Prunus cerasifera), 17

Cherrybark oak (Quercus falcata), 30

Cherrybark oak (Quercus pagodifolia), 160

Chestnut oak (Quercus prinus), 160

Chilean glory vine (Eccremocarpus), 147

Chilean jasmine (Mandevilla suaveolens), 67

Chimonanthus praecox, 42, 49, 57

China aster (Callistephus chinensis), 143, 167

China fir (Cunninghamia lanceolata), 21, 32, 37

China fleece vine (Polygonum aubertii), 67

China pink (Dianthus chinensis), 145

Chinese abelia (Abelia chinensis), 46

Chinese anemone (Anemone hupehensis), 89

Chinese astilbe (Astilbe chinensis), 82

Chinese bittersweet (Celastrus orbiculatus), 71

Chinese chestnut (Castanea mollissima), 22, 28, 32

Chinese dogwood (Cornus kousa), 24

Chinese forget-me-not (Cynoglossum amabile), 146

Chinese fringe tree (Chionanthus retusus), 7,

13, 17, 19, 25, 33

Chinese globeflower (Trollius chinensis), 90

Chinese ground orchid (Bletilla striata), 131, 132

Chinese holly (Ilex cornuta), 41, 47, 49, 170, 172

Chinese juniper (Juniperus chinensis), 36, 41, 46, 48, 64, 172

Chinese pistache (Pistacia chinensis), 7, 13, 23, 24, 29, 31

Chinese quince (Pseudocydonia sinensis), 25

Chinese redbud (Cercis chinensis), 20

Chinese sumac (Rhus chinensis), 58

Chinese wisteria (Wisteria sinensis), 67, 69, 163, 173

Chinese witch hazel (Hamamelis mollis), 52, 58, 65, 157

Chinkapin (Castanea pumila), 159

Chinkapin oak (Quercus muehlenbergii), 16, 31, 160

Chionanthus retusus, 7, 13, 17, 19, 25, 33

Chionanthus virginicus, 9, 13, 17, 19, 20, 24, 27, 28, 32, 33, 160, 166, 174

Chionodoxa (Chionodoxa), 132, 133, 171

Chionodoxa luciliae, 132

Chippendale zinnia (Zinnia haageana), 141

Chives (Allium shoenoprasum), 168

Chlorophytum comosum, 147

Choke cherry (Prunus virginiana), 15, 38

Chokeberry (Aronia arbutifolia), 53, 61

Christmas fern (Polystichum acrostichoides), 123, 124, 125, 126, 162

Chrysanthemum (Chrysanthemum), 19, 88, 98, 146, 164, 166, 170, 176

Chrysanthemum leucanthemum, 168

Chrysanthemum pacificum, 173

Chrysanthemum rubellum, 95

Chrysogonum virginianum, 80, 93, 97, 170

Chrysopsis villosa, 92, 95

Cigar plant (Cuphea ignea), 144

Cimicifuga, 90

Cimicifuga racemosa, 86, 91, 95, 161, 170

Cinnamon clethra (Clethra acuminata), 58

Cinnamon fern (Osmunda cinnamomea), 123, 124, 125, 126, 127, 162

Cinquefoil (Potentilla), 173

Cinquefoil (Potentilla tridentata), 76, 83

Cladrastis kentukea, 7, 9, 15, 19, 20, 22, 25, 26, 28, 30, 38, 156

Clarkia, 140

Claytonia virginica, 161

Clematis (Clematis), 19, 170

Clematis dioscoreifolia robusta, 68, 69, 70, 72

Clematis paniculata, 172

Clematis serratifolia, 74

Clematis texensis, 68, 69, 71, 73

Clematis virginiana, 69, 71, 74, 161

Clematis viticella, 156

Clematis x jackmanii, 68, 69, 70, 71, 72

Cleome (Cleome hassleriana), 136, 142, 167

Cleome hassleriana, 138, 139, 140, 141, 142, 143, 145, 167

Clerodendrum thomsoniae, 67, 70

Clethra acuminata, 58

Clethra alnifolia, 41, 42, 45, 54, 57, 58, 59, 61, 62, 156, 158, 160, 172

Clethra barbinervis, 51

Climbing aster (Aster carolinianus), 87

Climbing fern (Lygodium palmatum), 124

Climbing hydrangea (Decumaria barbara), 72, 161

Climbing hydrangea (Hydrangea anomala subsp. paniculata), 72

Climbing hydrangea (Hydrangea anomala subsp. petiolaris), 68, 69, 70, 72, 173

Climbing nasturtium (Nasturtium majus), 147

Climbing nasturtium (Nasturtium peregrinum), 147

Climbing nasturtium (Tropaeolum), 70

Climbing roses, 110, 111

Clinton wood fern (Dryopteris clintoniana), 162

Clinton's lily (Clintonia umbellulata), 161

Clintonia umbellulata, 161

Clover (Trifolium), 169

Clump verbena (Verbena canadensis), 93

Coast azalea (Rhododendron atlanticum), 56, 160

Coastal leucothoe (Leucothoe axillaris), 62, 160, 174

Cobaea scandens, 70, 147

Cockscomb (Celosia argentea var. plumosa), 148

Cockscomb (Celosia cristata), 139, 141, 148

Cockspur (Celosia argentea var. cristata), 143

Colchicum (Colchicum), 132, 133, 171

Coleus (Coleus x hybridus), 137, 140, 142, 148

Coleus (Solenostemon scutellarioides), 144

Coleus x hybridus, 137, 140, 142, 147, 148

Colocasia esculenta, 132, 144

Colorado blue spruce (Picea pungens glauca), 29

Colorado spruce (Picea pungens), 22, 32, 39, 172

Columbine (Aquilegia), 94, 96, 98, 166, 167, 170

Columbine (Aquilegia canadensis), 89, 94, 161

Columnar Oakleaf mountain ash (Sorbus thuringiaca fastigiata), 15

Comfrey (Symphytum grandiflorum), 86.97

Compact inkberry (Ilex glabra), 48

Concolor fir (Abies concolor), 21, 26, 36

Coneflower (Echinacea purpurea), 88, 161

Coneflower (Echinacea tennesseensis), 88

Coneflower (Rudbeckia subtomentosa), 86

Confederate jasmine (Trachelospermum jasminoides), 67

Consolida, 141

Consolida ambigua, 143

Consort black currant (Ribes nibrum), 164

Convallaria majalis, 78, 82, 90, 93, 95, 98, 100, 131, 133, 134, 170

Convolvulus tricolor, 139

Copper plant (Acalypha), 147

Copperleaf (Alternanthera ficoidea), 142

Coral bells (Heuchera), 19, 77, 82, 95, 97, 99, 100, 171

Coral bells (Heuchera americana), 161

Coral bells (Heuchera sanguinea), 90, 168, 173

Coral bells (Heuchera villosa), 161

Coral honeysuckle (Lonicera sempervirens), 72, 165

Coralbark maple (Acer palmatum), 25

Coralberry (Symphoricarpos orbiculatus), 59, 166

Cordyline (Cordyline), 147

Cordyline australis, 144, 145

Coreopsis (Coreopsis), 83, 92, 98, 167, 170

Coreopsis grandiflora, 91, 96

Coreopsis lanceolata, 94, 96, 165

Coreopsis tinctoria, 139, 141, 145, 173

Coreopsis tripteris, 161, 165

Coreopsis verticillata, 88, 91, 97, 98, 158, 161, 165, 168, 175

Coreopsis zampfir, 170

Cork tree, 9, 14, 15, 23, 24, 29, 31, 39

Corkscrew rush (Juncus effusus), 151

Corkscrew rush (Juncus effusus spiralis), 115, 175

Cornelia cherry dogwood (Cornus mas), 157